Witness to Reconstruction

Witness to Reconstruction

Constance Fenimore Woolson
and the Postbellum South, 1873–1894

Edited by Kathleen Diffley

University Press of Mississippi / Jackson

www.upress.state.ms.us

The University Press of Mississippi is a member
of the Association of American University Presses.

Copyright © 2011 by University Press of Mississippi
All rights reserved
Manufactured in the United States of America

First printing 2011

∞

Library of Congress Cataloging-in-Publication Data

Witness to Reconstruction : Constance Fenimore Woolson
and the Postbellum South, 1873–1894 / edited by Kathleen
Diffley.
    p. cm.
   Includes bibliographical references and index.
   ISBN 978-1-61703-025-3 (cloth : alk. paper) — ISBN 978-
1-61703-026-0 (ebook) 1. Woolson, Constance Fenimore,
1840–1894—Criticism and interpretation. 2. Woolson,
Constance Fenimore, 1840–1894—Travels—Southern
states. 3. Travelers' writings, American—History and criticism. 4. Reconstruction (U.S. history, 1865–1877) in literature. 5. Southern States—In literature. 6. Reconstruction
(U.S. history, 1865–1877) I. Diffley, Kathleen Elizabeth,
1950–
   PS3363.W58 2011
   813'.4— dc22   2010052084

British Library Cataloging-in-Publication Data available

For those, like Rodman, who are keepers of the dead as well as the living—that is, for Woolson scholars to come

Contents

3   "People Who Remember"
       The American South and Woolson's Postbellum Sojourns
       —Kathleen Diffley

"This Reserve of the North"
Reconstruction at Home

17   The Balances of Deceit; or, What Does Silver Mean to Me?
       Woolson's "Castle Nowhere" and the Money Question during Reconstruction
       —Michael Germana

"The Daughters of Carolina"
The South Beckons

37   Constance Fenimore Woolson and the Origins of the Global South
       —John Lowe

56   Tourism, Imperialism, and Hybridity in the Reconstruction South
       Woolson's *Rodman the Keeper: Southern Sketches*
       —Anne E. Boyd

73   Henry James, Constance Fenimore Woolson, and the Fashioning
       of Southern Identity
       —John H. Pearson

90   Woolson's *Two Women: 1862.*
       A Civil War Romance of Irreconcilable Difference
       —Caroline Gebhard

107   Zephaniah Swift Spalding
Constance Woolson's Cipher
—Cheryl B. Torsney

"A Shady Retreat"
Short Prose

129   Geology and Genre in Woolson's Southern Travel Sketches
—Timothy Sweet

147   Reconstructing Southern Hospitality
—Anthony Szczesiul

162   Imagining Sites of Memory in the Post–Civil War South
The National Cemetery in Woolson's "Rodman the Keeper"
—Martin T. Buinicki

177   Poking King David in His Imperial Eye/"I"
Woolson Takes On the White Man's Burden in the Postbellum United States
—Carolyn Hall

194   Cypresses, Chameleons, and Snakes
Displacement in Woolson's "The South Devil"
—Kathleen Diffley

"Burned into Us as by a Red-Hot Fire"
Novels of the South

215   The Portrait of a Southern Lady in Woolson's *For the Major*
—Janet Gabler-Hover

232   Northeast Angels
Henry James in Woolson's Florida
—Geraldine Murphy

249   The Merits of Transit
Woolson's Return to Reconstruction in *Jupiter Lights*
—Sharon Kennedy-Nolle

266 "Pioneers of Spoliation"
Woolson's *Horace Chase* and the Role of Magazine Writing in the Gilded-Age Development of the South
—Kevin E. O'Donnell

"Shimmering Inlets"
Remembering Back, Looking Forward

285 "A Modern and a Model Pioneer"
Civilizing the Frontier in Woolson's "A Pink Villa"
—Annamaria Formichella Elsden

293 Contributors

297 Index

Witness to Reconstruction

"People Who Remember"

The American South and Woolson's Postbellum Sojourns

—Kathleen Diffley

What days they were! After all, we *lived* then. It is in vain for our generation to hope to be any other than "people who remember." Sometimes even now, I wake early, and think I hear the distant call of the newsboy far down the street, "Extra! Extra! All about the last battle!"—And then how we rushed out to get it, how we devoured it, and then hurried down to the "Soldiers' Aid" rooms to do the little that was open to us faraway ones to do.

So Constance Fenimore Woolson wrote to Southern poet Paul Hamilton Hayne a decade after the Civil War ended, when she had paused at Goshen, Virginia, during a summer's travel with her ailing mother.[1] Born and raised in Charleston, Hayne had served on the staff of South Carolina governor Francis Perkins and had been assigned late in 1861 to Fort Sumter; he had good reason to recall the war's devouring rush. North in Cleveland during those four stirring years, Woolson had been in her early twenties and had spent her days over boxes of supplies for the front as well as preparations for the 1864 Northern Ohio Sanitary Fair that raised funds for Union troops in camp. But after the war ended in 1865 and her father died in 1869, she was among the first Northerners to look to the South for the warm springs that would ease her mother's rheumatism and the affordable lodgings she would soon find in Florida. For six years she would also tour by wagon, coach, railroad, and steamboat through the differing Southern landscapes that invited travel, travel sketches, and the unsettling problems of her postwar poetry and fiction. Beginning in 1873, then, Woolson sojourned in a reconstructing South that Northerners scarcely knew, a shrouded and partitioned territory that Northern troops would slowly leave and that Northern magazines were only beginning to discover.

Born in New Hampshire in 1840, before her family relocated that same year to Ohio, Woolson was the grandniece of James Fenimore Cooper. As a girl, she had stayed from time to time with her family in Cooperstown, and she would summer there with her mother after her father died and her writing career began. In "The Haunted Lake," one of her first contributions to *Harper's New Monthly Magazine* (December 1871), Woolson described the "secret depths" of Lake Otsego and the "magic" that infused both Cooper's fiction and New York's lake district.[2] The same literary eye for an inviting landscape would be evident in the Great Lakes pieces she began publishing in *Scribner's Monthly* and the *Atlantic*, *Harper's Monthly*, *Appletons' Journal*, and the *Galaxy*, before she collected nine stories in *Castle Nowhere: Lake-Country Sketches* (1875). By then, Woolson had already left New York for Hispanic Florida and was describing St. Augustine as "The Ancient City" (December 1874, January 1875), the first of several illustrated accounts she would write for *Harper's Monthly* as she traveled the southeast before turning her hand to fifteen short stories, a novella, and three novels about the postwar South. "I go about a great deal, but always as an 'observer,'" she wrote a family friend, likely in 1876.[3] Thanks to the money she earned by her pen, she and her mother could live quietly and just as quietly observe the social relations across races, classes, and regions that the Civil War had permanently disrupted.

Following Woolson's example, the essays in this volume set aside the shrill postwar agendas she meant to counter, especially those appealing to Southern apologists or Northern capitalists on the rise. Even before 1865, the shaping of a collective past was already a matter of rhetorical moment; as David Blight has observed, "the living were compelled to remember, and from the stuff of memory, create a new nation from the wreckage of the old."[4] But sectional memories did not readily jibe. In 1869, the year Woolson's father died, the Southern Historical Society was founded and Confederate general Jubal Early returned from exile thanks to federal pardon. He would shortly become the society's president and one of the most outspoken advocates of the Lost Cause, an abiding claim to white Southern chivalry, Confederate valor, and a patriarchal way of life. By contrast, in 1873, the year Woolson arrived in Florida, correspondent Edward King was declaring in the first installment of his Southern tour for New York's *Scribner's Monthly* that "a gigantic struggle" was underway, what amounted to "the battle of race with race, of the picturesque and unjust civilization of the past with the prosaic and leveling civilization of the present."[5] For King and the many readers of *The Great South*, which Jennifer Rae Greeson has described as a "global reframing of the relationship between the nation and its defeated, occupied southern states," the unfolding story of Reconstruction was driven by a near tropical indifference to labor acquiescing to the more vigorous enterprise of arriviste investors, who would reclaim the national Eden that bitter partisans like General Early continued to waste.[6] Fierce Southern honor, in short, was already pitched against fiercer Northern appetites.

But the postwar periodicals that circulated these emerging sectional narratives, now so familiar, also began circulating Woolson's less predictable reports. From the midst of her extended sojourns and continuing Southern travels, she offered an alternative and polyvocal account of Reconstruction, what Leonardo Buonomo has called a "counterstory." As he puts it, "the losers become individuals with a name and a story."[7] Persistently local and yet drawn from a sojourner's consecutive homes, Woolson's accumulating Southern history tended to favor limited perspectives, thwarted characters, ramshackle settings, and unanticipated options. During the 1870s and thereafter, she effectively opened a space for backwater listening, disintegrating social codes, and sustained literary endeavor, a quiet reckoning with sudden loss and even more sudden opportunity. As Henry James would later put it, she "perceived that no social revolution of equal magnitude had ever reflected itself so little in literature, remained so unrecorded."[8] Among the first visitors to notice what Reconstruction would entail and for whom, she drew the attention of Northern spectators to abrupt social changes that only seemed simple, transparent, and comfortably far away.

For Woolson's earliest readers and for those just discovering the scope of Reconstruction as she saw it, first in the former Confederacy for six years and then in print for years to come, the occupied South was a national social experiment, an indisputable part of the Union and yet a foreign country. "As the key space for nation (re)building in the 1860s and 1870s, before the emergence of an American empire in the late-nineteenth century," Jamie Winders has observed, "the postbellum South's paradoxical location both within and outside the nation-state created an opportunity for the U.S. to work out the details of its own imperial practices in an imperfect imperial holding and to do so without ever leaving home."[9] In that regard, the places Woolson brought to magazine life suggested at once an immediate summons and a permanent horizon that was forever receding further south, further west. "The U.S. South is not an enclave of hyperregionalism," Kathryn McKee and Annette Trefzer have declared, "but a porous space through which other places have always circulated."[10] As the essays in this collection reveal, Woolson acknowledged that wider transnational traffic as well as the orienting gaze of Northern eyes across the mysterious ravaged territory of a defeated nation.

This volume examines the portrait Woolson limned of the South she saw, a portrait that was always detailed and kaleidoscopic. As she was quick to reveal, Florida was not the Carolinas, Georgia was not Virginia, coastal "indolence" was not mountain hospitality or the dangerous fecundity of the swamps. And Northerners were not Southerners, as Woolson had already learned while a student at Madame Chegaray's well-heeled New York academy during the 1850s. The school was frequented by Southern girls, and Woolson herself would later write that she was "fascinated by their ways and grandiloquent style of talking," especially in casting themselves as "The Daughters of Carolina" since Woolson never considered herself a "Daughter of Ohio."[11]

After the war, when she also turned to the Carolina South as a "shady retreat," Woolson detailed the traditional manners and local speech she discovered anew, this time on behalf of a postwar audience intent on ready exotica.[12] For emerging American travel writers, that meant verbal pictures, which illustrated magazines regularly transformed into wood engravings. After "The Ancient City," Woolson's initial response to the South prompted three further travelogues, all lead essays in *Harper's Monthly* and all revealing notably different terrains, both geographical and cultural. In "The French Broad" (April 1875), she described the Blue Ridge summits of western North Carolina (Fig. 1) and the "hidden region locked up beyond mountain walls," where grass now grew on the earthworks of an old Confederate fort and Cold Mountain reared up in the distance. In "Up the Ashley and Cooper" (December 1875), she began instead with colonial Charleston, home of transplanted Roundheads and Cavaliers who moved up the Ashley (Fig. 2) to "patriarchal" estates and a scene of "great magnificence," where some residences now lay in ruins; on the Cooper, she noted in addition the old Goose Creek church, a plantation schoolhouse, and more aging mansions with their secret rooms for protection against Revolutionary danger. In "The Oklawaha" (January 1876), she replaced mountain roughness and colonial architecture with vistas along a meandering river (Fig. 3), whose Indian name recalled the Seminole wars and whose cramped steamboats encountered alligators and opossums, the flap of cranes and the hoot of limpkins. "Florida has always been a far-away land, a beautiful trackless tropical wilderness," she wrote, and she hesitated over the inland settlements and economic growth that would soon draw crowds of Northern tourists.[13] From the stern natural enclave of the Appalachians to the built world of colonial South Carolina and the lingering wilderness of Indian Florida, Woolson discovered the retreats that would catch the spirit of an enterprising *Harper's Monthly* and catch the fancy of its bustling readers.

Monied, curious, and leisured, such readers became at once Woolson's professional guarantee and her reason to pause. On the one hand, the postwar years across the decimated South were ripe with investment opportunities that travel accounts in Northern magazines encouraged, thanks to their pictures of fading Confederate strongholds and shared Revolutionary zeal. The very mobility of travelers like Woolson seemed to promise that postbellum violence was ebbing and that Northern travelers on Southern tours could revisit the civilities and languor that were fading elsewhere. "In the tourists' eyes," writes Nina Silber in *The Romance of Reunion*, "the South ceased to be a sectional problem and became more of a regional antidote to northern distress."[14] That meant, on the other hand, a necessary Northern blindness to unpicturesque social complications and a demanding intrusiveness sparked by the war's "red-hot fire," in Woolson's phrase.[15] Sharon Dean points to the disturbing upshot, what she calls "the inevitability of cultural bias" that Northern

Fig. 1, "Wildly Beautiful."
Constance Fenimore Woolson, "The French Broad."
Harper's Monthly (April 1875): 631.

Fig. 2, Magnolia, on the Ashley.
Constance Fenimore Woolson,
"Up the Ashley and Cooper."
Harper's Monthly (December 1875): 6.

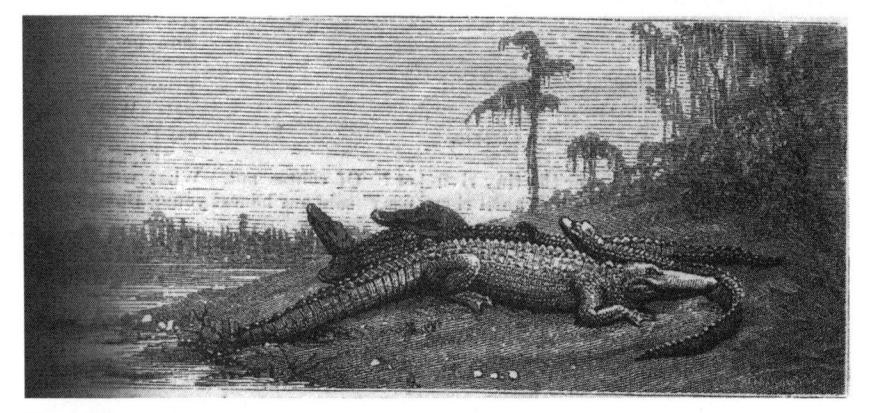

Fig. 3, Alligators.
Constance Fenimore Woolson, "The Oklawaha."
Harper's Monthly (January 1876): 165.

travelers could not set aside any more readily than Northern travel sketches with their fetching scenes.[16] At its most fraught, reconciliation on these terms became the imposed venture of a triumphant North with the strategic assistance of illustrated periodicals and their audiences. "Although there was, within the picturesque framework, some freedom to capture and convey local differences," writes Jeffrey Auerbach, "everywhere it was deployed it served to conceal the hardships and beautify the frequently unpleasant surroundings that characterized life in the imperial zone, refracting local people and conditions through a single, formulaic lens."[17] Scratch a travel sketch, as Auerbach sees it, and the designs of those in armchairs are suddenly less conciliatory than suspect.

Woolson's remedy for the inherent problems of an organizing gaze, particularly in the steady advance of travelogues that were generally tidy and continually on the move, lay most often in her postwar fictions, which probed the "local differences" as well as the "formulaic lens" that her travel accounts made whimsical. Left to her own devices in more elastic genres, she tended to favor inconvenient protests, dead ends, and counter purposes, usually for the same Northern readers and genteel magazines that welcomed her travel writing. "Old Gardiston," for example, appeared in *Harper's Monthly* (April 1876) and centers on a broken-down colonial mansion near Charleston where a proud Southern family has dwindled to an aging scholar and his cousin, a young woman who dusts inherited relics while resenting the kindnesses of the Northern captain she will reluctantly marry. "Rodman the Keeper," published in the *Atlantic* (March 1877), follows an ex-colonel who "keeps" the graves at a national cemetery beside a Georgia prison much like Andersonville. In the small cottage where he transcribes the names of 14,321 dead Union soldiers, a maimed Confederate officer lies dying, while his kinswoman gives way to "small venom" and his aging black servant learns to read. "King David," which appeared in *Scribner's Monthly* (April 1878), focuses on black "scholars" in the hands of a Freedmen's Bureau teacher, a New Hampshire transplant to the South's pine forests.[18] Despite his further efforts in the cotton field he rents and the crop he tries to work with the paid labor of recent slaves, his radical project fails, thanks largely to a carpetbagger's liquor.

In these and other Southern stories published by *Lippincott's*, *Appletons' Journal*, and the *Galaxy*, Woolson often focused on Northern vision eroding as Southern waywardness prevailed. Reviewing the book such stories would become in 1880, *Scribner's Monthly* (August 1880) commented on the "forlorn and broken lives" Woolson sketched, while the *Catholic World* (February 1887) noted her fondness for contrasting "the hard New England Puritan with the Creole Catholic." The *Literary World* (July 3, 1880) pointed to the difference between "Northern energy and Southern ease" and insisted that a Northern woman had written "the present desolation, the depression, the pathos, the loss and the anguish, the wounded pride, the ruined homes, [and] the stricken hearts" of the postbellum South. Speaking for other postwar commentators, the *Christian Union* (April 14, 1880) summed up her nomadic method and gathering success: "Miss Woolson in her residence at the South seems to have absorbed the Southern atmosphere; and whether it be the hot and sandy beach, the dank luxuriant swamp, or the dry and breezy uplands, she paints that all with equal skill and accuracy." Her purpose, concluded *Appletons'* (May 1880), was "to interpret the North and the South to each other," a project in national reconstruction that the essays in this collection reanimate.[19] But in Woolson's hands, the "shimmering inlets" of the defeated South and the economic appetites of the postwar North rarely enabled a simple story of Union triumphalism, of the intransigence of a Southern master class, or of the hard-won liberty that freedmen were daily interpreting for themselves.[20]

To demonstrate Woolson's unusual canvas and her reliance upon an unanticipated "reserve of the North,"[21] this collection opens with her early professional years as radical congressional policies began to coalesce, a perspective Michael Germana details in "The Balances of Deceit; or, What Does Silver Mean to Me?: Woolson's 'Castle Nowhere' and the Money Question during Reconstruction." Focusing on the Coinage Act of 1873 as a "crime" and contemporary monetary debates as they touched for Woolson on lingering sectional tensions and biblical paradigms, Germana reveals the postwar economic implications of the gold standard and the appeal of silver, especially amid the financial collapse of the planter South and the growing money hunger of the prospering North. Stretching across Woolson's career, this volume concludes with her late literary glimpse in 1888 of nineteenth-century Florida and its increasing lure, which Annamaria Formichella Elsden considers in "'A Modern and a Model Pioneer': Civilizing the Frontier in Woolson's 'A Pink Villa.'" Weighing issues of gender by contrasting Florida and Italy, fatherland and maternal space, she examines "civilizing" in its late-century contortions, a preoccupation that has also proved central in this volume for other contributors who trace Northern inroads into the unsettled South.

Between Germana's sectional tensions and Formichella Elsden's "maternal" frontiers, fourteen essays investigate what has long been considered a literary dead zone, the uneasy years between a fading Melville and a cresting Twain. Conventionally, those years have constituted a haphazard postwar period but, as it turns out, one that did not escape literary notice or cultural politics. After Germana's entrée, the first cluster of essays casts Woolson's literary career in relief with the help of remarkably different theoretical compasses. In "Constance Fenimore Woolson and the Origins of the Global South," John Lowe creates an expansive view of the Caribbean as another Mediterranean with its own Ottoman Empires and yet, thanks to Woolson, with an early sense of hemispheric connectedness. The result is a transformative return to Woolson's Great Lakes "islands" as well as a vision of

Florida as what Lowe dubs "the crossroads of culture," a matter of some moment for a transnational writer who would later embrace Europe. By contrast, and with a keen sense of Northern eyes, Anne E. Boyd surveys Woolson's short fiction in "Tourism, Imperialism, and Hybridity in the Reconstruction South: Woolson's *Rodman the Keeper: Southern Sketches*." Her essay focuses on Woolson's recurring efforts to "decenter" a Northern metropolitan perspective, a postcolonial strategy that allows Southern voices to "speak back" with a postwar counternarrative in which reconciliation scarcely figures.

Likewise surveying the arc of a career's imaginative engagements, John H. Pearson introduces an intellectual genealogy for Woolson's challenge to a nakedly cosmopolitan view of the South as sectional backwater. In "Henry James, Constance Fenimore Woolson, and the Fashioning of Southern Identity," Pearson weighs "new social identities" and the sense of improvisation that Stephen Greenblatt has described, along with the scrape of sectional and gender priorities. The play of gender was also uppermost for Woolson as Reconstruction was winding down, when she parlayed sectional clash into a dramatic dialogue that Caroline Gebhard takes up in "Woolson's *Two Women: 1862.*: A Civil War Romance of Irreconcilable Difference." Gebhard positions Woolson's long poem, which few scholars have read with care, as a tantalizing nod to Shakespeare's *Antony and Cleopatra*, especially in its erotic appeal, its mounting grief, and its reckoning with racial difference. For Gebhard, Woolson's railcar setting recalls both wartime troop movements and unthinkable social collisions in a border state like Kentucky.

The movements and collisions of the borderlands also orient Cheryl B. Torsney's more focused concern with John Hunt Morgan, who becomes the key to Woolson's wartime romance as well as her early poems and stories of border clash. In "Zephaniah Swift Spalding: Constance Woolson's Cipher," Torsney carries the shiver of Morgan's appeal and Woolson's infatuation with Zeph Spalding through Gilded-Age speculations to Spalding's marriage and later sugar plantation in Hawaii. Her sweeping development ties youthful days in Cleveland to the divided course of postwar celebrity—literary for her, political for him—and then ties her troubled artistry of empire to his brief for the continuing slavery of the global South.

In the wake of the broad arc these five essays build from the poetic *Two Women, 1862.* (1877) to Woolson's late novel *Horace Chase* (1894), the next cluster of essays focuses more narrowly on Woolson's short Reconstructive prose, from the travel essays of the 1870s to the stories she published in Northern magazines and then collected in *Rodman the Keeper* (1880) at the end of the decade. Orienting this early and revealing period with a shrewd assessment of magazine venues, Timothy Sweet's "Geology and Genre in Woolson's Southern Travel Sketches" examines the compositional dynamics of Woolson's approach to travel accounts with an intriguing consequence: as Sweet sees it, Northern nostalgia and Northern investment were intimately related when it came to appropriating the postwar South in print. Underlining a similar consumerist paradigm, Anthony Szczesiul's "Reconstructing Southern Hospitality" tracks the familiar marriage of Northern enterprise and Southern bloodlines in "Old Gardiston" and thereby establishes Woolson's place in "Lost Cause" pitches and the postbellum appeal of resorts like Virginia's White Sulphur Springs, particularly in a leisured world dominated by Saratoga and Cape May. Approaching his subject as a philosophical and ethical imperative, Szczesiul evaluates the white racial hegemony that was bolstered by the protocols of Southern hospitality, by class distinctions among whites (especially as hotel guests), and by the "foreignness" of a suddenly emancipated black population.

Shifting perspective with "Imagining Sites of Memory in the Post–Civil War South: The National Cemetery in Woolson's 'Rodman the Keeper,'" Martin T. Buinicki then considers Woolson's title story for the trap of nostalgia, as well as the ragged edge of continuing loss for ex-Confederates and of uncertain gain for ex-slaves. Buinicki is preoccupied, as Woolson was, with Northern sentiment about national cemeteries for the Union dead, and he investigates the ways in which Pierre Nora's "sites of memory" were fashioned once historical events began to fade. Carolyn Hall substitutes Northern bungling for Southern malice, and the advice of a black "scholar" for the instruction of a white "master" in "Poking King David in His Imperial Eye/'I': Woolson Takes On the White Man's Burden in the Postbellum United States." Enlisting Eric Cheyfitz's sense of "translation," she reads a teacher of freedmen as the projected figure of Northern deliverance, and she sees Reconstruction's miscarriage as a savior's comeuppance. My own essay, "Cypresses, Chameleons, and Snakes: Displacement in Woolson's 'The South Devil,'" concludes this sifting of short prose by reckoning with the Florida swamp, for Woolson the generative terrain of Southern opportunity and the terrifying site of Northern intrusion. Where Sweet sees the come hither of rudimentary tourism and Szczesiul parses Southern hospitality as advertising pitch, Buinicki introduces a mindfulness of the dead and of occupying troops, Hall investigates a Northern devotion to "duty" and racialist hauteur, while my pause on Florida's semi-tropical landscape links Woolson's sense of lush promise to the swamp's unnerving fangs.

Having measured in five different balances the Civil War's impact on Woolson and her generation before 1880, this collection provides a final cluster of essays that investigate the deepening Southern concerns of Woolson's longer and later works, which were at once apostrophes to waning local customs and harbingers of a new social order. In "The Portrait of a Southern Lady in Woolson's *For the Major*," Janet Gabler-Hover reads Woolson's novella, published in 1883, as a sustained effort to demystify the Southern "lady" cum regional type and to reassemble her appurtenances as consciously staged. Decidedly richer in her performative appeal and unexpectedly humble in her unmasking, Woolson's custodial mistress initiates for Gabler-Hover a series of orchestrated reversals that defy the reemerging plantation tradition of the 1880s and highlight Northern misperceptions. Geraldine Murphy's "Northeast Angels: Henry James in Woolson's Florida" then furthers the connection to Jamesian fiction by examining the "lapidary comedy of North/South manners" in *East Angels* (1886), before probing that novel's ultimate tragedy and, through it, Woolson's unsparing commentary on James.

Casting the literary net wider in "The Merits of Transit: Woolson's Return to Reconstruction in *Jupiter Lights*," Sharon Kennedy-Nolle grounds Woolson's 1889 novel in General Sherman's experiment with land redistribution among Georgia's freedpeople on Sapelo Island. For Woolson, Kennedy-Nolle argues, the narrative consequence was a kind of perpetual motion among all of the novel's postwar characters, and yet a disconcerting legacy of slavery in the seeming irrelevance of black death. On a similarly skeptical tack, Kevin E. O'Donnell concludes this section with a case for the connivance of genteel magazines in the postwar clear-cutting of Southern forests, a case that links Woolson's travel writing to the aid and comfort provided rising capitalists. With "'Pioneers of Spoliation': Woolson's *Horace Chase* and the Role of Magazine Writing in the Gilded-Age Development of the South," O'Donnell assails nineteenth-century industrialists like Woolson's title character for their expansionist designs, while he assesses Woolson for her facilitating enthusiasms and then subtler shadows.

Robust and variegated, this volume explores such postbellum complexities, particularly as seen by one of the first Northern writers to travel south during the neglected 1870s. Significantly before the wave of Northern tourists a decade later and the welter of invalids Nina Silber has called "sick Yankees in paradise," Woolson helped to limn the postwar South for those in Northern armchairs, especially as Northerners were weighing civil rights on the one hand against entrepreneurial opportunities on the other, what amounts to a continuing social revolution against a simpler economic shrug.[22] The witness she bore to the fumbling terms of a country's reconstitution is likely to appeal to those intrigued by the black hole before late-century literary celebrity, to readers of women's writing who are drawn by the political forum that nineteenth-century magazines provided, and to cultural historians preoccupied with the ways in which "the South" was reinvented in postwar print. Similarly, those intent on dawning African American possibilities in the wake of emancipation will be struck by Woolson's coalescing map of fractured social relations, which will be of interest to anyone caught up as Mark Twain was in Gilded-Age "sivilization" and its discontents. Taken together, these essays probe the various ways in which national reconstruction took shape and fell short, often with startling results that Woolson was quick to detail and that students of the war's social upheaval will follow with quickening interest.

Notes

A particular thanks to the University of Iowa's Special Collections librarian Kathy Hodson, who pointed out the color plate of yellow jessamine that lends a disquieting grace to this volume's cover and title pages. Woolson describes yellow jessamine in its "tangled wreaths," its "clustered gleaming stars" and "floating, curling sprays" as heralding the early Southern spring. It is also true that every part of the flower is poisonous, sometimes fatal. Yellow jessamine is the state flower of South Carolina.

Woolson's description appears in her poem "Yellow Jessamine," *Appletons' Journal* (March 21, 1874): 372. The drawing of yellow trumpet blossoms and green viney leaves was first printed in *Curtis's Botanical Magazine* (1799): Plate 461. The engraved portrait of Woolson was published in *Harper's Monthly* (March 1886): 559.

1. Constance Fenimore Woolson to Paul Hamilton Hayne, July 23, 1875, in Paul Hamilton Hayne Papers, Rare Book, Manuscript, and Special Collections Library, Duke University, Durham, North Carolina.
2. Constance Fenimore Woolson, "The Haunted Lake," *Harper's Monthly* (December 1871): 20, 21.
3. Constance Fenimore Woolson to Arabella Carter Washburn, [1876?], *Five Generations (1785–1923)*, ed. Clare Benedict, I: *Voices Out of the Past* (London: Ellis, 1930), 242.
4. David W. Blight, *Race and Reunion: The Civil War in American Memory* (Cambridge, MA: Harvard University Press, 2001), 6.
5. Edward King, "The Great South: Old and New Louisiana," *Scribner's Monthly* (November 1873): 2.
6. Jennifer Rae Greeson, "Expropriating *The Great South* and Exporting 'Local Color': Global and Hemispheric Imaginaries of the First Reconstruction," *American Literary History* 18.3 (Fall 2006): 499.
7. Leonardo Buonomo, "The Other Face of History in Constance Fenimore Woolson's Southern Stories," *Canadian Review of American Studies/Revue canadienne d'études américaines* 28.3 (1998): 16.
8. Henry James, "Miss Constance Fenimore Woolson," *Harper's Weekly* (February 12, 1887): 114. James's remarks have often been reprinted, by James himself in *Partial Portraits* (London: Macmillan, 1888), 177–92, a collection in which he offers similar profiles of writers like Emerson, Eliot, Trollope, and Turgenieff.
9. Jamie Winders, "Imperfectly Imperial: Northern Travel Writers in the Postbellum U.S. South, 1865–1880," *Annals of the Association of American Geographers* 95.2 (June 2005): 405.
10. Kathryn McKee and Annette Trefzer, "Preface: Global Contexts, Local Literatures: The New Southern Studies," special issue of *American Literature* 78.4 (December 2006): 679.
11. Constance Fenimore Woolson to Hjalmar Hjorth Boyson [Boyesen], August 9, 1881; Constance Woolson Papers, 1873–1893, Clifton Waller Barrett Library, Accession #7331, 7331a, Albert and Shirley Small Special Collections Library, University of Virginia, Charlottesville, Virginia. A cordial thanks to reference coordinator Margaret Downs Hrabe, who shared information about this letter's recipient.
12. Constance Fenimore Woolson to William Dean Howells, June 28, 1875, Howells Family Papers (Ms Am 1784), Houghton Library, Harvard University.
13. Constance Fenimore Woolson, "The French Broad," *Harper's Monthly* (April 1875): 618; "Up the Ashley and Cooper," *Harper's Monthly* (December 1875): 4; "The Oklawaha," *Harper's Monthly* (January 1876): 175.
14. Nina Silber, *The Romance of Reunion: Northerners and the South, 1865–1900* (Chapel Hill: University of North Carolina Press, 1993), 70.
15. Constance Fenimore Woolson to Hamilton Mabie, June 18, 1883, Constance Fenimore Woolson Papers, Rare Book, Manuscript, and Special Collections Library, Duke University, Durham, North Carolina.

16. Sharon L. Dean, *Constance Fenimore Woolson: Homeward Bound* (Knoxville: University of Tennessee Press, 1995), 51.

17. Jeffrey Auerbach, "The Picturesque and the Homogenisation of Empire," *British Art Journal* 5.1 (Spring/Summer 2004): 48.

18. For the white South's "small venom" in Woolson's story, see "Rodman the Keeper," *Atlantic Monthly* (March 1877): 270. For Woolson's description of one fictional Bureau teacher and his students, "scholars" as early as the story's first line, see "King David," *Scribner's Monthly* (April 1878): 781.

19. See "Culture and Progress," *Scribner's Monthly* (August 1880): 634; "A Chat about New Books," *Catholic World* (February 1887): 709; "Southern Sketches," *Literary World* (July 3, 1880): 223; "Rodman the Keeper," *Christian Union* (April 14, 1880): 350; and "Books of the Day," *Appletons' Journal* (May 1880): 479.

20. Constance Fenimore Woolson to Edmund Clarence Stedman, April 30, 1883, E. C. Stedman Papers, Rare Book and Manuscript Library, Columbia University in the City of New York.

21. Constance Fenimore Woolson to Paul Hamilton Hayne, September 10, 1876, Paul Hamilton Hayne Papers, Rare Book, Manuscript, and Special Collections Library, Duke University, Durham, North Carolina.

22. For the cascade of Northern visitors during the 1880s and 1890s, see Silber's ch. 3, "Sick Yankees in Paradise: Northern Tourism in the Reconstructed South," *The Romance of Reunion*, 66–92.

"This Reserve of the North"
Reconstruction at Home

But you warm hearted hospitable clan-gathering southerners do not understand this reserve of the north, particularly the New England north. I am very strongly "New Hampshire" in all my ways. I have a row of tall solemn Aunts up there,—silent, reserved, solitary, thin, and a little grim; I am as much like them as the kind of life I lead will allow.

—*Constance Fenimore Woolson to Paul Hamilton Hayne*

The Balances of Deceit; or, What Does Silver Mean to Me?

Woolson's "Castle Nowhere" and the Money Question during Reconstruction

—Michael Germana

When "Castle Nowhere" was first published in the collection of narratives that bears its name in 1875, critics singled out the novella as an aberration. William Dean Howells called it "the least satisfactory" of the lot, citing its "disagreeable fantasticality." Another reviewer writing for *Scribner's Monthly* lamented, "it is a pity it should occupy the first position in the volume, for its inferiority to the others may prejudice an impatient reader." When *Castle Nowhere* (the volume) was republished *in toto* in 1886, however, "Castle Nowhere" (the novella) was no longer dismissed as an anomaly, but praised as an integral part of the collection. This critical about-face is most easily explained by the surge in Woolson's popularity during the intervening years, which saw the publication of some of Woolson's most accomplished short stories. As a reviewer for *The Literary World* opined, the tales collected in *Castle Nowhere* "have a definite place and interest perhaps above their intrinsic value" when "viewed in the backward light of her recent successes." Extending this specular metaphor, Howells, who had written that "Castle Nowhere" harasses its readers "from beginning to end" in 1875, applauded the collection as a coherent whole in 1887, writing, "their assemblage under one cover somehow throws new light on all the stories, and one sees, or seems to see—it is best not to be positive—that their final value, or the merit that they have in supreme degree, is to have caught and recorded in very clear and impressive terms the finest poetry which stirs in the heart of wild, new countries." Howells must have conveniently forgotten that the stories gathered in *Castle Nowhere*, which he praises without qualification in 1887, were also assembled "under one cover" when they were published in 1875.[1]

The "backward light" Woolson's later work shines on "Castle Nowhere" acquires its brilliance, not from the author's increasing fame after 1875, but from her subsequent explorations of the theme of Reconstruction and its discontents. The subject of several of Woolson's "Southern Sketches," the Radical Republican project takes center stage in no less than four short stories she published between 1876 and 1878. "Castle Nowhere" looks good in the "backward light" of these stories, I argue, because it, too, is an allegory for Reconstruction. Only the allegory that had currency for reviewers in 1886 and 1887 was not an allegory Woolson necessarily intended to write. Instead, her novella became a site for the articulation of the era's dominant monetary ideologies following the Coinage Act of 1873, a legislative act known by its critics as the "Crime of '73." Woolson's "fantastical" story therefore not only improved in the "backward light" of her later narratives, it acquired a meaningful material context in the monetary debates that roiled the nation from 1876 to 1878.

The narrative's inflection in political economic accents by readers during the late 1870s and 1880s was facilitated by Woolson's incorporation of language and imagery from the Old Testament Book of Amos. In Woolson's tale, Amos Fog stands in for his biblical namesake, Amos of Tekoa, only his role in "Castle Nowhere" is an ironic inversion of the sentiments expressed by the prophet. When viewed through the lens of 1870s political economic ideology, the critique of class society expressed by the Book of Amos becomes an indictment of Reconstruction-era monetary politics, and Amos Fog's motives and actions are transformed into a satire on pro-silver producerism. Because the so-called money question divided the nation along the same sectional lines as the Civil War, "Castle Nowhere" joins "Old Gardiston" (1876), "In the Cotton Country" (1876), "Rodman the Keeper" (1877), and "King David" (1878) in reflecting lingering sectional animosities that would long outlive Reconstruction itself.

In my reading of "Castle Nowhere," Fog plays the role of a displaced Southerner who forges an eccentric alliance with the West that resembles the pact formed by Southern and Western agrarians against the fatted calves of Northeastern money interests, the gold standard in particular. The symbolism here is two-fold: Fog follows in the footsteps of Amos of Tekoa, who journeyed north from the southern kingdom of Judah to denounce Israel's predatory monetary politics and golden calves (literal and figurative) before being banished himself. And in picking up Amos's story where the Bible leaves off, Woolson places Amos Fog in the shoes of the postbellum Southern agrarian whose pro-silver stance puts him at odds with the architects of postwar U.S. monetary policies that favored Northern capital before Southern and Western labor. Woolson is neither a disinterested observer nor a great sympathizer with the agrarians, however. Rewriting the story of Amos from a Northern perspective, Woolson inverts the Southern bias of the Book of Amos that, because it originated in Jerusalem, paints Israel's cultic and economic activities in a negative light. In so doing, Woolson articulates her own Northern allegiances by satirizing Amos Fog and the politics that inform his symbolic role in "Castle Nowhere."

"Castle Nowhere" chronicles the adventures of Jarvis Waring, a young man with enough means—and few enough responsibilities—to spend his summer getting lost, literally, in the northern Michigan wilderness. Upon arriving at the shore of Lake Superior, Lake Huron, or Lake Michigan (he can't tell which), Waring is visited by a "shape," a weathered and graying sailor by the name of Amos Fog.[2] When "old Fog" steals some of Waring's belongings and swiftly steals away in a boat, Waring leaves behind his imaginary traveling companion, the Spirit of Discontent, and takes to the water to track down the thief. Serendipitously, Waring, who is just as lost on water as he was on land, happens upon the forecastle of a wrecked steamer far from the shore and hidden from view. Climbing aboard, Waring finds not Amos Fog but his adopted daughter, a young woman named Silver, happily consuming lumps of white sugar and reading a book of Shakespeare sonnets pilfered from Waring's knapsack. When Fog returns to his "castle" and discovers, to his dismay, that Waring has found his hidden fortress, a long battle of wills ensues during which Fog tests Waring's suitability as a husband for Silver (with whom he does not want to part), while Waring tries to convince himself that he does not love the young woman (whom Fog keeps isolated and inexperienced to the point of perpetual childishness). A key twist in the plot occurs when, following one of Fog's initial attempts to rid himself of Silver's reluctant beau, Waring discovers that Fog doesn't just hunt and fish to keep body and soul together; he also wrecks ships. Luring commercial vessels to the shore with a false light, Fog harvests the merchandise they carry as it washes up on shore. Silver, of course, remains ignorant of Fog's transgressions, which he performs in her service. But Waring, who comes into this horrible knowledge, is left to deal with its moral and ethical implications.

Woolson scholars, who have otherwise picked up on the author's penchant for economic metaphors, have not yet turned their attention to the symbolic significance of adopting and/or serving silver at a time when the monetary standard, like the future shape of the Union, was still in flux. As a result, critics have not yet examined how Woolson's fiction, and in particular "Castle Nowhere," articulates monetary ideologies that had currency among Woolson's contemporaries. For example, Carolyn VanBergen lucidly describes the symbolic exchange that occurs between financial and social economies in America during Woolson's productive years in her doctoral dissertation, "Legal Tender: The Search for a Just Social Economy in the Novels of Constance Fenimore Woolson." But when it comes to the "money question," VanBergen employs its rhetoric only as shorthand for the question of value it negotiates. So while she draws clear analogies between the "money question" and the "debate over varieties of values" that found sectional expression in the Civil War and its aftermath,[3] she does not extend this preoccupation to the actual currency debates that characterized the period. The same can be said of Peter Stephan's Ph.D. thesis, "Comparative Value Systems in the Fiction of Constance Fenimore Woolson," which examines, among other subjects, the economic systems of Northerners and Southerners in Woolson's fiction. Stephan is keen to show how Southerners are agrarians and Northerners are capitalists in Woolson's symbolic economy, but he is as unconcerned with the monetary politics that maintained this sectional division as VanBergen is.[4] This essay may not be the first to examine the role monetary metaphors play in Woolson's fiction or the first to illustrate how Woolson maps these metaphors onto social fissures, but it is the first to consider Woolson's story as a participant in, not merely a chronicler of, the monetary debates of the period. At the same time, the reflexive reading of "Castle Nowhere" I am promoting here contributes to the arguments of VanBergen and Stephan by adding another dimension to the discursive practices these scholars have already identified.

As with Woolson's economic symbolism, several critics have already examined the author's incorporation of the language and imagery of the Old Testament in her fiction. In the particular case of "Castle Nowhere," Sharon Dean describes the narrative as a commentary on the contradictory desire to recreate Eden after the fall:

> Despite his attempt to recapture Eden, Fog lives in a postlapsarian world, where he has assumed responsibility for, and control over, Silver. The only way he can support Silver is by murder—he lures ships to wreckage by using a false light and then uses the booty to build and maintain his ark. On the one hand, the ark represents salvation, the place Fog can survive as he expiates his guilt, but it also represents punishment because it is a confining home that is a necessary protection from an outside, hostile world. Fog takes control of the ark, trying to transform it to a prelapsarian Eden, but he can do this only by eliminating all references to religion.[5]

Clearly, Dean locates Woolson's inspiration for "Castle Nowhere" in the Book of Genesis, which might explain why, in accounting for the significance of Amos Fog's surname, she notes only that his name is taken for the weather that shrouds his "castle." Had Dean focused on Fog's first name instead of his last, she might have found an additional source for Woolson's inspiration in another book of the Old Testament: the Book of Amos.

Although it may seem incongruous to present-day readers, it would have made sense for Woolson to tie the discourses of Old Testament prophesy and monetary policy together since, as Walter T. K. Nugent has argued, the "money question" of Reconstruction was, at bottom, a moral issue.[6] Having been a student in the Cleveland Female Seminary during the early 1850s, Woolson was well versed in the stories of the Old Testament—an easy familiarity she demonstrates in her fiction.[7]

But even if she didn't consciously write the monetary politics of the era into the morality play that is "Castle Nowhere," her contemporaries would have had no difficulty making this connection on their own. The reason, as the following pages illustrate, is that it was a common practice among public figures of the era to articulate their preferences for one monetary standard over another by joining this discourse to the language and imagery of the Bible. The Book of Amos facilitates such grafting by taking as one of its principal subjects the standards of money and measure and the collusion of the powerful that leads to their abuse.

The Book of Amos and the "Crime of '73"

The Old Testament Book of Amos is informed by the era of Hebrew history it punctuates. This era began with the death of King Solomon around 920 B.C. and the ensuing division of the Davidic Kingdom. Following the ascension of Solomon's son Rehoboam to the throne, Israel's northern tribes seceded from the union to form an independent kingdom under King Jeroboam. The northern kingdom retained the title "Israel," while the southern kingdom took the name "Judah" after Rehoboam's tribe. Once enthroned, Jeroboam established a rival state religion— an independent Yahweh cult—in the northern kingdom. Aiming to counteract the prestige of Jerusalem to the south, Jeroboam had two golden calves built and installed at the Canaanite shrines of Bethel and Dan.[8] These golden calves weren't just icons of the new cult; they were symbols of the power and material wealth that had concentrated in the hands of the northern elite following the cession. This consolidation was at its zenith when Jeroboam's namesake, Jeroboam II, became king of Israel in 786 B.C. The rising tide of Israel's prosperity did not raise all ships in the northern kingdom, however. Instead, a great class divide opened up as the rich got richer and the poor got poorer, the nation's wealth having aggregated in the hands of a privileged minority.[9] Judah, meanwhile, was still reeling decades after Shisak, Pharoah of Egypt, invaded and plundered the southern kingdom during Rehoboam's rule. Judah never recovered from the loss of its national wealth and remained Israel's poorer neighbor to the south when Jeroboam II began his reign in the north and, like his predecessors before him, hailed the golden calf as the proper throne of God.

The events chronicled in the Book of Amos took place against this backdrop of ideological, class, and sectional tensions. Amos, one of the Minor Prophets of the Old Testament, was a laborer who hailed from the province of Tekoa in the southern kingdom. A "sheep-breeder" and "dresser of sycamore trees," Amos traveled north during Jeroboam II's reign to read an indictment against the luxury and corruption of Israel's moneyed elite. Called to prophesy (as opposed to claiming himself a prophet), Amos lamented the exploitation of the poor by the rich, and prophesied Israel's doom for this and other sins. Amos decried the rift that had opened up between rich and poor in the region, and he condemned the conspicuous consumption of Israel's small upper class, whose members did little to assist the impoverished majority. Of particular concern to Amos were the practice of predatory lending and the habit of relaxing the standards of money and measure in order to maximize profits—two procedures by which the rich exploited the poor. "Hear this, O ye that swallow up the needy," announces Amos,

> even to make the poor of the land to fail, Saying, When will the new moon be gone, that we may sell corn? and the sabbath, that we set forth wheat, making the ephah small and the shekel great, and falsifying the balances by deceit? That we may buy the poor for silver, and the needy for a pair of shoes; yea, and sell the refuse of the wheat? The Lord hath sworn by the excellency of Jacob, Surely I will never forget any of their works. Shall not the land tremble for this, and everyone mourn that dwelleth therein? and it shall rise up wholly as a flood; and it shall be cast out and drowned, as by the flood of Egypt. (Amos 8:4–8)[10]

Amos's prophecy of divine (and watery) judgment against Israel—a prophecy that included the inevitable fall of Jeroboam II's dynasty—was seen as an act of treason by Amaziah, the priest at Bethel. As the Book of Amos chronicles, Amaziah confronted Amos, denounced him as a false prophet, accused him of sedition, and banished him from the northern kingdom.[11] There is no record of what happened to Amos thereafter. Amos's unwritten future allows Woolson's "Castle Nowhere" to become a kind of postscript to the Book of Amos set in the postbellum West—a relocation in space and time that brings the rhetoric of the biblical text to bear on 1870s American politics.

The tale told by the Book of Amos would have struck a chord with Americans living at the tail end of Reconstruction because the narrative dramatizes sectional and economic tensions that bear more than a passing resemblance to their analogues in post–Civil War America. This resemblance was strengthened by an act of Congress popularly known by its critics as the "Crime of '73," which deserves a brief explanation. When the monetary system of the United States was established in 1792, gold and silver were legal tender—the monetary standard was bimetallic, and all debts could be paid in either gold or silver. Gresham's Law dictates that "bad" money drives "good" money out of circulation, so if the price of gold was low and the price of silver was high, gold would circulate as money while silver would be hoarded as bullion. This is exactly what happened after the Coinage Act of 1834, which revised the ratio of silver's value in relation to gold from 15:1 to 16:1. Silver dollars thereby became more valuable as bullion than as money and disappeared from circulation. The United States was still on this *de facto* gold standard—gold circulating, silver not—when the Civil War broke out in 1861 and all specie payments were suspended.

No sooner had the war ended than the debate began over how best to pay off the war debt (embodied by the "greenbacks," which were declared legal tender in 1862) and resume specie payments. Congress decided in 1873 that resumption should occur in gold only, so the silver dollar was demonetized and the nation put on a *de jure* gold standard. No one much minded the legislation when it passed in 1873. But when the price of silver plummeted and the value of a silver dollar dropped below its face value in 1876, many people were aggrieved to find that the silver dollars they had been hoarding for decades had been preemptively prohibited from increasing the money supply beyond the nominal sum of five dollars. Hence was born the conspiracy theory known as the "Crime of '73." To many Americans, the elimination of "cheap money" was a crime in and of itself. Others took stock in a popular myth about English financier and coinage expert Ernest Seyd, who, it was said, came to the United States in 1872 with $500,000 to bribe members of Congress into voting for gold standard legislation.[12] Whatever their reasons or rationale, the anger of individuals who felt they had been bilked by the government was palpable and, by 1876, had become a key component of American popular culture.

Not surprising, the battle lines over the Coinage Act of 1873 were drawn along class and geographical axes that exacerbated lingering sectionalist animosities between Northerners and Southerners, animosities that the Book of Amos prefigures and "Castle Nowhere" dramatizes. Gold monometalists or "gold bugs" were typically bankers, investors, and other members of the moneyed establishment concentrated in the urban Northeast, while the "silverites," members of the debtor classes, dominated the agrarian South and West. The class inflections of these competing monetary ideologies are readily apparent, especially in the producerist rhetoric of the pro-silver faction. Decrying the *laissez faire* politics of gold monometalists, pro-silver bimetalists accused the government of colluding with the business establishment and adulterating the monetary standard to benefit capitalists at the expense of laborers who *produced* goods and services for a living. An 1877 speech by John J. Ingalls, Republican senator of Kansas, exemplified the rhetoric of producerism, framing the "money question" as "the corn and wheat and beef and cotton of the country against its bonds and its gold; its productive industry against its accumulations. It is the men who own the public debt against those who are to pay it, if it is to be paid at all. If the bonds of this government are ever paid, they will be paid by the labor of the country, and not by its capital."[13]

Producerists like Ingalls often invoked the Book of Amos in their rhetoric and used the symbol of the golden calf to critique the gold monometalist establishment. Take, for example, a brief article simply titled "Silver" published in the February

21, 1878, issue of the *Christian Advocate*, which observed: "Some relief will come from the Silver bill [which reintroduced silver as a standard of value]. It will not do all its friends expect of it. It will not do all its enemies fear from it. It will do something. It will break the golden calf which the Jews have elevated in Wall-street." The article's author went on to rehearse familiar producerist rhetoric: "It will transfer the seat of legislation from Wall-street to Washington, and the seat of empire from the shop to the farm.... We hope to see capital go to work, to hear the hammers and spindles ringing and singing." If the commonplace articulation of religious discourse and producerist ideology in these debates weren't clear enough already, Kentucky representative Thomas Turner chimed in, "Let us force a square issue and make every one array himself either on the side of God or Mammon—the people or the gold ring."[14]

As the sectional inflection of these rhetorical performances demonstrates, the "money question" was inextricably tied to the broader policies of Reconstruction. Many Southerners saw Reconstruction-era federal monetary policy as another form of Union colonization because it mandated participation in an economic system that privileged Northern capital over Southern labor. This conflation of U.S. monetary policy with Union occupation of the South was made clear by an article entitled "The Currency Debate of 1873–74," in which Charles Francis Adams asks, "Why should the intelligent elements of the South, embittered by a sense of outrage and crushed under negro legislation, care to maintain those standards of value which represent only ruin to themselves?"[15] Adams's lamentation exemplifies a trope of Southern resistance to Union occupation that echoes the southern kingdom's vilification of northern kingdom money interests in the Book of Amos.

The regional and class dynamics of Amos of Tekoa's call for social justice would have had currency for Woolson's contemporaries regardless of the debates surrounding the Coinage Act of 1873. But Amos's critique of the adulteration of the standards of measure and value by those who stand to profit would have given the Book of Amos—and by extension Woolson's story—additional cultural currency after 1876. The key figure in "Castle Nowhere" that ties these biblical and monetary discourses together is Amos Fog's adopted child, Silver, whom Old Fog has been "hoarding" in his "castle" after forty years of wandering the proverbial desert. Without Silver, the similarities between Amos Fog and Amos of Tekoa remain largely superficial. But these similarities gain substance (and the story gains a whole new interpretation) when Amos Fog's diatribes about work and redemption are viewed alongside the tropes of producerism they appear to echo, and the role Silver plays in Woolson's story is compared with the role silver played in the monetary politics of the period.

"But what are they to Silver?": Debt, Resumption, and Redemption

Running throughout "Castle Nowhere" is a theme of debt that shapes the narrative as it informs the characters' names. Protagonist Jarvis Waring's last name means "cost" or "reckoning"[16]; Amos is Hebrew for "burden." And no sooner has Jarvis Waring been introduced than the reader finds the young man reciting lines from Shakespeare's Sonnet 30 to the rhythm of the waves lapping the shore of the lake. The full sonnet, which is only alluded to in Woolson's narrative, both reflects and extends this theme by deploying economic metaphors to liken the delayed expression of emotions to the cancellation of long-held debts:

When to the sessions of sweet silent thought
I summon up remembrance of things past,
I sigh the lack of many a thing I sought,
And with old woes new wail my dear time's waste:
Then can I drown an eye, unused to flow,
For precious friends hid in death's dateless night,
And weep afresh love's long since cancelled woe,
And moan the expense of many a vanished sight:
Then can I grieve at grievances foregone,
And heavily from woe to woe tell o'er
The sad account of fore-bemoaned moan,
Which I now pay as if not paid before.
But if the while I think on thee, dear friend,
All losses are restor'd and sorrows end.

Like the subject of this sonnet, Amos Fog is also looking back to the past and thus also to a long-held debt of his own. The reader learns of this debt when Fog tells Waring that he adopted Silver to expiate his guilt for a crime he committed forty years earlier in New York City. After fleeing the city with "the mark of Cain" on his brow (47), explains Fog, he "went to and fro on the earth" fearing to join the dead and face punishment for his mortal sin (47). But during his peregrinations Fog began to reckon with God's reckoning. "A crime is committed," he says to Waring, "perhaps in a moment; the ensuing suffering, the results, linger on earth, it may be for some years; but the end of it surely comes sooner or later and it is as though it had never been. Then, for that crime, shall a soul suffer forever,—not a thousand years, a thousand ages if you like, but forever?" (48). Eventually, says Fog, he convinced himself "that no punishment could endure forever, that somewhere in the future I, even I, should meet pardon and rest" (48–49). The same day, he recalls,

"I found by the wayside a little child, scarcely more than a baby; it had wandered out of the poorhouse, where its mother had died" (49), and the thought came to him: "expiation. I would take this forlorn little creature and bring her up as my own child, tenderly, carefully,—a life for a life" (49). If Fog's crime is his debt, then Silver is the medium he has chosen to pay it.

The resulting similarities between Fog, who adopts Silver to pay his debt to society, and the contemporary agrarian who adopted silver coinage as a means to pay the nation's debt are augmented by Fog's description of how he serves his adopted daughter—a description inflected in working-class accents. "I work, I slave," says Fog, who notes that his provisions are "honestly earned" (27). "I get out timber and raft it down to the islands sometimes," he tells Waring,

> although the work is too hard for an old man alone.... Ah, how I have labored! I have felt my muscles crack, I have dropped like a log from sheer weariness. Talk of tortures; which of them have I not felt, with the pains and faintness of exposure and hunger racking me from head to foot? Have I stopped for snow and ice? Have I stopped for anguish? Never; I have worked, worked, worked, with the tears of pain rolling down my cheeks, with my body gnawed by hunger. (27–28)

As a self-identified laborer working for Silver, Amos Fog resembles his working-class counterpart of the Reconstruction era. More important, he resembles his biblical namesake seen through the lens of 1870s political economic ideology. Accordingly, Amos Fog simultaneously appears as a stand-in for both Amos of Tekoa and the agrarian silverite of the mid-to-late 1870s.

With these motifs of obligation and redemption as a backdrop, Woolson's allegory explicitly invokes the discourse surrounding the Civil War debt in the form of Amos Fog's absent sister, Shadow. As the Thomas Nast cartoon reproduced below illustrates, the "greenbacks," whose legal tender status was acquired not by precious metal backing but by an act of Congress, were frequently lampooned as the "shadow" of specie, or a simulacral image of "real money" (see Fig. 1). The "greenbacks" weren't just signs of the Civil War debt, they were the embodiment of this debt. Because "Castle Nowhere" was published during the "greenback" era, the character of Shadow would likely have been read as a reference to the debt the "greenbacks" concretized—a claim supported by the fact that Shadow doesn't even exist in the story except as an afterimage and, in the context of Fog's service to Silver, an afterthought. Shadow's death would therefore have been interpreted as a metaphor for resumption, for like "greenbacks," which were retired when the debt they represented was erased, so too does Shadow's disappearance coincide with her demise.

To extend this allegory, Shadow's relationship to Silver in "Castle Nowhere" parallels the relationship of the national debt to the pro-silver political platform

Fig. 1, Thomas Nast, "A Shadow Is Not a Substance."
David A. Wells, *Robinson Crusoe's Money*.
(New York: Harper, 1876), 58.

of the mid-to-late 1870s in two ways. First, when Amos Fog and Shadow—burden and debt—first encountered Silver she was "wasted with illness and too far gone to talk" (49). But Silver begins her transformation from silence to speech thanks to Shadow, who "took to the child wonderfully" and nurtured her (49). Just as the Coinage Act of 1873 effectively silenced silver (if money speaks, demonetized dollars don't), the lingering Civil War debt figuratively gave silver a voice in the form of those who advocated for its return as a standard of value. Second, Shadow's disappearance (or placement under erasure) underscores Silver's persistence—another nod to the rhetoric of pro-silver advocates who were keen to point out that, as specie, silver was "real money," too.[17] However, like the silverites who continued to agitate for the white metal after resumption of specie payments occurred on the gold standard, Amos Fog's single-minded devotion to Silver leads him to erase the signs of Shadow's death. The debt may be gone, but the burden of serving Silver remains.

Given the sectional inflection of the "money question" during Reconstruction, Fog's role as a man who labors for Silver raises the enticing possibility that Fog may be a Southerner. This possibility is given credence by his given name of Amos, which he shares with another exiled Southerner, and reinforced by the presence of Lorez (a.k.a. Orange), the black servant and former Southern slave whom Amos Fog picks up in New York City, "*another* stray lost out of its place in the world, and suffering from want in the cold Northern city" (49; emphasis added). If Old Fog, like Lorez, traveled to New York City from down South, then "Castle Nowhere" chronicles a Southern laborer traveling north to a sinful city where the moneyed worship the proverbial golden calf, only to be cast out following a crime that stirred "the whole East" (47). These echoes of both the Book of Amos and the agrarian outcry against the "Crime of '73," which by now ought to be legible, would have been too resonant for Woolson's contemporaries to ignore, especially since readers of Woolson's magazine fiction were given regular lessons in the "money question" by the editors of, and other contributors to, the very periodicals in which her work was published.[18]

Fog's role as producerist prophet turns satirical, however, when Fog's talk butts up against his walk, for he's not a producer but a destroyer—his manna comes not from heaven, but from the ships he wrecks with false lights. And the fact that he does it all "for Silver" plays into the hands of the gold monometalist establishment's rhetoric. Fog's service to Silver, wrecking the ships of trade, has a distinct anticapitalist ring to it. The irony would not have been lost on critics of producerism who portrayed pro-silver agitators as advocates for policies that would drain the economy by stifling trade.[19] There's additional dramatic irony in the fact that the reader knows Fog has wrecked more ships than even he admits, which becomes clear when Waring complains that the "castle" is a clumsy imitation of the forecastle of a ship and the reader realizes that it *is* the forecastle of *yet another* ship wrecked by Amos Fog. So, Old Fog may invoke the spirit of Amos of Tekoa while speaking the language of pro-silver producerism, but his actions are inconsistent with the biblical Amos's message. The resulting disconnection between Fog's words and deeds lends credence to critiques of producerism articulated by the "gold bugs" of the era.

The documented Northern bias of Woolson's Reconstruction narratives, when examined alongside this reading of "Castle Nowhere," lends additional support to my assertion that Fog is a Southerner, not only by design but also by serendipitous coincidence.[20] For when viewed through the lens of the "money question" of the late 1870s, "Castle Nowhere" becomes a critique of Southern agrarian money interests, and Woolson sounds like a "gold bug" from her beloved North. In fact, this characterization might not be too far from the truth, as a letter Woolson wrote to the Southern poet Paul Hamilton Hayne illustrates. In this letter, dated April 16, 1876, Woolson quips, "Don't you think that for a red hot abolitionist, Republican *and hard-money advocate*, I have behaved well down here in Dixie during these last three long years?"[21] Woolson's claim to hard-money advocacy could only have meant supporting gold standard policies, for silver was inflationary at the time and would thus have been considered "soft money." Only gold was "hard money" in 1876. Besides reinforcing the regional inflections of the "money question"—Northern gold versus Southern silver—Woolson's letter sheds new light on that enigmatic moment in "Castle Nowhere" when Silver "saw at last how she had robbed him," "him" being her working-class champion, Amos Fog (62). Who else but a self-professed "gold bug" would portray the allegorical representative of silver feeling pity for a debtor who sought in the white metal a respite from the era's "hard times," or have such a character admit that it was she who robbed the misguided laborers for whom Amos Fog stands? These meaningful coincidences illustrate why "Castle Nowhere" should be treated as yet another one of Woolson's Reconstruction allegories, even if the novella's sectionalist inflections weren't articulated until the narrative became a palimpsest for participants in the monetary debates of the period.

Given the reflexive reading I am promoting here, it is only fitting that the resolution of the narrative should anticipate the resolution of the money question of Reconstruction, which was marked by the symbolic return of the bimetallic standard in 1878 and the resumption of specie payments thereafter. These events are prefigured in "Castle Nowhere" by the marriage of Fog's adopted daughter to protagonist Jarvis Waring—a wedding commemorated by a wooden ring on Silver's finger that will eventually be "coated over with heavy gold, just as it is" (61). This pledge of a bimetallic union ends Amos Fog's expiation—his debt is paid just as the Civil War debt was paid—and he can finally rest in peace because Silver is back in circulation with a solemn promise that she will be paired with gold forevermore. Because this matrimonial ending so closely prefigures the bimetallic compromise hammered out in 1878 and the erasure of the Civil War debt that followed, it is clear why reviewers in the 1880s no longer thought "Castle Nowhere" was disagreeably fantastic but in tune with Woolson's "Southern Sketches."

This harmonious resonance between "Castle Nowhere" and the "Southern Sketches" amplifies Woolson's ambivalence about the ultimate success of Reconstruction—an ambivalence that "Old Gardiston," "In the Cotton Country," "Rodman the Keeper," and "King David" articulate. "Castle Nowhere" may not be another romance about failed unions (as in the case of "Rodman") or uneasy national reconciliation (à la "Old Gardiston"), or even a commentary on Northern intrusion into Southern life, but the novella serves a similar function to Woolson's other Reconstruction narratives whose critiques share an economic foundation. In "Old Gardiston," for example, Gardis Duke's acceptance of Captain Newell's marriage proposal is predicated upon the death of her cousin and the destruction of her house—events which coerce rather than invite her to join hands with her Northern counterpart. The same is true for John, the orphaned Southern boy of "In the Cotton Country," who will have a future only if he escapes from poverty, and will escape from poverty only if he is adopted by the visiting narrator from the more prosperous North. Ex-colonel John Rodman's overtures of reconciliation to Miss Bettina Ward are forestalled, not by Rodman's Yankee paternalism but by the poverty that leads Bettina Ward to depart for Tennessee and a teaching job that will support her now that her cousin Ward De Rosset is dead. And David King's efforts to educate and enfranchise Southern freedmen fall short, not because his students are indolent but because, without wealth or power, feigned indolence is the only bargaining chip they have in their quest to have a colored teacher employed in King's stead.

In each of these allegorical tales, policies of Reconstruction and national reconciliation are either complicated or thwarted by material conditions created by agrarianism and the Civil War—conditions that postwar monetary politics exacerbated rather than ameliorated. The irony of the "Southern Sketches" is that the authorial "I" of Woolson's stories often rejects these material and monetary conditions as root causes of Reconstruction's shortcomings and cites something decidedly more ideological as the real source of Reconstruction's frustration. From the vantage point the reader is provided, Gardis Duke, like the South for which she stands, appears merely to cling to foolish pride and outdated tradition and is wise to accept Captain Newell's overtures of reconciliation once relieved of her obligation to maintain the pretense of independence. Similarly, the narrator of "In the Cotton Country," who serves as amanuensis for silenced Southerner Judith, tacitly affirms Judith's contempt for both the freedmen and the legislation that empowered them while echoing Judith's proclamation that national reunification will have to wait for future generations on account of the "sins" of the Confederate past—a past that "no one can help" Judith overcome.[22] And the efforts of both John Rodman and David King to educate ex-slaves appear futile when viewed through the racialist lens of "Rodman the Keeper" and "King David," which make black men like Pompey and Scipio appear inherently dim and prone to self-destructive behavior.

"Castle Nowhere" brings the performative contradictions of Woolson's subsequent Reconstruction narratives into bold relief. In fact, Old Fog embodies just such a contradiction as the materialist critique that his role as latter-day Amos facilitates is undermined by the passions that rule him and the murders he commits to quell them. The resulting ironic tension, which characterizes all of Woolson's

Reconstruction allegories, reveals the complexity of the issues these stories dramatize. Caught again and again between the demonstrative and the rhetorical, readers of Woolson's postbellum narratives find themselves in a position similar to that of Jarvis Waring, who reflects upon Fog's "strange life and its stranger philosophy" only to find "He could not judge them" (50). Instead, Waring is confronted with knowledge that precludes his ability to judge. The reader is placed in the same position when, upon describing Waring's newly cultivated inability to judge Fog's deeds, Woolson asks, "Can we?" (50). If readers judge Woolson's characters by relying solely upon the rhetoric of her narrators, then they have judged too hastily. For when the material conditions these stories portray are considered, readers find they cannot judge at all. Thus, Woolson's apparent condemnation of pro-silver agrarian politics is itself compromised and the reader's judgment, like the measure of Reconstruction's success, is deferred.

Notes

1. For Howells's initial dismissal of *Castle Nowhere*, see "Miss Woolson's *Castle Nowhere*," *Atlantic Monthly* (June 1875): 736. For the keener lament about the position of "Castle Nowhere" within the volume, see "Miss Woolson's Stories," *Scribner's Monthly* (September 1875): 647. For further commentary on the "backward light" of Woolson's later successes, see *The Literary World* (December 11, 1886): 466. For Howells's about-face, see "Editor's Study," *Harper's Monthly* (February 1887): 482.

2. Constance Fenimore Woolson, *Castle Nowhere: Lake Country Sketches* (1875; reprint, with a foreword by Margo Livesey, Ann Arbor: University of Michigan Press, 2004), 7. Subsequent references to and quotations from this collection are cited in the text.

3. Carolyn J. VanBergen, "Legal Tender: The Search for a Just Social Economy in the Novels of Constance Fenimore Woolson" (Ph.D. diss., University of Rochester, 1991), 1.

4. Peter Morris Stephan, "Comparative Value Systems in the Fiction of Constance Fenimore Woolson" (Ph.D. diss., University of New Mexico, 1976), 109.

5. Sharon L. Dean, *Constance Fenimore Woolson: Homeward Bound* (Knoxville: University of Tennessee Press, 1995), 17–18.

6. For an extended discussion of the rhetoric of morality that clung to the "money question" during Reconstruction, see Walter T. K. Nugent, *Money and American Society 1865–1880* (New York: Free Press-Macmillan, 1968), and *The Money Question during Reconstruction* (New York: W. W. Norton, 1967).

7. An account of the Seminary included in L. T. Guilford's *The Story of a Cleveland School, From 1848 to 1881* (Cambridge: John Wilson and Son, 1890) cites lessons in "Old Testament history and prophesy" as part of the curriculum (77).

8. The biblical scholar Mark S. Smith notes that because the foundations of the Hebrew Bible were laid in Jerusalem it is difficult to get an unbiased picture of northern cultic practice. He writes that the installation of the golden calves by Jeroboam I "evidently appeared in biblical books produced in the southern capital because these practices contained evidence of the northern kingdom's apostasy." See *The Early History of God: Yahweh and the Other Deities in Ancient Israel*, 2nd ed. The

Biblical Resource Series (Grand Rapids: Wm. B. Eerdmans, 2002), 12. "Castle Nowhere" inverts this geographical and moral compass by examining Southern politics through a Northern lens.

9. The biblical historian James Luther Mays uses archeological studies to confirm his assertion. "The excavations at Tirzah (Tell el-Farah) uncovered evidence of the social revolution that had occurred," he writes. "While the city's houses in the tenth century had been of uniform size, in the eighth century by contrast there was a quarter of large, expensive houses, and one of small huddled structures." *Amos: A Commentary*. The Old Testament Library (Philadelphia: Westminster, 1969), 2.

10. King James Version. For a modern translation of Amos 8:4–8, see Shalom M. Paul, *A Commentary on the Book of Amos*, ed. Frank Moore Cross, Hermeneia—A Critical and Historical Commentary on the Bible (Minneapolis: Fortress, 1991), 256.

11. Max E. Polley, *Amos and the Davidic Empire: A Socio-Historical Approach* (New York: Oxford University Press, 1989), 17.

12. For a thorough examination of the popular myth of the "Crime of '73," including a description of the role played by Ernest Seyd, see Allen Weinstein, "Was There a 'Crime of 1873'?: The Case of the Demonetized Dollar," *Journal of American History* 54 (1967): 319–20. Evidently, the Populist myth did not square with the actual role Seyd played. Weinstein writes, "Seyd's actual influence on the legislation was less sensational and did not fulfill the popular or Populist stereotype"; in actuality, "Seyd advocated retaining the silver dollar as a full legal tender although reducing its weight to 400 grains" (320n).

13. Quoted in M. W. Walbert, *The Coming Battle* (n.p., 1899), 178–79.

14. "Silver," *Christian Advocate* (February 21, 1878): 120. For another example of the connection of religious discourse and producerist ideology, see "Work and Bread" (July 11, 1878), in which another contributor to the *Christian Advocate* writes: "One of the sins of the Republican administrations has been *worshipping the golden calf*. It has sought too much mere respectability on the basis that gilding makes respectability. It has been allowed, under the lead of such men as Lincoln and Grant, to do a great work.... But when the party seeks respectability by forsaking the people who furnished the blood and honor to coin into liberties and victories and national credit, then the people will forsake the party" (440). Turner's speech is quoted in J. Laurence Laughlin, *The History of Bimetallism in the United States*, 4th ed. (New York: D. Appleton and Co., 1898), III.XIV.17.

15. "The Currency Debate of 1873–74," *North American Review* (July 1874): 117. Besides demonstrating the obvious sectional inflection of the "money question," Adams's observation is a reminder that the turning point of the "money question" occurred during the critical year of 1876, which saw the failed presidential election that would lead directly to the end of Reconstruction in the "Compromise of 1877."

16. *Oxford English Dictionary*, 2nd ed., s.v. "waring." The *OED* defines "waring" as "spending, investing (of money)" or "payment of a price." The definition is obscure, but relevant nonetheless.

17. As Nast's cartoon demonstrates, it was common during the period for money to be personified. It was also common for authors to create extended monetary allegories in their fiction. For a close reading of another monetary allegory that deals with the period 1873–1879, see my "Real Change: George Washington Cable's *The Grandissimes* and the 'Crime of '73,'" *Arizona Quarterly* 61.3 (2005): 75–108.

18. The editors of *Scribner's Monthly*, in which "Peter the Parson" (September 1874) and "Jeanette" (December 1874) appeared, were staunchly against pro-silver agitation. See "Topics of the Time" (October 1879), where the "silver question" appears "absolutely dangerous to every political, commercial and industrial interest" (936). The *Atlantic Monthly*, by contrast, published N. S. Shaler's pro-bimetallism article entitled "The Silver Question Geologically Considered" (May 1878), which concludes, "If steadiness in production over centuries of time is a necessary quality in the substance

taken as a commercial standard, then gold is not to be trusted out of the company of its steadier-gaited companion" (629). Woolson's "Solomon" (October 1873), "Wilhelmina" (January 1875), and "The Lady of Little Fishing" (September 1874) appeared in the *Atlantic*. *The Galaxy*, in which "The Old Agency" (December 1874) was published, took a more measured approach in "The Volume of the Currency" (June 1874), which weighed the pros and cons of increasing the money supply (830–40). *Appletons' Journal*, in which "St. Clair Flats" (October 4, 1873) appeared, published the much more topical "The American at Work: The Genesis and History of a Silver Dollar" (June 1878) by William H. Rideing, who more or less celebrated the return of the silver dollar after the Bland-Allison Act was passed (489–98). And finally, *Harper's Monthly*, which published "Misery Landing" (May 1874), usually stayed above the proverbial fray but published an article by Charles Barnard entitled "Silver" (December 1878), in which the author combines an appraisal of silver's value and a description of its extraction with producerist rhetoric. Barnard writes, "In the immense activities of our commerce and manufactures it often happens that we forget that it is the fisherman, the farmer, and the miner who create wealth" (82).

19. In a document published by *The Bankers' Magazine and Statistical Register*, representatives of banks from New York, Boston, Philadelphia, and Baltimore rehearsed a litany of catastrophes that would accompany the remonetization of silver. "A silver standard will be as mischievous in the domestic as in the foreign commerce of the country," they wrote before professing: "It has been demonstrated . . . that silver has not been fitted to serve as the standard of values; and that had it been used as such, the gravest disasters would have overtaken the Nation." See George S. Coe et al., "Memorial of Banks against the Silver Bill," *The Bankers' Magazine and Statistical Register* (March 1878): 726.

20. For an extended discussion of Woolson's alleged Northern bias, see Karen Weekes, "Northern Bias in Constance Fenimore Woolson's *Rodman the Keeper: Southern Sketches*," *Southern Literary Journal* 32.2 (2002): 102–15. Weekes points out that Woolson may have written her stories at a time when it was common for Northern writers to romanticize the South once it was no longer a political threat, but her "Southern Sketches" more closely resemble Northern fiction of the late 1860s that was "hostile to conciliatory representations of the region" (103). Woolson's biases are more complicated than they may at first appear, however, as I remark in the conclusion of this essay.

21. Quoted in Jay B. Hubbell, "Some New Letters of Constance Fenimore Woolson," *New England Quarterly* 14 (1941): 731. Emphasis added.

22. Constance Fenimore Woolson, "In the Cotton Country," *Appletons' Journal* (April 29, 1876): 551.

"The Daughters of Carolina"
The South Beckons

The very girls who, at school, had grandly called themselves "The Daughter of Carolina," (to the astonishment of the new western pupil, who had never thought of styling herself "The Daughter of Ohio"), proved themselves her daughters indeed, when the time came.
—*Constance Fenimore Woolson to Hjalmar Hjorth Boyesen*

Constance Fenimore Woolson and the Origins of the Global South

—John Lowe

Constance Fenimore Woolson's attempt to instill a new awareness of American identity, of hemispheric and Atlantic connectedness, is figured in her arresting metaphor for the shape of Florida, a "long, warm peninsula" that she sees "stretching like a finger pointing southward from the continent's broad palm into the tropic sea."[1] After years of living in Florida, where two of her novels and many of her short stories are set, Woolson was conscious of the state's relation to the Caribbean and the polyglot peoples of the Americas. The most obvious import of the peninsula's "finger" is the directed link with Cuba and the Antilles; but Florida also points to a Creolized culture, where the peoples of the Caribbean jostle, interact, and create new hybrid forms of expression and material culture. As the Caribbean writer Edward Kamau Brathwaite has noted, creolization amounts to "a cultural action—material, psychological, and spiritual—based upon the stimulus/response of individuals within the society of their environment and—as white/black, culturally discrete groups—to each other."[2] In several of her short stories, Woolson describes such communities, but the creolized town of Gracias (based on St. Augustine) in her novel *East Angels* (1886) proves exemplary. Two churches, Anglican and Catholic, sit side by side, as do their parishioners, and yet the public occasions of the town involve everyone. Although a perceived ethnic and racial hierarchy prevails, Woolson describes throughout her novel a site of cultural interdependency, hybridity, and often harmony.

Both *East Angels* and Woolson's Florida short stories reveal that her work is ripe for new critical assessment. Most scholars reasonably associate postcolonial theory with the literatures produced by formerly subject people in Asia, Africa, and the Caribbean. A few years ago, however, Walter Benn Michaels startled many of his American Studies peers by suggesting that Thomas Nelson Page's forgotten novel of Southern Reconstruction, *Red Rock: A Chronicle of Reconstruction* (1898), might profitably be read through the lens of postcolonial theory. After all, white Southerners saw their region as a victim of Northern invasion and colonization from 1865 to around 1917, and many Confederates migrated to Mexico and Brazil. The disenfranchised Confederates remaining, many without homes, were functionally or mentally "exiles," which Woolson discovered almost immediately upon her arrival in the postwar South.[3]

Most of the characters in Woolson's Southern narratives are in mourning for their "lost homeland," even if they are still living in it. The decaying mansion, the tattered rags of former finery, the barren fields, the empty quarters—all of these are decried by blacks, whites, Minorcans, and others. Many figures leave, in a Southern diaspora that extends into the American West, Europe, and often the tropics south of the South. But in Woolson's time, Florida was part of a similarly unknown territory, a virtual "tropical island." The Southern communities she depicts are far from the postwar nation's urban centers and most of them are "islands," either in reality or in function. As such, they bear comparison to what Antonio Benitez-Rojo has termed the "repeating island" aspect of Caribbean culture. Benitez-Rojo refers to the ways in which the cultures of the Caribbean have been ignored and marginalized, and he identifies several factors that have contributed to this condition, including fragmentation, instability, reciprocal isolation, uprootedness, cultural heterogeneity, lack of historiography and historical continuity, contingency and impermanence.[4] All of these conditions emerged in the postbellum South and in Woolson's fiction. She would seem to be playing a doubled role as author in these works—namely, to make artistic and aesthetic capital out of such conditions, but also to displace or reform them. Her histories of Florida highlight the long trajectory of events that began in the contact era and encompass the centuries of Spanish and/or Native American dominance. At the same time, she embraces cultural difference and takes her readers beyond the usual racial binary of reconstruction fiction and mythology.

Like Benitez-Rojo, Woolson recognized that this complicated, heterogeneous culture was awash in a "soup of signs," and she could hardly hope to decode them all. Like Woolson, Benitez-Rojo attempts to analyze aspects of Caribbean culture in an effort "not to find results, but processes, dynamics, and rhythms that show themselves within the marginal, the regional, the incoherent, the heterogeneous, or if you like, the unpredictable that coexists with us in our everyday world."[5] While it may be difficult to move outward from the nineteenth-century conventions of genre that tend to shape Woolson's fiction, it is wise to be newly attentive to the margins of her stories and, above all, to the details and methods in her mode of physical description, a mapping that gives context and sometimes revelation to ostensibly central plots.

Similarly intent on shedding light where none has been, Édouard Glissant and his fellow theorist, Antonio Benitez-Rojo, find a solution to the isolation of discrete islands in the Caribbean through the element that unites them—that is, the sea. This monumental fact of nature creates similarities for cultures, shaping and connecting them, particularly in terms of folklore and myth. Not surprisingly, Woolson's Florida characters travel on steamers, yachts, trawlers, fishing vessels, or canoes because, often as not, they too are surrounded by water—oceans, sounds, lakes, rivers, swamps. These bodies of water are described idyllically or realistically, as scenes of the sublime or as turbulent, dangerous cauldrons. They are links to the outside world, avenues into the primeval, sources of life through the harvest of the sea. They are also the watery paths to death, as is most dramatically seen in the story "Sister St. Luke" and in several inset stories in the novel *East Angels*. Perhaps because of this Atlantic ambiance, it is only in Florida settings that Woolson continually refers to Africa, a presence beyond the ocean that is suggested by the Africans and African Americans she encounters. This is but one of many ways in which the Black Atlantic registers in her work. Her waterway connectedness recalls Glissant's observation about the subterranean convergence of Caribbean history, particularly in terms of the thousands of black bodies thrown overboard from slave vessels. In Glissant's evocative formulation, these events have grown "submarine roots" that are "floating free . . . extending in all directions . . . through its network of branches."[6] As Woolson's characters suggest, these submarine histories link more than just African Americans.

For Benitez-Rojo and many others who have studied both the South and the Caribbean, the great engine that developed this broad region was the plantation. When Woolson chose to situate her fiction in her own time rather than in the antebellum period, it was inevitable that she would write about the temporary destruction of what has been called the "plantation-machine."[7] The great sugar mills, the cotton farms, the orange groves—all these are failing in Woolson's Florida, one reason many assume she was influenced by Thomas Nelson Page and Thomas Dixon, or perhaps Mary Noailles Murfree and others associated with the Appalachian school of romance, such as James Fox Jr. or James Lane Allen. All of these writers, however, published after Woolson's stories began appearing in the 1870s. By choosing this moment of decline and despair, she sets in motion the thematics she most cared about—namely, those of dignified poverty, renunciation, and constant struggle, including the struggle toward social progress, both personal and communal, which ultimately can lead to redemption and renewal. Her delineation of the coastal South—particularly Florida—is unique and comes from her own close inspection. She must therefore be considered as an inventor of Southern local color fiction, Appalachian writing, and (as I will argue) transatlantic fiction of the Global South basin.

As a case in point, her story "Rodman the Keeper" begins this way: "In the little town . . . Everything was monotonous, and the only spirit that rose above the waste was a bitterness for the gained and sorrow for the lost cause. The keeper was the only man whose presence personated the former in their sight, and upon him therefore, as representative, the bitterness fell . . . in sudden silences . . . in withdrawals and avoidance, until he lived and moved in a vacuum . . . so Rodman withdrew himself, and came and went among them no more" (11–12).[8] This opening tableau emphasizes "silences," one of Woolson's dominant motifs, for she constantly maintains that the people of the South—be they British, Spanish, cracker, African, or Native American—have been "silenced" by defeat and colonization. Henry James recognized this aspect of her work in speaking of her Southern tales' high value, "especially when regarded in the light of the *voicelessness* of the conquered and reconstructed South."[9] The silence of colonized/conquered people is a note frequently sounded in the theory and discourse of postcolonial peoples, whose chronic economic dependency has often been noted; in Martinique, for example, Aimé Césaire long ago remarked on a people "so strangely garrulous yet silent."[10] In all of his work, Martinique's Édouard Glissant has sought to rupture this silence. As he puts it, "Caribbean people should not entrust to others the job of defining their culture."[11] Similarly, the reactionary Virginian Thomas Nelson Page, speaking of the silencing of the South during Reconstruction, once noted, "We are not a race to pass and leave no memorial on our time. We live with more than Grecian energy. We must either leave our history to be written by those who do not understand it, or we must write it ourselves."[12] While Woolson, from New England and the Midwest, might be seen as one of Glissant's "others" or Page's "those who do not understand," her embrace of the South, and her presentation of both its virtues and vices through the eyes of her Northern characters, actually historicizes and ennobles Southern struggles. In her fiction, she gives the region a multitude of voices, many of them redolent of both the wider South below Florida and the myriad connections of the Atlantic world.

Woolson knew, of course, that a grieving North might lend a more sympathetic ear to Southern chronicles if approached through mourning, the very maneuver of postcolonial literatures that rehearse wars of oppression, exile, and genocide from a foundation in grief and memorial. The mood of death and ruin that dominates the beginning of "Rodman the Keeper" has a sequel later when the title figure relates his personal history, one that involves the deaths of his parents and his two brothers, the loss of the family home, his fortune, and his health, as well as the admission that he sought the Keeper's job because the Southern climate would aid his recovery. Miss Bettina, similarly grieving over her dead kin though obstinate in her loyalty to the Lost Cause, seems a possible mate for Rodman, especially after she comes secretly to the Union cemetery to honor the dead despite her pride. Yet Miss

Bettina's rituals of mourning and Rodman's take on very different meanings, and the two ultimately part; Rodman kisses her hand just before she leaves for a lonely teaching job in Tennessee. Still, Miss Bettina might return one day, a hope partly engendered when Rodman goes to the new Yankee owner of her old family home and requests cuttings of the vines she planted there.

In this story, Woolson atones for her "darky" imagery by featuring a moving procession of the town's black folk to honor the fallen Yankees who helped set them free. On national memorial day, they ask Rodman to "head . . . de processio'" so they can scatter flowers on the graves. As Woolson describes the scene, "It was a pathetic sight to see some of the old men and women, ignorant field-hands, bent, dull-eyed, and past the possibility of education even in its simplest forms, carefully placing their poor flowers to the best advantage. They knew dimly that the men who lay beneath those mounds had done something wonderful for them and for their children; and so they came bringing their blossoms, with little intelligence but with much love" (33).

Woolson's attention to the alternate perspective of nondominant ethnic peoples takes a different form in the collection's second story, "Sister St. Luke." The story opens by confronting three pairs of "Spanish eyes" on an island near Pelican Reef in the former Spanish territory of Florida. Carrington and Keith, two Anglo friends vacationing at the lighthouse, are the real narrative focus, not the "swarthy Pedro" or the "figure in black" of the nun Woolson's title references. Sister St. Luke is at odds with Pedro's wife, who is not Spanish or Catholic but a fierce Vermont Protestant who married Pedro unaccountably since she hates the "lazy tropical island" and the Catholic Church in equal measure. As keeper of the old lighthouse that was built by the Spanish, remodeled by the British, and then redone by the United States, the Minorcan Pedro echoes Rodman's "keeper" role. What is "kept," in both the lighthouse and the Union cemetery, is a marker of history and a symbol of warning, here against the reefs of the world. Woolson signals the link to the Caribbean by referring to the ships that sweep by on their way to the "Queen of the Antilles" (presumably Cuba) and the "far Windward and Leeward Islands" (44). Later, Keith imagines a sea-bean drifting from "one of the West Indian islands . . . let us say Miraprovos—a palmy tropical name, bringing up visions of a volcanic mountain, vast cliffs, a tangled gorgeous forest, and the soft lapping wash of tropical seas" (62). This image is in keeping with Keith's romantic view of nature; upon finding Pedro's lost boat in the marsh, he had earlier rhapsodized, "a salt marsh is not complete without . . . an abandoned craft, aged and deserted, aground down the marsh with only its mast rising above the waste" (56). The figure rehearses the basic elements of the Romantic ruin as a metaphor of the relation between man and nature; however, the mast rising above the waste also mirrors the situation of the story's virtually abandoned lighthouse. Woolson pauses on the history of that tower attached to a crumbling Spanish fort: early "keepers" evidently kept a sharp eye out for "damnable Huguenot" sails, which find their current referent in Pedro's New England Puritan wife. Woolson also acknowledges the rest of the Atlantic; the waves in "Sister St. Luke" surge from "the distant African coast," which had, of course, occasioned the great war a century before that had devastated the United States.

The story also provides a detailed description of the twenty-mile-long island, with its salt marsh, plants, crabs, jellyfish, gulls, pelicans, hawks, and eagles, and the varieties of its seaweed. Sister Luke stands in for the reader as Carrington and Keith educate her about the Florida world that seems so strange, a world that helped encourage the tremendous postbellum vogue for travel writing that Woolson had already mined. Building by accretion, the story conversely strips away the nun's habit. Pedro's Protestant wife removes the wimple, leaving only a veil and, during the jaunt to the ridge and marsh, Keith sweeps that off, too. This effort to remake and educate the nun works contrary to the recognition of a wider world and the uncovering of a Spanish past, specifically a Spanish galleon that emerges from the eroding sands. As the sunbathing Keith puts it, "I never imagined I was lying on the bones of this old Spaniard" (63). In Woolson's story, history becomes a palimpsest, for Sister St. Luke is essentially a descendant of the old Spanish sailor, and the Minorcans like Pedro have helped create the paradise that the Anglos gratefully inhabit away from Northern snow and ice. All these factors gradually erode any concept of a "superior" Anglo "race."

Instead, Woolson paints a portrait of Sister St. Luke's convent life that is serene and beguiling, replete with doves, the convent garden, orange trees, and soft music. As a site of global reckoning, the convent belongs to Florida's complex history, which is seen through those early "Spanish eyes." But the story also reads Florida as Northerners Keith and Carrington see it: what they "teach" Sister St. Luke proceeds from the "lessons" they have learned themselves. Pedro's actual marriage to his Vermont Protestant and the impossible marriage Woolson nevertheless imagines between Keith and Sister St. Luke both cross cultural and religious lines, and they point to the suddenly hybrid nature of American history and society.

Woolson's fascination with tropical landscapes takes a different and disquieting turn in "The South Devil," a tale that opens at the edge of a burned plantation home, as robust orange grower Mark Deal and his consumptive sibling Carl enjoy the warm December sun. The house was burned by Indians and the narrator recalls the Spanish past when plantations flourished: "the belief is imbedded in all our Northern hearts that, because the narrow, sun-bathed State is far away and wild and empty, it is also new and virgin, like the lands of the West; whereas it is old—the only gray-haired corner our country holds" (142). Woolson excels in her description of this cypress-shadowed realm, with its myriad plants and animals that insinuate an atmosphere of menace. Yet Carl sees beauty where Mark sees danger.

Both, in fact, are present. Mark shoots a moccasin that is about to spring, but Carl has climbed the swamp canopy where "the long moss hangs in fine, silvery lines like spray . . . mixed with . . . air-plants, sheafs, and bells of scarlet and cream-colored blossoms" (149); but dreaming or dozing, he fell. Here Woolson rehearses the thematic from Melville's great chapter in *Moby-Dick*, "The Mast-head," where Ishmael warns "pantheists" at watch atop a ship about dreamily gazing at a moonlit sea and then falling to their death. Mark also sees nature as his enemy because he has to hack his living out of it. Woolson's detailed description of the moccasins Mark kills repeatedly shows both her revulsion and her fascination, almost admiration.[13]

Woolson's scenes in the Southern swamp exemplify what other narratives of exploration and travel made of the postwar South and anticipate later encounters with the exotic and even the surreal. In 1939, Aimé and Suzanne Césaire began publishing a journal in Martinique entitled *Tropiques*, which featured the work of surrealists such as André Breton. On their behalf, Suzanne urged readers to embrace "the domain of the strange, the marvelous and the fantastic, a domain scorned by people of certain inclinations. Here is the freed image, dazzling and beautiful, with a beauty that could not be more unexpected and overwhelming. Here are the poet, the painter, and the artist, presiding over the metamorphoses and the inversions of the world under the sign of hallucination and madness."[14] The Césaires saw surrealism operating as a revolutionary force; for Aimé, it was part of a "call from Africa." Certainly Woolson's presentation of the swamp and its flora and fauna in these fantastic scenes resonates with the methods of African writers whose native landscapes speak so seductively to the aesthetic imagination.

The intoxicating beauty of the South Devil is enough to lure Carl, but in Woolson's story and elsewhere the setting proves even more laden. As a psychologically symbolic site, the swamp often embodies the repressed in human consciousness, which Freud has treated as a central concern. More historically, the swamp has been seen as both refuge and site of freedom, one that had already registered powerfully in Harriet Beecher Stowe's *Uncle Tom's Cabin* (1852) and *Dred: A Tale of the Dismal Swamp* (1856) as well as in antebellum slave narratives and the fiction spun out of the Haitian Revolution.[15] But there Woolson hesitates. The crisis of her story comes when a false friend named Schwartz gets Carl drunk, cheats him at cards, and demands Mark's hidden money. Instead of fleeing to the swamp, Schwartz books passage for Key West, where "smuggling and illegal trading" abounded and "all the harbors, inlets, and lagoons of the West Indies were open" (163). For Woolson, South Florida and the islands beyond extend the negative figuration of the American tropics, whose serpents are men. The portrayal of the South Atlantic as a lawless terrain allies that alternative Florida to mythologies of the frontier and has much to do with the tangled web of imperialistic conquest and piracy that was well established by the mid-nineteenth century.

As "The South Devil" demonstrates, Woolson examines Florida's peninsular topography from swamps to palm regions, from scrub to shore, and discovers what Mark's New England leaves out, the Caribbean waterways that ushered Carl into the wetlands and took Swartz south.[16] In the story "Felipa," in fact, the title character is so racially marked as "dark-skinned, yellow-eyed" that she seems almost a part of the landscape. A fisherwoman dressed in men's clothing, she has only seen three women in her life when vacationers Catherine and Christine arrive at their enchanted Florida "Paradise" with their prejudices intact. As is usual with Woolson, they disparage Felipa's Minorcan relatives as "slow-witted . . . part pagan, part Catholic, and wholly ignorant; their minds rarely rose above the level of their orange-trees and their fish-nets" (199). It is therefore no surprise when Christine confides to Catherine, "Teach a child like that, and you ruin her . . . ruin her happiness" (200), a convenient twisting of Rousseau's theory of the Noble Savage that has been repeated for centuries in colonial cultures.

The comment also suggests the story's multiple perspectives. When Catherine finally paints Felipa and her dog Drollo, Christine sees an image of "an ugly little girl," where Catherine means to embody "latent beauty, courage, and a possible great gulf of love" (203). Just as in "The South Devil," friends view the same thing very differently, a point Woolson makes repeatedly, as her fiction circles round an object or idea from various angles. Even Felipa contributes: when she dresses up in borrowed finery and Catherine laughs, she drags the artist to the mirror and cries, "You are not pretty either . . . Look at yourself!" (209). Here the colonizing gaze is reversed. With these shifts in perspective, Woolson reveals not only contrary opinions but also unpleasant truths about the dominant culture and perhaps the complicity of her readers. Although narrated in English, Woolson's story is actually multilingual: the Anglo characters all speak Spanish with Felipa, but when she appears to be learning the English they use to shut her out, they resort to French. Spanish, English, French—these are, of course, the languages of the colonized Caribbean.

The story ends shockingly when Felipa, who has adored both Christine and her lover Edward, turns on the latter after Christine agrees to marry him, thereby shutting Felipa out of what she had seen as a trio. Having eaten paints and let a snake bite her, Felipa stabs Edward in the arm, then asks to die at Christine's feet with "her white robe over me" (220). Although the girl recovers, the confrontation gains in dimension as Woolson's readers acknowledge their own assumptions about Felipa's "dog-like" devotion, which has become suicidal rage. It is further worth pondering how the great slave revolts of the South and the Caribbean put an end to such assumptions when the myth of black devotion evaporated.

The gulf between white authority and black agency also informs the most problematic story in Woolson's collection, "King David," which concerns a white Northern teacher in a black Southern school. Woolson initially deals in stereotypes;

students are as "black as the ace of spades" and as wild as "mustangs." Yet the story has a Black Atlantic ring: the teacher tells his charges they should strive for an education so they may become agents of change in Africa. Unfortunately, says the story's narrator, "Cassius and Pompey had only a mythic idea of Africa; they looked at the globe as it was turned around, they saw it here on the other side, and then their attention wandered off to an adventurous ant who was making the tour of soodan and crossing the mountains of Kong as though they were nothing" (255). Sharon Dean has tartly—and correctly—observed that David King's mission is the ultimate form of colonialism, since he seeks to create disciples who will serve as ambassadors for his idea of an even more debased culture, that of Africa.[17] Commenting from a related angle, Édouard Glissant speaks of the attempt to instill mimicry in the colonized. "Because the method of transformation (domination by the Other) sometimes favors the practice of approximation or the tendency to derision, it introduces into the new relationship the insidious promise of being remade in the Other's image, the illusion of successful mimesis" (15).[18]

The arrogance of colonial authority is just as evident in "Up in the Blue Ridge," perhaps the collection's most impressive story. It's a small detail that interests me, but it orients my conclusions about the collection as a whole and it comes in the story's brief final line: "The wild, beautiful region is not yet conquered" (338). In this last pronouncement, the moonshiners are seen as representative, not only of the mountain people but of the proud, blue-hazed mountains themselves. The Appalachian mountaineers, although Americans, are in effect in a world apart, a world they protect against the encroachments of the outside civilization. Woolson seems to be paying tribute to a Southern variant of the maroons, those bands of escaped slaves who populated the swamps and mountains of the South and the Caribbean alike. Similarly, maroon culture had been crucial to Nat Turner's band in Virginia and Toussaint L'Ouverture's army in Saint Domingue, as it still was to the Seminoles in the Florida swamps. In Woolson's story, Wainwright accuses the moonshiners of murder, but Brother Heade points out that what has been going on is "war."

This host of Southern stories leads to several conclusions. First, Woolson obviously drew from the Plantation tradition but with a difference; she approached it with Northern eyes and through Northern characters. Second, she was keenly conscious that Florida was a different part of the South, and her constant concern for the Spanish and Indian past—even if she tended to portray both heritages, along with African American culture, as racially inferior—speaks to her interest in transnational issues that would eventuate in her removal to Italy. Third, her almost biological fascination with Southern flora and fauna dictates that she be considered, perhaps for the first time, as part of the group of Caribbean writers who have made capital out of the basin's ecology.

What is more, Woolson's stories of the postwar South paved the way for *East Angels* (1886), whose stern binaries dissolve in the circumCaribbean sun. Henry James reserved his highest praise for this novel when he wrote of Woolson that "she has expended on her subject stores of just observation and an infinite deal of the true historical spirit."[19] Like "The South Devil," *East Angels* opens with a meditation on the difference between the tropic blue skies of Florida and faraway ice and snow. The Northern visitor, now with the historic Puritan name of Winthrop, basks in the sun while the Southern Garda yearns to experience winter, perhaps because her New England mother has told her about the colder climes. The exotic, Spanish aspect of Garda's home, "East Angels," is signaled by the name of the hamlet, Gracias-a-Dios, and Woolson will elaborate the transatlantic and Caribbean influences on this place throughout the narrative. Despite her displacement in Florida, Garda's mother, Mrs. Thorne, was a staunch Confederate during "the late unhappy context" (6), and she applauds the British for their sympathy with the Lost Cause: "they were with us—all their best people—as to our patriarchal system for our servants" (6). The Thorne family, however, has been in Florida for generations, first during the British occupation and then afterward under the Spanish, when a Thorne married a Duero; their son also married a Spaniard, which accounts for Garda's doubled ancestry. As Mrs. Thorne puts it, "Edgarda is the portrait of her Spanish grandmother painted in English colors" (7), a clever construction that embeds an assertion of racial purity. Garda hardly makes Florida attractive to Winthrop, for she asserts that the cultivation of cotton and cane is impossible now without slaves, and that the new industry of orange growing requires advisors not yet present. Moreover, there are the heat, the swamps, the snakes.

The exotic nature of Garda, who is not at all the usual plantation belle, is reinforced when Winthrop associates her "naturalness" with Native American maidens he had encountered and did not much care for out West. But Garda is somehow different, which indicates a shifting racial line in Winthrop's categories of exotica. His ethnic spectrum, as is usual in Woolson's postwar stories, includes African Americans. Despite their poverty, the Thornes have a "jet-black" retainer named Raquel, a fourth-generation servant who is loyal to the family. Significantly, she and her husband, the gardener Pablo, both have Spanish names, hinting at cross-racial sexuality during the Spanish regime.

Winthrop's tour of East Angels allows Woolson to display her expertise with flora and fauna, as the avenue of live oaks, the cultivated magnolias, the Cherokee roses, the romantic ruins, the towering palms, the orange arcade, and pet crane Carlos all get considered. The house, though decayed, has a specifically tropical magnificence; with pomegranate wainscoting and shell masonry construction, the building forms a parallelogram around a Spanish courtyard and features a balcony with green blinds. Winthrop's introduction to this and other such houses is a revelation:

he discovers "tradition and legend ... which had nothing to do with Miles Standish ... [having] more richness of color and a deeper perspective than that possessed by any of the rather blank ... American history farther north." Woolson continues, "Like most New-Englanders, he had unconsciously cherished the belief that all there was of historical importance ... was associated with the Puritans." Thinking of Europe, he muses, "When Raphael was putting into the backgrounds of his pictures those prim, slenderly foliaged trees which he had seen from Perugino's windows in his youth, the Spaniards were exploring this very Florida shore" (16). This reference to the Italian Renaissance brings a forceful congruity to privileged art and New World conquest, while drawing the parameters of the Americas into a different configuration. Before the Puritans sailed for New England, Winthrop sums up, "on this Southern shore had been towns and people, governors, soldiers, persecutions, priests" (16). Woolson takes care to extend the Atlantic world when she describes the sea as stretching "eastward to Africa," thereby establishing a link that is manifest in her black characters and the qualities they have contributed to a hybrid Southern culture.

Woolson also brings Indians into the narrative through the romantic ruin Winthrop sketches, now grown over with the yellow jessamine that was Woolson's favorite flower and the subject of one of her best poems. The ruin is an old sugar mill destroyed by the Seminoles, a site whose history is related somewhat impressionistically by the biased local doctor, Reginald Kirby. "Canebrake, swamp, hammock ... ague, sunstroke, everglade; fever, scalping, ambuscade—and massacre, massacre, massacre!" (28). Winthrop actually has an ancestor named "Dizzy Dick" who fought in these wars, and Dr. Kirby remembers the magical Indian words: "the Withlacoochee, the Caloosahatchie, the Suwanee, the Ocklawaha" (28). As it turns out, Dizzy Dick fought side by side with the doctor's brother, and the uncle for whom Winthrop was named went to Central America to "see the Aztecs" (69), proof positive that it's a small transnational world.

Garda's grandmother taught her Spanish, and Kirby's sister taught her French. Thus, Garda commands the three languages of the Caribbean and can converse with her neighbor, Adolfo Torres, born in Cuba but educated in Spain; he speaks only Spanish, and his last name has several meanings in that language: tower, tower block, castle, and rook. Perhaps to reflect the suspected African heritage of Cubans, Woolson describes him as a "dark-skinned youth, with dull black eyes ... ungainly" (38–39). He strongly contrasts with the Spaniard Manuel Ruiz from a neighboring estate, a "remarkably handsome young man" who is compared to a romantic Italian tenor; Manuel is also an English-speaking American. While Woolson's characterization of Torres might raise some eyebrows, it is important to note that Garda is preparing to marry him, not Ruiz, at the end of the story. As the most "Spanish" of the characters and the darkest one among them, he represents the Moorish taint of

Spain. A "tower" of sorts, he is associated with one of the key icons of the Spanish flag, the tower of Castile, but perhaps also with Moro Castle in Havana, his hemispheric reference. Edgarda Thorne, his beloved, has a feminized form of Edgard for her moniker, but everyone calls her Garda, which relates to the Spanish verb "guardar" (to keep, to put away, to look after, to guard, to observe) and with the reflexive "se" (to be careful not to). Garda, more than any of the other characters, truly "sees" nature, and she guards against yielding to the conventional strictures of her culture(s). As a child of a New Englander, she naturally inherits Emersonian traits of self-reliance and independence, which many readers have translated as egoism and selfishness.

But Woolson clearly invites readers to see both her and Torres as *criollos* of the Americas, and it is not surprising that they wind up together. Only the fact that Woolson is an Anglo author suggests that she might be expected to "improve" her characters, as Mrs. Thorne might say, by further "Saxonizing" them. To be fair, the silencing of Torres, a "rook" who must play a patient waiting game, demonstrates Woolson's broader pattern of silencing the Latino culture that is dominant in Gracias-a-Dios. And yet her linkage of this community with both Latin America and Spain—and, through racial suggestiveness, with Africa—recalls Glissant's insistence on the subterranean links of related cultures, a reference that is similar to Deleuze and Guattari's concept of cultural rhizomes with their underground connections between blades of grass.[20] *East Angels* discourses at length on the history of Gracias-a-Dios, which was named by grateful Spanish sailors fleeing a storm. Woolson delineates between the original British and later immigrants from Georgia and the Carolinas, thus elevating the Thornes. But there are more recent newcomers: predators who want to open health resorts, land speculators, builders of canals, and drainers of swamps who want to rape the landscape and ignore its history while pronouncing gracias "grashus." This further delineation has frequently been voiced by natives of the Caribbean, and in fact the "invaders" in both Florida and points south had counterparts in the earlier pirates, wreckers, and smugglers who holed up (as Schwartz of "The South Devil" well knew) in the Florida Keys. This range of attitudes toward ethnicity means that when Mrs. Thorne tells Garda, "Mr. Winthrop is not another Manuel or Torres" (52), Garda agrees. She *and* Manuel and Adolfo see that this ultra-Anglo must be respected like a father, a remark that is far from what her mother intended. Garda ignores the racial aspect of the older woman's distinction, while simultaneously acknowledging hierarchy among New World cultures.

Woolson situates connections between persons of African descent in this way as well. *East Angels* makes comedy out of the contrast of Celestine, a Yankee really named Minerva Poindexter, and the black servants of the nearby Seminole Inn, which furnishes meals for the visitors; these servants, including Telano Johnson, have never seen a white retainer before (Celestine is Winthrop's aunt Katrina's maid). Here Woolson inserts more Caribbean color, for Telano, thinking Minerva a witch, shakes a voodoo fetish at her and practices conjure, what Woolson terms "pagan rites." Minerva, by contrast, loves Telano's songs and hums "these bones," thinking the words refer to rheumatism. A fervent Protestant, Minerva is appalled that they are living over an old Franciscan monastery. It is significant that Woolson's ethnic humor often comes at the expense of the ostensibly "white" figures, who offer comic relief but who also provide a sense of the multiethnic texture of the community and its complicated class totem pole.

Throughout the novel, the theme of courtship and marriage nonetheless predominates, spiced by the possibilities of cross-ethnic unions. The complications surrounding Garda are increased when Lucian Spenser joins the circle, for he incites jealousy, particularly from Manuel and Adolfo; Spenser is deemed just as handsome as Manuel, and he is an Anglo descended from Virginia's Byrd family. Once again the racial line of distinction emerges, although it is complicated by the fact that Spenser speaks Spanish and takes an interest in Torres. This "mixing" thematic takes a further linguistic turn in Woolson's description of the fishermen: "their English was by no means clear, it was mixed with Spanish and West Indian, with words borrowed from the not remote African of the Florida negro, and even with some from the native Indian tongues; it was a very patchwork of languages" (180). The metaphor is an interesting one, in that quilted patchwork forms a unity—in fact, a useful one. Woolson's reference is not to Babel or to impurities; she comments instead on the *métissage* of circumCaribbean languages.

It is a mingling with a motive. When Winthrop buys East Angels from Mrs. Thorne, Woolson has another tailor-made opportunity to provide Spanish-era history as the deeds are examined. The original grant to Admiral Juan de Duero in 1585 was directly from the Spanish crown and was regranted later by the British sovereign. The property survived three raids by buccaneers and several by Indians. Some of the latter group, in fact, are still in the area; it turns out the Northern visitor Margaret has made a shirt for the Sioux chieftain Spotted Tail, which prompts Winthrop's declaration, "they don't want shirts, they want their land . . . We should have made them take care of themselves long ago, but we shouldn't have stolen their land" (207). Yet Winthrop himself has not paid much for East Angels. The colonization of Indian lands thus seems a parallel to the Northern colonization of Florida. Here Woolson comments on the ways in which legal maneuvers play key roles, often corrupt and corrupting, during eras of transition and colonization.

In a similar fashion, she undercuts the Northern-born Mrs. Thorne, who declares as she lies dying:

in my heart I have always hated the whole thing . . . I have always ranked the lowest Puritan far, far above the very finest Spaniard they could muster . . . they caught the poor Indians and made them work for them; because they imported Human Flesh, they dealt in negro slaves! . . . Their country here will be opened up, improved; but not by them. It will be made modern, made rich under their very eyes; but not by them . . . They will dwindle in numbers, but they will not change . . . *Could* I leave Garda to that? Could I die, knowing that she would live over there . . . on that forlorn Ruiz plantation, or . . . in that tumble-down house of the Girons—that Manuel with his insufferable airs, or that wooden Torres with his ridiculous pride, would be all she should ever know of life and happiness—my beautiful, beautiful child? (220–21)

This arrogant Saxon also provides a moving and extensive list of the labors and thrifts she has had to endure to make ends meet over the years, with the idea that her sacrifices have been exceptional. She confesses that, in her determination to make herself over as a Thorne, "I even swallowed slavery—I, a New England girl . . . abolitionist to the core! . . . I covered every inch of myself with a southern skin. But if any one thinks that it was easy or pleasant, let him try" (224). She never considers that her neighbors must have gone through similar trials.

Tellingly, when Mrs. Thorne is buried, her coffin is borne by eight former slaves, who have not appeared before in the narrative. In the cemetery, the tombs have a local touch: they are made of coquina, a stone generated from shells and shell fragments, and the characters one by one follow the Florida custom of casting handfuls of sand into the open grave. As is so often the case, the black characters are not portrayed individually, but in anonymous groupings: "the negroes of the neighborhood . . . sang their own funeral hymn; their voices rose with sweetness in the wildly plaintive minor strains" (231). The group of eight blacks is then repeated when Torres comes courting, rowed by eight negroes who have been taken from their work in the sugar fields. In *East Angels*, Torres is "dark," so having eight black men row him to Kirby's situates him as "white" in the bichromatic arrangement of power in the postbellum South. When Garda's guardian Kirby rejects Torres, it is apparently because of his age, but that rationale is a cover for a deeper-seated bias, as the use of the coded term "boy" confirms. This scene is followed, however, by the novel's presentation of Torres's thoughts as he reacts to Manuel's fury at being rejected in favor of Lucian; here Woolson reveals a more cerebral side of Torres that the monolingual English-speaking world does not suspect.

Woolson's examination of racial "types" would hardly be complete without a consideration of poor whites. In the pine barrens where Winthrop canters, he meets for the first time a "cracker" who is "astride his sorry pony," while "[p]acked into the two-wheeled cart behind him, [are] all his family, with their strange clay-colored complexions and sunburnt light hair." Woolson continues, "They were a gentle, mummy-like people, too indolent even to wonder why a stranger should wish to know [directions]" (274). There is reason to wonder at the way Woolson constantly applies the epithet "indolent" to most of the residents of Florida, including Latinos, blacks, whites, and Indians, especially when her wealthy Northern main characters (who might expend energy on walks and rides) are hardly fountains of industry. Later, a boating party composed of Garda's friends, together with Lucian and Rosalie Spenser, encounters poor-white "squatters" in the ruin of a house, where the father has just arrived with a bear killed in the swamp and the older boys add their fish. Lucian imagines they are happy: "if I had to be very poor... let it be in Florida! ... I don't want them to rise... too much 'rising,' in my opinion, is the bane of our American life. The ladder's free to all, or rather the elevator; and we spend our lives, the whole American nation, in elevators" (314). As Lucian has just married an heiress, his remarks could hardly be more callous or hypocritical.[21]

Woolson creates yet another shock when Lanse Harold finally appears after adulterous years in Rome. Winthrop, now in love with Lanse's wife, Margaret, meets him in the little post office on the pier at the St. John's River, where Lanse is sitting in the United States chair. This location suggests the transatlantic correspondence and travel that dominates the novel and creates the suggestion of a crossroads, one that had long been open to the Indians, the Spanish, the frontiersmen, and now the modern folk changing the face of the state and the postwar South. Winthrop's arrival on the *Hernando* (named after De Soto) and the coonskin-wearing postmaster suggest this rich past, but the postmaster's archaic dress also contrasts sharply with the wardrobe of the present. Amazingly, Woolson's Europeanized Lanse takes Winthrop in a birchbark canoe to an inlet, where old Joe (born in Africa) shows them a huge rattlesnake and alligator he has killed. It is an odd place for what turns out to be a confession: "Great turtles swam along... water-moccasins slipped noiselessly into the amber depths from the roots of the trees as the canoe drew nearer; alligators began to show themselves" (412). Moored among the reptiles, Lanse tells the story of his rupture with Margaret years before and thereby reveals his adulterous conduct as well as Margaret's saintly silence about the matter. In a further unexpected development, a black boy (speaking heavy dialect, of course) comes by with the white girl he is baby sitting, and a moccasin falls into their boat. Lanse dives in, saves them, and eventually is stricken and paralyzed. Margaret must come to him, but only after Winthrop apologizes to her for the long years of his scorn. To her credit, Woolson refuses to make Lanse a simple villain; the incident, at once exotic and riveting, complicates his character while adding much to the intersecting vectors of nature and ethnicity.

Woolson's Florida fictions are actually akin to concepts of nature that had been retained by Africans in the New World. The bond between man and a sacral natural world is at the center of various forms of New World religions such as Vodun and religious figures such as Loco, the "he of the trees."[22] Woolson's fiction displays a fixation with trees, especially the pine but also the palm, the palmetto palm, the live oak, and, most mystically, the orange tree. Indeed, East Angels has always depended on the cultivation of orange trees; the property, which has been owned in turn by Native Americans, the Spanish Douros, the New Englander Mrs. Thorne, and the New Yorker Evert Winthrop, is finally owned by Margaret Harold, who announces her intention to replant the orange orchard. She thereby prefigures the Northern exodus to Florida in the years to come. More specifically, Woolson makes the nearby swamp a site of refuge, reverie, and meditation. When Margaret and Winthrop must brave bad weather in a swamp canoe to find the missing Lanse, old Rose, terrified, won't go: "Please missy, *no*. Not inter de Munloons in der *night, no! Ghosessess dar!*" (464). She and Dinah sing a spiritual as Winthrop and Margaret push off: "Didn't my Lord delibber Dan-yel, Dan-yel?" (470). But the desperate trip into the heart of swamp darkness brings out the full arsenal of Woolson's tropical colors as she sketches a scene less Southern than Caribbean in its tangled vegetation, strange beauties, and morbid reptilian dangers.

In addition, the swamp has always been the locale for numerous love stories, among other freedoms. It is no accident that the search for Margaret's husband in the nocturnal world of the tropical swamp waters engenders the most intimate scenes between Margaret and Winthrop, much as a dangerous voyage would later engender a fated love story for Humphrey Bogart and Katherine Hepburn in *The African Queen*. Henry James commented on Woolson's "remarkably fine" interlude when he observed: "the picture of their paddling the boat by torchlight into the reaches of the river, more or less smothered in the pestilential jungle, with the personal drama, in the unnatural place, reaching an acute stage between them—this whole episode is in a high degree vivid, strange, and powerful" (14). Although the swamp has been a locus for refuge and freedom in African American literature, white Southern writers have taken a more gothic view of this terrain. In this regard, a novel like *East Angels* has a great deal in common with John Pendleton Kennedy's *Swallow Barn* (1832), which is often seen as the first great example of the plantation genre. Kennedy's Northern participant-observer takes readers on an exhaustive tour of plantation cultures (replete with stereotypes of poor whites, black slaves, and white Southern belles) that reveals the self-sufficient nature of the rural South. As in Woolson's Florida, a swamp then plays a doubled role in the narrative: the poor are sustained by its resources, but the more aristocratic characters fear it and are sometimes sickened. As always, the need for a guide, a local who knows the landscape, introduces a Dantean aspect to Kennedy's narrative that the Renaissance "wood of error" in epics like Ariosto's *Orlando Furioso* and Spencer's *The Fairie Queen* makes all the more familiar. Woolson thus draws on a rich heritage in

East Angels, where the struggle against an extravagant, beautiful, dangerous, and seductive environment offers a metaphor for unruly emotions.[23]

Like "Rodman the Keeper" as well as Henry James's *Portrait of a Lady* (1881), Woolson's novel concludes with a scene of rescue, which brings Margaret and Winthrop's love into crisis and eventuates in their honorable if bitter accession to Lanse and social norms. While Margaret and Lanse as transplanted Anglos play central roles, Woolson imagines a social fabric that includes Native Americans, Latinos, African Americans, Africans, and the rural poor of the Midwest and the South. Moreover, these figures are often connected to other lands—to Cuba, Mexico, the West Indies, and Spain. With so strong a presence of Southern cultures in *East Angels*, Woolson almost turns her deracinated white Protestants into disasporan wannabes. Ultimately, her refusal to imagine a single identity for the South brings her in congruence with a later age and the postnational study of the Americas. As Glissant has stated, "the struggle against a single History for the cross-fertilization of histories means repossessing both a true sense of one's time and identity: proposing in an unprecedented way a revaluation of power."[24] Woolson did not quite share this agenda, but she let her strong feeling for Florida guide her to a surprisingly broad vision of its peoples and landscapes. It was a vision that followed the pointing finger of the state southward in a proleptic gesture, one fraught with the problems and possibilities she was among the first to engage.

Notes

1. Constance Fenimore Woolson, *East Angels* (New York: Harper & Brothers, 1886), 26.

2. Edouard Kamau Brathwaite, *The Development of Creole Society in Jamaica* (New York: Oxford University Press, 1971), 296.

3. As I recently noted elsewhere, Edward Said has remarked that exile is strangely compelling to think about but terrible to experience, the stuff of both romanticism and modernism. Yet today exile is generally conceived in political terms. The current age "with its modern warfare, imperialism, and the quasi-technological ambition of totalitarian rulers," Said has observed, "is indeed the age of the refugee, the displaced person, mass immigration." See John Lowe, "Reconstruction Revisited: Plantation School Writers, Postcolonial Theory, and Confederates in Brazil," *Mississippi Quarterly* 51.1 (Winter 2003/2004): 6. Said's comments first appeared in *Reflections on Exile and Other Essays* (Cambridge, MA: Harvard University Press, 2000), 174. As my earlier essay demonstrates, the era of Southern Reconstruction can easily be read through the lens of displacement, disruption, exile, and loss, the postcolonial quandary that begins as William Safran sees it with "expatriate minority communities" that seem strangely appropriate in the occupied South. Defeated by war and displaced by peace, Confederates lost their nation and then their homeland when Union troops patrolled postwar military districts while white Southerners were disenfranchised and emancipated slaves were elected to political office. The resulting diaspora of Confederates was nonetheless tied, as Safran predicts of all displaced communities, to a "myth about their original homeland," which encouraged a

conscious hope of restoration binding stranded Confederate communities together and buoying those "exiled" even in the homeland they knew. For Safran's more elaborate discussion, see "Diasporas in Modern Societies: Myths of Homeland and Return," *Diaspora* 1.1 (Spring 1991): 83–84. In Plantation School narratives, ex-Confederates retain a powerful memory of an exalted pastoral past.

4. Antonio Benitez-Rojo, *The Repeating Island: The Caribbean and the Postmodern Perspective*, trans. James E. Maraniss (Durham, NC: Duke University Press, 1992), 1.

5. Benitez-Rojo, *The Repeating Island*, 3.

6. Édouard Glissant, *Caribbean Discourse: Selected Essays*, trans. Michael J. Dash (Charlottesville: University Press of Virginia, 1989), 67.

7. Benitez-Rojo, *The Repeating Island*, throughout.

8. Constance Fenimore Woolson, *Rodman the Keeper: Southern Sketches* (1880; rpt. New York: Harper & Bros, 1886), 11–12. Woolson's title story was first published in the *Atlantic Monthly* (March 1877): 267–77. Page references will be noted parenthetically in the text and will be to the later collection in which Woolson's several Southern stories appeared.

9. Henry James, "Miss Woolson," in *Constance Fenimore Woolson*, ed. Clare Benedict (London: Ellis, 1930), 9.

10. Cited in Michael J. Dash, "Introduction," in Glissant, *Caribbean Discourse*, xxii.

11. Glissant, *Caribbean Discourse*, 6.

12. Cited in John Lowe, "Re-Creating a Public for the Plantation: Reconstruction Myths of the Biracial Southern 'Family,'" in *Bridging Southern Cultures: An Interdisciplinary Approach* (Baton Rouge: Louisiana State University Press, 2006), 221.

13. Woolson's focus on consumptive Northerners coming to Florida in a desperate effort to shake their disease has a parallel in George Washington Cable's classic "Jean An-Poqueline" (1883), a story set in a Louisiana leper colony and centered on two devoted brothers, one strong and one afflicted. The brothers also live on the edge of a swamp, which is eventually drained as New Orleans advances. Since Woolson's story was published first, it is worth wondering about her spreading influence. Carl's desire to make music for his violin from the sounds of the swamp also recalls the method of modern composer Messiaen, whose "Oiseaux Exotiques" (1955-56) does exactly what Carl intends, but for an orchestra.

14. Cited in Robin D. G. Kelley, "A Poetics of Anticolonialism," in Aimé Césaire, *Discourses on Colonialism*, trans. Joan Pinkham (1933; rpt. New York: Monthly Review Press, 2000), 15.

15. Just a few years ago, the Guadeloupian writer Maryse Condé invoked the swamp in a similar fashion for its maroon communities of escaped slaves. In her novel *Crossing the Mangrove*, translated by Richard Philcox (New York: Anchor-Doubleday, 1995), a central character feels that "[o]nly there, among the giant trees, the mabri, châtaignier, candlewood, mastwood and Caribbean pines, did he feel at home" (48). Glissant puts this summons in another way: "The forest of the marron was thus the first obstacle the slave opposed to the *transparency* of the planter. There is no clear path, no *way forward*, in this density. You turn in obscure circles until you find the primordial tree. The formulation of history's yearned for ideal, so tied up with its difficulty, introduces us to the dilemma of peoples today still oppressed by dominant cultures" (83).

16. An anthology like *Caribbean Literature and the Environment: Between Nature and Culture*, recently assembled and edited by Elizabeth M. DeLoughrey, Renée K. Gosson, and George B. Handley (Charlottesville: University of Virginia Press, 2005), could have profited from acknowledging writers such as Woolson. Though not Caribbean themselves, they detail a terrain that must be considered, especially as Florida has become more, rather than less, Caribbean in both population and culture.

17. Sharon L. Dean, *Constance Fenimore Woolson: Homeward Bound* (Knoxville: University of Tennessee Press, 1995), 64.

18. Glissant, *Caribbean Discourse*, 15.

19. James, "Miss Woolson," 10.

20. Gilles Deleuze and Félix Guattari developed the concept of the rhizome—the interconnected systems of underground roots that link surface vegetation—as a way of conceptualizing a sense of myriad and nonhierarchical approaches to and departures from discrete points, particularly as they appear in the processes of evaluation and interpretation. Deleuze and Guattari's system was created in order to avoid the frequent impasses of binary categories and to achieve a horizontal spectrum, rather than the more traditional vertical and linear systems of prior analysis. Their most cogent expression of this system is found in *A Thousand Plateaus: Capitalism and Schizophrenia*, trans. Brian Massumi (Minneapolis: University of Minnesota Press, 1987), 7–13.

21. Decades later, by contrast, another Northern transplant to Florida, Marjorie Kinnan Rawlings, made these "crackers" her main characters and depicted a hard-working and resourceful folk, whose way of life is threatened by the advent of Northern industrialists and entrepreneurs.

22. See Lizabeth Paravisini-Gebert, "'He of the Trees': Nature, Environment, and Creole Religiosities in Caribbean Literature," in *Caribbean Literature and the Environment: Between Nature and Culture*, ed. Elizabeth M. DeLoughrey, Renee K. Gosson, and George B. Handley (Charlottesville: University of Virginia Press, 2005), 32.

23. Anthony Wilson has recently noted how a long declension of Southern writing has used the swamp as a bivalent symbol, both refuge and zone of infection. The dichotomy, as Wilson points out, stretches back to the mapquests of William Byrd and William Bartram before getting codified in novels by Kennedy, Simms, and Stowe, then reinvoked in the travel writings of Frederick Law Olmstead and Frances Kemble. These are all writers that Woolson likely knew well. See *Shadow and Shelter: The Swamp in Southern Culture* (Jackson: University Press of Mississippi, 2006). As Rayburn Moore has observed, Woolson repeatedly focuses on characters whose strength is seen through "self-denial, renunciation, marginality, or 'heroic sacrifice.'" See *Constance Fenimore Woolson* (New Haven, CT: Twayne, 1963), 127. Such noble qualities, Moore points out are customarily found in characters that are in some way social "outcasts."

24. Glissant, *Caribbean Discourse*, 93.

Tourism, Imperialism, and Hybridity in the Reconstruction South

Woolson's *Rodman the Keeper: Southern Sketches*

—Anne E. Boyd

> Now that the little monkey has gone, I may be able at last to catch and fix a likeness of her.
> —"Felipa"

At their core, issues of imperialism coalesce around such concepts as center and margin, dominance and subjugation, self and other, binaries at the heart of the ten stories collected in Constance Fenimore Woolson's *Rodman the Keeper: Southern Sketches* (1880).[1] I am interested not only in excavating these binaries in Woolson's Southern fiction, but also in examining what happens to the tensions between them. Ultimately, these tensions are not neatly resolved, as they often were in popular postwar reunion romances. As many postcolonial theorists have noted, sooner or later the encounter between cultures and peoples results not only in clashes but also in a mingling that creates forms of doubleness or hybridity, a term often used today to connote the mixture of cultures, but which has its origins in nineteenth-century conceptions of racial difference. A reading of Woolson's fiction in this context suggests her discomfort with the effects of imperialism, particularly a form of hybridity predicated on an inequality that blurs cultural and racial distinctions. In the process of registering this discomfort, Woolson also manages to decenter her texts in ways that challenge her Northern readers' presumed cultural superiority in the wake of the Civil War and Reconstruction.

As a prologue to my examination of the entire volume of Southern stories, I will briefly examine how "Felipa" (1876), one of Woolson's most frequently anthologized Southern stories, can be read in a postcolonial/anti-imperialist context. The story's narrator, a white, Northern artist who struggles to "catch and fix" the image of a Spanish-speaking Minorcan girl (203), epitomizes the "imperial eyes" of the colonizer, to borrow Mary Pratt's phrase, not least in her use of an animalistic metaphor—"little monkey"—often employed in racist portrayals of dark-skinned peoples. The girl, Felipa, whose gender identity is blurred by the boy's clothing she wears, is "a small, dark-skinned, yellow-eyed child, the offspring of the ocean and the heats, tawny, lithe and wild, shy yet fearless—not unlike one of the little brown deer" (197). Like many colonized natives, she is described as a product of the landscape around her, even as a type of the region's fauna; thus she is the typical exotic "other." Felipa is also a product of Florida's colonial past: her father was a Spanish sailor, and she is now being raised by her Minorcan grandparents, members of an ethnic group brought as indentured servants from the isle of Minorca off the coast of Spain to the British colony of Florida in 1768.[2]

Almost nothing is revealed about the artist and narrator, Kitty, who is convalescing as well as vacationing in Florida with two other friends: Christine, a "Pre-Raphaelite" beauty (202), and Christine's persistent suitor, Edward. In fact, so little is revealed about Kitty and her friends that they become ciphers of the imperial presence of Northern tourists in the South after the Civil War, unlooked-for guests imposing themselves on a native population that contains no other whites. Of Felipa, Kitty explains, "She did not come to us—we came to her; we loomed into her life like genii from another world" (197). The magical effect they have on her, however, is anything but benign. Felipa becomes obsessed with Christine, who is so different from any woman she has ever seen, and aspires to attain her beauty. She is thus educated in the standards of western beauty and art but ultimately realizes her inability to measure up. When Felipa learns of Christine and Edward's engagement and impending departure, she attempts to kill herself with the very tools of western art (poisonous paints) to which Kitty has introduced her, and then she stabs Edward in the arm. Her weapon, a "Venetian dagger" (219), may be a reference to *Othello*, which also suggests a love triangle featuring two whites and a dark-skinned person. Similar to Shakespeare's play, Woolson's "Felipa" presents a range of imperialist responses to the colonized other, taking as its subject, in the words of Shakespearean critic Edward Berry, the "tragedy of perception" (318).[3]

For the two lovers, Felipa is not much more than a sometimes annoying pet. Christine, in particular, cannot perceive Felipa outside a perpetual present. She explicitly declares that educating the girl would be a harmful waste: "Teach a child like that, and you ruin her.... Ruin her happiness" (200). Felipa should remain an ignorant savage, untroubled by the complexities of civilization from which the tourists presumably have fled. In another sign of her colonial attitude toward Felipa, Christine views her as irredeemably "ugly" (203), while her suitor, Edward, cruelly points out to Felipa, "You could not look much like this lady [Christine] ... because you are so dark, you know" (207). Felipa, who was not aware of her darkness, is ultimately "ruin[ed]" by the mirror these Northern tourists hold up to her. Christine and Edward make her conscious of her difference and the unbreachable gulf between races.

Kitty's perception of Felipa is more complicated but not less destructive. She ultimately has more respect for Felipa than her friends, although she portrays the girl as part wild animal—her arms "terminated in a pair of determined little paws" (202)—and as an object of her gaze—"although ugly, Felipa was a picturesque little object always" (200). However, Kitty develops an appreciation of her subject's "full-curved, half-open mouth of the tropics" and "low Greek forehead," suggesting they are "pretty" (201–2). When she finally completes her portrait, she challenges Christine's reading of Felipa, saying, "You do not see the latent beauty, courage, and a possible great gulf of love in that poor wild little face?" (203). There are signs, in other words, that Kitty (whose name also signifies the status of a pet) sees in Felipa familiar qualities. Whereas Christine sees only difference, Kitty recognizes similarities, "latent" potential and therefore the capacity for "improvement." Thus Kitty takes up the project of civilizing Felipa (*fixing* her in another sense) by instructing her in the conventions of western beauty and gender. Consequently, the two women represent alternative approaches to the colonial or racialized "other": Kitty wants to help Felipa assimilate, to become more like them, while Christine rejects the child as irredeemably separate and virtually inhuman. Yet Woolson does not privilege Kitty's view over Christine's. On the contrary, Kitty's attempt to civilize Felipa proves equally damaging.

Furthermore, Woolson complicates the imperial stance of her story by forcing her artist narrator to recognize her own marginality, and by making Felipa the agent of that awareness. In a stunning reversal of the recognition of otherness that has been thrust upon Felipa, the girl calls attention to Kitty's own difference and inadequacy. When Kitty laughs at Felipa's attempt to dress in a western feminine way, the "wild little phantom . . . seized me by the skirts and dragged me toward the looking-glass. 'You are not pretty either,' she cried. 'Look at yourself! look at yourself!'" (208–9). What Kitty sees therein is not explicitly stated, but Felipa's subversive act of turning the mirror on the artist/colonizer ultimately forces Kitty to recognize her own inability to measure up to the standards of western beauty as well as her exclusion from the heterosexual world that Christine and Edward represent. Kitty cannot comprehend their romance—"I do not understand you two," she tells Edward. "What do peaceful little artists know about war?" (204), Edward responds, calling to mind the recent Civil War that has made the South a quasi-colony of the North. Nor can Kitty ever be as attractive as Christine. Like Felipa, Kitty yearns to be "one of those long, lithe, light-haired women" (216), an equally impossible transformation. As an artist, Kitty casts her imperial gaze on the other, only to discover her own otherness.

In the end, after it is clear that Felipa will survive her suicide attempt, Kitty realizes the folly of her efforts to study or civilize Felipa: "there was nothing for us to do but go away as quickly as possible and leave her to her kind" (220). Kitty's final attempt to comprehend Felipa also fails. Kitty sees her only as a child who "does not know." Yet the hitherto voiceless grandfather declares, "I know," and explains that Felipa's passion for Christine was stronger than her love for Edward (220). By giving the colonized perspective, through the voice of the grandfather, the final word in the story, and by showing the colonizers to be not only harmful but uncomprehending of the native other, Woolson challenges the imperial eyes of the Northern visitors, the narrator, and her contemporary readers. A similar dynamic is visible in nearly all of the stories collected in *Rodman the Keeper*, which portray a wide range of interactions between Northerners and Southerners, from a Northern abolitionist who starts a school for freed slaves to a Northern veteran who keeps a cemetery for the Union fallen in the heart of the South and a Northern spinster who adopts a Spanish gentleman's son in Florida.

Postcolonial Studies and the Reconstruction South

Scholarship at the intersection of postcolonial and U.S. literary studies has brought to light the nation's empire building overseas as well as the "internal imperialism" of manifest destiny and Euro-American hegemony. More important, scholars have begun to excavate the patterns of European imperialism reinscribed by slavery, the myth of the frontier and westward expansion, the conquest and relocation of indigenous peoples, responses to immigration and miscegenation, and territorial wars of annexation.[4] The examination of internal forms of U.S. imperialism must also include discussion of the Reconstruction South, which was perceived by Northerners and Southerners as an occupied colony of the North. Consider, for instance, the Northern journalist Sidney Andrews's claim in 1866 that "we may treat this State [South Carolina] as we please,—hold it as a conquered province or restore it at once to full communion in the sisterhood of States," or, in a more figurative vein, George M. Barbour's book *Florida for tourists, invalids, and settlers* (1884), which declared that "Florida is rapidly becoming a Northern colony."[5] The rhetoric of colonialism also has been part of white Southern self-fashioning at least since the Civil War, and was central to constructions of Southern literature in the twentieth century, from Charles William Kent's reference to the South in the *Library of Southern Literature* (1907) as "an imperial territory," to Jay B. Hubbell's claim in 1954 that the South after the war "was once more reduced to the intellectual status of a colony," to Richard Gray's formulation in 1986 of Reconstruction as "reducing the South to a colonial status and fastening on it a colonial psychology."[6] More recently, scholars in the fields of history and geography have examined "the South's position as a post-Civil-War imperial holding," just as literary scholars have used postcolonial theory to examine white male writers' resistance to imperialism in Reconstruction novels of the 1890s and 1900s. However, very little scholarship exists on imperialist discourses in Reconstruction-era texts.[7]

The limits of comparison between the Reconstruction South and traditionally identified colonies, however, are also apparent. As Scott Romine explains, white Southern resistance to Northern hegemony cannot be equated with the experiences of racialized others in former European colonies, the traditional terrain of postcolonial theory, let alone the experiences of Native or African Americans in the United States.[8] Nor can the ways that Northern and Southern whites found common ground in the oppression of African Americans be overlooked. In addition, the North did not actually colonize the South after the war in the same way the United States colonized Puerto Rico at the end of the century. As Amy Kaplan emphasizes, the U.S. Supreme Court cast Puerto Rico as a "foreign" yet "domestic" territory, a state of inbetweenness which to some extent also characterizes the U.S. South, although not in the legal sense. Puerto Rico would be held legally apart from the nation as an "incorporated territory,"[9] whereas the Confederate South was reintegrated into the nation. The metaphors of reunion after the war made it clear that the North and South were once again one country, legally if not culturally; "the union" had been preserved, however much white Southerners still perceived of themselves as inhabiting a separate country. The South also regained a certain amount of regional autonomy with the end of Reconstruction. The ousting of Northern politicians and the removal of federal troops effectively ended the South's colonial status as an occupied territory. The South would ultimately accept its condition as again unified with the North, particularly as the region became "an equal and willing partner in imperialist expansion" during the Spanish-American War at the end of the century.[10]

Acknowledging that discourses of imperialism both do and do not apply to the Reconstruction South, I wish to borrow Jamie Winders's formulation of "the region's double placement as both 'insider' and 'outsider' within the nation immediately after the Civil War,"[11] and, arguably, up to the present day. Woolson's position vis-à-vis national and literary cultures was also both inside and outside, making her sympathetic with displaced, exiled, marginalized white Southerners after the war yet also aware of her difference from them. According to Sharon Dean, scholars should not "overlook the colonialist implications in Woolson's position as a representative of the victorious North," but, she cautions, "Woolson was never a part of the eastern establishment tradition. Aware of her position as an outsider, a single woman who has lost her home, she was sensitive to southern loss."[12]

As an accomplished travel writer who utilized her Southern sojourns to make a name for herself in the pages of *Harper's Monthly* and other esteemed Northern literary magazines, Woolson was certainly aware of the portrayals of the South in travel narratives written for Northern consumption after the war. A key element of these narratives as well as fiction portraying the defeated South is their function as the dominant postwar narrative and their displacement of the voices of the conquered region. As Edward Said declared in his classic *Culture and Imperialism*, "The power to narrate, or to block other narratives from forming and emerging, is very important to culture and imperialism, and constitutes one of the main connections between them." The South's condition of voicelessness after the war is characterized by one Georgia girl who wrote in her diary, "I hate the Yankees more and more, every time I look at one of their horrid newspapers and read the lies they tell about us, while we have our mouths closed and padlocked. The world will not hear our story, and we must figure just as our enemies choose to paint us."[13] The fear of being represented by the enemy is a powerful postcolonial sentiment for which Woolson expresses sympathy in her fiction. She understood that her pen had the power to describe what few Southerners could portray for themselves.[14] In various ways, then, Woolson decenters the metropolitan perspective of her texts by giving voice to continued white Southern animosity after the war. Henry James recognized this important cultural function of the stories in *Rodman the Keeper*: "As the fruit of a remarkable minuteness of observation and tenderness of feeling on the part of one who evidently did not glance and pass, but lingered and analysed, they have a high value, especially when regarded in the light of the *voicelessness* of the conquered and reconstructed South."[15] Woolson's stories attempted not merely to speak for the desolated region but to allow Southern voices to speak back, particularly to Northern insistence on a narrative of defeat, humiliation, and, ultimately, assimilation to the dominant (Northern) culture and economy.

In addition to writing the conquered region's story from the victor's perspective, Northern postwar travel writing regularly adopted a variety of other colonial attitudes toward the South. Jamie Winders has provided a useful inventory of such attitudes, which included describing the South as "uncivilized or primitive" and criticizing it for "backward lifestyles and social practices"; positioning Northern women as "'the active agents of civilization'"; "tapp[ing] well-known tropes of black subjects in need of white aid"; and depicting the land as virtually uninhabited, wild, pristine, feminine, and sexual, awaiting the improvement of (male) Northern capitalists or the enjoyment of (masculine) explorers and tourists.[16] Each of these attitudes is adopted by the narrators or major and minor characters in Woolson's Southern fiction, although in each story, as I will demonstrate, these stances are exposed as naive, inadequate, or harmful.

Rewriting Imperial Narratives of Northern Tourism

As Sharon Dean has noted, Woolson was aware of the ways in which literature, particularly travel literature, opened up new territories for tourism, thus contributing to the destruction of land and culture.[17] Woolson's ambivalence about this situation likely accounts for the relative inaccessibility of the remote regions in which she sets her Southern fiction: islands, coastal marshes, swamps, and mountain terrains predominate. Rather than portray virgin lands awaiting male exploration and cultivation, Woolson casts Southern regions as not merely uninviting but also forbidding: "the poisonous swamp—the beautiful, deadly South Devil" (146) in "The South Devil," or the "purple-black, wild, and pathless" (279) mountains of "Up in the Blue Ridge," which harbor murderous men protecting the locations of their illegal stills. In "In the Cotton Country," the lowlands are a "barren waste" (181) rather than a fecund wilderness inviting exploitation. As Nina Silber has documented, Northern reconciliation with the South was predicated on domesticating and feminizing the region,[18] just as the Northern travel writers' imaginative ownership of the land entailed a process of domestication and feminization. Woolson, however, complicates the Southern landscape, making it less familiar and more dangerous; if it is feminine, it is certainly not domestic. Ascent into the mountains or descent into the swamp are fatal or nearly fatal enterprises.

The swamp in "The South Devil" is perhaps the most explicitly feminized landscape: "the Spirit of the Swamp," the failed musician Carl rhapsodizes, "[is] a beautiful woman falsely called a devil by cowards, dark, languorous, mystical" (154). For his stepbrother, Mark, the swamp is not only seductive but deadly: "Death lives there" (145), he insists. Indeed, Carl, who is seduced by the swamp and allows himself to be drawn into it, dies, while Mark survives by resisting the allure of "its intoxicating perfume" (177) and returning North to marry his cousin. Their taste in landscapes is mirrored in their tastes in women; while Carl's "fancy was for something large and Oriental" (165), Mark remains entranced by the "icy looks of a certain blue-eyed woman" (175). Thus Carl's undoing is not merely the consumption from which he suffers but also his taste for the "Oriental" and the tropical. His attractions clearly mark him as an imperial wanderer, who, Woolson suggests, is in danger of being destroyed by the seductive landscape he so admires. In the end, Mark, also an imperial wanderer who has laid claim to Florida's orange groves and employs a former slave as cook, rejects the "wild ... over-ripe" oranges for the "firm ... cool" apples growing in a neat orchard up north (176).

The setting of "Sister St. Luke," the coastal marshes and islands off Florida, is similarly treacherous for two Northern "city men" (49), who also figure as imperial explorers. Keith is the prototypical "seeing-man," as Mary Louise Pratt defines him: "he whose imperial eyes passively look out and possess."[19] For Keith, "A salt marsh is not complete without a boat tilted up aground somewhere, with its slender dark mast outlined against the sky" (56). His friend, Carrington, is almost a caricature of white manliness, a "vigorous young Saxon" (49) who hacks his way through the wild brush and knows no limitations, physical or geographical. "The two men led a riotous life; they rioted with the ocean, with the winds, with the level island, with the sunshine and the racing clouds. They sailed over to the reef daily and plunged into the surf; they walked for miles along the beach, and ran races over its white floor; they hunted down the center of the island, and brought back the little brown deer" (51). Yet the landscape itself warns them of its recalcitrance. The only vegetation on the island is a "rope-like vine" in the sand: "try to tear it from the surface of the sand ... and behold, it resists you stubbornly. You find a mile or two of it on your hands, clinging and pulling as the strong ivy clings to a stone wall; a giant could not conquer it, this seemingly dull and half-dead thing" (52). In other words, the ostensibly innocuous vine will resist any attempt to remove it, a metaphor for the way the land itself resists appropriation by adventuring tourists who come to claim its material and aesthetic enjoyments. Near the end of the story, the two men are made violently aware of their impotence in the landscape when a tornado strands them at sea. They are reduced to "two dark objects ... clinging" to the reef now barely visible above the furious waves (71). Unable to save themselves, they are ironically rescued by the timid nun they have unsuccessfully been trying to "convert" (48), a female personification of the seemingly placid land. But the land and the nun, like the vine in the sand, have hidden resources the men cannot fathom, as well as the capacity to resist their influence. As in so many of Woolson's stories, the would-be colonizers of the region are reduced in power. In this case, it is the land itself that seems to reject them. They admit defeat in the end, sending the nun back to her convent and returning to New York.

Even more important, Woolson explained to her Northern readers that the South was not a blank slate on which the nation could (re)write its national narrative, as the West appeared to be. In "The South Devil" she admonishes her readers with a history lesson:

> It is all natural enough, if one stops to remember that fifty years before the first settlement was made in Virginia, and sixty-three before the Mayflower touched the shore of the New World, there were flourishing Spanish plantations on this Southern coast ... But one does not stop to remember it; the belief is imbedded in all our Northern hearts that, because the narrow, sunbathed State [sic] is far away and wild and empty, it is also new and virgin, like the lands of the West; whereas it is old—the only gray-haired corner our country holds. (142)

The South, she insists, is not another frontier for national expansion. Instead, the region has an alternative history, older than the dominant U.S. narrative, and its inhabitants have their own narratives and regional (even national) identities. Accordingly, Bettina in "Rodman the Keeper" claims, "the South *is* our country, and not your North" (40), and Gardis in "Old Gardiston" insists on calling the South "[m]y country" (129). Although Gardis is forced to abandon her allegiance to her "country" and marry a Northern officer, the story also contains a counter narrative to their reconciliationist marriage. The archetypal plantation home from "colonial days" (105) virtually self-combusts on the eve of its transfer to a Northern woman, "the wife of an army contractor" (136). Burning down, the house resists appropriation by its new colonizers.

"In the Cotton Country" similarly portrays white Southern refusal to adapt to Northern occupation and narrative-making. The disembodied narrator, a Northern visitor, is the essence of Pratt's "seeing-man," roaming the desolate landscape, admiring "the beauty and the fancies that come with the soft after-glow and the shadows of the night" (179), much in the fashion of postwar travel writers. However, when the narrator is confronted with a "solemn, lonely old house" (181) unexpectedly inhabited by "a white woman, tall, thin, and gray-haired" (182), distant aesthetic observation is no longer possible. The narrator acknowledges the woman's despair: "The eyes haunted me; they haunt me now, the dry, still eyes of immovable, hopeless grief. I thought, 'Oh, if I could only help her!'" (182). Stirred by her emotions, the narrator speaks directly to readers and reveals her own gender for the first time: "shall we not, we women, like Sisters of Charity, go over the field when the battle is done, bearing balm and wine and oil for those who suffer?" (184). But the woman does not welcome the intruder's presence or aid, and the narrator must return daily to "build . . . up a sort of friendship with this solitary woman of the waste" and elicit "her story" (184). From here, the narrator surrenders authorial control to the white Southern woman, who tells her own tale of the war and defeat, thus transforming the imperial travel narrative into an empathic, almost sentimental, first-person account of loss and grief.[20] Quite dramatically, Woolson counters the Northern narrative of conquest and possession with one of victimization and desolation. "Bitter, am I?" the woman asks her interlocutor. "Put yourself in my place" (195). Thus, as in "Felipa," Woolson turns the tables on the Northern reader and reverses the direction of the imperial gaze, modeling empathy rather than objectification by, here, granting the white Southern victim a voice.

Interestingly, while Woolson's Northern tourists are able to achieve momentary empathy with the "other," her Northern transplants exhibit less ability to understand or adapt to the region. Like many Northern postwar travel writers, these characters (usually female) position themselves as "the active agents of civilization"[21] against indolent and slovenly locals. Melvyna, from "Sister St. Luke," the transplanted Vermont wife of a Minorcan light-house keeper, "hated the lazy tropical land" (43). Her futile efforts to change her husband's slothful habits are echoed in one of the collection's most complex stories, "Miss Elisabetha." The eponymous heroine, from New York, attempts to transport her strict notions of housekeeping and the refinements of civilization to the tiny town of Beata, Florida. As the town's name suggests, everyone in this place is happy except Miss Elisabetha, who is "striving always against the current" (104); she scolds the "colored population" for their idleness (79) and bemoans the Minorcan "lazy housewives" (81).

Perhaps more important, Miss Elisabetha, the guardian of an orphaned son of Spanish parents, has imported a piano and music books to this benighted backwater. Although "the ancient piano has lost its strength" (76), it functions as a kind of fetish of middle- or upper-class respectability and is used as a marker of refinement and civilization that distinguishes Miss Elisabetha and her ward Theodore from the African Americans and Minorcans who hover at the story's edges. Miss Elisabetha "tunes it herself, protects its strings from the sea-damps, dusts it carefully, and has embroidered for it a cover in cross-stitch" (76). As Jamie Winders explains about the postwar Northern travel narrative, "as in other colonial settings, material objects associated with a white, northern middle-class lifestyle held the capacity . . . to signal the civil in white northerners."[22] Miss Elisabetha's authority as the lone representative of Northern respectability is challenged by an opera singer, whose voice and style of singing seduce Theodore. But Miss Elisabetha sends her away, determined to provide for him the life of "a gentleman's son" (102). When Theodore falls in love with Catalina, a beautiful Minorcan girl, who "sang as the bird sings, naturally, unconscious, for the pure pleasure of singing," Miss Elisabetha recognizes "a certain element of the *sauvage* in [her voice]. No lady, no person of culture would permit herself to sing in that way" (100), she tells herself, insisting upon her own status as a "lady of culture" and casting the girl as a native savage. She rejects Theodore's plan of marriage, reminding him, "Child, you have seen nothing—nothing" (103), suggesting that he doesn't recognize the difference between his status and Catalina's because he has not been exposed to the class and ethnic hierarchies that are more rigid in the rest of the United States.

Ultimately, Woolson turns that hierarchy on its head, allowing Theodore to marry Catalina and foster a "careless, idle, ignorant happy brood, asking nothing, planning not at all, working not at all, but loving each other in their own way, contented to sit in the sunshine, and laugh, and eat, and sing, all the day long" (104). While this description at first replicates the trope of the ignorant native also seen in "Felipa," Woolson stresses that this lifestyle prevails while Miss Elisabetha's values exert no influence. Catalina, in fact, breaks the piano. Although Theodore continues to use it, he plays Minorcan melodies rather than the French ballads Miss Elisabetha held up as the highest form of civilized music. Despite the fact that she has devoted her life to him, she has failed to instill in him the refinements of civilization. He has, in a sense, gone native, while she unhappily clings to her outmoded way of life. Her status is reduced to the point that she is cast as a kind of slave at the end of the story: "The tall, gaunt figure that came and went among them, laboring ceaselessly, striving always against the current, they regarded with tolerating eyes as a species differing from theirs, but good in its way, especially for work" (104). Miss Elisabetha is thus the object of their gaze, the dehumanized figure of another species who is only good for labor. In this passage, Woolson most explicitly inverts the usual order of colonizer and colonized, giving Theodore and his Minorcan family the normative position and defining the white Northern woman as the "other." "Miss Elisabetha" thus undercuts the civilizing mission of white Northern women in the South, reflecting the large presence of (often female) teachers, nurses, and missionaries following the war.

Woolson's story "King David" more overtly deals with this cultural phenomenon. Although the missionizing educator in this story is male, he is feminized as a "narrow-chested . . . country student" from New Hampshire, whose "near-sightedness and an inherited delicacy of constitution . . . kept him out of the field during the days of the war" (255). Yet his abolitionist sentiments are complicated by his racism. David King is physically repelled by his black students. He throws away the food they have touched and makes himself a separate meal, "for he still shrank from personal contact with the other race" (259). The farmers back home scoff at David's feeling of responsibility toward the freed slaves. "Let the blacks take care of themselves" (255), they chide. In the end, David comes to the same conclusion, but less out of a conviction that he was mistaken in his responsibility than out of a new awareness of his inability to help them. As one of his pupils, Uncle Scipio, tells him, "You hab nebbber *quite* unnerstan us, suh, nebber quite; an' you can nebber do much fo' us, suh, on 'count ob dat fack" (274). Therefore, David determines to send for "a man of your own people" (273).

Uplift must come from within, not from without, this story suggests, rejecting the imperial missionary impulse replicated in the U.S. South after the war. But more than skin color is at issue here. Uncle Scipio explains, "a color'd man will unnerstan us, 'specially ef he had lib'd at de Souf; we don't wan no Nordern free niggahs hyar" (274). In other words, region and legal status (free or slave) matter just as much as race. Meanwhile, Uncle Scipio gratefully sends David back to the North: "we hopes you'll go j'yful back to your own people, an' be a shining light to 'em for ebbermore" (274). Uncle Scipio talks back to the would-be colonizer, just as Felipa's grandfather does to the Northern tourists. Woolson thereby rewrites the imperial texts of Northern exploration and tourism of the Reconstruction South by sending her missionaries, adventurers, and tourists back home and making space for local characters to voice their resistance.

Anxieties of Hybridity

By ejecting her Northerners from the South or portraying their civilizing missions as ineffectual, Woolson takes an anti-imperial stance in her Southern stories. Yet the discomfort she displays with the mingling of cultures and races is also apparent. Most of these stories end with separation and acknowledgment of irreconcilable difference rather than coexistence or the possibility of cross-fertilization. Those that do end in union also stress the dissolution of one identity into another and thus do not portray a hybrid formation of mixed identity. It is therefore difficult to see Woolson advocating the forms of hybridity that are today celebrated in postcolonial literary studies. Yet an examination of the anxieties surrounding nineteenth-century hybridity and its colonial context can help us understand the basis for Woolson's discomfort as both conservative *and* anti-imperialist.

The term hybridity is often employed to convey the annihilation of difference as two distinct entities combine to create a new form, or the embodiment of difference as one entity contains elements of previously separate identities. However, as Robert Young explains in *Colonial Desire: Hybridity in Theory, Culture and Race*, the concept of hybridity, which today connotes the mixing of cultures, originated in discussions of racial distinction. "[T]he preoccupation with hybridity in the mid-nineteenth century," he writes, centered on the question of whether Africans were a separate species, which "stood or fell over the question of hybridity, that is, intra-racial fertility." Hybrids, or crosses between species, are doomed to extinction because they are sterile. For contemporary theorists, hybridity has much more fertile connotations. Linguistic or cultural hybridity is essentially a challenge to the hegemony of the dominant culture, a way of opening up the supposedly homogenous "dominant cultural power" and changing it from within. Andrew Smith explains that "the idealized liberal view [of] *hybridization* occurs on a level ground of equality, mutual respect and open-mindedness."[23]

However, in Woolson's day, such progressive notions of hybridity were not current. Racial and ultimately cultural mixture were associated with the tropical regions of the South, colonial regions where imperial dominance dictated relationships. As Barbara Ladd has argued, colonies are sites of amalgamation, of racial and cultural mixing, whereas nations are sites of racial segregation and (forced) cultural unity:

> In a racist and xenophobic culture, the creation of a "creole" caste makes sense only when a region is defined as a colony, or a borderland. When a nationalistic United States expands its own territory into what used to be a "colony," when it pushes back the frontier, the creole caste has to be either assimilated completely by the national culture or displaced in order to preserve the integrity/unity/homogeneity of the nation, which supposedly comprises the state.[24]

Ladd is concerned primarily with Louisiana, which Woolson did not visit on her Southern sojourns. However, Florida was also a contested colonial region subsequently incorporated into the United States. In Woolson's stories, Florida is similarly portrayed as a site of racial and cultural mixing that raises questions about how difference is incorporated into the national narrative.

Woolson's Southern stories tend to reject hybridity due to the imperial damage it inflicts on local cultures. In her stories of contact between Northern and Southern whites, Woolson critiques the inevitability of enforced assimilation. But her stories portraying encounters between different races attempt to preserve racial boundaries; thus they could be read as anticipating the "separate but equal" logic of segregation. Rejecting the model of colonial hybridity predicated on inequality and coercion, Woolson nonetheless falls back on what Ladd identifies as national models of preserving homogeneity through assimilation or separation. It was not possible for her to anticipate notions of hybridity grounded in equality or counter-hegemony.

In her "southern sketches," intersectional encounters between upper-class whites, even those resulting in marriage, are not successful attempts at the mingling of disparate entities. In the collection's title story, the keeper of a Union cemetery learns to respect a white Southern woman's faithfulness to the memory of her dead father and brothers, which prevents her from writing her name in the cemetery's visitors' log. The story forecloses the possibility of a union between North and South as Rodman tells Bettina, "Nothing can change you . . . you are part of your country, part of the time, part of the bitter hour through which she is passing. . . . Yet do not think, dear, that I have not seen—have not understood" (40). Understanding must keep its distance, however, as mutual respect can blossom but not love. In "Old Gardiston," the white Southerner Gardis does marry the Northern officer. But "[s]he never was a real Gardiston" (138), so she can shed her familial affiliations and adopt a new cosmopolitan identity as the officer's wife. The Southern girl, Honor, in "Up the Blue Ridge," is similarly robbed of her separate identity when she marries a Northerner: he "took her away to the North, and was, on the whole, a good husband. But, from first to last, he ruled her, . . . she was too devoted to him, too absorbed in him, too dependent upon his fancies" (338). In "Bro," although the male character is not from the North, he does represent the "bohemian" wanderer. His childhood friend from Georgia falls in love with him only to lose her vitality: "she was not what she had been. She seemed to have become timid, almost irresolute; . . . she seemed disposed to sit more in the shadow, or half behind the curtain, or to withdraw to her own room" (242). In the end, he takes her away to Europe. Thus these women, with the exception of Bettina in "Rodman the Keeper," are absorbed by their husbands and removed from the South, losing their distinct identities and identification with the region.

Woolson's Florida stories, each of which touches on the issue of racial mixture, more overtly express her discomfort with hybrid identities. Her depiction of mixed-race or Minorcan characters is marked by a mixture of distaste and ambivalence. Sister St. Luke, who is an orphan of unknown parentage—"she don't know herself what she is exactly" (48)—speaks Spanish but could be Minorcan or even Creole, which may explain why Keith and Carrington think of her condescendingly as "a gentle being of inferior race" (49). The mixed-race hunter in "The South Devil" is a particularly unsavory character. As "an old man of unknown, or rather mixed descent, having probably Spanish, African, and Seminole blood in his veins" (165), he is a Creole; instead, however, Woolson repeatedly refers to him by the derogatory term of "mongrel" (170, 171, 177). He is also portrayed stereotypically—"The mongrel had no idea; he had not many ideas" (171)—and somewhat threateningly—he "looked around stealthily, stole several small articles, and hastened away" (177). A mulatto also appears briefly in this story and is likewise pejoratively described as "a bronze piece of insolence" (162). Nowhere else in the collection does Woolson overtly portray a Creole or mixed-race character, despite her acknowledgment of "this vast, many-raced, motley country of ours" (43).

However, Woolson does recognize the significant Minorcan presence in Florida, thus unsettling the black-white binary typical in portrayals of the South. Her Minorcans inhabit a kind of middle ground between whites and blacks, similar to Kate Chopin's Cajun characters or George Washington Cable's Creoles of color. Contemporaries of Woolson identified Minorcans as a "sub-Spanish population" or as "Greek and Italian in type." These ethnic identities were not necessarily considered "white" in Woolson's day, which may explain why she portrayed Minorcans as potentially mixed-race in two works published early in the period of her Southern travels.[25] Her poem "Dolores" describes Minorcans as "A simple folk c[o]me from the Spanish sea-isles, / Now tinged with the blood of the creole quadroon" (34). In her travel narrative "A Voyage to the Unknown River," Woolson included an "olive[-]skin[ned]" woman whom the narrator assumes is Minorcan. However, the woman insists she is Spanish, "throwing back her head, with a quaint little air of *hauteur*." "[A]ll the Minorcans are invariably 'pure Spanish,'" the narrator comments, suggesting an element of passing that carried a racial subtext.[26] Although the stories in *Rodman the Keeper* do not overtly identify Minorcans as racially mixed, Woolson repeatedly distinguishes Minorcans from descendants of the Spanish and marks them as "dark" or "yellow," slow-witted, Catholic, and indolent.

Woolson portrays two marriages between "whites" and Minorcans, and, again, neither suggests a positive form of hybridity. Melvyna's marriage to Pedro in "Sister St. Luke" has resulted in only a still-born child, evoking the sterility of the union between separate species. She also is not transformed by her marriage to Pedro. As the story concludes, "Melvyna went every Sunday to the bare, struggling little

Presbyterian mission over in town, and she remains to this day a Sawyer," a reference to her maiden name (74). Thus no merging or mixture has resulted from their union, merely a toleration of the other and a fierce resistance to change. Theodore's marriage to Catalina in "Miss Elisabetha" is more fruitful, yet it seems to reflect the fears of those who objected to amalgamation as the potential extinction of the white race, for Theodore blends into the Minorcan community, and his children are raised as Minorcans. His identity as a descendant of Spanish colonists has been easily submerged into his wife's Minorcan cultural background, suggesting a further distinction between the whiteness that Miss Elisabetha represents and her ward's more easily assimilable cultural/racial status. Closer in language and coloring, Theodore and Catalina can mix. But Miss Elisabetha remains a distinct "species." Felipa, as the product of a Minorcan mother and Spanish father, is similarly portrayed as simply Minorcan. Thus, in her portrayals of Minorcans, Woolson allows for the possibility of cross-cultural/racial mixture, yet she displays anxiety about such unions.

Despite the warnings her stories encode of the dangers of imperial appropriation or hybridization, Woolson also understood that such processes would inevitably transform the region. The South will have "her new dawning," the forlorn woman of "In the Cotton Country" concedes, only when "new blood . . . come[s] to her" (196). Ultimately, Woolson's anxiety about racial or cultural hybridity is eclipsed in *Rodman the Keeper: Southern Sketches* by the acknowledgment of new voices and "new blood" like that of the potentially mixed-race Felipa, who asserts her power not only to reverse the mirror on the artist narrator but also to attempt the destruction of the male adventurer who told her she could never measure up to Western standards of womanhood. As her grandfather tells Kitty, Felipa is not a child. Although she is only twelve, "[h]er mother was married at thirteen" (220). His (and Felipa's) assertion of an alternative notion of womanhood displaces the normative logic of the colonizers, challenging Woolson's readers to acknowledge the South's resistance to a hegemonic homogeneity. Although Woolson's Southern stories may call to mind the coming era of racial segregation, they can also be considered an acknowledgment of the South's hybridity. As Andrew Smith explains, "hybridity" has come to mean not only mixture but "an arena of struggle," in which the voice of the "other" can be heard.[27] In this sense, Woolson's Southern stories do perform a type of hybridity in their acknowledgment of multiple, conflicting subject positions in a quasi-colonial context. They therefore anticipate our early-twenty-first-century preoccupation with global cultures and the interplay of hegemonic and postcolonial voices.

Notes

1. I am grateful to John Lowe for sharing with me his essay for this volume. His keynote speech inspired me to read Woolson in a postcolonial context. While his essay focuses more on the context of the "global South" in her fiction, I have emphasized the imperial dynamics of her Southern stories. I am also grateful for helpful comments on earlier drafts of this essay by Kathleen Diffley, Doreen Piano, Elizabeth Steeby, Nancy Easterlin, and Catherine Loomis.

2. Constance Fenimore Woolson, "Felipa," *Rodman the Keeper: Southern Sketches* (1880; rpt: New York: AMS Press, 1971), 203, 197. All further references to Woolson's fiction come from this collection and will be made parenthetically in the text. The phrase "imperial eyes" is borrowed from Mary Louise Pratt, *Imperial Eyes: Travel Writing and Transculturation* (London: Routledge, 1992). For information on Minorcans, see "The Minorcans in Florida," Amelia Island Genealogical Society Web site: http://www.aigensoc.org/story_minorcans.asp; and Patricia C. Griffin, *Mullet on the Beach: The Minorcans of Florida, 1768–1788* (Gainesville: University Press of Florida, 1991). For a compelling reading of "cultural alterity" in "Felipa," which came to my attention after I had completed this essay, see Neill Matheson, "Constance Fenimore Woolson's Anthropology of Desire," *Legacy* 26.1 (2009): 48–68.

3. Edward Berry, "Othello's Alienation," *Studies in English Literature, 1500–1900* 30.2 (1990): 318. Berry goes on to summarize the "paradigm of early colonial attempts to rationalize contact with the 'other'" in Tzvetan Todorov, *The Conquest of America* (New York: Harper & Row, 1984). Berry's explication of "the two opposing ways of defining and ultimately oppressing the 'other'"—to view them as "essentially the same . . . and therefore worthy of assimilation; or as essentially different" and thus not human (318)—has informed my reading of "Felipa."

4. See, for instance, *Cultures of United States Imperialism*, ed. Amy Kaplan and Donald E. Pease (Durham, NC: Duke University Press, 1993); John Carlos Rowe, *Literary Culture and U.S. Imperialism: From the Revolution to World War II* (New York: Oxford University Press, 2000); and *Postcolonial Theory and the United States: Race, Ethnicity, and Literature*, ed. Amritjit Singh and Peter Schmidt (Jackson: University Press of Mississippi, 2000).

5. Andrews is quoted in Jamie Winders, "Imperfectly Imperial: Northern Travel Writers in the Postbellum U.S. South, 1865–1880," *Annals of the Association of American Geographers* 95.2 (2005): 396. George M. Barbour, *Florida for tourists, invalids, and settlers.* (New York: D. Appleton, 1884), 225.

6. Kent is quoted in John Lowe, "Introduction," *Bridging Southern Cultures: An Interdisciplinary Approach*, ed. John Lowe (Baton Rouge: Louisiana State University Press, 2005), 3. Jay B. Hubbell, *The South in American Literature* (Durham, NC: Duke University Press, 1954), 709. Richard Gray, *Writing the South: Ideas of an American Region* (1986; rev. ed., Baton Rouge: Louisiana State University Press, 1997), 88.

7. A notable exception is the article by the geographer Jamie Winders, cited above. For the South as an "imperial holding," see Winders, "Imperfectly Imperial," 392. Literary analyses include Walter Benn Michaels, "Anti-Imperial Americanism," *Cultures of United States Imperialism*, 365–91; and Scott Romine, "Things Falling Apart: The Postcolonial Condition of *Red Rock* and *The Leopard's Spots*," *Look Away!: The U.S. South in New World Studies*, ed. Jon Smith and Deborah Cohn (Durham, NC: Duke University Press, 2004), 175–200.

8. Romine, "Things Falling Apart: The Postcolonial Condition of *Red Rock* and *The Leopard's Spots*," 176.

9. Quoted in Amy Kaplan, *The Anarchy of Empire in the Making of U.S. Culture* (Cambridge, MA: Harvard University Press, 2002), 7.

10. Nina Silber, *The Romance of Reunion: Northerners and the South, 1865–1900* (Chapel Hill: University of North Carolina Press, 1993), 11.

11. Winders, "Imperfectly Imperial," 392.

12. Sharon L. Dean, *Constance Fenimore Woolson: Homeward Bound* (Knoxville: University of Tennessee Press, 1995), 34.

13. Edward W. Said, *Culture and Imperialism* (New York: Vintage, 1993), xiii. Diary quoted in Gray, *Writing the South*, 75.

14. As Hubbell has documented in *The South in American Literature*, Southern writers only slowly gained access to Northern periodicals by refraining from "'unreconstructed' point[s] of view" (728).

15. Henry James, "Miss Woolson" (1887); reprint in *Women Artists, Women Exiles: "Miss Grief" and Other Stories*, ed. Joan Myers Weimer (New Brunswick, NJ: Rutgers University Press, 1988), 271–72. The perception of Woolson as a sympathetic observer has prevailed in Woolson scholarship. A notable exception is Karen Weekes, "Northern Bias in Constance Fenimore Woolson's *Rodman the Keeper: Southern Sketches*," *Southern Literary Journal* 32.2 (2000): 102–15.

16. Winders, "Imperfectly Imperial," 396, 397, 401–2.

17. See Sharon L. Dean, *Constance Fenimore Woolson and Edith Wharton: Perspectives on Landscape and Art* (Knoxville: University of Tennessee Press, 2002), 47–48. Timothy Sweet complicates this view in his essay for this volume.

18. Silber, *The Romance of Reunion*, 9–10.

19. Pratt, *Imperial Eyes*, 7.

20. Leonardo Buonomo, in "The Other Face of History in Constance Fenimore Woolson's Southern Stories," *Canadian Review of American Studies* 28.3 (1998): 19, views the narrator's "surrender" as a kind of defeat. Instead, I see Woolson portraying a victory of empathy over imperialism.

21. Mona Domosh quoted in Winders, "Imperfectly Imperial," 397.

22. Winders, "Imperfectly Imperial," 398.

23. Robert Young, *Colonial Desire: Hybridity in Theory, Culture and Race* (London: Routledge, 1995), 9, 8, 22–23. Andrew Smith, "Migrancy, Hybridity, and Postcolonial Literary Studies," *The Cambridge Companion to Postcolonial Literary Studies*, ed. Neil Lazarus (Cambridge: Cambridge University Press, 2004), 251. On hybridity and doubleness, see also Kenneth Mostern, "Postcolonialism after W. E. B. Du Bois," *Postcolonial Theory and the United States*, 258–76; and Steven G. Yao, "Taxonomizing Hybridity," *Textual Practice* 17.2 (2003): 357–78.

24. Barbara Ladd, *Nationalism and the Color Line in George W. Cable, Mark Twain, and William Faulkner* (Baton Rouge: Louisiana State University Press, 1996), xiv–xv.

25. James Dabney McCabe, *The Great Republic: A Descriptive, Statistical and Historical View of the States and Territories of the American Union* (Philadelphia: William B. Evans, 1871), 661; and Edward King, *The Great South* (Hartford, CT: American Publishing Co., 1875), 396.

26. Constance Fenimore Woolson, "Dolores," *Appletons' Journal* (July 11, 1874): 34. Constance Fenimore Woolson, "A Voyage to the Unknown River," *Appletons' Journal* (May 16, 1874): 616.

27. Smith, "Migrancy, Hybridity, and Postcolonial Literary Studies," 252.

Henry James, Constance Fenimore Woolson, and the Fashioning of Southern Identity
—John H. Pearson

Although Europe remained a fashionable destination of monied Americans in the late nineteenth century, the postbellum South became a popular alternative for increasing numbers of middle-class Americans. Nina Silber explains that many Americans traveled the South for the benefit of sunshine, the slower pace, and the ease with which they could get there. The Old South seemed new again to those arriving by train, travelers who sought "strange and unusual scenes in comfortably predictable tours" that they first read about in *Harper's New Monthly Magazine* and other popular magazines and newspapers.[1] Richmond, Charleston, and St. Augustine developed nascent tourist industries toward the end of the century, thanks in large part to the ways in which the reconstructed South was reclaimed and reincorporated into the Northern imagination of writers like Henry James and Constance Fenimore Woolson.

In *The American Scene* (1907), which was first published in the United States serially in two of the Harper publications (*Harper's Monthly* and the *American Review*), James observes that the South had become the new Europe: "It was American civilization that had begun to spread itself thick and pile itself high, in short, in proportion as the other, the foreign exhibition had taken to writing itself plain.... Europe had been romantic years before, because she was different from America; wherefore America would now be romantic because she was different from Europe."[2] No place seemed as romantic as the South, especially the "compromised South" that revealed to James "by a turn of my hand, or of my head" its former glory and its current defeated and debased state (371–72). James identifies the tragic fall as a gender switch that for him explains what had been lost in the South and what was left behind: "the ancient order" of the South, which James describes unequivocally as "masculine, fierce and moustachioed," had become "feminized" in the aftermath of the Civil War (417). In this newly feminized geography, James initially found little to incite his usually active imagination. Eventually, however, he discovered what he had imagined, and this postbellum construction of the South as well as the nostalgia for what it replaced would dominate the national narrative at least until World War II.

If the South was a feminized space that signaled little but loss of a more masculine fixity to Henry James, it became for Constance Fenimore Woolson a space of possibility for the fashioning of identity, particularly of women's identity, in the postwar era. Like James, Woolson eventually acknowledged the dominant Northern perspective of her readers, but she acknowledged it as a perspective rather than as an objective truth. Initially, she attempted to write the South without channeling it through a distinctly Northern consciousness. Her novel *For the Major* (1882), which was serialized in *Harper's Monthly* twenty-five years before James's *American Scene*, attempts to obviate the dominant Northern perspective on regional conflict that is typically found in late-nineteenth-century writing about the South. Certainly regional conflict informs the relationship of Major and Madam Carroll as they eke out their lives in decline. In this novel, however, the focus is most squarely on one woman's struggle to fashion a self within the existing hierarchical social system, and most particularly to fashion that self through the outward signs of clothing, gesture, demeanor.

Seven years later, Woolson returned to the subject of Southern female subjectivity in *Jupiter Lights* (1889), also serialized in *Harper's Monthly*. Rather than avoid the conflicting regional perspectives of the South, however, in this story of a Northern woman who travels to the coastal South to meet her sister-in-law and young nephew, Woolson calls attention to them as forces that construct often artificial identities for self and others. She understood, moreover, that the fashioning of identity was an entirely different enterprise when practiced by women than when practiced by men. Woolson and James both argue that women's identities are often contingent on men, and in the postbellum South this frequently meant that their identities were contingent on absent men. Where James saw depletion and tragic loss, however, Woolson saw possibility.

Following the war and Reconstruction, the undermining of Southern traditions and conventions that had been formed over several generations provided opportunities for Southern women willing to risk their received identities for something self-fashioned. Suzanne W. Jones and Sharon Monteith call the South of this period a "site of exchange" where "new coordinates of southern identity" were developed and learned.[3] Woolson understood this, and in her fiction of the South she offers a valuable, preemptive correction of the prevailing Northern (re)construction of Southern identity that James and others articulated in the late-nineteenth and early twentieth centuries. In both of her Southern novels, *For the Major* and *Jupiter Lights*, Woolson depicts a region where the old determinants and signs of identity were losing their meaning, and new social identities were being self-fashioned. These in turn called for a new heuristic, a way of reading the new signs of identity aright. Unlike James, who favored a nostalgic construction of the South to suit Northern readers, Woolson considered the ways in which identity is constructed by uncontrollable circumstances that the individual—particularly the individual woman—could use to self-fashion an identity out of a combination of old remnants and new cloth.

Self-fashioning, a term coined by Stephen Greenblatt, is the understanding of personal identity as what Greenblatt calls "a manipulable, artful process," one in which the public presentation of the self (including the body and speech) is recognized as a semiotic field.[4] Greenblatt explains the concept as the product of historical dialectic process. In the Middle Ages, individual identity was understood as an external characteristic and fixed by God at birth. Attempts to alter or control identity were acts of hubris doomed to failure and eventual damnation. As Greenblatt observes, Augustine admonished his readers to leave themselves alone: "Hands off yourself. Try to build up yourself, and you build a ruin."[5] This notion of identity externally controlled and therefore not approved for action by the self began to change in the sixteenth century, when the connotation of *fashion* changed to reflect a growing sense of individual agency. Previously applied to the manipulation of appearance and adornment, *fashion* came to be used widely as "a way of designating the forming of a self" (2). This notion of individual agency over the self passed through the lenses of eighteenth-century Enlightenment and early nineteenth-century Romanticism, crossing the Atlantic and informing Benjamin Franklin's systems of self-improvement and the rise of Freemasonry in the United States, with its similar doctrine of the self as a stone to be hewn.[6]

Identity signification systems are determined by culture, history, and individual will. When cultures, historical trajectories, and wills collide, however, identity signification systems can be misunderstood and misrepresented, which was often the case in literature from and about the postbellum South. In the forty years following the Civil War, the South underwent tremendous change resulting in "acute self-consciousness and an even greater pluralism than ever before," Richard Gray explains, as well as rapid shifts in the determinants of individual identity (race, class, gender, economic status) and in the signs of it.[7] As might be expected, this provided unusual opportunities for self-fashioning as well as for misreading, particularly as the signs were manipulated by the selves being fashioned. Gray argues that the emerging South was multiple—the self-fashioned that was always both antebellum and "marginal" postbellum, and the "reverse image of itself" due to the conflicting perceptions of others, especially in the North.[8]

James and Woolson both attempted to connect their ideas to palpable reality, but they worked in opposite directions. James worked deductively, beginning with his long-held beliefs about the character of the South. In the first decade of the twentieth century, James wrote about his travels south from Baltimore in search of a romantic vision of the Confederate states that he admitted to having formed "as long ago as the outbreak of the Civil War, if not even still more promptly," and he found himself "romantically affected" by those youthful fantasies of Southern abundance, elegance, and masculine gentility (369, 365). Woolson worked inductively, creating ideas about the South and about women's lives there based on her observations and experiences living in many areas of the nation, including Florida.

Such varied approaches reflected a larger conflict over postbellum Southern identity. James located agency over Southern identity in the Northern literary imagination; he thereby reinscribed the lines of the dominant national narrative of his time. Woolson sought signs of agency in the lives of women whose identities were self-fashioned in a matrix of "family, social convention, and deontological morality" that was often challenged by what Jil Larson calls the new "focus on the inner life" characterized by "introspection, rebellion, and self-fashioning."[9] This tension between external force and internal agency mirrors the "resolutely dialectical" view of the early modern period that Greenblatt describes: "If we say that there is a new stress on the executive power of the will, we must say that there is the most sustained and relentless assault upon the will; if we say that there is a new social mobility, we must say that there is a new assertion of power by both family and state to determine all movement within the society" (1–2). He might as well have been writing about the postbellum South, and particularly about its Northern construction in *The American Scene*. There, James conjures a preconceived South in buildings and gardens, and he observes Southern men and women already defined by his sense of who they were or must be, for he comprehended Southern white identity based largely on his own antebellum notions.

His accounts of Richmond and Charleston, in particular, reveal a Northern traveler consciously reading through the "feminized" present to discover a South shaped by his distinctly Northern, richly literary, and undeniably cosmopolitan imagination; he ultimately encounters a South fashioned according to the masculine past that he desires (417). Upon alighting from the train in Richmond, James finds himself not only enduring unseasonably cold weather but facing "a picture charmless at best," a "desert" that looked "simply blank and void" (368, 370). Richmond disappoints and disorients him because he could find nothing to objectify the "mystic virtue" that he attached to "the very name of Virginia" (370). He acknowledges his romantic conception of the former capital of the Confederacy when he asks, "How was the sight of Richmond not to be a potent idea; how was the place not, presumably, to be interesting." After all, he expected Richmond to be "lurid, fuliginous, vividly tragic" (369). However, James's "reverse images" of the South, as Gray calls them, find no objective correlatives in the Southern space he explores. Try as he may, James cannot find the potent, poignant, tragic South for which he longs. Instead, he succumbs to disappointment: the Richmond before him offers "the shallow vistas, the loose perspectives, [which] were as sadly simple as the faces of the blind" (370). A large, new hotel is the only building of note, and even this is "a huge well-pitched tent, the latest thing in tents, proclaiming in the desert the name of a new industry" (370). Perhaps most disappointing of all to James is that Richmond turns out to be little different than a "Northern city" with no pretence to Northern cultural resources (370). He cannot find the "'old Southern mansions' on the wide verandahs and . . . the rank, sweet gardens" (370–71). Because "there were no *references*" to the South as it was constructed in the imagination of a young Henry James before and during the Civil War, Richmond threatens to become for him the geography of personal loss—loss of his romantic illusion of a South that retained its difference from the North, loss that brings James near to "intellectual bankruptcy" (371). He searches Richmond for the city of his adolescent fantasies but can locate none of its signs.

And then in an instant, everything changes. James suddenly understands that the South he cannot find is actually immanent in the scene. He peers through the insipid and oddly familiar urban landscape of Richmond and spies behind it "the very essence of the old Southern idea . . . [of] the immense, grotesque, defeated project—the project, extravagant, fantastic, and to-day pathetic in its folly, of a vast Slave State" (371). In *The American Scene*, James arrives in Richmond so utterly prepared to discover a "defeated project" that he finds what he is looking for in the very absence of all markers. The memory of wide verandahs and sweet gardens becomes an "immense, grotesque" postbellum Richmond that can never become itself because, in Gray's words, its past is constantly "altering" and leading away from the idealized Richmond of James's youthful fantasy.[10] Still, James finds his way back to his ideas of the South through some athletic leaps of imagination. Richmond's residents are "such pathetic victims of fate, as so played upon and betrayed, so beaten and bruised, by the old burden of their condition" that James feels sorry for them, but he is relieved that this lost generation of Southerners gestures toward a former rebellious if not righteous glory (374–75). In short, James reads these postwar Virginians as signs of what they have forfeited. By working back through this dialectic, he finds a semiotic path to his original destination, a path that later leads through Charleston's tea-houses to proprietors dressed in aging gowns and thus to women of commerce who trade on the residual signs of a time and position now lost.

In this manner, James looks through the signs of female self-fashioning in front of him to discover the thetic masculine for which he was originally searching. James's willful act of sublation—the preservation of the thesis even as it was overwritten through the dialectical process—marks perfectly the conceptual site of the conflict between a Northern fashioning of the postbellum Southern self and the Southern self-fashioning within a frame that offered little semiotic certainty. In Charleston at least, Southern women of commerce might manipulate the signs of their identity in the "ancient order" that James—the Northern tourist—longed to experience. This suggests the possibility that the old order had carnivalized itself, creating a new, commercial order in the South that catered to (while ironizing) the Northern romantic ideal of Southern womanhood, and, to a certain extent, Southern manhood. When James says that his Richmond hotel proclaimed "the name of a new industry," after all, he was acknowledging the new industry of tourism and business that brought Northerners to the South (370).[11] For James, *a priori* ideas of the South always dominated whatever he discovered there, and so he brought a conceptually conquered South home to his readers.

In an oeuvre that also presents the postbellum South to Northern readers, and does so long before James wrote *The American Scene*, Constance Fenimore Woolson attempted to unsettle the Northern gaze as the ruling fashioner of Southern identity. She was deeply concerned with the necessities and possibilities of female self-fashioning, and she looked always to the geographical spaces where identity was in flux. Woolson's fiction of the Michigan frontier, of the South, and of the Europe discovered by nineteenth-century Americans privileges place as the context that sometimes throws identity construction into the light and sometimes constructs identity itself. In *For the Major*, Woolson asks how Southern women created makeshift selves immediately after the war; in *Jupiter Lights*, she asks how women—Southern and Northern—reconstructed their identities in a postwar nation that normalized aggressive, "moustachioed," absent masculinity and rendered women as either dependent and helpless or independent and degraded, but in either case as nothing more than signs of the men they had lost.

In the opening pages of *For the Major*, Woolson describes the process of self-fashioning that accounts for individual autonomy and external forces.[12] This process begins with the broadest geographical terms and gradually hones in on the individual locating herself on the map. Woolson affects a tone that is mildly ironic and exquisitely careful as she presents the Southern hillside towns of Edgerley and Far Edgerley, which seem to foreshadow James's dialectic of the commercial desert that Richmond would become and the old Confederate capital it once was. Simultaneously lower on the mountain and closer to "the high civilization of the State capital," Edgerley "had two thousand inhabitants, cheese factories, saw-mills, and a stage line across Black Mountain to Tuloa" (November 1882, 907, 908). Lacking these markers of nineteenth-century progress, Far Edgerley defines itself by contrast. It is higher up the mountain and, as Woolson explains, "it had no factories, no sawmills, no stage line to Tuloa, and no necessity for one, and no two thousand inhabitants" (908). While the merchants of Edgerley pride themselves on their progressive spirit of commerce and their relatively close connection to the state capital, the inhabitants of Far Edgerley boast a reactionary antebellum social identity that they consider virtuous and superior. In Far Edgerley, *commerce* is a social slur reserved for its nearly named neighbor downhill. With this comparative and cartographical construction of identity, Woolson offers a corrective to the reconstruction of the South in the Northern imagination. She begins to weave the thread of Southern self-fashioning that appears throughout *For the Major*, demonstrating the inefficacy of an insular identity with no connection to national contexts—historical and conceptual—from which it must derive some of its signification.

For the Major presents the processes of postwar self-fashioning via two dominant metaphors—one geographical, to indicate the external forces that shape identity, and one sartorial, to indicate identity self-construction. The geographical metaphor begins with the opening comparison of Edgerley with Far Edgerley and extends throughout the narrative to reveal that identity exists always already in context, which acts of self-fashioning may in turn re-form. Setting aside a dominant Northern perspective, Woolson examines the geographical underpinnings of identity apart from national politics and more broadly, even as she focuses more narrowly. The "prejudiced creed," as Woolson calls it, of the citizens of Far Edgerley enables them to construct a group social identity that depends upon geographical relations to other Southern places (Tuloa, the state capital, Edgerley). The carriage that the coachman Inches drives through Far Edgerley offers one revealing source of geographical pride: its steps "impart an especial dignity to 'the equipage'" that does not derive from its near approximation to some platonic ideal of carriage steps. Comparing places instead, the narrator explains, "No other carriage west of the capital had steps of this kind" (909). The prodigal daughter, Sara Carroll, who returns to Far Edgerley and brings readers with her, makes a map of her father's house and its environs so that she will understand herself as "home" when she gets there. Both of these instances suggest that identity is neither autonomous nor strictly individual but an understanding of the self's place in a larger context and a manipulation of the significance of that place as well as of other signs. Identity is contingent on location, here a single regional location that at first seems invisible because it is not contrasted with the North.

Woolson then uses a sartorial metaphor to present individual self-fashioning and refashioning as an ongoing project, one that is caught in a broader social narrative sometimes authored by others. Not surprisingly, therefore, self-fashioning is sometimes about actual fashion. When Sara Carroll returns home to the Farms, her stepmother insists that the occasion requires an "especial reception." As Madam Carroll explains, "There are, you know, in every society certain little distinctions and—and differences, which should be properly marked; the home-coming of Miss Carroll is one of them. I suppose you have without doubt an appropriate dress?" (909). The undertones are clear: Sara is not only an autonomous, individual subjective consciousness; she is also an important part of the lexicon used by her stepmother as she tells the story of her own self to the community.

Woolson understood the semiotics of self-fashioning and the need for "an appropriate dress." As it turns out, *appropriate* is a matter of distinction within context, for Sara's "best" dress is "severely plain," which her mother decides "will have the added advantage of being a contrast." As if discussing her own identity, she says about Sara's clothing, "We have few contrasts in Far Edgerley, and I may say, no plainness . . . Rather, a superabundance of trimming. . . . But even with the best intentions you can not always construct new costumes from changes of trimming merely; there comes a time when the finest skill will not take the place of a little undoubted new material, no matter how plain it may be" (910). This is not merely a metaphor: it is Woolson's understanding that self-fashioning requires "a little new material," an appropriate dress (which is to say a form or base on which to build), and particular skill. Perhaps most important of all, self-fashioning requires a readership that understands the language of female self-presentation.[13]

Woolson here rehearses self-fashioning as contiguous and relative to, if not contextualized within, the fields of family, social convention, and duty-bound morality because, like the two Edgerleys, the self exists and understands itself in these contingent relations. Indeed, Sara Carroll "believed that her tastes, her wishes, her ideas, possessed rather a superior quality of refinement; but far beyond this did her pride base itself upon the fact that she was her father's daughter" (911). In *For the Major*, Madam and Sara Carroll present their fashioned selves through their clothing, which they adjust to express exquisite differences and refinements. Yet identity is at least in part derived through familial relations; the Carroll clothes anticipate the ghostly moustachioed Southern gentlemen that James would see in the ragged gowns of Charleston's women of commerce, their cultural widows. Woolson actually takes a much stronger stance in portraying the Major's second wife. Madam Carroll has fashioned herself as a young(er) woman of some means to secure for herself a family connection. Rather than judge her self-fashioning as deceitful, immoral, and doomed, Woolson suggests that Madam Carroll maintains a sure hand in her self-creation. As Cheryl Torsney explains, Madam Carroll "successfully asserts selfhood, having acquired the authority that attends its discovery in choosing both to write the fiction of her life and to reveal its made-up character. . . . Marion Carroll is an essential, creative spirit."[14] By foregrounding Southern women in their inventive artistry, Woolson's narrative suggests triumph rather than tragedy.

For the Major casts the self as a semiotic field in which the "I" is both author and authored. Greenblatt calls this understanding of self-fashioning *improvisation*—"the ability both to capitalize on the unforeseen and to transform the given materials into one's own scenario" (227). This is made possible, he explains, "by the subversive perception of another's truth as an ideological construct[;] that construct must at the same time be grasped in terms that bear a certain structural resemblance to one's own set of beliefs."[15] Madam Carroll fashions herself as a woman born into the Southern gentry by dressing herself accordingly. She manipulates the ideological constructs of class just as Charleston's women of commerce would manipulate the constructs of Southern identity that Northern tourists brought with them to the tea-houses. In both cases, the manipulative play bears "a certain structural resemblance" to their own sense of self and yet reveals the sometimes stunning disconnect between Northern and Southern constructions of Southern identity. Woolson and then James find the significant overlap—the structural resemblance—that offers at least the possibility of a common language as well as a common interpretive heuristic.

Woolson demonstrates in *For the Major* that *self-fashioning* is, as Stephen Greenblatt says, "the fashioning of human identity as a manipulable, artful process," but it is a process bound within the confines of semiotic fields that are as large as history and as complex as society (2). The authoring self places and replaces the frame over that field to determine semiotic boundaries. Self-fashioning in Woolson thereby combines what Julia Kristeva describes as the symbolic and the semantic—the externally authored self and the individually authored self—and perhaps Woolson shows this most clearly at the end of *For the Major* through a small outward ornament. With a gesture that signifies greatly in Madam Carroll's authoring and authored self as she exchanges wedding vows with the Major, she "drew off her own wedding ring, and guided his feeble fingers to put it back in its place again" (April 1883, 763). Woolson refers to her as "the wife" in this sentence, naming the contextual identity that she effects with the work of her own artful hand.

The gender politics of self-fashioning and family relations thus appear in a new light, apart from social privilege. With the loss of the Major's sight and hearing, Madam Carroll is, in Lyndall Gordon's gorgeous phrase, "release[d] from the laborious falsities of femininity."[16] Enacting the earlier contention that self-fashioning sometimes requires "undoubted new material, no matter how plain it may be," Madam Carroll "pins back her hair and bares the lined face of a woman who has grieved over the deaths of children; she extends to visitors a worn hand, no longer covered by muslin frills."[17] Individual will and exigent circumstances team up to empower her self-fashioning or, more exactly, to empower the fashioning of self. Changing the style of her clothing, like changing her physical appearance, Madam Carroll indicates a significant re-fashioning of the self that acknowledges her own history as well as her place in the Carroll family. With this scene, Woolson completes her earliest examination of Southern self-fashioning among women: it is geographical, which is to say relational, and it is sartorial, which is to say representational.

In *Jupiter Lights*, less than a decade later, identity and self-fashioning would have everything to do with geography and perspective. The novel begins with Eve Bruce, an American Yankee residing in London and readying herself for a trip to the American South, where she hopes to take custody of her late brother's infant son. When Eve first arrives at her Southern destination, which her English maid marks as exotic by referring to it as "the farawayest place," she appears as an excessively displaced figure alienated from the natural world around her.[18] The maid, frightened and quivering at the sight of largely unindividuated, scantily appareled, African American men who try to help with the luggage, launches her bag into the air as a diversionary missile before running off.[19] Apparently she is equipped with no intellectual framework with which to comprehend the South. The Northern American woman, however, understands the region as the idea with which she, like Henry James, was raised. Eve comes to the South equipped with romantic *a priori* notions, and she imposes these constructs on the place and the people she encounters, beginning with her sister-in-law Cicely. As the smoke from the ferry engines clears, the young, self-absorbed, and not especially interesting Cicely appears to Eve, "one of Diana's young huntresses, a creature light, fleet, and cool as the wind of dawn, untrammeled by too much womanhood"; she becomes mythic only "to a person with an eye for such resemblances"—the Northern Eve—and not to Cicely herself, who seems utterly unaware of analytical and mythic perspectives (249). Cicely's lack of self-consciousness registers her inability to comprehend the project of conceptual reconstruction of herself and the South, whereas Eve's constant discernment and evaluation are reminiscent of James, "the anxious explorer" who learns to "see straight" by grasping "the whole piece at a series of points that are after all comparatively few."[20]

Eve grasps "the whole piece" by relying on familiar myths. She calls upon these throughout *Jupiter Lights* and transforms the South through an act of artistic will into a place already seen. Woolson thereby reveals, on the one hand, the mythic structures of which Eve's apparently singular narrative is a part and recalls, on the other, the authorial eye through which her readers see and understand the novel's world, in particular the South. Woolson's use of free indirect discourse in much of the narrative further identifies this perspective as dominant among her readers. From the beginning, the use of imported myth as the conceptual framework for the postbellum South requires a place that does not have its own indelible identity with which to contend—at least in the minds of mythmakers like Eve. To many like her after the Civil War, the South was a devastated land that was conceptually rehabilitated through such means, the very reason James sought the tragic in Richmond.[21]

It isn't surprising, then, that Woolson would draw on music and myth, particularly when focalizing the narrative through a Northern visitor who holds the region (and its embodiment in the Southern ingenue) responsible for the death of the man on whom her identity had long depended.

Eve's perspective is privileged because the novel begins with her trip across the Atlantic, and the South first materializes as she sees it. Through Eve, Woolson establishes early on a series of oppositions that set up the novel's eventual clash of perspectives and ideas: North/South, analytical/mythic, and Eve/Cicely. These are gradually dismantled as disabling to the self-fashioning of regional and individual identity, a dismantling process that eventually encourages Woolson's readers to reflect on their own practices. At first, however, she appears to be engaged in the same project as Northern writers who, like James, brought the South home in their work by privileging a Northern, geographically defined identity. This is why the initial oppositions are so stark: they must be perceived and acknowledged before they can be examined critically and, in some cases, defused if not dismantled.

The problem with reading identity geographically, Woolson reveals, is that the reader's own identity is partially contingent on location and environment, and this contingency becomes an important but unstable variable in comprehending what is read. Woolson shows this repeatedly in *Jupiter Lights*, particularly when Eve finds herself increasingly affected and gradually refashioned by her location. Soon after settling in with her in-laws on Abercrombie Island, she is nearly swept up in a reverie with Cicely that foregrounds Eve's struggle to remain steadfastly *herself* in this land she has half discovered and half constructed. Late at night, Cicely finds Eve alone in her room, and then takes her through the dark house, lit mostly by moonlight, to an old ballroom where Cicely puts on an "old-fashioned ball dress made of lace interwoven with silver threads and decked with little silvery stars" (January 1889, 254). The dress is a clear sign of the antebellum South for both Cicely and Eve, but the meaning and value of this sign are quite different for the two women. For Cicely, the dress signifies her freedom from social restraint and responsibility: she is free to become the wind, to "run and shriek," but she dances to a tune called "Niggerless" (255); in short, she is what Richard Gray would predict—a version of her antebellum self. Cicely takes up a silver streamer and begins "moving over the moonlit floor" to Eve, whom she sweeps up in her arms and dances across the room "in a wild gallopade," as she simultaneously lets loose Eve's hair (254).

Yet Eve cannot give in to this impulse to lose her self-restraint and, with it, her Northern difference if not her Northern identity. Cicely's dress appears almost mythic, but Eve cannot participate in this myth. She reminds herself of her role as the scene's critical reader, specifically by inciting a self-protecting fear of the consequences that chased the first Eve out of that other Eden. "Suppose a dark figure should appear on the veranda and peer in at us through one of the windows!" she exclaims to Cicely, fearful of discovery by a predatory figure as much from her dream world as from the dark Southern landscape. In this way, her conscience functions to maintain her Northern distance.[22] In turn, Cicely takes an almost intoxicated bacchanalian stand: "I don't care about it, really; I don't care about anything!" She seems thoroughly a part of a natural world that orients the geography of her long-held identity: "It's the wind, you know," she explains to Eve: "When it blows like this, I always have to do something. Sometimes I call out and shout" (255). Cicely seems utterly in sympathy with the forces of the Southern landscape and able to communicate with them; her will is expressed as one small note in the music of the wind. For a brief moment, Eve is joined with her and experiences at least the possibility of self-forgetting. But the moment is cut short by her insistence on remaining apart, fashioned as she and her background have made her.

The early tension between characters begins to collapse, not because Eve gives in to the allure of the Southern landscape, with its moonlight and wind, but because she asserts a conscious agency over the South as semiotic construct, an agency more in tune with her own sense of self. Instead of ignoring the geographical forces at work, Eve transforms the South into a world she recognizes: England, where she last lived with her brother. She traces Southern place-names to their English origins and even begins to predict what she will find based on her knowledge of the similarly named places in England. Because "the South had forgotten her beginnings" (April 1889, 708), Eve is able to control the region as her own semiotic field and as a reflection of her will. By contrast, "Cicely's imagination took no flight toward" such an act of artistic will (February 1889, 436) because she has no desire to change herself or her sense of place.

In fact, finding the right *place* becomes the greatest challenge in Eve's quest to fashion her own postbellum, post-brother identity, in part because she discovers the limits to the fashioning influences of place. The singular act of shooting Cicely's first and murderous husband, Ferdie, to save Cicely and her son becomes an act that she can never separate from her sense of self no matter how far she travels. At first she attributes her actions to her location—the South and, most particularly, Abercrombie Island. From the moment when Eve picks up the gun, she is no longer acting singularly according to her subjective will but, instead, seems to be entranced by her dream of the place where she now resides. Even the initial description of the shooting fails to attribute individual agency: "there was a crack, not loud, of a pistol discharged very near" (March 1889, 602). As Eve runs through the brush, a hand reaches out and a gun goes off. It's as if the place itself channels its will through her. Thereafter, Eve struggles to make sense of this event and to determine what it signifies in the semiotics of self that she had previously taken for granted. In an effort to re-compose her self-portrait, she runs from one location to another—to the northwest, to the South, and eventually to Italy. There she isolates herself within the most limiting and barren geographic space, a cell, as if desperately trying to determine if a new location will help her construct a new self that bears no visible reminders of what she has done.

A change of location does seem to bring about at least a change of behavior, and this is the lesson that Eve learns about the limits of self-fashioning. After she and Cicely race northward to the Great Lakes and the safety of Ferdie's brother, Paul Tennant, Eve becomes uncontrollably anxious, the result of her past action and a suffocating fear of its moral and legal consequences. Woolson's narrative doubles back on itself as Eve, within range of a Northern Jupiter Light that matches its Southern counterpart at least in name, takes up Cicely's role and nearly loses herself in a Dionysian reverie: aboard ship in the Northern wilderness, "the river growing constantly more wild as they ascended it, the high Northern air ... was like an intoxicant—all of these seemed to her wonderful. She breathed rapidly; it seemed as if she must clasp her arms about herself to hold herself in" (April 1889, 713). And then, just as Cicely had done in the warm Southern wind, full of self-forgetfulness, Eve knocks on Cicely's door with an invitation to walk in the dark.

Cicely, however, refuses. "I am in bed already," she says, before turning her back on Eve. Despite repeated promises to herself that she will return to bed (to "that narrow shelf" in her "cell") and that she will not wander about on deck at night, Eve finds herself alone as she once was that night on Abercrombie Island, where she feared a dark and critical stranger (714). In this scene, a figure in the dark unexpectedly lights his cigar. It's Cicely's brother-in-law, Paul Tennant, and in the brief conversation that ensues, Eve quickly admits to Paul, "'I control no one,'" and to herself "('Not even myself')," as if she were admitting that she could not create and control her own identity (714). Eve learns that the possibilities of self-fashioning are limited by geography and by personal as well as national history.

In the Northern wilderness, Eve allows the boundaries of self to become porous because she senses the possibility of being made anew in a landscape she endorses: "here was the freshness of a new world" and so of a new self (708). When she returns with Cicely to the South, she returns with a new sense of what it means to self-fashion and to read and interpret others within a context that includes the external forces that shape the self. She no longer assumes a privileged, judgmental position toward the South and its inhabitants. With the Southern Jupiter Light in view, "Eve remembered that less than a year before she had landed here for the first time, a woman imperious, sufficient to herself; a woman who was sure that she could direct her own course.... How like child's play did this all seem now" (September 1889, 585). At this point, Eve understands that identity is not a fixed mark like the Jupiter Light but is partly fashioned by the self and partly fashioned by the context in which it stands. As a result, Eve no longer sees Cicely as the *other*, the *Southern* woman she preconceived, but as another *self* who, like her, is contextualized by the place and the history they now share.

As Eve learns that identity can be shaped by geographical and historical contexts, she also learns the possibilities of self-fashioning within those parameters. After Cicely and Eve return South, Cicely demands that they take a walk one night to reenact the shooting of Ferdie. The moon "silvered the forest," recalling of that first strange pas de deux in the old ballroom (587). Once again, Eve's sense of self is influenced by geography: she is under "the spell of the place" much as Cicely had been in the first scene, but there is a notable difference: "She felt herself forced by some inward compelling power to go through the whole scene" (587). Although Eve is swept up by a tide that she cannot finally control, it is not the wind or the landscape that pushes her; the power of place is now felt as an *inward* compulsion. She again expects to see a dark figure observing her, but this time she has a name for it—Ferdie, the man she shot in this same spot.

This time, Cicely does not dance her way to Eve. Instead, she "came rushing ... and with quick force bore her to the ground" and began strangling her sister-in-law and crying, "'Do you like it? Do you like it? Do you *like* to be dead?'" as if the deed were already done (587). Eve exercises no will to define herself in this scene; she allows herself to become part of another's scenario. As quickly as she gives up her self, she is released. "Like a person in a dream," Eve gets up from under the limp, now almost mindless Cicely, goes to the beach, dampens her kerchief, and returns to cool Cicely's feverish brow (587). Then she carries Cicely to the verandah. Because she accepts the external forces beyond her control, she can now harness the power to self-fashion that also shapes identity.

While the regional conflict of North and South, particularly as it fuels the geographical determinants of identity in *Jupiter Lights*, seems to reinforce the dialectic that dominates the national narrative in the latter half of the nineteenth century, Woolson suggests a more productive way of thinking in this novel. The two Jupiter Lights, one south and one north, overlook nearly identical scenes in which each of the two women takes her turn at fusing her identity with the natural forces around her. Eve and Cicely, moreover, dance and fight their way like sister states to become the single unifying figure of Eve carrying her dazed sister-in-law. No man watches or threatens to watch since Ferdie, the imagined observer, is dead and gone. The absence of the fierce masculinity for which James searches becomes an opportunity for Woolson: a world of absent men recalls the subject of *For the Major*, the novel in which Woolson began her examination of identity formation in the South. Woolson returns to this subject because there, and not within the dialectic of North and South, is where she locates the possibility for female self-fashioning.

It would take more than a change of clothing or a change of place to settle Reconstruction's battle for signification and interpretation. As James's account of his Southern sojourn suggests, the "latent poetry" of the South remained a fixed conceit in the Northern imagination. James and Woolson focus on the fashioning of Southern women, however, to suggest that what remained after the Civil War was a place—a nation—with a future that was not so fixed to the assumed certainties of the past. If as Madam Merle explains to Isabel Archer in James's *The Portrait of a Lady*, "'a woman . . . has no natural place anywhere; wherever she finds herself she has to remain on the surface and, more or less, to crawl,'" then the identity of the postbellum United States was not rooted in the places themselves—the North, the South, the West—but in the *idea of place*, in the movement from location to location, and in the possibilities of self-fashioning that presented themselves.[23] The cultural project of the late nineteenth century that sought the familiar and the strange at home rather than abroad was aimed largely at Northerners and aimed to reaffirm the sense of Northern normativity. That postwar project also asserted the combination of individual autonomy and external forces that shape identity, at least for Woolson, and this implies the possibility of change within the larger boundaries that define self, region, and nation.

Notes

1. Nina Silber, *The Romance of Reunion: Northerners and the South, 1865–1900* (Chapel Hill: University of North Carolina Press, 1993), 67. For a discussion of print culture as a means of shaping ideas about the South, particularly in regard to self-fashioning and slavery before the Civil War, see David Waldstreicher, "Reading the Runaways: Self-Fashioning, Print Culture, and Confidence in Slavery in the Eighteenth-Century Mid-Atlantic," *William and Mary Quarterly* 56.2 (April 1999): 243–72.

2. Henry James, *The American Scene* (Bloomington: Indiana University Press, 1968), 366. All subsequent references will be to this edition and will be made parenthetically in the text. For a succinct publication history of *The American Scene*, see Rosalie Hewitt, "Henry James, the Harpers, and *The American Scene*," *American Literature* 55.1 (1983): 41–47.

3. Suzanne Jones and Sharon Monteith, "Introduction: South to New Places," *South to a New Place: Region, Literature, Culture* (Baton Rouge: Louisiana State University Press, 2002), 10, 9.

4. Stephen Greenblatt, *Renaissance Self-Fashioning: From More to Shakespeare* (Chicago: University of Chicago Press, 1980), 2. All subsequent references will be made parenthetically in the text.

5. Quoted in Greenblatt, *Renaissance Self-Fashioning*, 2.

6. I am indebted to Carol Del Vitto's work on Freemasonry in nineteenth-century America. See especially "The Symbolic Masonic Initiation of Herman Melville's *Pierre*" (MA thesis, Stetson University, 2007).

7. Richard Gray, "Inventing Communities, Imagining Places: Some Thoughts on Southern Self-Fashioning," *South to a New Place: Region, Literature, Culture,* ed. Suzanne W. Jones and Sharon Monteith (Baton Rouge: Louisiana State University Press, 2002), xx.

8. Gray, "Inventing Communities, Imagining Places," xxiii. Gray contends that the idea of the South "has become a vital instrument of knowledge, linked to the broader human project of trying to spin a sense of reality out of language. It is also a palpable sign of ignorance to the extent that the histories it maps must remain irreducibly other" (xxii).

9. Jil Larson, *Ethics and Narrative in the English Novel, 1880–1914* (Cambridge: Cambridge University Press, 2001), 32–33; quoted in Annette Federico, "Irony, Ethics and Self-Fashioning in George Moore's *Confessions of a Young Man,*" *Marketing the Author: Authorial Personae, Narrative Selves and Self-Fashioning, 1880–1930,* ed. Marysa Demoor (London: Palgrave Macmillan, 2004), 97.

10. Gray, "Inventing Communities, Imagining Places," xxii.

11. For more information on postbellum tourism in the South, see Silber, *The Romance of Reunion,* and Jamie Winders, "Imperfectly Imperial: Northern Travel Writers in the Postbellum U.S. South, 1865–1880," *Annals of the Association of American Geographers* 95.2 (2005): 391–410.

12. All reference to *For the Major* are to the novel's first serialized publication in *Harper's Monthly*: 65 (November 1882): 907–18; 66 (December 1882): 93–105; 66 (January 1883): 243–51; 66 (February 1883): 405–14; 66 (March 1883): 564–71; and 66 (April 1883): 749–64. Page references will be made parenthetically in the text.

13. In *Constance Fenimore Woolson: The Artistry of Grief* (Athens: University of Georgia Press, 1989), Cheryl B. Torsney points out that Henry James noted the focus on fashioning the self in *For the Major*. In "Miss Woolson," James claims that "it is the first time that a woman has been represented as painting her face, dyeing her hair, and 'dressing young,' out of tenderness of another." See *Literary Criticism: Essays on Literature, American, English Writers* (New York: Library of America, 1984), 643. Quoted in Torsney, *Constance Fenimore Woolson,* 128.

14. Torsney, *Constance Fenimore Woolson,* 131.

15. Greenblatt, *Renaissance Self-Fashioning,* 228.

16. Lyndall Gordon, *The Private Life of Henry James: Two Women and His Art* (London: Norton, 1998), 214.

17. Gordon, *The Private Life of Henry James,* 214.

18. Constance Fenimore Woolson, *Jupiter Lights, Harper's Monthly* (January 1889): 247. Woolson's novel was first serialized in this and subsequent issues: (January 1889): 240–55; (February 1889): 435–53; (March 1889): 589–611; (April 1889): 703–22; (May 1889): 951–58; (June 1889): 114–23; (July 1889): 265–82; (August 1889): 415–32; and (September 1889): 582–99. Page references will be made parenthetically in the text.

19. In *Constance Fenimore Woolson: Homeward Bound* (Knoxville: University of Tennessee Press, 1995), Sharon Dean reads this scene as evidence that Woolson "understood the degree to which one's own ethnicity shaped social attitudes" and that she attended "to issues of race . . . [and] social class" (70).

20. James, *The American Scene,* 368.

21. In *The Birth of Tragedy,* Friedrich Nietzsche argues that "music and tragic myth . . . transfigure a region where dissonance and the terrible image of the world fade away in chords of delight; . . . both justify by their play the existence of even the 'worst of all worlds.'" See *The Birth of Tragedy and Other Writings,* trans. Ronald Spiers, ed. Raymond Geuss and Ronald Spiers (Cambridge: Cambridge University Press, 1999), 115. In *Jupiter Lights,* Eve invokes myth to transform the terrible image of the South that she carries with her as a Northern visitor, making the South at once both less palpable and more familiar.

22. Caroline Gebhard notes that this scene offers a moment of intimacy between the women approaching "a triangulation of lesbian desire" that is actively repudiated in the novel, especially here by Eve. I would argue that she further reasserts her Northern identity by inciting a kind of homosexual panic and fear of discovery. See "Romantic Love and Wife-Battering in Constance Fenimore Woolson's *Jupiter Lights*," *Constance Fenimore Woolson's Nineteenth Century: Essays*, ed. Victoria Brehm (Detroit: Wayne State University Press, 2001), 90.

23. Henry James, *The Portrait of a Lady* (London: Penguin, 1984), 248.

Woolson's Two Women: 1862.

A Civil War Romance of Irreconcilable Difference

—Caroline Gebhard

Constance Fenimore Woolson is not remembered as a poet but, in the decade following the Civil War, her poems captured the imagination of her countrymen and -women. By 1877, she had published close to 50 poems in leading literary magazines such as the *Atlantic Monthly*, *Harper's Monthly*, and *Appletons' Journal*. A reviewer for the *Boston Globe* commented, "There are certainly very few American women who can write both prose and verse as well as she."[1] Impressed with her poetry, Paul Hamilton Hayne, the best-known Southern poet of the day, praised her poems as "full of 'grit,' vigor, and almost manly verve."[2] And Charlotte Cushman, a famous actress of the time, paid her the highest compliment of all by appropriating a number of Woolson's poems for her own public performances.[3]

This essay will explore why she abandoned poetry at the height of her popularity as a poet and how Woolson's most ambitious poem, *Two Women: 1862.* (1877), responds to the "romance of union" popular in the aftermath of the Civil War. Woolson, who was twenty-two when the war began, poured herself into the war effort, imagined herself in love with a soldier, and never felt anything quite lived up to being a part of the great unfolding drama of our country's Civil War.[4] *Two Women* represents Woolson's attempt to craft a bold tragic heroine modeled not a little upon Shakespeare's Cleopatra, who embodied the wartime experience of her own generation. Yet ultimately Woolson's Civil War romance unfolds as a drama of difference that exposes a gulf between North and South, and between old-fashioned ideals of femininity and new possibilities for women's lives.

Woolson's Different Romance of Union

When Woolson published her dramatic poem a dozen years after Robert E. Lee's surrender to Ulysses S. Grant, Civil War love stories were in vogue. Scholars have long recognized that romance and marriage in popular fiction register the ways in which postbellum American culture came to grips with the recent past. For Northerners, as Nina Silber points out, stories of Southerners marrying across the Mason-Dixon Line became "a way to convey their image of a Union victory, one which was not rooted in greed but in feelings and emotions."[5] Between 1861 and 1876, Kathleen Diffley observes, "the romance of union had become a prevailing cultural figure for Reconstruction policy."[6] As the 1870s wore on, however, military occupation of the South became more politically unpalatable. Nevertheless, those in the North clung to the idea of their moral superiority, even as it became clear that Federal troops would soon be withdrawn. Silber notes that in this climate, Northern versions of North-South romances favored images of reunion that cast Northern manhood as virile, principled, and dominant while the South was "assigned the weaker and more emotional role,"[7] naturalized as the woman properly conquered by love. Diffley, however, points out that by far the most common fictional "union" during the postwar period was not North and South at all; she writes that the majority of romantic tales published in magazines during the 1860s and 1870s did not bring Northern and Southern lovers together but matched couples from the same region: "Girls from Massachusetts chose boys from the Bay State, girls from Virginia chose boys from the Old Dominion."[8]

Woolson's poem both fits—and does not fit—the paradigmatic "romance of union" that Diffley, Silber, and others have identified. Unlike most such romances, this narrative takes place in the early days of the war, when the outcome was uncertain, and when John Hunt Morgan's notorious Raiders crossed into Kentucky and even Ohio at will. Indeed, the poem does not emphasize reunion or opposites reconciled as do so many Civil War stories: instead, Woolson's long "play-poem" dramatizes the uncertain, tense territory of the border, where opposites meet and mingle but do not become one. From its inception, *Two Women: 1862.* underlines division and difference in an encounter of two women who meet by chance on a train. The mobile setting—a train on which one woman, "The Maiden," traveling south from the Great Lakes, meets another, "The Lady," from Washington, DC—underscores the shifting battlefield of the war as well as the unthinkable social collisions it has begun to unleash: women traveling alone far from home in a time when who is friend, who foe, is no longer clear. Their destination, Kentucky, is also telling. Literally a border state during the war, Kentucky was officially still a part of the Union but also a haven for Confederate sympathizers, and the state became the scene of Rebel raids and Union counterinsurgency operations.

Kentucky thus provided Woolson the perfect setting for a poem about divided loyalties and the chaos the war brought. Morgan's Raiders, outlaws or heroes, savages or gentlemen, depending upon one's vantage point, similarly embody the

Janus-like figures the poem portrays. From the Rebel side, the Raiders were gallant fighters against desperate odds for love, honor, patriotism, duty, and the future. In one of Woolson's travel sketches, a Confederate veteran points out the town where Morgan was shot and killed; Uncle Jack, the older Northerner in the piece, views Morgan as a traitor who deserved his fate, but the Southerner still sees Morgan's choice as honorable, if ultimately mistaken.[9] Although his adopted state of Kentucky did not elect to secede from the Union, John Hunt Morgan joined the Confederate army and from July 4 to August 1, 1862, commanded a feared cavalry brigade that raided central Kentucky and hindered the Union advance into Tennessee.[10] Woolson deftly drew upon Morgan's raids in the summer of 1862 as a dramatic way to link the fates of her two women and to symbolize how war makes evil and good dependent in part upon one's vantage point.

Although the poem carefully avoids making Morgan into either a hero or a villain, Woolson was well aware that Morgan had become in Union eyes a notorious figure. During the late summer of 1862, *Harper's Weekly* published an illustration of the "SACKING OF A CITY IN THE WEST BY THE GUERRILLAS under John Morgan," claiming, "Such God-forsaken wretches can not be found any where in the world out of the Feejee Islands and the Southern Slave States."[11] Against this historical backdrop, Woolson begins her story with sharp contrasts: North and South, rural and urban, fundamentalist zeal and free thinking, but her purpose from the outset is to complicate all simple notions of friend and foe, love and hate, good and evil. From the poem's opening lines, "The Maiden" from the North is identified with daylight, ripening corn and wheat, Protestant thrift, and innocence, while "The Other" from the South and traveling west from Washington is identified with nighttime, urbanity, pleasure, and danger. Their paths first cross in "The Western city with the Roman name," presumably Cincinnati.[12] They do not yet know that they are seeking the same wounded Union soldier, felled by a bullet from Morgan's raiders.

In some respects, *Two Women* does follow the plot delineated by Silber of a Southern girl conquered by love for a manly Northern soldier. Woolson's poem also plays into conventional views of the Southern belle. In a letter for the *Cleveland Herald* excerpted in the *New York Times*, Woolson herself claimed, "You can tell a Southern girl at once," describing her this way:

> She is rounder than her Northern sisters; indeed she is never thin or lank; she walks with a languid step.... She has fine soft eyes ... very different from the quick, keen eyes of the North; she has not the beautiful red and white complexion of New-York and New-England, rather she is sallow, with few rose tints; you might call her cream color.[13]

Woolson also hints at the legendary sensuousness of Southern women; the Southern girl, she claimed, "dresses picturesquely rather than trimly . . . [with] brighter colors and more floating ends and curls about her than a Northern belle allows." Southern women, Woolson wrote, were not "particular" about the gloves that covered their "pretty, plump hands," seemingly indifferent to "Fifth avenue rules," or high fashion. Not surprisingly, Southern women objected to Woolson's representations of them.[14]

The reader's first tantalizing glimpse of this Southern type of beauty in "The Other" (or "The Lady," as she is later called) is by the light of the conductor's lantern. The sensuality of her figure is accented by the "shimmer of lace," the "sheen of silk," and the "India shawl" that only "half concealed / The curves superb which the light revealed" (8–9). In the first of many images that suggest her erotic power, all the men in the car are transfixed by this slumbering "Milo Venus" who awakes to show "Dark-brown, sleepy, velvet eyes" and "Bold features, Nubian lips, a skin / Creamy pallid, the red within / Mixed with brown" (9–10). We see her through admiring male eyes—the "city thief," the "traitor spy," the "correspondent with quick, sharp eye," the "man of God," and the soldiers present, all alike under her spell (8–9). With her creamy skin, dark eyes, and languid grace, The Lady evokes stereotypical Southern beauty; later named Helena, she recalls legendary queens such as Helen of Troy or the Egyptian Cleopatra. Yet The Lady's identification with the South is complex and ambiguous. It is never clear if she is even a native Southerner, although many indications suggest that she is.

In the course of conversation with "The Maiden" (the only name Woolson gives her Northern counterpart), we learn, for example, that The Lady loves Kentucky and has a taste for horse racing, gambling, and plays. She seems taken aback by The Maiden's description of John Morgan's men as "guerrillas," demurring that "Maybe so, / and maybe not; they bear a seven-leagued name / That many hide beneath . . ." (21). She defends Morgan's raiders as not guilty of every crime assigned to them, and she sees it as natural that Kentuckians would aid and abet them: "Kentucky knows her own" (22). Such comments lead The Maiden to suspect that The Lady is "that mythical adventuress" (22), the Confederate female spy. The Lady, however, evades the question of whether she is "Kentucky-bred," saying only that she is coming from Washington. Nor does she admit to being a spy; instead, she changes the subject (22–23).

We never learn for sure how far her allegiance to the South goes,[15] but it is clear her Northern lover has utterly won her heart despite their differences. She tells The Maiden how, almost against their wills, the two fell in love in Washington: "We met, we two so far apart / In every thought, in life, in soul, in heart— / Our very beings clashed" (35). Yet she affirms that both were mutually struck as if by "lightning from a cloudless sky, / So sudden, strange, the white intensity— / Intensity resistless!" (37). Her lover was overcome by "a force unknown before" just as she was likewise humbled by love, and, she proudly confesses, she "gave him—all!" (37). She asks her companion on the train to forgive her: "Sweet girl, / Forgive me for the guiltless robbery, / Forgive him, swept by fateful Destiny!" (37).

However, The Lady's insistence in this scene that she gave her Northern lover "all" raises more questions than it answers. Have they become engaged? Have they consummated their relationship? Does this mean—if she is working for the Confederacy—that she puts love for him above all else? There is an ambiguous moment when she recalls watching him leave with his regiment; she says, "Love for my country burns / Within my heart; but this was love for him" (42). One reading is that, despite their troth, she expects him to do his duty for his country (and hers, the Union?), yet the same lines could also suggest she is torn between love for her country (the Confederacy?) and love for him, though ultimately love for him trumps all else. Like those of Cleopatra, The Lady's political motives remain murky but not her passion, which is paramount.

Yet unlike the classic romance of union, this story does not end conventionally with the marriage of a Northern officer to a Southern belle. Instead, the Northern officer whom the women both claim dies of fever from an infected bullet wound in his arm. Indeed, the only marriage in the poem follows the more common pattern noted by Diffley: At the end of the poem, the Northern maiden puts aside her grief over the loss of her soldier-sweetheart and marries another local boy from the Lake Erie region. Thus, the figure the poem makes is hardly one of national reconciliation. For Woolson's two women, there is no real reunion possible on earth. The Federal soldier is dead and the two women, read as North and South, are still divided over him and what he really stood for; they even call him by different names. The Lady resolves never to marry but to be true to his memory, her only hope of reunion being in paradise.

Her refusal to go back on the past recalls the legendary commitment of Southern women to the Lost Cause, depicted elsewhere in Woolson's work. In "Rodman the Keeper" (1877), love between the Southern woman and the Northern keeper of a national cemetery in the South cannot grow because of her loyalty to the Confederate dead; similarly, "In the Cotton Country" (1876) tells the story of a Confederate widow in a state of perpetual mourning. Woolson's "Old Gardiston" (1876) does feature marriage between a Southern girl and a Yankee officer, but the story also shows that this daughter of the South pays a high price for agreeing to marry the former enemy: the total loss of her proud family heritage represented by the old house's self-immolation. None of Woolson's Southern fictions project an image of untroubled national reunification but rather portray a country still riven by deep divisions. Another tale offers the most chilling prediction for the nation's future. Woolson's

"King David" (1878) ominously predicts that "hundreds" of freedmen "will die, nay, must die violent deaths before their people can learn what freedom means, and what it does not mean," accurately forecasting the failure of Northerners to stop postwar Southern violence, the rise of the Ku Klux Klan, and the endemic lynching of black men to come.[16]

In *Two Women*, ironically, the tug-of-war over the Union soldier is not resolvable even in the afterlife; like The Lady, The Maiden also plans to rejoin him in heaven. The poem's ending appears closer to what really happened in Northern and Southern households in the postbellum era: though both alike recognized the ultimate authority of the federal government as a reality, very different narratives arose about who had kept the true faith and why.

Woolson's Rare Hero: A Southern Cleopatra

Although *Two Women: 1862.* tells a Civil War love story, the poem also takes aim at the conventional morality of romances popular in postbellum America. Woolson once wrote a girlhood friend, "I want you to think of me not as your old friend, when you read my writings, but as a 'writer,' like anyone else." Citing George Eliot's *Adam Bede* (1859), in which a young woman pregnant out of wedlock commits infanticide by abandoning her child at birth, Woolson explains her own position: "Would you like to have a friend of yours the author of such a story? Dealing with such subjects? And yet it was a great book." She places herself firmly in Eliot's camp: "I would rather be strong than beautiful, or even good."[17]

Most striking, then, in this poem written by a self-professed "red hot abolitionist" and staunch Union supporter is the critique of pious Northern womanhood.[18] Reversing the stereotype of the passionate dark lady losing out to the blonde and blue-eyed virgin, the poem portrays the Northern "Maiden" not as the ideal of Christian femininity but instead as a puritanical prig. Easily scandalized, this prim girl is shocked by the jocular swearing of the young soldiers on the train, just as she judges her rival harshly. *She* is sure that horse racing, plays, wine, and dancing are very wicked and that The Lady is Hell-bound. "I *know*," she tells The Lady, that "my Willie" "your evil smiles he spurned" (38–39).

When confronted with love letters that prove otherwise, The Maiden says that even if he has fallen under this "sorceress's" spell she will not leave him to her rival; she asks God to "let him die" rather than be with such a woman (45). The most generosity she can muster is praying that if "My poor boy loves this woman," "Change her, Lord—make her good!" (62). Yet even at this moment, she cannot resist thinking herself superior: "if [she] be fair, though I / Think her too brown" (62). Ultimately, her self-righteousness proves chilling: unlike The Lady, she quickly resigns herself to the soldier's death. This brand of piety, Woolson suggests, is self-deluded and self-serving. The Lady proves the stronger and the more generous of the two. When both are forced to ride horseback because Morgan's Raiders have destroyed the rail bridge, The Lady must rescue The Maiden who, no judge of horseflesh, has chosen the poorer steed. So they arrive together, only to find that the man they are seeking has died the night before.

The Northern girl, certain her letters and her picture on the soldier's bedside table are proof that he loved only her, soon departs, leaving The Lady to bury him. In the meantime, The Lady has interviewed the surgeon and learned it is *her* name that the dying man spoke. She also learns that he instructed the doctor to place her picture and letters next to his heart. In another twist, The Maiden never learns the truth because The Lady chooses not to disillusion her, believing that her lover would have wanted to spare his childhood sweetheart another blow. Woolson's poem thus defies readerly expectations that the "good," Christian, blonde, Northern maiden must be the true heroine; instead, the poem reveals the dark lady to be superior in strength, love, and, ultimately, self-sacrifice. Reversing expectations by allowing the dark Lady to outshine the fair Maiden, Woolson's poem participates in a transformed understanding of gender roles that emerged amid civil upheaval.

After Appomattox, Nina Silber points out, defeat as well as the emancipation of the slaves "propelled the postwar South into a multifaceted 'gender crisis,' with ex-slaves working . . . to hold onto wartime gains, defeated white men working to reassert their positions of prominence . . . and white women working to both restore features of the status quo and advance some of their own ideas about independence." The complex contestations over gender, race, and power were not just confined to the postwar South, as new scholarship on the Civil War suggests; Northern men and women were also affected by what Silber has recently dubbed a "climate of intense virility," which emerged from the militarization of Northern society as a result of the Civil War.[19]

John Stauffer argues that writers of Woolson's generation who came of age during the war turned away from the sentimental ideal of femininity celebrated by women writers of the previous generation, like Harriet Beecher Stowe and Lydia Maria Child. In particular, he contends that Louisa May Alcott "led the way in transforming the representations and roles of women" by "creating manly women and womanly men."[20] Although Woolson, too, creates a virile female hero of decided strength and independence—a "manly woman"—, she draws more boldly upon a richly ambiguous ancient figure, one whose nineteenth-century iconography not only signals a transformation of traditional gender roles but also underscores the country's continuing racial divide.

The grandeur and glamour of Cleopatra, directly descended from Shakespeare's character in *Antony and Cleopatra*, provided a touchstone for many nineteenth-century literary characters as well as for the paintings and sculptures of contemporary artists.[21] For this era, Cleopatra was, in the words of Anna Jameson, the "most wonderful" of all of Shakespeare's women:

> I have not the slightest doubt that Shakespeare's Cleopatra is the real historical Cleopatra—the "Rare Egyptian"—individualized and placed before us. Her mental accomplishments, her unequalled grace, her woman's wit and woman's wiles, her irresistible allurements, her starts of irregular grandeur, her bursts of ungovernable temper ... her magnificent spirit, her royal pride, the gorgeous eastern colouring of the character; all these contradictory elements has Shakspeare [sic] seized, mingled them in their extremes, and fused them into one brilliant impersonation of classical elegance, Oriental voluptuousness, and gipsy sorcery.[22]

Woolson's friend Henry James would later turn to "The Rare Egyptian" in *The Ambassadors* (1903) to represent the devious sexual power and sophistication of women—in this case, European women. Woolson's daring was to project her Cleopatra as an American, specifically a Southern woman with a past.

There is something Shakespearean in The Lady's soliloquy over her lover's dead body.[23] In sharp contrast to The Maiden's calm acceptance is The Lady's wild grief. She rages at God, "Who makes us at his will, and gives us hearts / Only to rend them in a hundred parts" (72). When Shakespeare's Antony dies, his Cleopatra rages "at the injurious gods," suggesting they have purposefully stolen her "jewel."[24] The Lady feels similarly bereft, implying that God has unfairly taken her lover from her (72). Having previously married young, The Lady is a widow who, like Cleopatra, wed in "her salad days." Like Cleopatra learning of Antony's marriage to Octavia, she lashes out violently: "Scarce can I refrain / My hands from crushing you!—" (33) she tells The Maiden, practically ripping the locket from the girl's neck when she sees that it contains the likeness of Meredith Wilmer Reid, her lover. "Give it me forthwith!" she demands, adding: "The 'pet name Willie!' Would you try to chain / Phoebus Apollo with your baby-love / And baby titles?" (32–33).

Cleopatra recurs in Woolson's work, not only as a figure of erotic power[25] but also as one of a solitary and markedly masculine strength. In "St. Clair Flats," for example, Raymond apostrophizes the water lilies: "Cleopatra art thou, regal blossom," stressing the toughness of the flowers ("Fiery sun himself cannot subdue thee") and their solitude ("Haughty empress of the summer waters / Livest thou, and diest all alone").[26] In *Two Women*, her regal heroine is also portrayed as exercising a strikingly unconventional freedom of thought and action. Sizing up the "dreamless ignorance" of the Northern girl, she thinks to herself, "I must put out / My eyes to live with you again" and even defends religious doubt as "upward growth

/ Of the strong mind" (25). She has braved temptations that The Maiden is not even capable of feeling. She tells her nunnish rival:

> ... *You* never yearned
> For freedom, born a slave! You never felt
> The thrill of rapture, the wild ecstasy
> Of mere existence that strong natures know ... (40)

Significantly, though, the recurring trope of freedom in the poem is not linked to black slaves at all, but to women, especially women's erotic power, even though the poem's time frame (1862 to 1864) spans Lincoln's Emancipation Proclamation of 1863.

Yet Woolson's trope of freedom embodied by a regal woman who recalls the Queen of the Nile is problematic on many scores. After all, Cleopatra famously "unmanned" Antony in battle, when he fled the contest to follow her and left behind a disastrous defeat at sea. To deflect attention from the threat of emasculation suggested by such a strong image of female eros and power, Woolson makes use of yet another classical image. At a key moment, The Lady claims: "No Omphale I, / Though he be Hercules," adding, "his passion must not dim / The soldier's courage" (42). Ironically, the very mention of Omphale here could likely have had the opposite effect: Woolson reminded her nineteenth-century readers of the mythical Lydian Queen who in enslaving Hercules through erotic mastery, usurped his signature animal skin and club, thereby forcing him into female clothing so that the allusion intensifies the threat of emasculation rather than lessens it.[27] Apart from this indirect allusion to enslavement, however, there is only one brief and ambiguous mention of chattel slavery in Woolson's poem, just when Morgan's men also make their final appearance.

Struck by the sight of the burial attended by a regal lady alone, the raiders gallantly dismount and pay their last respects, unaware of their own lethal part in this scene. The grave diggers suspect that these men ride with Morgan; among them is a lone slave who confirms that Morgan himself was there: "'That was him— / Young Cap'en Morgan's self!'" He adds, "'These eyes is dim, / But they knows Morgan! Morgan!—what! why, bless / Your hearts, *I* know him, and I know Black Bess— / 'Twas Bess he rode'" (86). The slave's presence at the grave scene Woolson imagines is an uneasy reminder of what romance can and cannot incorporate. David W. Blight powerfully underscores the tendency of popular Civil War fiction to gloss over the brutal realities of slavery in favor of fictions more agreeable to white audiences. In *Race and Reunion: The Civil War in American Memory*, Blight argues that "the intersectional wedding that became such a staple of mainstream popular culture ... had no interracial counterpart in the popular imagination." As he goes on to point out, "The memory of slavery never fit well into a developing narrative in which the Old and New South were romanticized and welcomed back to a new nationalism."[28] *Two Women: 1862.* thus reaches for an unusual reckoning, especially in 1877.

The picture that Woolson paints in this scene—the gallant Confederate raider, the grieving lady, the knowing slave—resists easy interpretation. Does the slave's speech suggest affection for the rebel leader? Or does it rather signal that there are things he cannot say while enslaved in Kentucky, a border state that was largely Confederate in its sympathies? The slave knows Morgan and the horse he rides, but of what does this knowledge really consist and where do his loyalties lie? It is impossible to tell from his statement. Woolson's inclusion of an unreadable black figure registering the unknowable subjectivity of the racial other is repeated elsewhere in her work.[29] Here the slave intensifies the illegibility of all three figures: Does *Two Women: 1862.* romanticize this reviled rebel leader who penetrated even farther into Union territory than Robert E. Lee at Gettysburg? Or does Woolson's poem merely record the brutality as well as graceful gestures that Morgan was known for? A measure of the terror Morgan spread was recorded in a cover story published by *Harper's Weekly* during the late summer of 1862, the year emphasized by Woolson's title. The story, devoted to the man labeled "guerrilla" and "bandit," nonetheless admitted he was "said to possess some of the chivalrous qualities of his namesake and prototype, Morgan the Buccaneer of the Caribbean Sea."[30] The unresolved tension of these opposing readings even apparent in the newsmagazine's profile is, perhaps, the point of Woolson's depiction of the Civil War: during those "strange and breathless days" (8) of that internecine war, any place, Woolson's poem revealed, might become a shifting, dangerous borderland, where allegiances did not always surface quickly, where friendship, love, and enmity overlapped in strange ways.

Just as the poem's slave and its planter-turned-guerrilla-fighter remain opaque figures, The Lady proves to be enigmatic, ultimately moreso than either the slave or the Confederate raider. Inscribed with the adjective "Nubian" and thus evoking Cleopatra, Woolson's Lady becomes a figure for the American conundrum of race. As Francesca T. Royster has argued in *Becoming Cleopatra: The Shifting Image of an Icon*, in Shakespeare's hands the exotic, non-Roman, non-Western otherness of Cleopatra assumed for the first time a racial significance; thus *Becoming Cleopatra* follows a line of critical interpretation that sees the Egyptian queen's allure as dependent "on her racial and cultural instability." Even though African Americans, beginning in the nineteenth century, were appropriating Cleopatra as "black," Royster contends that the real issue was not whether she was "white" or "black," but how, from Shakespeare onward, this iconic figure's race remained "problematically unstable."[31] Royster draws upon Arthur Little's work to show that, even within a single text, Cleopatra could exhibit a range of racial and ethnic identities; she quotes

Little: "'Sometimes this racially othered Cleopatra adeptly occupies a number of cultural and racial positions in a single text, as she does in Elizabeth Cary's *Tragedy of Mariam* (1613), where she is variously described as brown, black, Egyptian, and Ethiopian. But her tendency toward cultural and racial polymorphous perversity extends, too, to white Cleopatras who are no less secure in their cultural and racial positions and often seem just a step away from the cultural/racial border or having about them at least a hint of color.'"[32] Both Royster's and Little's insights into the racial and cultural confusion that Cleopatra cannot help but signify in the West underscores Woolson's boldness in connecting her hero with the "Rare Egyptian."

The "Nubian" lips, "too brown" complexion, and passionate attachment to freedom link Woolson's Lady not only to a Cleopatra, whose racial identity is inherently unstable and "polymorphously perverse," but also to the enslaved African Americans largely absent from this poem.[33] Telling, too, are other characters in Woolson's fiction whose skin color and physiognomy hint at the secret of African ancestry. The doomed heroine of the story "Wilhelmina," for example, not only has a "Nubian head" and "creamy skin," but also uncertain parentage.[34] In *Two Women*, even if Woolson does not consciously intend to inscribe her heroine as a racial other, The Lady as a version of Cleopatran "white" womanhood—albeit Southern "white" womanhood and therefore supposedly more "exotic" and "emotional"—is inevitably haunted in a racist society by the specter of blackness.[35]

Perhaps that is why in a poem that celebrates this unconventional female hero, she is not vouchsafed the final word. Instead, it is the conventionally "good" woman who stands at the end "in bridal white" (91). The reader's last view of "The Lady" shows her continuing to play her part, that of the endlessly fascinating "queen" who must not "lay down / Her long-used sceptre," who must, that is, go on receiving the flattering attentions of men—in this instance, a "Count" "with smiles that are not wholly feigned, / For life is strong, and I am young" (89). Woolson's Nubian queen may protest that she will be true to her vow never to marry even as she admits a male admirer, but a Cleopatra who does not die becomes a hopelessly paradoxical figure to serve as the highest representation of female fidelity. The last scene is given to "The Maiden" who has burned the soldier's picture in preparation for her wedding to another. Cheering herself that she (unlike The Lady, whom she still refuses to recognize as "fair") has not "wronged the dead / With many lovers" (90–91), The Maiden receives the blessing of her mother, who tells her, "Never has mother blessed / A child more dutiful, more good" (92). Thus Woolson ends the poem as she began it, with clashing images of womanhood. If The Lady incarnates a new and virile female freedom, her figure is nevertheless still hedged in by the age-old anxieties about emasculation that female power arouses, and she is still bound by the perils of crossing the gender and race lines that she also embodies. Yet The Maiden in figuring the traditional feminine path represents an equally perilous choice for women: living according to such narrow strictures requires blindness and severe limits to freedom, a straitjacket for women of any imagination and feeling.

Popular Acclaim and Critical Neglect

Two Women: 1862. was a popular poem; it was reprinted more than once before Woolson died, the last time with a frontispiece of the author in 1890. However, the reviews it garnered sound as if they were written by the male reviewers in Woolson's "Miss Grief," where they pronounce a woman writer's work fatally flawed even as they recognize its power. Critics of *Two Women* declared it "strong" and "rugged" with "a force and strength beyond the common," yet also "defective," "abounding in 'faults' and 'crudenesses.'"[36] Despite publishing poetry in major literary magazines, Woolson was never confident of its worth. She asked Hayne what he thought of her poems, confessing, "I have not yet decided whether I can write verses or not. Perhaps you can help me to a decision."[37] She feared, she told him, that her poems were too "dramatic."[38]

When *Two Women* was published in 1877, Woolson was publishing almost as much poetry as she was fiction. Yet from 1878 until her death in 1894, her poetic output dropped precipitously to only four poems, the last printed in 1884.[39] She also declined the chance to publish her collected poems.[40] Is "Miss Grief" (1880), written while the sting of reviews of *Two Women* was still fresh, an oblique comment on the poem's mixed reception? Perhaps these reviews confirmed for Woolson that her "dramatic" tendency was not under tight enough control; perhaps she decided her poetry was dangerously close to melodrama. She later said that she "didn't think much of" "Kentucky Belle," a dramatic monologue that draws yet again upon Morgan's Raiders, even though it was one of her best-known pieces.[41]

One further hint that publishing a book of poetry was a painful, not to be repeated, experiment occurs in "At the Chateau of Corinne" (1887). Its heroine, Katharine Winthrop, gives her anonymously published book of poetry to a suitor for his honest opinion and is attacked for the poem's naked, unwomanly ambition: "a woman should not dare in that way. Thinking to soar, she invariably descends."[42] We might agree that Woolson was in the end a more gifted prose writer than she was a poet, but *Two Women*, the work she counted as her second book,[43] was a vital artistic experiment for her although it has been ignored by modern critics.[44] It is where she first developed her full-length portrait of a lady, and where she explored the meaning of the Civil War to her own generation.

In expressing what the war meant to her, The Lady voices sentiments very close to the author's own. Woolson wrote in a letter, "Sometimes even now, I wake early, and think I hear the distant call of the newsboy far down the street, 'Extra! Extra!

All about the last battle!'—And then how we rushed out to get it, how we devoured it," yet the letter's recipient whom she is confident will fully share her feelings is no Northerner but the South Carolina poet Hayne: "What days they were! After all, we *lived* then," she writes, speaking for both.[45] The letter attests to her own conviction, surely shared by those who had borne the brunt of the war's monumental sacrifice and suffering, that the Civil War was the great crucible through which the country had passed to become one—indivisible—nation.

Yet, to invoke D. H. Lawrence's dictum, if we trust the tale and not its teller, we must recognize that Woolson's remarkable poem resists such a hopeful closure. Instead of representing North and South merging into one country, into a union that transcends sectional differences, *Two Women: 1862.* dramatizes deep and irreconcilable differences as well as parallel, not convergent, narratives. In our own time, in a nation still so often bitterly divided by race, region, gender, and creed, Woolson's work testifies to an uncomfortable truth—that even the most terrible war ever experienced on American soil did not make the country truly one. Until we face the polarizing persistence of our most divisive narratives, we will not make good on our pledge to become one Nation, indivisible, with liberty and justice for all.[46]

Notes

1. This review is excerpted in *Five Generations (1785–1923)*, II: *Constance Fenimore Woolson*, ed. Clare Benedict (London: Ellis, 1930, 1932), 555.

2. Jay B. Hubbell, "Some New Letters of Constance Fenimore Woolson," *New England Quarterly* 14 (December 1941): 717.

3. Woolson admitted ruefully that the actress's reading "made" "Kentucky Belle," "and now that one little ballad is better known than anything I have written." Letter to Hayne, February 13, [1876], in Hubbell, "Some New Letters of Constance Fenimore Woolson," 730.

4. For Woolson's life during the war, including her infatuation with Zeph Spaulding, see Rayburn S. Moore, *Constance Fenimore Woolson* (New York: Twayne, 1963), 22–24, as well as Cheryl B. Torsney's essay in this volume.

5. Nina Silber, *The Romance of Reunion: Northerners and the South, 1865–1900* (Chapel Hill: University of North Carolina Press, 1993), 63–64.

6. Kathleen Diffley, *Where My Heart Is Turning Ever: Civil War Stories and Constitutional Reform, 1861–1876* (Athens: University of Georgia Press, 1992), 76.

7. Silber, *The Romance of Reunion*, 65.

8. Diffley, *Where My Heart Is Turning Ever*, 58.

9. Constance Fenimore Woolson, "The French Broad," *Harper's Monthly* (April 1875): 636.

10. See James M. McPherson's *Battle Cry of Freedom: The Civil War Era* (New York: Oxford University Press, 1988), 513–16.

11. *Harper's Weekly* (August 30, 1862): 548, 555.

12. Constance Fenimore Woolson, "Two Women: 1862," first published in *Appletons' Journal* (January 1877): 60–67, and (February 1877): 140–47. The poem was republished that same year as a book, *Two Women: 1862*. (New York: D. Appleton, 1877), where the "Western" reference occurs (11). Hereafter, the first book edition will be cited parenthetically in the text.

13. "Southern Women and Men," *New York Times* (1857-Current File), July 31, 1875, ProQuest Historical Newspapers, *New York Times* (1851–2003), 5.

14. Woolson wrote to Hayne, All Saints Day 1876 [1875?], explaining how her "harmless little paragraph ... about 'Southern girls'" had been copied in newspapers "all over the country," provoking outrage in the Southern press, especially from Southern women. See Hubbell, "Some New Letters of Constance Fenimore Woolson," 726.

15. She also calls upon "chivalrous Kentucky" to aid "the bride" [herself] / though thou hast wounded with thy rebel sword / the foeman bridegroom" (47), again allying herself with the "rebel" state, though Kentucky did not officially join the Confederacy.

16. Constance Fenimore Woolson, "King David," *Rodman the Keeper: Southern Sketches* (New York: D. Appleton, 1880), rpt. The American Short Story Series, vol. 87 (New York: Garrett, 1969), 259. All of the stories cited above were collected in this volume.

17. Benedict, *Five Generations*, II: 20. This volume edited by Woolson's niece is often the only published source for her letters. Unfortunately, Benedict often censored her aunt's writings.

18. Woolson to Hayne, April 16, 1876, in Hubbell, "Some New Letters of Constance Fenimore Woolson," 731. Critics have argued that Woolson often betrayed a Northern bias. According to Silber, Woolson characterized Southern women as having "weak moral fiber and poor work habits" as well as a "spiteful" character (9, 6). Sybil B. Weir argues that "the strong, mature women are all Northern; the self-indulgent, irresponsible women ... are all Southern." See "Southern Womanhood in the Novels of Constance Fenimore Woolson," *Critical Essays on Constance Fenimore Woolson*, ed. Cheryl B. Torsney (New York: G. K. Hall, 1992), 141. See also Karen Weekes, "Northern Bias in Constance Fenimore Woolson's 'Rodman the Keeper,'" *Southern Literary Journal* 32.2 (Spring 2000): 102–15. In my view, these critics overstate the case and flatten the complexity of Woolson's characters, although many of her female heroes—Anne Douglas in *Anne* (1882), Margaret Harold in *East Angels* (1884), and Eve Bruce in *Jupiter Lights* (1889)—are exemplary Northern women.

19. Nina Silber, "Introduction: Colliding and Collaborating: Gender and Civil War Scholarship," *Battle Scars: Gender and Sexuality in the American Civil War*, ed. Catherine Clinton and Nina Silber (New York: Oxford University Press, 2006), 9, 14. The entire collection paints a complicated, sometimes contradictory, picture of gender roles being redefined in the postwar period.

20. John Stauffer, "Embattled Manhood and New England Writers, 1860–1870," *Battle Scars*, 131, 134.

21. For example, William Wetmore Story's famous *Cleopatra* (1858) greatly impressed contemporaries like Nathaniel Hawthorne, who included a description of the sculpture as the work of Kenyon in *The Marble Faun* (1858). Edmonia Lewis, of mixed Native and African American ancestry, also sculpted the African Queen in "The Death of Cleopatra" (1876), a celebrated work only recently rediscovered. See John Carlos Rowe, "Hawthorne's Ghost in Henry James's Italy: Sculptural Form, Romantic Narrative, and the Function of Sexuality," *Henry James Review* 20.2 (1999): 107–34; and Charlayne Hunter-Gault, "Testament to Bravery," available online at http://www.pbs.org/newshour/bb/entertainment/edmonia_8-5.html.

22. Anna Jameson's popular musings upon Shakespeare's heroines, including Cleopatra, first appeared in her *Characteristics of Women, Moral, Poetical, and Historical* (1832), reprinted in *Women Reading Shakespeare 1660–1900: An Anthology of Criticism*, ed. Ann Thompson and Sasha Roberts

(Manchester: Manchester University Press, 1997), 78–79. Jameson pays particular attention to Cleopatra's capacity for violence (79 n. 6).

23. Shakespeare, of course, was a familiar nineteenth-century frame of reference, and there are many reminders of his work throughout Woolson's writings. For more on her masterful use of allusion, see *Constance Fenimore Woolson: Selected Stories and Travel Narratives*, ed. Victoria Brehm and Sharon L. Dean (Knoxville: University of Tennessee Press, 2004).

24. William Shakespeare, *The Tragedy of Antony and Cleopatra*, IV: xv, 75–78, *The Riverside Shakespeare*, ed. G. Blakemore Evans et al. (Boston: Houghton Mifflin, 1974), 1381.

25. For how Shakespeare's *Antony and Cleopatra* served a female-centered eroticism in the poetry of another nineteenth-century woman, see Kristin M. Comment's "Dickinson's Bawdy: Shakespeare and Sexual Symbolism in Emily Dickinson's Writing to Susan Dickinson," *Legacy* 18.2 (2001): 167–81.

26. Constance Fenimore Woolson, "St. Clair Flats," *Appletons' Journal* (October 4, 1873): 423. There are allusions to Cleopatra throughout her writings. In "Duets," a young woman declares she would rather be herself alive "than dead Cleopatra," *Harper's Monthly* (September 1874): 580. In "The Ancient City: Part II," Sara prefers *Antony and Cleopatra* to *Romeo and Juliet*; see *Harper's Monthly* (January 1875): 177. Woolson also evokes the doomed lovers in "The Florida Beach," a poem that appeared in the *Galaxy* (October 1874): 482–83. Later, with a humorous allusion in "At Mentone," a provincial American tourist connects a convent with Shakespeare's play via this erotic figure: "'the grapes, the wine, and the frescoes'—reminded Mrs. Trescott of 'Cleopatra,'" *Harper's Monthly* (February 1884): 380. Perhaps Woolson's last allusion to Shakespeare's queen occurs in "Cairo in 1890," where a palace conjures "Oriental scenes" that a visitor imagined across a lifetime but "no more expected to see . . . than to behold the silken sails of Cleopatra furled among Cook's steamers on the Nile"; see *Harper's Monthly* (November 1891): 841.

27. Emil Krén and Dániel Marx, creators of the Web site *Web Gallery of Art*, explain that the "essential feature" in many representations of the myth of Hercules and Omphale is "the exchange of attributes," as in a painting by François Lemoyne. The Lydian Queen wears "his lion's skin and holds the club" while Hercules becomes her emasculated slave lover: "While in her service he grew effeminate, wearing women's clothes . . . and spinning yarn." See "LEMOYNE, François, Hercules and Omphale," *Web Gallery of Art*, Computer Networking Center of KFKI Research Institute for Particle and Nuclear Physics of the Hungarian Academy of Sciences, March 15, 2009, http://www.wga.hu/frames-e.html?/html/l/lemoyne1/apotheos.html.

28. David W. Blight, *Race and Reunion: The Civil War in American Memory* (Cambridge, MA: Harvard University Press, 2001), 4.

29. In "King David," the Northern teacher compares the older ex-slaves to tortoises, "half-crippled, poor old creatures," even though he also notes that sometimes "a fine old black face was lifted from the slow-moving bulk, and from under wrinkled eyelids keen sharp eyes met the master's, as intelligent as his own" (260). The description of former slaves as animals reveals David's uneasiness at racial otherness—and, I argue, his creator's as well. At the same time, Woolson's story endows the Other with an equal subjectivity, impenetrable and therefore separate.

30. *Harper's Weekly* (August 30, 1862): 555. Two years later, the same newsmagazine reported that Morgan, after being captured and imprisoned in Ohio, had escaped to conduct more raids. But on September 4, 1864, near Greenville, Tennessee, where Morgan was unwittingly lodging with the wife of a Union soldier, he met his fate: "When MORGAN was asleep Mrs. WILLIAMS procured a horse, rode fifteen miles, and returned with a company of Union soldiers. . . . He drew his revolver and undertook to escape, when he was fired upon and killed." See *Harper's Weekly* (September 24, 1864): 609.

31. Francesca T. Royster, *Becoming Cleopatra: The Shifting Image of an Icon* (New York: Palgrave Macmillan, 2003), 18.

32. Royster, *Becoming Cleopatra*, 19.

33. See Carolyn Hall, "An Elaborate Pretense for the Major: Making up the Face of the Postbellum Nation," *Legacy* 22.2 (2005): 144–57, among the first readings of the racial subtext in Woolson's work.

34. "Wilhelmina," *Atlantic Monthly* (January 1875): 44. In "Woolson's 'Wilhelmina' and Reconstruction's Egypt," a paper delivered to the Constance Fenimore Woolson Society in October 2002, Kathleen Diffley was the first to suggest that Woolson's use of "Nubian" would have indicated black ancestry.

35. An exhibit organized in 2002 at the Field Museum of Art in Chicago traced Cleopatra's many incarnations and noted a shift in the nineteenth century when she began to be depicted with dark skin and sometimes notably African features. See Lamaretta Simmons, "Cleopatra: The Enduring Icon," *F Newsmagazine*, The School of the Art Institute of Chicago, 2002, retrieved September 17, 2007, http://www.artic.edu/webspaces/fnews/2001-December/decfeatures1.html. See also Toni Morrison, *Playing in the Dark: Whiteness and the Literary Imagination* (Cambridge, MA: Harvard University Press, 1992), for how an "invisible" black presence has shaped the fiction of white American writers.

36. I am quoting from reviews in the *New York Evening Post* (January 15, 1877) and *Appletons' Journal* (June 1877): 570–71, both reprinted in *Critical Essays on Constance Fenimore Woolson*, 19–22. My first edition (see n. 12) includes an excerpt from the *Springfield Republican*'s review in the same vein: "To read it in completeness gives one, beyond its faults ... a sense of power in character-drawing ... which is rarely met with."

37. She continued, "Such as they are they come of themselves without the slightest effort; whereas my prose is always the result of long and careful thought." See Hubbell, "Some New Letters of Constance Fenimore Woolson," 720.

38. Hubbell, "Some New Letters of Constance Fenimore Woolson," 722.

39. "To Certain Biographers," *Appletons' Journal* (September 1878): 376; "An Intercepted Letter," *Harper's Bazar* (September 7, 1878): 578; "In Remembrance," *New York Evening Post* (October 18, 1878): 2; and "Mentone," *Harper's Monthly* (January 1884): 216.

40. While in Europe, she was approached by both the Appletons and the Harpers, but she declined "to allow the collection of all my scattered verses in a volume." See Woolson's letter to Samuel Mather, March 31, [1887?], Mss. 3735, Western Reserve Historical Society.

41. Hubbell, "Some New Letters of Constance Fenimore Woolson," 730. The poem, told by a farm wife who was raised in Kentucky but lives in Ohio, tells how she gave up her favorite horse, "Kentucky Belle," so that a Rebel youth who had been with Morgan's riders could go home.

42. "At the Chateau of Corinne," *Harper's Monthly* (October 1887): 789. Significantly, Woolson's *Two Women* also first appeared anonymously.

43. Benedict includes extracts taken from Woolson's notebooks that list *Castle Nowhere* as her first book and *Two Women* as her second (*Five Generations*, II: 553).

44. Her first biographer, John Dwight Kern, concluded, "In the case of Miss Woolson's verse, the reader can safely ignore virtually all of it," except four poems, including "Kentucky Belle." See *Constance Fenimore Woolson: Literary Pioneer* (Philadelphia: University of Pennsylvania Press, 1934), 175. Rayburn Moore's influential Twayne volume includes no discussion of Woolson's poetry. Later critics have mostly followed suit. Woolson's poetry was, however, selected for a modern encyclopedia of American verse; see my entry, "Constance Fenimore Woolson," in *Encyclopedia of American Poetry: The Nineteenth Century*, ed. Eric L. Haralson (Chicago: Fitzroy Dearborn Publishers, 1998), 503–8.

45. Letter to Hayne, July 23, 1875, in Moore, 145 n. 15. Compare her letter to The Lady's description:

The distant cry of "Extra!" down the street
In the gray dawnings, and our breathless haste

To read the tidings—all this mighty power
Hath burned in flame the day of little things ... (51)

46. I am alluding to the Pledge of Allegiance as first composed by Francis Bellamy in 1892; the phrase "under God" was not added until almost fifty years later. What the Pledge reiterated for Woolson's contemporaries was that the nature of the Union had been decided for all time by the Civil War: America was *one Nation, indivisible*. According to John W. Baer, Bellamy himself underscored this point by commenting on why he chose the words he did for the pledge: "And what does that vast thing, the Republic[,] mean? It is the concise political word for the Nation—the One Nation which the Civil War was fought to prove. To make that One Nation idea clear, we must specify that it is indivisible, as Webster and Lincoln used to repeat in their great speeches." See *The Pledge of Allegiance: A Short History*. 1992. http://www.oldtimeislands.org/pledge/pledge.htm (accessed October 30, 2010).

Zephaniah Swift Spalding

Constance Woolson's Cipher

—Cheryl B. Torsney

Speculation about Constance Woolson's lovers—their existence, their gender, how they are coded into her writing (or not)—has occasioned both scholarship and fiction. One of Woolson's earliest commentators, Rayburn Moore, continues to tantalize contemporary readers with his mention of Woolson's Army of the Republic soldier boyfriend, Zephaniah Swift Spalding (Fig. 1). In a number of her early Civil War poems and stories, I will argue, Woolson's affection for Zeph Spalding gets displaced onto the Confederate brigadier general John Hunt Morgan, the celebrity soldier with the name recognition of a pop idol. In this guise among others, Zeph haunts Woolson's writing throughout her career: in *Anne* (1880), Woolson's first novel, as Captain Ward Heathcote, and in *Horace Chase* (1894), Woolson's last novel, as the eponymous Yankee businessman. Throughout, Zeph functions as a cipher that reveals Woolson's understanding of the Civil War and its aftermath, the economic expansion that followed, and the imperialist zeitgeist of nineteenth-century America.[1]

Zephaniah Swift Spalding, son of the Honorable Rufus P. Spalding (1759–1823), was named after his father's mentor Zephaniah Swift, chief justice of Connecticut. Rufus Spalding served three years on Ohio's supreme court beginning in 1848. He and his family moved from Warren, Trumbull County, to Summit County, where he joined the Free Soil party and, as an outspoken critic of slavery, served as counsel for at least one fugitive slave. He was a delegate to the Republican National Convention that nominated Abraham Lincoln; following the Civil War, he represented Ohio's Eighteenth District in Congress, where he led debates on Reconstruction.

His son, Zephaniah or Zeph, was a bright young man. Born in Akron, he was two years older than Woolson. By 1860, the Spaldings lived in Cleveland's Fourth Ward and the Woolsons in Cleveland's Sixth Ward. The families vacationed together at Mackinac Island, where the young Connie and Zeph worked together on a newspaper distributed to their families. Given the small size of Cleveland in general and the political and business communities in particular during the 1850s, it

Fig. 1, Zephaniah Swift Spalding in his twenties or thirties.
Photo courtesy of the Kauai Historical Society.

would be no surprise that the teenaged Connie and Zeph were wrapped up in each other's lives.[2]

Cut to 1861: Woolson was twenty-one years old; Zeph was twenty-three. Both were unmarried. Zeph enlisted in the Twenty-seventh Ohio Volunteer Infantry (Fuller's Brigade) on July 25, 1861. A member of Company G, he did well; his father wrote Ohio governor David Tod on July 17, 1862, to request that his son be given command of one of the new Ohio regiments. The Twenty-seventh OVI was organized at Camp Chase in Columbus, where Wilhelmina's lover Gustav from Woolson's early story "Wilhelmina" (1875) would be mustered in. The regiment was sent to Missouri but eventually participated in the siege of Corinth in 1862 and Grant's Mississippi Campaign thereafter, as well as the fall of Atlanta in 1864. Before mustering out at war's end, the Twenty-seventh OVI was headquartered in Louisville, the Kentucky home of General Morgan.

Very little is known directly about Woolson's wartime experience outside of the short discussion in Rayburn Moore's ever-valuable Twayne volume. Moore cites Woolson's description of the war's early days in *Anne* and her singing old Civil War tunes around a piano during her Cairo sojourn in 1890. In letter after letter, she lamented that the war had indelibly marked her generation. To her former

Cleveland schoolmistress, Miss Linda Guilford, she waxed nostalgic, "I belong to the generations, you know, who felt those years [of the war] as I have felt nothing since." To the Southern poet Paul Hamilton Hayne, "It is in vain for our generation to hope to be any other than 'people who remember.' Sometimes even now, I wake early, and think I hear the distant call of the newsboy far down the street, 'Extra! Extra! All about the last battle!' —And then how we rushed out to get it, how we devoured it, and then hurried down to the 'Soldier's Aid' rooms to do the little that was open to us faraway ones to do,—prepare boxes of supplies for the soldiers." To Hamilton Mabie, who served on the staff of the *Christian Union* and then as associate editor of *The Outlook*, she wrote from Venice on June 18, 1883: "I have a theory, too, that those of us who remember the war,—who were old enough to be stirred by it, yet, at the same time, young enough to have it the first great event of our lives,—we of that generation, are the most deeply-dyed 'Americans' that exist. We cannot help it. Our 'country,' and all that means,—patriotism in its warmest form, was burned into us by a red-hot fire, and the results are ineffaceable."[3]

On December 10, 1893, just weeks before she died, Woolson told her nephew Samuel Mather,

> I should like to see [Zeph] again.... If I could get him alone, I dare say we should have a very friendly and funny talk. But, meanwhile, we should both be inwardly thinking "Great heavens — what an escape I had!" It was only the glamour of the war that brought us together. Every girl wanted to have a soldier-lover in those intense years, and every soldier (especially the volunteers) was wrought up to the highest point of excitement & romance.[4]

Romantic it was, at least at the beginning of the war. Connie, the confessed "red-hot abolitionist," would have seen Zeph, the Ohio volunteer, as Rufus P. Spalding's son, fighting on the battlefield instead of in the courtroom for the freedom of the slaves.

At the same time, a separate albeit related narrative competed for Woolson's attention and the attention of the country: the romance of Confederate brigadier general John Hunt Morgan, the Rebel Raider. Woolson's local Cleveland papers and the national press were obsessed with General Morgan, both during and after the Civil War. And why not? A bad-boy celebrity of his day, he was handsome, rakish, bold, and dangerous: a cross between a pirate and one of Dumas's musketeers, with piercing eyes, flowing hair, and a neatly trimmed goatee. He sported his signature hat folded up on one side (Fig. 2). The *Cleveland Plain Dealer*, Woolson's hometown paper, featured between one and three articles a day on him and his 2,460 men when he launched a raid into Kentucky, Indiana, and Ohio during July 1863; accounts told repeatedly of heroic local efforts to hide livestock from the raiders, as

Fig. 2, Brigadier General John Hunt Morgan, Rebel Raider.
Photo courtesy of Special Collections, University of Kentucky Libraries.

Morgan's wiliness was widely touted. In 1862 C. D. Benson published music for the "Captain John Morgan Schottishe," with the subtitle "Now you've got him, / Now you hav'nt," to commemorate Morgan's escape from the Ohio State Penitentiary following his capture. Morgan was the hero of "The Kentucky Partisan" (1862), a bloody, passionate, nationalist poem by Paul Hamilton Hayne, Woolson's postwar friend and correspondent, whose second stanza reads in part:

> Well done, gallant Morgan!
>   Strike with might and main,
> Till the fair fields redden
>   With a gory rain;
> Smite them by the roadside,
>   Smite them in the wood,
> By the lonely valley,
>   And the purpling flood;

Given Woolson's frequent correspondence with Hayne over a short period in the mid-1870s, she must have known this poem and would have been as impressed as readers are today by its vivid, bellicose imagery.[5]

Seward did not believe that the American public was ready to entertain either a reciprocity agreement or annexation. As he wrote in a confidential communiqué to Spalding on July 5, 1868:

Without going into an explanation of the causes for the condition of national sentiment which temporarily exists, it is enough to say that the public attention sensibly continues to be fastened upon the domestic questions which have grown out of the late civil war. The public mind refuses to dismiss these questions even so far as to entertain the higher but more remote questions of national extension and aggrandizement. The periodical Presidential and Congressional elections are approaching. Each of the political parties seems to suppose that economy and retrenchment will be prevailing considerations in that election and the leaders of each party therefore seem to shrink from every suggestion which may involve any new national enterprise, and especially any foreign one. How long sentiments of this sort may control the proceedings of the Government is uncertain, but, in the meantime, it will be well for you not to allow extravagant expectations of sympathy between the United States and the friends of annexation in the islands to influence your own conduct.[10]

Two years after the war, as Seward saw it, the country was still focused on civil disruption. But as Zeph Spalding was beginning to discover, sugarcane was already developing in Hawaii as an international cash crop, the Hawaiian trade was in the ascendant and politically vexed, while new labor opportunities were opening for freedmen amid accusations that their treatment in the cane fields recalled their lives as slaves. Already in 1867, the United States was seeking a global economy in the Pacific.

To understand the implications for Spalding's future and Woolson's future writing, it is useful to understand something of the business of growing, harvesting, refining, and marketing sugar. As Francine du Plessix Gray explains, cane from which sugar is extracted had always grown wild in Hawaii but had not been exploited until after the disintegration of the Pacific whaling industry in the 1840s and 1850s, which impacted the economies of whaling nations from Norway to Russia. Hawaii needed another source of support for its economy, and sugar was another natural resource. By 1853, sugar was the chief export of the islands, with almost three thousand acres planted in cane. According to Gavan Daws's *Shoal of Time: A History of the Hawaiian Islands*, "The Civil War . . . made the Hawaiian sugar industry. Southern sugar disappeared from the market in the northern states of the Union, and prices climbed so high that planters in the islands could make good profits even after paying heavy tariffs at American ports of entry." Daws goes on to note that thirty-two plantations and mill companies conducted business in would also provide Woolson's rugged landscape for Anne Douglas's nursing experience in Anne. Her patients are first from western (i.e., Ohio) regiments and then from New York regiments: Zeph actually served in both. Woolson's first novel casts Anne as a nurse first in Weston, now West Virginia, then further south in a field hospital, and finally in a private home near the Virginia border, where she tends to Captain Ward Heathcote, her fever-ridden lover. Both Zeph, Woolson's personal connection to the war, and Morgan, her fictionalized Zeph, were present in Mississippi on October 2 and 4, 1862, for the Battle of Corinth. Moreover, both men were imprisoned during the war; Morgan quickly escaped from the Ohio penitentiary, while Spalding was eventually released through an exchange for "a Southern prisoner who also had a distinguished father."[7]

General John Hunt Morgan was betrayed and killed on September 2, 1864, at Greeneville, Tennessee, when the owner of his billet, Mrs. Williams, alerted Union soldiers. His death made the front page of the September 24, 1864, issue of Harper's Weekly. A longer piece in Harper's Monthly, John S. C. Abbott's "Heroic Deeds of Heroic Men: The Pursuit and Capture of Morgan," detailed Morgan's final days. Well after the war, Morgan continued to enthrall. The Ohio Farmer, a Cleveland magazine that published reviews of Woolson's work, featured two articles about Morgan in a column for younger readers, "Talks with the Children: The Morgan Raid," and "An Incident of Morgan's Raid." In January 1891, the Century printed a twenty-three-page piece entitled "A Romance of Morgan's Rough Riders: The Raid," by Basil W. Duke, Morgan's brother-in-law. Woolson surely had access to all of these periodicals. John Hunt Morgan thus remained on the stage—and elided with Zeph in Woolson's mind—from the early days of the war to the last decade of the century.[8]

As for Zeph, he was discharged from the Twenty-seventh OVI in February 1864. For the next three years, until late 1867, there is no record of his whereabouts; however, because his father Rufus was serving as a congressman at the time, the well-respected Colonel Spalding may have returned to his home in Cleveland and would have encountered young Constance Woolson, who had been following his Civil War exploits and writing poetry and sketches. In December 1867, no doubt as a result of his influential father's efforts in Washington, Zeph was called upon by Secretary of State William H. Seward to travel to Hawaii, serve as a "secret agent," and determine "what effect the reciprocity treaty would have on the future relations of the United States and Hawaii." In the guise of a cotton speculator, Zeph was to investigate the local sentiment regarding whether Congress should sign a trade agreement with Hawaii, a "reciprocity treaty," which would allow Hawaiian sugar to enter the United States duty-free in exchange for access to Pearl Harbor; or whether the United States should instead begin the process of annexing the Sandwich Islands.[9]

Zephaniah Swift Spalding: Constance Woolson's Cipher   113

love with the same wounded volunteer. The narrative begins on a train with a meeting between the only two women aboard, among groups of soldiers. Unbeknown to them, both are traveling to see the same man. The backdrop is "The wild adventurous cavalry campaign / That Morgan and his men, bold riders all, / Kept up in fair Kentucky all those years" (61). The country girl is naive and knows nothing of horses while the city lady is, like Morgan himself, a fair judge of racing flesh. As it turns out, the lover has been shot by John Morgan's troops. When the lady discovers this, she champions Morgan and his riders:

> . . . Morgan's men
> Are bold Kentucky riders; every glen
> Knows their fleet midnight gallop . . . . (63)

Morgan, then just a captain, makes an appearance at the end of the poem, when the soldier is buried. He and a band of men arrive graveside, dismount, honor the fallen, and then ride away.

> . . . And one, a slave,
> Looks down the road and mutters: "That was him,
> Young Cap'en Morgan's self! These eyes is dim,
> But they knows Morgan! — what! why, bless
> Your hearts, I know him, and I know Black Bess—
> 'Twas Bess he rode." (146)

Readers today will recognize this hushed awe as akin to the response of those left in the wake of a superhero.

Morgan and Spalding merge into a single romantic hero in Woolson's imagination regardless of the fact that one fought for the Confederacy and the other for the Union. Although the men did not resemble each other physically—Morgan was dark complexioned and compactly built, Spalding was blonde and husky—both adored horses. Morgan's horsemanship is well documented, and there is lingering evidence of Spalding's tastes as well. A letter in the Kauai Historical Society from Lydia Hoy, Spalding's great-granddaughter, reveals that Spalding also appreciated fine horses: "Col. Spalding was very interested in horse racing and he imported the 'Norfolk Strait' to Kauai from Calif. where he made the purchase from Gov. (then) Leland Stanford. He had a racetrack called Waipoli by the Wailua River." The two men were further linked geographically. Spalding led the Twenty-seventh OVI; Morgan's northernmost foray was into Ohio. His famous blunder occurred at the Battle of Buffington Island (July 1863), which was fought over an Ohio River island between Marietta, Ohio, and Parkersburg, West Virginia. Current West Virginia

In fact, the number of references to Morgan in Woolson's writing betrays a fascination with his guts and gallantry. As Patti Capel Swartz has noted, Woolson builds her narratives around Morgan in "Told in a Farm-House" (1873), a long poem often referred to as "Kentucky Belle," in which an Ohio farm woman finds one of Morgan's raiders injured, takes him in, nurses him back to health, and sends him back to Morgan on her own horse, Kentucky Belle. Swartz notes as well that "Matches Morganatic" (1878), a short romance, is set in Ohio against the background of Morgan's Raid. Further examination of Woolson's *oeuvre* reveals that General John Hunt Morgan also looms in the short story "Crowder's Cove" (1876) and in the long poem *Two Women* (1877) subtitled "1862," both published in *Appletons' Journal*. Evidently the success of "Crowder's Cove" left the Appletons asking for more of the same from Woolson, who may have returned, yet again, to the Morgan myth she had used in "Told in a Farm-House" only three and a half years earlier.[6]

In "Crowder's Cove," Sally, an orphan "fresh from boarding-school," has been sent to the Tennessee mountains to board with John Crowder and his sister-in-law Elinor Kent, originally from New Hampshire (like the Woolson family). The young women couldn't be more different: "one girl was rich, the other was poor; yet the rich girl's possessions looked like rags, and beggar's gatherings, beside the neat belongings of the other" (357). Elinor develops a plan to aid the Union and to cross the Ohio River on a horse that she convinces her brother-in-law to purchase, a white mare named Bess. Sally is rather disengaged with the progress of the war, which disgusts Elinor. Partisans come to the farm twice: ununiformed Confederate sympathizers for horse feed and uniformed Union soldiers for livestock. Bushwhackers claiming to be neutrals come a third time and burn Crowder's barns. At this point, the Crowders are forced to take in a wounded Southern soldier, Cameron Halisey, whom Sally nurses back to health. When Halisey receives intelligence about a surprise attack, both girls overhear and saddle horses to alert the troops: Elinor, the Union; and Sally, the Confederate.

Sally, the Southern girl who is the better rider with the stronger horse, wins the race, and Morgan's troops capture the Yankee band. Sally is "the pride, and the belle, and the glory of Morgan's men that night" (362). Because of her bravery, a Yankee general is captured. The denouement reveals that Elinor, like Woolson, worked in hospitals throughout the war and doesn't marry, while Sally weds a well-to-do gentleman and gains a reputation for voluptuous beauty. Like Morgan and his men, Sally becomes the subject of narrative. Moreover, a conflation of the names of Sally's and Elinor's mounts—Black Tom and Bess—produces the name of Morgan's famous horse, Black Bess.

In "Two Women," Woolson reprises the premise of two very different women—a brunette and a blonde in the first, a country girl and a city lady in the second—in

Constance would have been reminded of Zeph frequently upon reading *Harper's Monthly*. A cursory glance at issues from February 1855 to October 1893 reveals no fewer than fifteen articles devoted at least in part to the Hawaiian Islands, including pieces on volcanoes, horse-taming, diplomatic service, sugar growing, and the Hawaiian monarchy, as well as a long article in October 1893 by Carl Schurz on Manifest Destiny, William Seward, and territorial expansion. Surely these articles, with their Spaldingesque subtext, would have touched Woolson personally.

In 1882, Zeph himself penned a defense of the Reciprocity Treaty that had made him a rich man. His observations were published by the *Cleveland Leader*. Although Constance was already living abroad, someone may well have forwarded Zeph's treatise, which rebutted an article published by the *San Francisco Chronicle* on the topic of a *Leader* story about Hawaiian sugar production and labor practices in Hawaii. The *Chronicle* had called the sugar industry "the worst system of slavery ever known," and Spalding took affront. Further, he declared that the Reciprocity Treaty had not made sugar more expensive as a result of the production falling into the hands of a monopoly headquartered in the United States. He retorted, "I am one of many Americans engaged in the production and manufacture of sugar at the Hawaiian Islands, and flatter myself that I am well enough known to many of your readers to have my word taken as truth, in preference to the sweeping assertions of a newspaper whose career has been marked by demagoguism, slander and blackmail."[17] Most of the letter, however, deals with the *Chronicle*'s charge that the planters of Hawaii were employing a labor system "'of the most abject slavery'" (7). He went on, "I am happy to assure you, on the contrary . . . that I am to-day as firm an abolitionist as when I gave my sanction and adherence to the emancipation proclamation of Father Abraham!" (7). Spalding explained that Hawaiian landowners contracted with laborers, and he included in an appendix the contract itself. Further, he discussed the need for American financial support through the Reciprocity Treaty because laborers were difficult to keep and even more difficult to replace: "[T]he number of available laborers in the country has never been in excess," Spalding wrote, "nor even equal to the wants and demands of the various industries pursued" (9–10).

The *Chronicle* had charged that the sugar magnates "'buy up' the poor, ignorant natives of the Southern Islands, and even inveigle the innocent and unsuspecting Norwegians from their fatherland to work out their lives under a burning sun upon our desert plains!" (10). Spalding responded that his climate was mild, and his laborers were able to save because there was "little call for spending money" (10). He concluded by begging the question: "How many Norwegians or Portuguese could do it in their own over-crowded and time-worn lands?" (10). Both the defensive tone of the open letter and Zeph's overstatement about living conditions in Norway suggest that he was protesting too much.

With its charges and countercharges regarding contract labor and cultural conflict, Zeph's history in Hawaii has all of the makings of Woolson's fiction, especially to readers familiar with her Civil War stories and novels. While several of her earliest stories, like "Old Gardiston" (1876), "In the Cotton Country" (1876), "Rodman the Keeper" (1877), "King David" (1878), and "Bro" (1878), touch the plight of the former slaves and interrogate racism, sectionalism, and freedom in complex ways, none deals specifically with Hawaii and the planters' difficulty in finding laborers for the cane fields. Nonetheless, Zeph's protestations in his letter to the *Leader* can be read as a response not only to the *Chronicle* but also to Woolson's stories, where the former slave workforce is not what the Woolson characters had hoped. King David cannot teach his freedmen pupils and returns to his New Hampshire school. At about the same time, the native Hawaiians who worked as cowboys, the Japanese who worked in island homes, and the Filipinos who worked the fields—in other words, those who supplied the uneducated labor for the island workforce—were thought to be "lazy, not good workers."[18] Such paternal perceptions bespeak the plantation's familiar social economy, which persisted in Hawaii for some time. Like many of his class in the antebellum South, Zeph's grandson Rufus had a local wet nurse, though he was born in Hawaii after the twentieth century began. While it is important to recognize that island laborers had contracts, the Hawaiian economy was firmly modeled on the role of a black workforce in the nineteenth-century South.

Strikingly, some of the most recent scholarship on the Civil War situates that conflict in a global context. Gerald Horne's *The White Pacific: Imperialism and Black Slavery in the South Seas after the Civil War* demonstrates that American blacks found a kind of open society in nineteenth-century Hawaii and could be mistaken for ethnic Hawaiians.[19] Following the Civil War, sugar plantation owners encouraged freed slaves to emigrate and sign labor contracts, while prominent American blacks like Frederick Douglass disapproved of the "unwarranted intermeddling of Americans in Hawaiian affairs" (130). Still, the conflation of black labor in the American South and contract labor in Hawaii was exemplified when Mark Twain called indigenous Hawaiians "niggers" in his journals (139). The Lihue plantation that eventually encompassed Zeph Spalding's properties actually hired former slaves from the American South but later determined that they were "unreliable and indolent," the same conclusion drawn by Hawaiian Sugar Company agents who believed that Negroes were "no good whatever on Hawaiian plantations" (140). Thus, thinking about Zeph and the turns his life had taken, particularly his life in Hawaii, must have further complicated Woolson's responses to postwar race relations and the possibilities for reconciliation and a lasting peace.

In Woolson's last novel, *Horace Chase* (1894), published the year she died, Zephaniah Swift Spalding makes a final appearance. In the guise of capitalist hero,

Woolson offered one last look at the successful industrialist and at herself as she felt her career coming to an end. In a letter to nephew Sam Mather, dated January 9, 1893, she discussed her last fictional creation and how he had been inspired:

> Horace Chase ... has a dozen other interests besides this steamboat firm. At the time of this conversation (1874), he is about embarking in a new business in California, — "a big thing." — If I could have got at you, I should have taken your advice, & then said more clearly what the big thing was. As it is, it is left in the dark. The only big California business I know anything about, is sugar, & it is more connected with the Sandwich Islands, after all, than California, — though I believe Claus Spreckels is a Californian, is'nt he. But I thought Col. Spaulding [sic] would be too much amused by my making use of sugar, —! Which is the business in which he has made all his money.[20]

Clearly, Woolson had the stocky, blond Zeph in mind. Clearly, too, she had a sense that he was following her work.

The enduring role Zephaniah Spalding played in Constance Woolson's life and work—and Woolson's sense that *Horace Chase* would be her last novel—reveals the narrative as a *roman à clef* with an autobiographical subtext. Woolson, whose letters reveal a compulsive attention to her weight, might herself be cast as Ruth Franklin, whose older sister remarks that Ruth is "a whalelike creature."[21] Woolson's description of Ruth is close to a youthful self-portrait: "The girl had a dark complexion with a rich color, and hair that was almost black; her face was lighted by blue eyes, with long thick black lashes which made a dark fringe around the blue" (3). The text positions Ruth and Miss Billy as diametrically opposed personalities—Ruth abhors knick-knacks while Wilhelmina worships them (14)—and as competitors for Chase's affections. If Ruth bears a close resemblance to Woolson, Miss Billy (a.k.a. Wilhelmina) recalls Wilhelmina Makee Spalding (Fig. 3). Moreover, the novel's Ruth owns a dog named Petit Trone, Esq., the very name of Woolson's pet in Gertrude Van Rensselaer Wickham's "Dogs of Noted Americans" (Fig. 4) and the name of the little dog that appears in *The Old Stone House* (1873), Woolson's early novel.[22]

Most significant, Horace Chase stands in for Zeph. Both have California connections. Chase is a rich industrialist who has made his fortune in railroads and baking powder. Like the real Zeph—and John Hunt Morgan—he loves and keeps horses. Like Zeph, he is also linked to roses: in the first pages of Woolson's novel, he sends an extravagant bouquet of hot-house roses to Ruth (32), just when the Makee Plantation was becoming known as Rose Ranch for the roses first brought to Maui by Zeph Spalding's mother-in-law. While sugar was the source of Zeph's fortune, according to his obituary in the *Pasadena Star-News*, he shared Chase's

Fig. 3, Spalding Family at Valley House.
Wilhelmina Makee Spalding, with her
hair tightly knotted, is seated at center.
Zephaniah stands in profile at left.
Photo courtesy of the Kauai Museum.

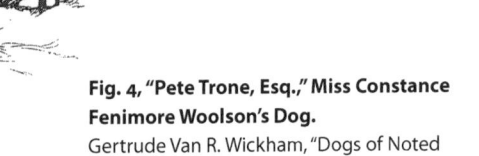

Fig. 4, "Pete Trone, Esq.," Miss Constance Fenimore Woolson's Dog.
Gertrude Van R. Wickham, "Dogs of Noted Americans, Part I."
St. Nicholas (June 1888): 599.

"business investments in various parts of the United States and Canada." Although it is not clear whether Zeph invested in railroads like Chase, he did arrange to have both his sugarcane and his paralyzed wife transported around the plantation on a flatcar, which rode on portable rails. The inside joke undoubtedly escaped her editors and readers, but Woolson must have been amused by her own pun when Chase remarks "'I'm only a civilian myself,' in a *pacific* voice" (112, my emphasis). A lover of animals, flowers, and music, Chase is a pacifist, a "civilian" with whom the reader is to sympathize. Through Chase, Woolson presents Zeph as a complex soul who has moved beyond his Civil War identity and his resemblance to Rebel Raider John Hunt Morgan to become a real estate developer destined to link the North and the South. As Chase reasons about turning Asheville, North Carolina, into a summer resort, "[I]t isn't only the Southerners who will come here.... Northerners will flock also, when they understand what these mountains are" (29). Is it possible to imagine a more prescient statement about both North Carolina and Hawaii in the twenty-first century?[23]

One of the most provocative subplots in *Horace Chase* involves Ruth's brother Jared, who is "tall and broad-shouldered, with dark eyes whose expression was always sad" (95). His glory days have been his international travel while serving in the navy, and he has not been happy since. Horace Chase hires Jared to direct the Charleston office of the Columbian shipping line at a salary of $3,000 a year. Jared is unsuccessful, however, and when Chase visits him in Charleston, Ruth's brother is "wasted. His eyes had always been sad; but now they were deeply sunken, with dark hollows under them and over them" (267). Chase devises a story about needing an "experienced officer" to take over commanding one of his steamers from San Francisco to the Sandwich Islands; there is a quiet suggestion that Jared is suffering from a fever, which leads to raving and a near suicide. But readers familiar with the Woolson family history of depression may read Jared as Charlie, Woolson's ne'er-do-well brother who was removed from his position as executor of Charles Jarvis Woolson's estate and died in California.[24] No public records reveal what happened to Woolson's only brother—and her mother's favorite child—but Zeph may have offered Charlie work through one of his California interests.

Horace Chase is the culmination of Constance Woolson's lifelong connection with Zephaniah Spalding, and he reprises Spalding's early conflation in Woolson's work with John Hunt Morgan as well. By the end of the novel, Chase has given his prize mare to his wife, Ruth Franklin, who rides *Kentucky Belle* to her tryst with Walter Willoughby. Years before, Woolson had invoked the same horse in her early poem "Told in a Farm-House" (1873), where Morgan's soldier is returned to his brigade on another Kentucky Belle. In this way, Woolson's *oeuvre* comes full circle, with the horse and Morgan/Spalding appearing once again as icons of romantic daring.

In Woolson's last work, however, Horace Chase as a latter-day Zeph Spalding has outgrown the flamboyance of John Hunt Morgan. Like Zeph, Chase is a New World postwar industrialist. Having matured beyond the sectional arguments that brought national disruption, he yearns to unite the North and the South with the West on a pacific road to economic prosperity. His creative sensibilities promise a future secured by invention and the sort of imagination on display at Chicago's Columbian Exposition in 1893, the year before Woolson's death and the publication of *Horace Chase*. In fact, if there is a Morgan whom Zephaniah Swift Spalding resembles in the 1890s, it is industrialist John Pierpont Morgan, who had connections with Woolson's nephew Samuel Mather.[25]

Since the beginning of the renaissance of Woolson studies in the mid-1980s, Constance Fenimore Woolson has been seen as a quiet innovator. Recent scholarship has noted that Woolson pioneered realism when other women were still writing sentimental novels. Upending novelistic conventions that required heroines to marry happily, her women characters did not. In Woolson's fiction, the Civil War does not result in regional reconciliation; instead, like Woolson herself, her characters retreat to Europe and older sin, deeper suffering, and suffocation.

Woolson, however, proved even more revolutionary, more political, than scholars have thus far revealed. From the beginning of her career to its sudden end, her references to her childhood friend Zephaniah Swift Spalding place her on a global stage that stretched across the Pacific as well as across the Atlantic. She followed Zeph's life in Hawaii, America, and Italy: in "A Pink Villa" (1888), an American family eager to marry their daughters to titled Europeans encounters an American who, like Spalding himself, was educated at a small Methodist college and plans with his partner to clear a "large farm" and "put it all in sugar." Woolson obviously knew about Zeph's marriage and his growing wealth. Into the 1890s, her childhood sweetheart continued to appear in her fiction. His role need no longer be covert. In 2007, Victoria Brehm observed, "I now believe that Constance Fenimore Woolson created her stories with a subtext from the beginning of her career, that she wrote very, very few stories that didn't have a political agenda. My guess is that she learned to do this from reading Melville."[26] In the 1870s, when Woolson's work began to appear in print, she knew that Melville had earned international fame as the author of *Typee* (1846), a novel of the Sandwich Islands. Like Melville, Woolson understood the country's interest in Hawaii. Through her lifelong relationship with Zephaniah Swift Spalding, she also understood, even before Hawaii's annexation in 1898, that the western territory was connected to the reemerging nation; and that the Civil War, ironically fought over transatlantically transported slaves, would have reverberations in the Pacific. Spalding, the blond counterpart to the dark John Hunt Morgan, evolves in Woolson's work from Civil War soldier to Gilded-Age industrialist and thereby illuminates the whole of Woolson's work, an intricate political and economic assembly of bodies, feelings, and history, of global supply and demand.

Notes

I would like to acknowledge the research assistance of Dr. Jessika Thomas, West Virginia University; Rhea Palma, Kauai Historical Society; and Chris Faye, Kauai Museum; and the editing assistance of Emily Smead.

1. For tempting speculation about Woolson's amours, see, for example, my *Constance Fenimore Woolson: The Grief of Artistry* (Athens: University of Georgia Press, 1989); Kristin Comment, "The Lesbian 'Impossibilities' of Miss Grief's 'Armor,'" in *Constance Fenimore Woolson's Nineteenth Century: Essays*, ed. Victoria Brehm (Detroit: Wayne State University Press, 2001), 207–23; and Colm Tóibín, *The Master* (New York: Scribner, 2004). For mention of Spalding, see Rayburn Moore, *Constance Fenimore Woolson* (New York: Twayne, 1962), 23. As to Spalding's recurring appearances, Victoria Brehm has discovered a number of blond Zeph-like figures in some of Woolson's earliest work, including Hugh in *The Old Stone House* (1873), Max Ruger in "Flower in the Snow" (1874), and Rast Pronando in *Anne* (1882).

2. Sandol Stoddard's biography of Zephaniah Spalding explains that Spalding did not get along with his stepmother and so left home at an early age. He attended Ohio Wesleyan College for a time, moved to New York in 1858 to work as a clerk, and joined New York's Seventh National Guard unit as a private to meet influential people who might assist him in finding a job. With the outbreak of the Civil War, he returned to Ohio, where he enlisted in the Twenty-seventh OVI as a second lieutenant on his way to becoming a major. See "Biography of Col. Spalding [sic]." Unpublished ms, n.p., October 31, 1991, Kauai Historical Society, Lihue, Hawaii. For the newspaper at Mackinac, see Moore, *Constance Fenimore Woolson*, 23.

3. For Woolson's pastimes in Cairo, see Moore, *Constance Fenimore Woolson*, 22–23; for her letter to Guilford, see Moore, *Constance Fenimore Woolson*, 23. Permission is granted by Duke University for use of Woolson's letters to Paul H. Hayne, July 23, 1875, and to Hamilton Mabie, June 18, 1883.

4. Moore, *Constance Fenimore Woolson*, 23.

5. For Benson's "Schottish," see *Historical American Sheet Music*, http://scriptorium.lib.duke.edu/sheetmusic/conf/conf01/conf0126/ (accessed January 2, 2007). For Hayne's poem, see the *Southern Literary Messenger* (April 1862): 229; reprinted in *Anecdotes, Poetry and Incidents of the War: North and South 1860–1865*, ed. Frank Moore (New York: Printed for the subscribers, 1866), 403.

6. For Swartz's observation, see "The Complex Loyalties of War: Constance Fenimore Woolson's 'Matches Morganatic' and 'Kentucky Belle.'" Unpublished ms. For "Kentucky Belle," see "Kentucky Belle (Told in a Farm-House, 1868)," *Appletons' Journal* (September 6, 1873): 289–90; for "Matches Morganatic," see *Harper's Monthly* (March 1878): 517–31. For "Crowder's Cove," see *Appletons' Journal* (March 18, 1876): 357–62; and for *Two Women, 1862*, see *Appletons' Journal* (January 1, 1877): 60–67, and (February 2, 1877): 140–47. Further references will be to these editions and will be made parenthetically in the text.

7. Hoy's observation may be found in Lydia Hoy, Letter to Mr. Arruda, February 3, 1970, Kauai Historical Society, Lihue, Hawaii. For Spalding's release, see Stoddard, "Biography of Col. Spalding [sic]," n.p.

8. For Abbott's "Heroic Deeds of Heroic Men," see *Harper's Monthly* (August 1865): 287–97. For "Talks with Children: The Morgan Raid," see *Ohio Farmer* (May 31, 1879): 347; for "An Incident of Morgan's Raid," see *Ohio Farmer* (July 18, 1885): 43. Duke's narrative appears in the *Century* (January 1891): 403–12. This is the first of three accounts in the same issue. See also Orlando B. Willcox's "II: The Capture," 412–17; and Thomas H. Hines's "III: The Escape," 417–25.

9. For Spalding's charge from Seward, see Sylvester K. Stevens, *American Expansion in Hawaii: 1842–1898* (Harrisburg: Archives Publishing Co. of Pennsylvania, 1945), 106. Further information on the Reciprocity Treaty and the fate of the Sandwich Islands appears in Ruth Tabrah, *Hawaii: A Bicentennial History* (New York: Norton, 1980), 82. A reciprocity treaty had been approved by the Senate Committee on Foreign Affairs in 1855 but was then defeated by the Senate. In 1864, the idea of such a treaty was resurrected without consequence, given the attention and funding to the war effort that Edmund Janes Carpenter has noted. See *America in Hawaii: A History of United States Influence in the Hawaiian Islands* (Boston: Small, Maynard & Co., 1899), 41. In 1867, the treaty was revived but failed again to be ratified in the Senate, although the Hawaiian government approved it on July 30.

10. Appendix 2, *Foreign Relations of the United Stated 1894: Affairs in Hawaii* (Washington, DC: Government Printing Office 1895), 144.

11. Gray's description of the sugarcane industry appears in *Hawaii: The Sugar-Coated Fortress* (New York: Random House, 1972), 50. For the sudden growth in acres planted, see Carpenter, *America in Hawaii*, 30. Daws's observations may be found in *Shoal of Time: A History of the Hawaiian Islands* (New York: Macmillan, 1968), 174–75, observations that are usefully augmented by data from "Domestic Sugar Production," *Manufacturer and Builder* (January 1882): 17.

12. For the conclusion of Spalding's covert activities and the beginning of his career as a sugar planter, see Daws, 187–88. For his investment in Maui's sugar industry, see A. Grove Day, *History Makers of Hawaii* (Honolulu: Mutual Publishing of Honolulu, 1984), 116. Day also profiles the career of Captain James Makee, 93.

13. See the *San Francisco Daily Morning Call*, July 30, 1864, http://www.twainquotes.com/18640730d.html (accessed June 7, 2007).

14. An early Woolson story entitled "Wilhelmina" appeared in 1875. "Wilhelmina" was not a familiar name of the age, with 487 names per one million births. Compare this to 35,350 instances of Jennifer per one million births in the early 1970s via http://www.thenamemachine.com/baby-names-girls/Wilhelmina.html. Given that the top girls' names of 1850 were Anna, Emma, Elizabeth, Minnie, Margaret, Ida, Alice, Bertha, and Sarah, Woolson's use of the unusual Wilhelmina suggests that she knew the name of Zeph Spalding's bride. See http://www.ssa.gov/cgi-bin/popularnames.cgi.

Wilhelmina is a name Woolson would return to repeatedly. In "Cicely's Christmas," a Wilhelmina Van Airytop gains the affections of a rich and charming gentleman; in *Horace Chase*, Miss Billy's real name is "Wilhelmina."

It is also worth noting that Samuel Clemens spent time during 1866 with Captain Makee at his thousand-acre Rose Ranch. Clemens noted "two pretty & accomplished girl's [sic] in the family & the plantation yields an income of $60,000 a year—chance for some enterprising scrub." See his letter to Jane Lampton Clemens and Pamela A. Moffett, May 4, 1866, Mark Twain Project, www.marktwainproject.org/xtf/view?docId=lettters/UCCL00099.xml. Zephaniah Spalding turned out to be that "enterprising scrub," marrying the musical—and rich—Wilhelmina.

15. William G. Irwin and Co. is documented in Jacob Adler, *Claus Spreckels: The Sugar King in Hawaii* (Honolulu: University of Hawaii Press, 1966), 87. For the emergence of the Makee Sugar Company, see Lihue Plantation Company History, *Hawaii Sugar Planters' Association Plantation Archives*, ed. Deborah Saito and Susan Campbell, UHM Library Hawaiian Collection, http://www2hawaii.edu/~speccoll/p_lihue.html (accessed January 23, 2008). H. P. Baldwin describes

Spalding's diffusion process in "The Sugar Industry in the Hawaiian Islands," *Overland Monthly* (June 1895): 666.

16. For the Spalding family's residence in Paris, see Lydia Hoy, Letter to Mr. Arruda, February 3, 1970, Kauai Historical Society, Lihue, Hawaii. It is also of interest that Woolson and Spalding shared a silverware fetish. Although she could barely afford it, Woolson insisted upon purchasing Christofle flatware when she set up her Venice apartment. According to Sandol Stoddard, one of Zeph's European purchases was five complete sets of family silver in a pattern reserved for English nobility. Zeph had assured the silversmith that he would not be using the silver in England and so convinced the craftsman to fill his order ("Biography of Col. Spaulding [sic]," n.p.).

17. Zephaniah Swift Spalding, *Letter from Col. Zeph. Swift Spalding to the Cleveland Leader upon the reciprocity treaty with the Hawaiian government. Dated at Honolulu, November 30, 1881* (Cleveland: Leader Printing Co., 1882), 5–6. Subsequent references will be made parenthetically in the text.

18. Stoddard, "Biography of Col. Spaulding [sic]," n.p.

19. Gerald Horne, *The White Pacific: Imperialism and Black Slavery in the South Seas after the Civil War* (Honolulu: University of Hawaii Press, 2007), 130–40.

20. Letter to Samuel Mather, January 9, 1893, Mather Family Papers, Western Reserve Historical Society.

21. Constance Fenimore Woolson, *Horace Chase* (New York: Harper & Brothers, 1894), 2. Subsequent references will be made parenthetically in the text.

22. Woolson published *The Old Stone House* under the pseudonym Anne March (Boston: D. Lothrop, 1873). Gertrude Van R. Wickham's "Dogs of Noted Americans, Part I" appeared in *St. Nicholas* (May 1889): 595–600. Van Wickham refers to Woolson's terrier as Peter Trone, Esq. In a letter to magazine editor Mary Mapes Dodge, Woolson wrote, "Pete Trone's name was never Peter; do correct it won't you?" Woolson's descendant, Gary Woolson, has privately printed a charming chapbook excerpting Van Wickham's paragraphs about Pete Trone, Esq.

23. Rose Ranch is described by Stoddard, "Biography of Col. Spaulding [sic]," n.p., where the plantation's flatcar is also noted. For the scope of Zeph's investments, see "Death Calls Prominent American," *Pasadena Star-News*, June 20, 1927, 1. An air of nostalgia surrounds Horace Chase's appearance in Buncombe County, yet another facet of the complex character he shares with Zeph Spalding. Not only are the black retainers featured but also Chase's presence is noted by the locals: "Chase, did you say the name was? That's a hoax. It's General Grant himself, I reckon, coming along yere like a conqueror in disguise" (93). Interestingly, Zeph once had a Confederate flag that he had captured framed and hung at Valley House according to Chris Faye at the Kauai Museum. E-mail correspondence with the author, March 8, 2008.

24. Recently discovered texts at the Western Reserve Historical Society detail how Charlie was removed from his position as executor of his father's estate.

25. Because the Mathers were known as the first family of the Great Lakes iron-ore trade and J. P. Morgan owned U.S. Steel, it is not surprising that Woolson's nephew Samuel Mather and J. P. Morgan shared business and social circles. Among the instances reported, all following Woolson's death, are the following: on February 27, 1902, they dined together to welcome Prince Henry of Prussia; they also worked together to fund life insurance for Episcopal clergy, as reported in the *New York Times*, June 3, 1922, 9.

26. Victoria Brehm, personal correspondence, January 5, 2007.

"A Shady Retreat"
Short Prose

We came up from Charleston last week, and finding here a shady retreat, a primitive hotel in the heart of the woods with sulphur springs and baths, with utter quiet, not even the country turnpike in sight, with a circle of blue mountain-peaks on the horizon-line, we decided to remain for the present.
—*Constance Fenimore Woolson to William Dean Howells*

historical, or scientific sources, or to bracket that sort of information as intervening in the immediate aesthetic or social experience of travel, or, in some cases, to challenge the ambitious reader by way of incomplete allusion.

Woolson first tries out the ensemble technique in a Northern setting with "Round by Propeller," a tour of the Great Lakes by steamboat published in *Harper's Monthly* in September 1872. For example, as the boat sails out of St. Clair Flats, Miss Key, a schoolteacher, embarks on a learned lecture about the "history of Pontiac's conspiracy," a topic quite pertinent to the locale as she repeatedly points out.[5] However, readers hear no more than snippets of the lecture, as the narrator directs our attention instead to the flirtations of the schoolgirls in Miss Key's charge. In this way, Woolson reminds readers of important historical associations while positioning such associations as a mere backdrop to social interactions. Some readers, however, may be frustrated by this choice and may prefer sophisticated nonfiction or picturesque aesthetics to a comedy of manners. Woolson sympathizes with these readers as well. So, for example, she gives a reasonable amount of detail on topics such as the process of refining petroleum through the character of Major Archer, uninterrupted by any such frivolity. Yet even here, aesthetics remains important, as narrative description in the vein of the technological picturesque embellishes the Major's information: "we could still see the prismatic tints made in nature's laboratory ... the purified oil shimmering and shining in rare shades of color—blue, purple, and gold" (522).[6]

In subsequent travel sketches for *Harper's Monthly* set in the South, Woolson assigns the role of pedant to Professor Macquoid, a polymath who travels "for two reasons": for his health and for "the pleasure of imparting information."[7] Although the Professor seems capable of lecturing on any topic, his particular specialty is geology. This detail of characterization suggests that Woolson found geology to be an especially productive topos for exploring the complexities of the travel genre, especially the tension between experiential and informational modes. Through Professor Macquoid, Woolson brings the geological interest already evident in her picturesque Great Lakes writings to the sometimes less aesthetically promising landscapes of the South. Where Woolson foregrounds the experiential mode in her quasi-fictional pieces on St. Augustine and the French Broad River region, she abandons the ensemble technique, with its pull toward the experiential, for a more purely informational mode in her piece on Charleston. Yet the modes converge again in Charleston's rich historical associations. Woolson manages these associations so as to produce an experiential effect of nostalgia, eliding the ugly history of slavery to focus on a shared national past located in the colonial and Revolutionary eras. In the conclusion of the piece, the geological topos confirms this convergence of informational and aesthetic-experiential approaches to the South, promising a new shared nationalism in the exploitation of economic resources while naturalizing antebellum nostalgia against the alienating void of geological deep time.

The Magazine Context of the 1870s

The tension between experiential and informational travel has a long history, its roots running deeper even than, say, Laurence Sterne's *Sentimental Journey* (1768). In Reconstruction-era locodescriptive pieces published in the illustrated magazines, experiential travel most often took the form of aesthetic tourism, while informational travel concerned economic speculation, scientific reportage, or historical narration. Economics motivated the earliest of the postbellum illustrated magazine projects on the South, *Harper's Weekly*'s "Our Maps of the South." This project, launched in January 1866, surveyed the "material condition of the Southern States" and gave "industrial statistics," both emblemized on state maps. Aesthetic tourism soon followed, as *Harper's Weekly* sent Theodore R. Davis and Alfred Waud on sketching tours of the South, though the picturesque views and genre scenes sent back from these tours often carried economic information as well as visual pleasure.[8] The most ambitious of all such projects, *Scribner's Monthly*'s "Great South" series, interwove aesthetic, scientific, and historical strands into a primarily economic fabric. Written for the most part by Edward King and illustrated by numerous artists, the series ran to eleven installments from July 1873 to December 1874 before being published in book form in 1875. Proposing the development of the South's abundant natural resources, portraying Southerners both white and black as incapable of accomplishing this development, giving scientific bases for economic projections where appropriate, and occasionally enlivening statistical accounts with picturesque scenes, *The Great South* offered a complete carpetbagger's guide to Reconstruction.[9]

Appletons' Journal, by contrast, approached the South via aesthetic tourism, embarking in 1870 on the "Picturesque America" series that would grow into a two-volume book by 1874. Assistant editor Oliver Bell Bunce initially conceived the series as a means to encourage Southern tourism.[10] Bunce launched the series by featuring destinations that had been well established before the war, albeit frequented more by Southerners than Northerners. Florida was the first featured destination: pieces on the St. Johns and Oklawaha Rivers and St. Augustine, written by Thomas Bangs Thorpe and illustrated by the renowned artist Harry Fenn, ran in the November 12 and December 31, 1870, issues. During the 1869–1870 season, a contemporary guidebook estimated, only about four hundred Northern tourists had visited St. Augustine; the number increased dramatically with the opening of a railroad spur from the St. Johns River, and by the 1873–74 season (when Woolson and her mother took up semi-residence) St. Augustine hosted six thousand tourists.[11] The second destination featured in the "Picturesque America" series was the French Broad River region near Asheville, North Carolina, a resort popular with antebellum Southerners for its warm mineral springs. The French Broad was featured from late November 1870 through early January 1871.

In the illustrated magazines, aesthetic considerations necessarily inflected scientific reportage. While most of the scientifically oriented locodescriptive pieces published during the 1860s and 1870s explored the West, the South also offered itself to scientific curiosity, especially in combination with economic development. A beautifully illustrated example is "Along the Florida Reef," a five-part series that ran in *Harper's Monthly* from February through July 1871.[12] Combining scientific, economic, and aesthetic modes, the series integrates highly detailed natural history (much of it quite unfamiliar to Northerners) with an interest in exploitable resources, be it sponge diving or pineapple farming, as well as a brief foray into history (Fort Jefferson on the Dry Tortugas). While the initial impetus for the series came from development opportunities promised by the laying of a telegraph cable from Key West to Cuba, the treatment of natural history becomes less economically motivated as the series progresses; by the later installments, text and illustration focus extensively on flora and fauna of shore and reef with no apparent economic value. However, the prospect of tourism itself suggested an economic value underlying even the most apparently unmotivated locodescriptive or aesthetic accounts.

Of all the sciences, perhaps geology offered the greatest aesthetic possibilities for illustrated travel pieces.[13] Here, however, the South paled in comparison to the picturesque and sublime West. Illustrated magazine pieces included several by prominent scientists and explorers: Clarence King's report of the California Geological Survey for the *Atlantic Monthly* during 1871; John Wesley Powell's account of his Colorado River expedition for *Scribner's Monthly* during 1875; John Muir's rather technical series on the formation of the Sierra Nevada range for the *Overland Monthly* during 1874–1875. These accounts (even Muir's) necessarily carried an economic subtext in view of the nation's postwar western expansion. The economic dimension of geology was more immediately evident, however, in numerous articles on mineral resources: for example, an 1872 article in *Harper's Monthly* on deep mining for gold in the Grays Peak region of Colorado, which was amply illustrated by panoramic mountain views, aesthetically pleasing maps and diagrams, and genre scenes of mining operations.[14]

Woolson's piece on "Lake Superior" for *Picturesque America* easily fell in line with the western standard, the granite cliffs of the locale offering numerous opportunities for illustration.[15] As in the case of western pieces, geology here provided a common terrain on which the scientific, economic, and aesthetic modes of travel writing could intersect. Lake Superior had been treated as a site for picturesque tourism as early as 1867, when an illustrated wilderness-adventure story set amid the "Pictured Rocks" had appeared in *Harper's Monthly*.[16] Where Woolson's text incorporates the economic perspective that was so important in the definition of the upper Great Lakes region's identity, the accompanying illustrations adhere strictly

Fig. 1, Sail-Rock, Lake Superior.
Constance Fenimore Woolson, "Sail-Rock, Lake Superior."
Appletons' Journal (July 12, 1873): 33.

to the agenda of aesthetic tourism set by Appleton and Company. Journeying from venue to venue around Superior's shore via steamer or canoe, Woolson reports on the mineral "treasures" of each—from Iron Mountain near Marquette ("a ridge of ore eight hundred feet high, which sends its thousands of tons year after year down to the iron mills of Cleveland, Pittsburg [sic], and Cincinnati, and scarcely misses them from its massive sides") to speculations on silver and gold mines and other hints of mineral wealth, such that Superior "now needs only a diamond to complete its encircling crown of treasures."[17] At the same time, Woolson suggests that greater attention to aesthetics could improve the scientific accounts of this region on which her reportage has drawn: the "brilliancy of the coloring" of the granite formations of Pictured Rocks, for example, "charms the traveller [sic], and so astonishes the sober geologist that his dull pages blossom as the rose" (1: 396). Aesthetic motivations have the last word, as Woolson ends this account with the history of mining on Isle

Royale, which failed to yield the great "treasures" speculators had projected: "in spite of this ignominy," the island "is full of beauty, with castellated and columned cliffs of trap-rock" (1: 411). Yet any such tension between economic and aesthetic geology is absent from the accompanying illustrations, which make no allusion to mining but, rather, present rock formations purely as aesthetic objects.

Woolson's poem "Sail-Rock, Lake Superior," published in *Appletons' Journal* in 1873, is perhaps even more fascinated by the region's mineral ores. In this just-so story—purportedly an Indian legend in which the eponymous formation took shape when a ghost boat was "turned to stone" by the "Great Spirit's hand"—the landscape is prominently characterized by mineralogical features such as "ravines of iron," a peninsula's "copper arm," and "rocks where virgin silver shines." The mineralogical content of such topographic features is not visible to the eye and thus cannot be a part of any visual aesthetic: to name the features as such is to open the landscape to mining. The accompanying three-quarter-page illustration (Fig. 1) removes the economic dimension of Woolson's mineralogical references, presenting Sail-Rock as an object for distanced contemplation.[18]

Woolson's Southern Travels

Although the South might be thought to offer little in the way of aesthetic or economic geology, as compared with the Great Lakes and the West, Woolson identifies a stratum of geological interest in all of her Southern travel sketches for *Harper's Monthly*. Cropping out in various locales, geology becomes a topos for the challenges of the genre, a site where the interplay of informational and experiential travel are especially evident. The first of Woolson's sketches, "The Ancient City," addresses these challenges, by way of geological reference, through the quasi-fictional, ensemble technique Woolson had developed in "Round by Propeller." In "The Ancient City—Part I," we meet Sara St. John (a friend of the narrator, Miss Martha), a character disdained by Aunt Diana because she "wrote for the magazines" (3). For Aunt Diana, the mental labor of writing occludes the leisurely experience of aesthetic travel. (We might speculate whether a similar tension between travel as labor and travel as leisure inflected the relationship between Woolson and her mother during their semi-residence in the South.) Sara, who speaks in a "lead-pencil voice" when inquiring about any local feature, regards the landscape only as material for sketches: "the inevitable descriptive article . . . lurked behind every bush and waved a banner of proof-sheets at her from every sunshiny hill" (6, 3). As a steamboat carries the party on a well-traveled tourist route up the St. Johns River toward St. Augustine, Sara declares, "The question is, . . . *is* there anything one ought to know about these banks?" (2).

Woolson's guidebook and scientific voice, Professor Macquoid, points out that "the fresh-water shell heaps of the St. Johns River, East Florida...should be—should be somewhere about here" (2). The Professor's redundancy in naming the location (for the company and Woolson's readers all know full well where they are) signals a source text. The phrasing is verbatim from Daniel Brinton's *A Guide-Book of Florida and the South*, the first such guide published to encourage the postwar tourist trade on the St. Johns River route; or perhaps the Professor has in mind Brinton's source, Jeffries Wyman's pamphlet on the topic, entitled *An Account of the Fresh-water Shell Heaps of the St. Johns River, East Florida*.[19] The rest of the party are less than eager to find the shell heaps, however. Even the governess, "emerging reluctantly" from her early morning repose, only "stood prepared to do her duty"—that is, to educate her charge, young Iris—"by the fresh-water shell heaps or any other geological formation" (2). Though perhaps not a "geological formation," strictly speaking, the shell heaps are named as such, rather than as a historical artifact. These great piles of oyster shells, midden heaps left by ancient Native American towns, would, over eons, sink and become sedimented to form something like coquina, the characteristic building material of St. Augustine's Spanish-era architecture (see below). Woolson does not, however, draw the connection here—and in any case another traveler gives us a snippet of a different history, the sixteenth-century founding of a French Huguenot colony, until he too is cut off by the narrative's social flow.

Geology, or at least a landscape feature classified as "geological," is thus the site at which Woolson introduces the generic tension between informational and experiential-aesthetic travel. The layout editor at *Harper's Monthly*, however, bypassed this site altogether, no doubt because the shell heaps do not offer much in the way of picturesque scenery. Instead of shell heaps (or Huguenots, for that matter) we get a genre scene of "Shooting Alligators on the St. Johns," which follows the treatment of the St. Johns River as picturesque swamp established by *Appletons' Journal*.[20] The sophisticated reader might notice that Woolson avoids any mention of alligators at all here, perhaps as being too hackneyed.

A reader familiar with St. Augustine from a guidebook or a travel sketch (or from personal experience as a tourist) might expect some account of coquina, especially its use as a building material and one of the locale's characteristic features. Thus after several passing references, Woolson finally gives the Professor an opportunity late in the piece to define the substance as "a most singular conglomerate of shells cemented by carbonate of lime." At a quarry site, he gives the topic a more scientific inflection than other contemporary accounts by alluding to geohistory: "a recent formation, evidently, of the post-tertiary period. You are aware, I suppose, that it is found nowhere else in the world? It is soft, as you see, when first taken out, but becomes hard by exposure to the air" (23).[21] The *Harper's* illustrations fail to make anything of the locale's characteristic geology, however. The feature on St.

Augustine in *Appletons' Journal*, by contrast, had included a half-page sketch by Harry Fenn of workmen digging coquina out of a quarry—although this illustration was cut from the St. Augustine's segment for *Picturesque America*.[22]

Coquina also provides an occasion for a local color sketch in part 2 of Woolson's article, as the party visits the "studio" of a local artist, "a colored man and a cripple," who works small sculptures in "cokena," as his hand-lettered sign puts it. Reminiscent of the scene in Rebecca Harding Davis's *Life in the Iron Mills* in which owning-class characters comment on the rude korl sculptures of the untutored Welsh ironworker Hugh Wolfe, here the narrator observes that "it must require no small amount of skill to cut anything out of this crumbling shell rock." The evidence of native talent invites political commentary, in the authoritative, male voice of John: "Ignorant as he is, that man is not without his ideas of beauty and symmetry—another witness to the capability for education which I have every where [sic] noticed among the freedmen of the South."[23] Thus the aesthetic-experiential mode of travel merges into the informational-economic, as Woolson's assertion of a progressive view of race implies a corresponding need for Northern superintendence of social structures.

The geological topos would seem to offer greater range in Woolson's next piece for *Harper's Monthly*, "The French Broad," since mountains and hot springs are the region's primary attractions. The most accessible area of the Southern Appalachians, the region was second perhaps only to the White Mountains of New Hampshire of all travel destinations in the eastern mountains. Woolson's narrator (Miss Martha of the St. Augustine pieces) proposes, with an implicit nod to the superiority of the West, that the French Broad provides "the most magnificent scenery to be found in the old States—scenery which has remained undiscovered."[24] The region can only be called "undiscovered" from the perspective of the new Northern tourist: before the Civil War, it had been a long-established summer resort of South Carolina planters.[25] *Appletons' Journal* was among the first to recognize the region's potential as a destination for Northerners, running three pieces in November and December 1870 and January 1871. The region's geological and economic interest was especially noted in *Scribner's Monthly*'s "Great South" feature on western North Carolina, where Edward King finds the mountaineers' first question to the flatlanders is inevitably, "Air ye rock huntin'?"[26] That the mountains contained gold had been legendary long before the Cherokee Removal. King affirms that "there is no danger overestimating the mineral wealth of this country; it is unbounded," comprising not only gold and silver, but industrial minerals as well: iron, copper, coal, limestone, and so on (526). "Wherever we went," King reports, "we found the 'rock hunters' had been there ahead of us" (526). Even so, the French Broad installment of the "Great South" project contains more picturesque scenery and less economic information than other installments, for much of the region remained undeveloped, still wanting railroads.

In the wake of *Appletons'* and *Scribner's* accounts of the region, Woolson's Professor Macquoid approaches the French Broad oddly oblivious to its aesthetic and economic prospects. "Engaged upon the composition of a Great Work," the Professor has traveled here primarily to take geological measurements (635). Woolson evidently imagines the Professor as working in the vein of Arnold Guyot, a Princeton professor of geology and physical geography who had established elevations for the entire Appalachian chain in an attempt to ascertain its geological age.[27] In one humorous episode, the Professor is so keen to measure "a remarkable dip in the strata" that he crawls out onto a rock ledge, suffers an attack of "vertigo, ... the result of an overworked brain," and has to be led back to safety (622, 625). Over dinner, he hopes to entertain the company with an account of the region's geology. Recognizing the topic's potential interest, Woolson lets the Professor lecture longer than she usually does. Here is a sample:

> These mountains, my friends, ... form the eastern margin of our continent, ... extending from Vermont to Alabama; the coast follows their direction, curving in at Hatteras as they trend off to the westward. The rocks in this neighborhood belong to the most ancient of the azoic series. In the language of an eloquent spokesman among our band of geologists, "As North America is the eldest born of the continents, so the Black Mountain region is the eldest born of its giant brotherhood and was the first to emerge from the face of the water when the command went forth, Let the dry land appear!" In the group of the White Mountains, Mount Washington is the only one that rises above six thousand feet, while here there are peaks in all directions that rise above that height— (625)

The age of various formations was, contemporarily, a matter of some scientific controversy. To support his claim that the Black Mountain was the oldest formation in North America, the Professor quotes from a report issued by the Geological Survey of North Carolina.[28]

Woolson's travelers, however, are impatient to hear about a geological topic of more immediate interest: "Is the Bald Mountain in sight? ... *the* Bald, the volcano, you know, Professor." The travelers allude to an earthquake that struck western North Carolina the previous winter (February 1874) with enough force to have made the national newspapers. There was a good deal of speculation on whether the cause was volcanic, for the existence of live volcanoes in the continental United States would be exciting indeed. And volcanoes are of course more popularly

VIEW FROM TOP OF BLACK MOUNTAIN.

Mountains and many minor groups are crowded with visitors and dotted with easels."

In the morning we began our search for the river. We asked no questions, but walked a mile to the east, a mile to the north, a mile to the south, in vain; at last we found it down in the west, hidden so cunningly that we were on its very bridge before we saw the water. "The witch!"

Fig. 2, View from the Top of Black Mountain.
Constance Fenimore Woolson, "The French Broad."
Harper's Monthly (April 1875): 619.

compelling than the chronology of sedimentary strata. Curiously, however, none of the newspaper discussions attempted to correlate the question of volcanic activity with the presence of hot springs in the region.[29] The Professor too confesses ignorance. He refuses to comment on the question of volcanoes and cannot even identify the Bald from among the other peaks. Disappointing as this is, at least the Northern tourists, representatives of Woolson's readers, manage to fill in some information. Through the character of the Major, Woolson reminds us of the *New*

York Times's indulgence in a bit of local color in its scientific reportage, noting that "the people in the neighborhood" knew "less than the outside public, who at least gained some idea" from the New York newspapers (625). The *Times* had reported that the locals were ignorant of earthquakes as a geological phenomenon and so concluded "one and all . . . that the end of the world was near at hand. . . . Baptist and Methodist clergymen were sent for to pray with them."[30] The Professor, undaunted by the party's clamor for scientific sensationalism, pulls from his pocket a volume of Guyot's writings, whereat one of the young ladies prevails on him to read a poem instead. Her choice, Edmund Clarence Stedman's "Bohemia," redirects our attention to New York as cultural center: Stedman (whom Woolson had met the previous season in St. Augustine) was a member of the "Bohemian" crowd that congregated at Pfaff's saloon on lower Broadway.

For all this talk of geology, sensational or sober, the illustrations to "The French Broad" are unsuccessful in displaying either the informational or aesthetic aspects of the region's mountains. Overburdened by foreground detail and offering bland prospects, the images probably derive from original sources in photographs rather than artists' drawings (Fig. 2). In "View from the Top of Black Mountain," for example, the proliferation of tree trunks in the foreground clutters the space that in a picturesque sketch would conventionally be reserved for contemplative repose. Yet the distant mountains are not rendered with sufficient clarity, contrast, or scale to evoke the sublime.[31] By comparison, illustrations for *Appletons' Journal*'s 1870 pieces on the French Broad had used long lines, stark contrasts, and closer prospects to aestheticize the region's rock formations. In a pair of images of a sheer cliff illuminated by sunrise and moonlight, a foreground road and a single tree are key elements in picturesque composition.[32] (Curiously, neither *Harper's* nor *Appletons'* provided any visual account of the hot springs that were the locale's primary tourist attraction.)

Charleston, the destination of Woolson's next travel piece, might seem to offer minimal opportunity for picturesque illustration. *Appletons' Journal*, for example, reported that its best artist, Harry Fenn, had spent three days wandering the city before finally finding inspiration in an elevated view of the harbor from a belfry tower.[33] Woolson found the plantation country upriver to provide better opportunities. Focusing on the locale's colonial and Revolutionary era history, her text implicitly reconstructs a common American past for her Northern readers. Illustrations include images of mansions by moonlight, magnolias, live oaks with moss, coats of arms, churches, cemeteries, and the old fort at Dorchester (though of course not Fort Sumter). The legacy of slavery and other challenging political topics remain invisible: such topics would disrupt the article's historical-picturesque approach, especially since race relations in Reconstruction Charleston were notoriously tense. Shorn of the cast of characters that Woolson had used in previous pieces to dramatize the competing demands of the travel-sketch genre, the sketch

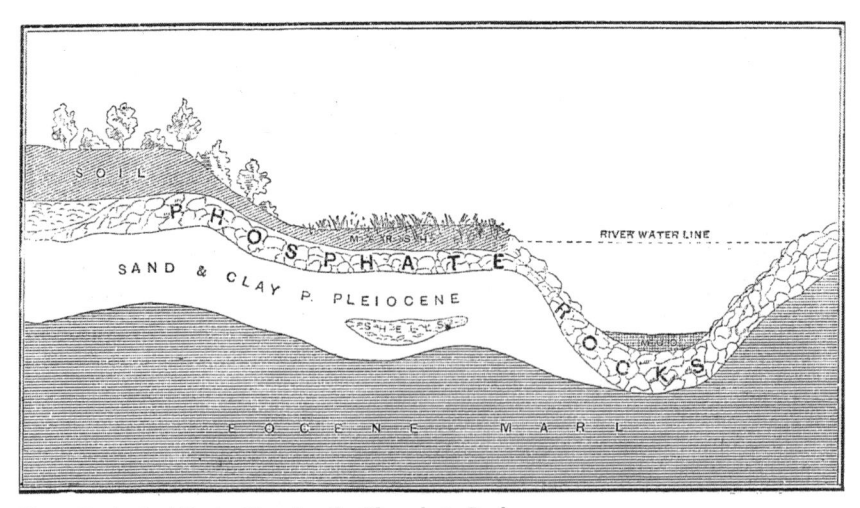

Fig. 3, Geological Strata, Showing the Phosphate Rock.
Constance Fenimore Woolson, "Up the Ashley and Cooper."
Harper's Monthly (December 1875): 22.

presents the South in a monologic voice as a Northern object of nostalgia for a less hurried, more socially stable chronotope, a refuge from the strains of industrial capitalism.[34] If there is a good deal more informational content than in Woolson's previous, quasi-fictional sketches, the exposition of (selective) historical detail in itself becomes the primary means of producing this nostalgia: the locale is "rich in colonial memories and Revolutionary legends, verified and emphasized by the old houses and gardens which still remain, not having been swept away by the crowding population, the manufactories, the haste and bustle, of the busy North."[35]

At the end of the piece, however, Woolson turns abruptly from the historical picturesque to the North's current economic interest in the South: "But something else belongs there [i.e., to the history of the Ashley River] which is in itself so wonderful, as well as valuable to South Carolina, that it may well find mention here" (23). This is the deposit of phosphate rock, from which can be manufactured a fertilizer richer in phosphorus than the mid-nineteenth-century standard, South American guano. The accompanying illustration, occupying the top third of the previous page, gives a technical diagram of the bed of the Ashley River in cross-section (Fig. 3). The phosphate deposit is associated with the strata of marl (anciently sedimented mollusk shells and clay) extant along the entire southeastern coast. (In fact, St. Augustine's coquina is a related geological formation.) Thus visual and verbal registers both shift from picturesque tourism to economic incorporation, as Woolson describes Northern capital investment in mines and fertilizer factories. The phosphate rock deposit is a resource "which seems to have waited until it was sorely needed before it made itself known, just as petroleum was discovered when the discouraged whalemen were coming home with ships half empty, declaring that the useful whales were nearly extinct" (24).

Woolson's material and two accompanying illustrations here derive from Francis Simmons Holmes's book, *The Phosphate Rocks of South Carolina*.[36] Holmes, a professor of natural history who had published several other books on geology and paleontology, was one of two remaining representatives of antebellum Charleston's lively intellectual circle. After the war, as mining began on a large scale, Holmes became involved in a quarrel over who could claim first discovery of the economic value of the phosphate deposits. He published *The Phosphate Rocks* to solidify his claim and to serve as a promotional tract (the last fifteen pages detail the extent of Northern capital already invested in the development of this natural resource), as well as a scientific work describing the riverbed's geology.[37] Holmes was probably eager to give Woolson a copy of this book and have her publicize his story in a magazine article. Although Woolson does not mention the book by title, she does cite Professor Holmes as the source for the more technical geological descriptions in the passage ("we use his own language," 23) and credits him with the discovery of the deposit and the promotional efforts resulting in its first development by Philadelphia investors who opened a mining operation in 1867. The engraving does not credit Holmes's book or any other source.[38]

This turn to economic geology bears comparison with Edward King's account of Charleston in *The Great South*.[39] Both King and Woolson present the South as needing Northern care and guidance. Often Woolson's Reconstruction-era Southern stories feature Northern caretaker figures who look after debilitated or otherwise incapable Southerners, as for example "Rodman the Keeper."[40] Where King addresses the politics of Reconstruction Charleston head-on, noting Klan violence and legislative corruption, Woolson approaches indirectly. Both are keen to show how much Northern capital has been invested in phosphate mining and fertilizer production: some six million dollars by Woolson's (that is, Holmes's) estimate, four to five million by King's. In the overall context of King's account of Charleston, the section on the phosphate rocks and fertilizer fits well with the rest of the economic material on cotton and rice production and so on. Woolson brings the notice of economic development into direct contrast with the historical-picturesque mode of the rest of her article by observing that "the trenches of the [phosphate] mines are invading the grounds of our old plantations," thus claiming, by means of the possessive pronoun, a nostalgia for the antebellum South as national property (24). (See figure 4.) Meanwhile, a new, industrial agricultural system is being produced literally out of the "grounds" of "our" old plantations, through the agency of Northern capital investment and Southern manual labor. In a similar move at the end of "Rodman the Keeper," an industrious Maine carpetbagger sets about "pulling down

Fig. 4, Phosphate Mine.
Constance Fenimore Woolson, "Up the Ashley and Cooper."
Harper's Monthly (December 1875): 23.

the old house" of the De Rossett plantation; he sells Rodman a piece of nostalgia, some vines that had shaded the piazza, for twenty-five cents.[41] As in "Rodman," then, Woolson suggests that Northern nostalgia for the Old South and the economic progress of Reconstruction under Northern initiative are two sides of the same coin.

Yet this turn to economics carries with it a larger geological frame, which includes not only the present reciprocation of progress and nostalgia, but the much longer temporal perspective of deep time. Woolson delves into the geohistory omitted by King, describing not only the aesthetics of the marl beds, source of "beautifully preserved forms of shells, teeth, and bones, mingled with the rocks filled with the casts of shells, corals, and corallines," but also their scientific significance for the question of human origins (23). She reports that stone tools and human bones have been found "in the same matrix or mother bed of clay" as "bones and teeth of the mastodon," an association confirmed by similar discoveries in Europe and proving that humankind had lived at the same time as now-extinct Pleistocene-era megafauna, a point that was still under some debate in the paleontological literature (23).[42] Holmes may have been Woolson's source for some of this information, though as we know from her other sketches, she was well versed in geology.[43]

Geology thus extends the overall historical theme of "Up the Ashley and Cooper" back beyond human prehistory as well as up through the postwar present of Northern economic development. The experiential-aesthetic and the informational-scientific modes merge, as Woolson frames both nostalgia for an antimodern South and Reconstruction economic appropriation within the larger imagination of deep time that reinforces the sketch's sense of place through multiple temporal references:

> At Drayton Hall children run after the visitors to sell "shark's teeth." One of these teeth weighed two pounds and a quarter, and measured six inches from tip to tip. The shark in whose terrible mouth it belonged must have been one hundred feet in length. On the whole, what with these sharks, with zeuglodons, squalodons, huge alligator-like creatures of giant size, and lizards eighteen feet long, one is glad not to have lived in those days on the banks of the two beautiful rivers, the Ashley and the Cooper. (24)

The creatures mentioned here all have distinctly Southern references: the megalodon shark is especially associated with the Cooper River, the zeuglodon with the Sintabogure River, Alabama, and the squalodon with Calvert Cliffs, Maryland. Sequentially, the three creatures cover nearly the entire tertiary period, from circa 50 million to circa 1.6 million years ago—that is, up nearly to the edge of human time. The primitive artifacts, "stone arrowheads and a stone hatchet," and human bones found associated with the remains of mastodons, described earlier, bring the temporal reference up from human prehistory to the Native American past, followed by the Old South plantation past evoked by Drayton Hall, to the postwar present of tourism and industrial development.

"Deep time is so alien that we can really only comprehend it as metaphor," observes Stephen Jay Gould.[44] Here, as temporalities expand and collapse on a single site, Woolson uses the inherent incomprehensibility of deep time to refamiliarize an antebellum South lately alienated from the North. In the form of tours of Drayton Hall and souvenirs of megalodon sharks' teeth—"our" plantation past and the pre-human past—Charleston, the seat of the Rebellion, now produces objects for the Northern tourist trade. (Diving the Cooper River to recover megalodon teeth is a popular tourist activity today.) The naming of a plantation house is as close as Woolson comes to mentioning slavery. With shark's tooth in hand as material token while strolling the grounds, it is easier to connect to the deep past than to the realities of antebellum life at Drayton Hall. How much less "terrible" does the history of slavery become when placed alongside a world terrorized by prehistoric monsters?

Notes

1. James Buzard observes that this sort of response begins in the early nineteenth century. See "The Grand Tour and After," *The Cambridge Companion to Travel Writing*, ed. Peter Hulme and Tim Youngs (Cambridge: Cambridge University Press, 2002), 37–52, esp. 48–50.

2. Nina Silber identifies a shift from information- to entertainment-oriented travel writing after about 1870; see *The Romance of Reunion: Northerners and Southerners in the South, 1865–1900* (Chapel Hill: University of North Carolina Press, 1993), 66–70. On the rapid growth of tourism in the 1870s, see 70–74. Henry Shapiro puts entertainment-oriented travel accounts of the Mountain South from the 1870s and following into a longer trajectory, contrasting local color sketches with antebellum informational accounts; see *Appalachia on Our Mind: The Southern Mountains and Mountaineers in the American Consciousness, 1870–1920* (Chapel Hill: University of North Carolina Press, 1978), 3–10.

3. On character and persona in the travel sketches, see Dennis Berthold, "Miss Martha and Ms. Woolson: Persona in the Travel Sketches," *Constance Fenimore Woolson's Nineteenth Century: Essays*, ed. Victoria Brehm (Detroit: Wayne State University Press, 2001), 111–18. Sharon Dean remarks on Woolson's "struggle" with the guidebook approach; see *Constance Fenimore Woolson and Edith Wharton: Perspectives on Landscape and Art* (Knoxville: University of Tennessee Press, 2002), 29.

4. Frank Luther Mott notes that *Harper's Monthly* was especially known for illustrated travel pieces in the 1870s and 1880s, including foreign and exotic travel; see *A History of American Magazines*, 5 vols. (Cambridge, MA: Harvard University Press, 1930–68), II: 397–98.

5. Woolson, "Round by Propeller," *Harper's Monthly* (September 1872): 518–33, 527, hereafter documented parenthetically.

6. Although Leo Marx argues that technology was accommodated to nature through a rhetoric of the technological sublime, Woolson's description here seems more picturesque than sublime. See *The Machine in the Garden: Technology and the Pastoral Ideal in America*, 2nd ed. (Oxford: Oxford University Press, 2000).

7. "The Ancient City, Part I," *Harper's Monthly* (December 1874): 1–25, 1, hereafter documented parenthetically.

8. Timothy Sweet, *Traces of War: Poetry, Photography, and the Crisis of the Union* (Baltimore: Johns Hopkins University Press, 1990), 156–61; quotations from *Harper's Weekly*, 157, 158.

9. Edward King, *The Great South* (Hartford: American Publishing, 1875). Jennifer Greeson argues that through such projects, the North came to imagine itself as an imperial nation, poised for hemispheric expansion; see "Expropriating *The Great South* and Exporting Local Color: Global and Hemispheric Imaginaries of the First Reconstruction," *American Literary History* 18 (2006): 496–520. For a survey of imperialist themes, see Jamie Winders, "Imperfectly Imperial: Northern Travel Writers in the Postbellum U.S. South, 1865–1880," *Annals of the Association of American Geographers* 95 (2005): 391–410.

10. Sue Rainey, *Creating* Picturesque America: *Monument to the Natural and Cultural Landscape* (Nashville: Vanderbilt University Press, 1994), 46–73.

11. John Whitney, *Whitney's Florida Pathfinder* (New York: Pathfinder's, 1876), 29.

12. J. B. Holder, "Along the Florida Reef," *Harper's Monthly* (February, March, April 1871): 355–63, 515–26, 706–19; (June, July 1871): 26–36, 187–95.

13. On the aesthetic appeal of geology in the nineteenth century, see Barbara Novak, *Nature and Culture: American Landscape Painting, 1825–1875*, 3rd ed. (New York: Oxford University Press, 2007), 41–70; Noah Heringman, *Romantic Rocks, Aesthetic Geology* (Ithaca, NY: Cornell University Press, 2004).

14. Verplanck Colvin, "The Dome of the Continent," *Harper's Monthly* (December 1872): 20–37.

15. See Kathleen Diffley, "'Clean Forgotten': Woolson's Great Lakes Illustrated," *Constance Fenimore Woolson's Nineteenth Century: Essays*, 119–39. On differences between illustrations of eastern locales (picturesque) and western locales (sublime) in *Picturesque America*, see Rainey, *Creating*, 203–73.

16. A. L. Rawson, "The Pictured Rocks of Lake Superior," *Harper's Monthly* (May 1867): 681–97.

17. Woolson, "Lake Superior," *Picturesque America*, 2 vols. (New York: D. Appleton and Co., 1872, 1874), I: 393–411, I: 400, hereafter documented parenthetically.

18. Woolson, "Sail-Rock, Lake Superior," *Appletons' Journal* (July 12, 1873): 33–34. On the interplay of text and illustration, see Diffley, "Woolson's Great Lakes," 134.

19. See Daniel Brinton, *A Guide-Book of Florida and the South, for Tourists, Invalids, and Emigrants: With a Map of the St. Johns River* (Philadelphia: Geo. Maclean, and Jacksonville: Columbus Drew, 1869), 54; and Jeffries Wyman, *An Account of the Fresh-water Shell Heaps of the St. Johns River, East Florida* (Salem, MA: Essex Institute, 1868). Woolson's description of the river's color and course in this passage also seem borrowed from Brinton, *A Guide-Book of Florida*, 52.

20. On *Appletons'* treatment of the St. Johns, see Rainey, *Creating*, 52–54.

21. Neither King, *Great South* (394), nor Whitney, *Whitney's Florida Pathfinder* (26), gives any information on the geology of coquina.

22. "Scenes in St. Augustine," *Appletons' Journal* (July 1, 1871): 17; cf. *Picturesque America* I:191.

23. Woolson, "The Ancient City—Part II," *Harper's Monthly* (January 1875): 165–85, 172.

24. Woolson, "The French Broad," *Harper's Monthly* (April 1875): 617–36, 619, hereafter documented parenthetically.

25. See, e.g., Henry E. Colton, *Mountain Scenery* (Raleigh: W. L. Pomeroy, and Philadelphia: Hayes & Zell, 1859), 13–14.

26. King, "Among the Mountains of Western North Carolina," *Scribner's Monthly* (March 1874): 513–44, 517, hereafter documented parenthetically.

27. See Arnold Guyot, "On the Appalachian Mountain System," *American Journal of Science and the Arts* (March 1861): 157–87.

28. W. C. Kerr, *Report of the Progress of the Geological Survey of North-Carolina* (Raleigh: William E. Bell, State Printer, 1866), 34. Woolson's source for the quotation, however, may have been an extract from the *Report* published in *Littell's Living Age*; see "The Oldest Spot of Earth," *Littell's Living Age* (January 15, 1870), 186. The idea that North America was the eldest among continents was closely associated with Louis Agassiz; see, e.g., the first of a series of articles on geological history, Agassiz, "America, the Old World," *Atlantic Monthly* (March 1863): 373–82. Guyot, "On the Appalachian Mountain System," had argued—contrary to the Professor's claim—that the Black Mountain region was the youngest of the Appalachian chain.

29. The *New York Times*, which covered the story in several short news items, ran a scientific feature arguing in favor of subterraneous volcanic activity, "North Carolina's Volcano" (July 20, 1874): 5. By contrast, "Scientific Intelligence," *American Journal of Science and the Arts* (July 1874): 69, reported that there was no sign of volcanic activity.

30. "Earthquakes," *New York Times*, December 20, 1874, 10.

31. During the production process, in-house artists could alter the source image by adding or subtracting detail before the image went to the engraver, but they would not substantially alter the basic compositional form. In this case, the art department could have chosen to simplify the composition of the left foreground by removing some of the trees but did not do so. On the production process, see Joshua Brown, *Beyond the Lines: Pictorial Reporting, Everyday Life, and the Crisis of Gilded Age America* (Berkeley and Los Angeles: University of California Press, 2002), 32–40; and Mott, *History of American Magazines*, III: 187–90.

32. See Rainey, *Creating*, 55–57.

33. Rainey, *Creating*, 114–16.

34. On the Reconstruction South as an antimodern refuge for the Northern tourist, see Silber, *Romance of Reunion*, 66–92.

35. Woolson, "Up the Ashley and Cooper," *Harper's Monthly* (December 1875): 1–24, 22–23, hereafter documented parenthetically.

36. Francis Simmons Holmes, *The Phosphate Rocks of South Carolina and the "Great Carolina Marl Bed"* (Charleston: Holmes' Book House, 1870). The *Harper's Monthly* illustration of "Phosphate Rock—Natural Size" (24) is taken from the frontispiece color plate; the stratigraphic section of the Ashley riverbed (22) is taken from the plate facing 71.

37. On Holmes's career and the controversy over his claim to first discovery of the deposit, see Lester D. Stephens, *Science, Race, and Religion in the American South: John Bachman and the Charleston Circle of Naturalists, 1815–1895* (Chapel Hill: University of North Carolina Press, 2000), 127–45, 226–35.

38. The engraving bears the mark of "Russell & Struthers, N.Y.," a firm that supplied engravings of maps and diagrams to *Harper's*; e.g., a map of the Lexington battlefield for an illustrated piece on "The Concord Fight," *Harper's Monthly* (May 1875), 884.

39. King, *Great South*, 449–50. Curiously, the *Scribner's* piece that was the basis for the book chapter on Charleston does not mention the phosphate rocks at all; cf. King, "The South Carolina Problem; the Epoch of Transition," *Scribner's Monthly* (June 1874): 129–60.

40. Karen Weekes, "Northern Bias in Constance Fenimore Woolson's *Rodman the Keeper: Southern Sketches*," *Southern Literary Journal* 32 (2000): 102–15. However, Anne E. Boyd argues against any oversimplified, imperialist reading of Woolson's Southern fiction; see her essay in the present collection.

41. Woolson, *Rodman the Keeper: Southern Sketches* (New York: Garrett Press, 1969), 41.

42. See Donald K. Grayson, "Nineteenth-Century Explanations of the Pleistocene Extinctions: A Review and Analysis," *Quaternary Extinctions: A Prehistoric Revolution*, ed. Paul S. Martin and Richard G. Klein (Tucson: University of Arizona Press, 1984), 5–39.

43. Among Holmes's books is *Post-Pleiocene Fossils of South-Carolina* (Charleston: Russell & Jones, 1860).

44. Stephen Jay Gould, *Time's Arrow, Time's Cycle* (Cambridge, MA: Harvard University Press, 1987), 3.

Reconstructing Southern Hospitality

—Anthony Szczesiul

In a sermon delivered at St. Mary's Church of Keyport, New Jersey, on January 27, 1867, the Reverend Telfair Hodgson, a Confederate veteran, made an emotional appeal to the Northern congregation about charitable aid for his fellow Southerners. Hodgson's "A Sermon in Behalf of Southern Sufferers" painted a dire picture of the South in the two years since the war ended, with floods and droughts and impending famines adding to the grim reality of an already devastated economy and defunct social system. With this picture in mind, Hodgson reminded his readers of the Christian imperative of hospitality by citing Matthew 25:43: "I was a stranger and ye took me not in; naked, and ye clothed me not; sick and in prison and ye visited me not." Although Hodgson acknowledged that his Northern listeners "may ... regard these people as enemies" and may feel that the Southern sufferers have "made the bed upon which they lie," he urged his listeners to remember the divine injunction, "I will have mercy, and not sacrifice."[1]

But Hodgson's persuasive appeal went beyond biblical injunctions by trading on the legendary Southern reputation for hospitality. After describing the Atlantans forced to live in tent cities in the dead of winter, he reminded the Northern congregation of the privileged position hospitable Southerners once enjoyed before they lost everything:

Many of these same persons have been as well, or better off than you or I, and we would have esteemed it a privilege to enjoy their company, or to extend to them the hospitality of our table. These, too, were men noted for their generosity, for their hospitality to strangers. No one, I may safely assert, has ever been turned away by them hungry, when they had it in their power to feed them. And how low they have fallen now. Men of education, and women of refinement, with nothing to clothe their nakedness, with nothing to feed their hunger. Should it be that you hate these people, it seems to me that they have newcomer that I welcome is perfectly harmless, innocent, that (s)he will be beneficial to me ... it is not hospitality. When I open my door, I must be ready to take the greatest of risks."[5] With this unconditional ethical standard in mind, it is no wonder that Derrida repeatedly says, "We do not yet know what hospitality is."[6]

Keeping this distinction between the ethics and the politics of hospitality in mind can help us to understand both the persuasive appeal and the cultural work of the postbellum discourse of Southern hospitality during Reconstruction and the early era of segregation. While the vaunted claims of Southern hospitality had been vigorously and openly contested on ethical grounds in the antebellum period, these debates were largely forgotten after the Civil War, when the South was increasingly seen as the home of hospitality.[7] With the growth of tourism and travel in the South and in the emerging national consumer culture, the discourse of Southern hospitality was transformed into a free-floating nostalgic image, an effective commercial concept, a consumer commodity, and a form of political persuasion. To Northerners, this view of the South provided a nostalgic image of a simpler, better time and a regional ideal upon which to hang the hopes of regional reconciliation following fratricidal war. To Southerners, a reasserted self-image stood as a confirmation of regional pride, exceptionalism, and superiority. To both, the gathering perception of Southern hospitality provided an adaptable discourse for reimagining postwar political and social relations.

The journalist Edward A. Pollard's *The Virginia Tourist* (1870) reveals the historically situated racial and political dimensions of the discursive practices engendered by Southern hospitality in the postbellum decades.[8] Directed to visitors from the North, Pollard's volume provides a comprehensive tour of the mineral springs resort areas of Virginia, combining detailed information on hotels, traveling arrangements, the medicinal qualities of the springs' waters, descriptions of natural scenery, overviews of local and natural history, discussions on the possible economic development of the region, and a large number of local color scenes and sketches based on firsthand experience and secondhand knowledge. In the concluding chapter, titled "Practical Hints," Pollard goes to great lengths to reassure his readers of the warm and hospitable reception they will receive from Southerners, who customarily make "a special and sedulous effort" to accommodate Northern visitors:

> [P]ersons in the North ... will be received there with the most cordial welcome, will enjoy the advantages of marked efforts to please them, and will have the satisfaction of assisting in a social "reconstruction," in which the people of the South are prepared to meet them with gracious readiness and with grateful alacrity....

> To the peaceful and richly-endowed spaces of her springs and mountains and scenery the State invites all comers; and what nature has bestowed, a generosity that does not encumber with its obligations, and a hospitality that never wearies of its offices, unite to dispense. (277)

Not only would the immediate needs of travelers be met, but "the social reunion of the two sections" would naturally ensue.

Through the genres of popular fiction and travel writing that would be Woolson's initial stock in trade, most Americans of the nineteenth century would have recognized the long-held assumption of Southern hospitality, which Pollard here rhetorically transforms into both an enticing tourism pitch and a patriotic call to the duty of social reconstruction. On the one hand, Pollard's rhetoric reflects the post–Civil War culture of reconciliation described by Nina Silber in *The Romance of Reunion*. As Silber demonstrates, both the tourism experience and tourism literature allowed middle- and upper-class Northerners "to view the South and reconciliation through a romantic and depoliticized prism."[9] On the other hand, Pollard's allusions to Southern hospitality also forecast the more modern tendency to transform Southern hospitality into both a compelling advertising strategy and a consumable product.

At the same time, when Pollard suggests that visiting Northerners will be participating in the "social 'reconstruction'" of the nation, the social reconstruction he has in mind is decidedly retrograde. Following the publication of *The Lost Cause* (1866), his history of the rebellion, Pollard had written *The Lost Cause Regained* (1868), a work that outlines a comprehensive national political agenda based on the doctrine of white supremacy. For Pollard, the end of slavery only clarified the central political issue facing the country, that of white racial purity and dominance: "When [the South] defended Slavery by her arms, she was single-handed, and encountered the antipathies of the world; now, when she asserts the ultimate supremacy of the white man, she has not lost her cause, but merely developed its higher significance, and in the new contest she stands, with a firm political alliance in the North, with the binding instincts of race in her favour, and with the sympathies of all generous and enlightened humanity drawn upon her."[10] With this political agenda in mind, we can look at his comments in a new light; for Pollard, the "social reconstruction" which Southern hospitality can help to secure is the reconstruction of the white race on a national level.

This depiction of Southern hospitality as a statement of white solidarity is seen in a more blatant manner in texts promoting Northern and foreign emigration to the South after the Civil War. In Frederick B. Goddard's *Where to Emigrate and Why*, for example, the introduction to the book's Southern section concludes that "the Southern people will extend to the immigrant of every land and condition, their far-famed hospitality and welcome."[11] This promise is echoed again and again in the numerous letters from Southern officials that follow and that detail the South's climate, social customs, and economic opportunities. For example, in a letter detailing the potential for immigration in Virginia, the State Agent for Immigration, J. D. Imboden, writes that there is a "universal" desire for immigration in the state, whether immigrants are foreign-born or from the North, and he promises these potential immigrants a "cordial welcome" (358). But again there is a racial logic to this promise of Southern hospitality. Tellingly, he draws his letter to a close with a promise of white supremacy that includes the potential immigrant (even the foreign-born) in its power structure:

> This too will always be a white man's State. The white male population of voting age exceeds the negroes more than 40,000 in the State, and the majority will rapidly increase as white population flows in, and the negroes move southward, as is now their tendency. They will be harmless here. No immigrant need fear any trouble from them, and the whites will welcome all you can send with open arms. (359)

For Pollard and like-minded Southerners, then, the discourse of Southern hospitality was about establishing boundaries. While the sense of who could belong in these texts is fluid and depends largely upon political or economic needs, the sense of who does not belong—the black population—remains constant.[12]

With the war lost, the old social verities largely destroyed, and the free black population exerting an unforeseen pressure, Pollard's *Virginia Tourist* tries to imagine a new social and political order. As David Blight writes in *Race and Reunion*, Pollard's *Lost Cause Regained* "counseled reconciliation with conservative Northerners on Southern terms," and it is not surprising, then, that his tour book published only two years later is primarily addressed to Northerners, but particularly those of the white upper classes.[13] His representation of life at the Springs resorts emphasizes conspicuous consumption, elegance, refinement, exclusivity, and "gay society" (29). At the same time, Pollard is noticeably ambivalent about the possibilities of more fluid relationships among the middle and upper classes. So while he insists upon white solidarity in the face of a free black population, he also wants to maintain clear class distinctions among whites.

In his introductory chapter, for example, Pollard describes at great length the opportunities for economic development and speculative investment in the Springs, which he believes can compete with Northern resort areas such as Saratoga and Cape May. A factor preventing this is the Southern one-rate system, which puts all guests on the same level as consumers. Pollard urges Virginia's resort hotels to favor a more Northern model of "adaptation to different classes of customers." As things currently stand, Pollard complains that there are "no degrees of comfort, or what is more, degrees of privacy" (28). Later, in a description of social life at the Montgomery White Sulphur Springs, he hints at a fear of class fluidity infecting the life at the Springs, particularly in the form of the newly wealthy from the North: "The social life here, high as it is, is peculiarly Southern, drawing its animation from the principal Southern cities, such as New Orleans, and having little of that Northern shoddyism which it has been attempted to import into some of our summer resorts in Virginia. Our Southern belles might, perhaps, improve their taste in decoration, but we are sure that people of fashion in the North might improve their own style by imbibing some of that earnest and natural gayety and enthusiasm, that unconcealed sense of happiness and enjoyment, which characterizes the more impulsive and demonstrative people of the South in places designed for pleasure and recreation" (122).

Pollard's comments on "Northern shoddyism" carried very particular meaning in the years after the war, for the word was "first used in the United States with reference to those who made fortunes by army contracts at the time of the Civil War, it being alleged that the clothing supplied by the contractors consisted largely of shoddy," a type of cheap, recycled woolen yarn.[14] Pollard, then, is criticizing the nouveau riche of the North. More specifically, he points to those whose sly wartime trickery enabled their social climb, and his critical comments here reveal the anxiety that runs beneath his case for social reconstruction with the North. Pollard desires white political solidarity, but he fears the loss of rigid class distinctions in the more fluid postwar economy. And yet Nina Silber's assessment of travel and tourism in the South following the war reveals that this criticism of Northern shoddyism actually proved effective with Northerners—or at least the Northerners that Woolson also addressed. Writing of the burgeoning success of the Southern tourism industries following the Civil War, Silber points out that "the South held a unique class appeal which other tourist spots seemed to lack. . . . [for] the South could offer an association with true aristocracy, even if it meant the remnants and ruins of an aristocratic past. . . . Consequently, for middle- and upper-class Northerners, the South became a land in which the class tensions of their own industrializing and stratified society could evaporate."[15] Considering this aristocratic appeal, it is not surprising that Pollard then turns to a long description and "knightly" defense of a "Grand Tournament" held at the White Sulphur Springs, a spectacle which hearkens back to antebellum plantation practices and what Twain termed the "Sir Walter Scott disease."

At another point in *The Virginia Tourist*, these romantic visions of the antebellum past are counterpointed with the postwar threat posed by a free black population. Pollard describes traveling in a remote and mountainous area of Bedford County, where he unexpectedly comes across a mansion in the mountains:

(119). Following the dinner she is further horrified when Saxton extends his hand in friendship. She does not deign to acknowledge his efforts, and later she burns the "desecrated" clothes she wore for the dinner. Gardis's posturing may seem melodramatic, even pathetic.

It is worth recalling, however, the overriding politics of Southern hospitality. In *Honor and Slavery*, Kenneth Greenberg shows that antebellum social practices functioned as part of a "system of gift exchange" that signified social position. Gifts could flow downward from master to slave, or sideways among men of honor. Consequently, there was a "double quality" to any gift; it could be "potentially degrading and divisive on the one hand and potentially defining of a community of free men on the other."[19] In "Old Gardiston," receiving aid from her sworn enemies carries a sense of degradation for Gardis, particularly since she had earlier denied them hospitality. As Bertram Wyatt-Brown explains, "Whether [Southerners] . . . competed gracefully under the formal rules of hospitality or furiously in the violence that sometimes resulted, the drama of these strategies was their appeal, and status their prize."[20]

But "Old Gardiston" does not simply debunk Southern hospitality by portraying it as a hypocritical and self-serving myth. If that were the case, Woolson would not have given voice to Gardis's aging Cousin Copeland, who rebukes her when she fails to welcome strangers. "Hospitality has ever been one of our characteristics as a family," he asserts. Ensconced in the house and removed from the war, Cousin Copeland seems momentarily incredulous: "it is a very sad state of things, my dear—very sad. It was not so in the old days at Gardiston House; then we should have invited them to dinner" (114). Rather than simply dismissing Southern hospitality out of hand, then, Woolson here offers two contrasting dimensions: Gardis's sense of hospitality's recent politics and Cousin Copeland's sense of hospitality's abiding ethics. In "Old Gardiston," politics and ethics seem peculiarly at odds.

Can Northerners and Southerners move beyond the trauma and resentment of the war and see one another as equals? This enduring ethical possibility is illustrated in a humble exchange of hospitality that takes place between Captain Newell and Cousin Copeland later in the story. When the family loses its one remaining source of income—rent from a warehouse tenant—Copeland is forced out of his house to seek employment in town. Newell comes upon the dejected Copeland sitting on the steps of a church after a degrading and unsuccessful job search. In contrast to Gardis's politically charged efforts to maintain a sense of superiority, the present exchange is marked by a sense of equality and mutual respect. Describing Newell as he approaches Copeland, Woolson introduces an unusual scene:

> With the rare courtesy which comes from a kind heart, he asked no questions regarding the fatigue and dust-powdered clothes of the little bachelor, and took

a seat beside him as though a church-step on a city street was a customary place of meeting.

"I was about to—to eat a portion of this corn-bread," said Cousin Copeland, hesitatingly; "will you taste it also?"

The young officer accepted a share of the repast gravely, and then Cousin Copeland told his story. He was a simple soul. Miss Margaretta would have made the soldier believe she had come to town merely for her own lofty amusement or to buy jewels. It ended, however, in the comfortable eating of a good dinner at the hotel, and a cigar in Captain Newell's own room. (127)

Since the two men see each other as equals, Copeland has no qualms about accepting Newell's offer of assistance in finding a new tenant. He even goes so far as to invite Newell to spend the night during a later visit to the chagrin of his cousin. Anticipating the promise of a budding romance between Newell and Gardis, Copeland helps bring the story to a permanently hospitable close, just as Nina Silber might have predicted.

The politics of hospitality were not so easily banished, however, even in the South that Woolson imagined. In "Old Gardiston," the reconstructive pressure of new black citizens intrudes only briefly with the rioting freedmen and only to encourage white solidarity and a grudging "noblesse oblige" that brings Gardis and Captain Newell together. Old resentments can be eased through a newly national ethic of hospitality, it seems, as long as new political burdens do not frustrate a sense of well-heeled resolution. But the "pure, unconditional or infinite hospitality" that Derrida sees based on "an acceptance of risk" elsewhere complicates Woolson's postwar scene. In "Rodman the Keeper," her collection's title story, prejudices run too deep for characters to move forward, particularly when the politics of hospitality are tied to a more complex handing of race than Gardis Duke allows.

At first, a similar but more dramatic instance of hospitality's ethics makes a new household possible without marriage. In a small cabin at Andersonville National Cemetery, the Union veteran John Rodman opens his door to his former enemy, the dying Confederate veteran Ward De Rossett. For a tenuous moment, the "house divided" by sectionalism and war is made whole under one roof that also extends to an "old black freedman" named Pomp, at least as long as he plays the part of faithful slave for De Rossett and missionary subject for Rodman. But on Memorial Day, a parade of freed blacks comes to honor the cemetery's dead.

Woolson describes the "new-born dignity of the freedman" and portrays the African American community as a vital, self-directed presence full of potentially equal partners in the American political landscape.[21] Unfortunately, this is a possibility which Bettina Ward, the story's Gardis Duke, is too Southern to tolerate. When it comes to racial difference, she cannot accept the risk that unconditional hospitality requires. After the parade, Rodman ruefully notes to himself, "Not a white face," and Bettina Ward coolly responds, "Certainly not" (34). Indeed, the "rampant little rebel" cannot even bring herself to sign the cemetery's registry of visitors, and the story ends with no sense of closure.

If we compare the African American presence from one story to the next, the results are telling. In "Old Gardiston," freed blacks are seen to pose a threat in the form of a mob, which in turn brings the Northern and Southern characters together. In "Rodman the Keeper," envisioning the freed black population as a parade, as potentially equal partners in the political process, drives a divisive wedge between the Northern and Southern characters, who are likelier to foster a reunited national household only if "Pomp" remains a projection of white desires. Taken together in her collection, Woolson's stories prod her readers to imagine the possibilities of a civil society in which hospitality is a national ethical principle because national politics have been transformed.

In "Manifest Domesticity" Amy Kaplan shows how the antebellum discourses of domesticity and empire were inextricably linked and how both were "dependent upon racialized notions of the foreign." While domesticity was typically seen as an "anchor" or "feminine counterforce to the male activity of territorial conquest," Kaplan asserts that "domesticity is more mobile and less stabilizing; it travels in contradictory circuits both to expand and contract the boundaries of home and nation and to produce shifting conceptions of the foreign."[22] The discourse of hospitality in the nineteenth century was likewise bound up in conceptions of both domestic and national spaces and in conceptions of native and foreign populations, and it was similarly mobile in its construction of otherness. In fact, the question of what constitutes true hospitality was extremely important to Americans throughout the nineteenth century, and discourse on the obligations and limitations of hospitality could inform different cultural spheres, from the religious and the social to the economic and the political.[23]

Southern hospitality formed only a small part of this much larger body of ethically charged discourse in nineteenth-century American culture, and Woolson's Southern sketches a smaller part still. Yet in the years following the Civil War, the discourse of hospitality was adapted to articulate complex and often shifting fault lines between self and other, between region and nation, between upper and lower classes, and—inevitably—between white and black Americans.

Notes

1. Telfair Hodgson, "A Sermon in Behalf of the Southern Sufferers, preached by the Rev. Telfair Hodgson, at St. Mary's Church, Keyport, N.J., January 27, 1867" (Princeton, NJ: Printed at the Standard Office, 1867), 11. Further citations are indicated parenthetically in the text.

2. For example, Hodgson at one point declared, "The failure was owing in part too to the disorganized state of society, in which not even the United States forces stationed there could render all the protection required. There is in these states a dense negro population. Lately released from slavery, they but imperfectly understand the nature of their new found freedom. It seems that they intend to enjoy it to its fullest extent. They look upon liberty as an immunity from work. I myself have often heard them define 'freedom' as 'plenty to eat, plenty to wear and nothing to do.' With many of these people freedom has made no change. They work with the same docility and earnestness as before. But with the mass it has wrought a great change, which we hope may only be temporary. However, they still continue to indulge their favorite theory of freedom, and are of no use to the social community at the South. They continue to be consumers while they are not producers. At length they begin to be in want, and when there is little restraint they unhesitatingly appropriate the effects of the white population, which is struggling for a bare subsistence" (12).

3. Historians who have written about Southern hospitality have limited themselves almost exclusively to the antebellum period and have concerned themselves only with determining the origins and cultural meanings of the social practices associated with Southern hospitality. Economic historians such as Eugene Genovese and Raimondo Luraghi have portrayed Southern hospitality as evidence of conspicuous consumption and competition among wealthy planters. Cultural historians—most notably Bertram Wyatt-Brown, Kenneth Greenberg, and Rhys Isaac—have treated such priorities peripherally as a symptomatic expression of the Southern code of honor, and have also pointed to circumstantial factors such as the large distances between plantations, the dearth of public inns, and the relative lack of public welfare, all of which resulted in more pressure on the plantation home. While historians offer different theories on the origins and practices of hospitality in the antebellum South, they generally agree that the mythic dimensions of Southern hospitality eventually outran its practices. Indeed, in *The Transformation of Virginia*, Rhys Isaac goes so far as to claim that the social reality upon which the myths were based went out of fashion as early as 1800. See Eugene Genovese, *The Political Economy of Slavery*, 2nd ed. (Middletown, CT: Wesleyan University Press, 1988); Raimondo Luraghi, *The Rise and Fall of the Plantation South* (New York: Franklin Watts, 1978); Bertram Wyatt-Brown, *Southern Honor: Ethics and Behavior in the Old South*, anniversary ed. (Oxford: Oxford University Press, 2007); Kenneth S. Greenberg, *Honor and Slavery: Lies, Duels, Noses, Masks, Dressing as a Woman, Gifts, Strangers, Humanitarianism, Death, Slave Rebellions, the Proslavery Argument, Baseball, Hunting, and Gambling in the Old South* (Princeton, NJ: Princeton University Press, 1996); and Rhys Isaac, *The Transformation of Virginia: 1740–1790*, new ed. (Chapel Hill: University of North Carolina Press, 1999).

4. Jacques Derrida and Anne Dufourmantelle, *Of Hospitality: Anne Dufourmantelle Invites Jacques Derrida to Respond*, trans. Rachel Bowlby (Stanford: Stanford University Press, 2000), 25.

5. Qtd. in Mirielle Rosello, *Postcolonial Hospitality: The Immigrant as Guest* (Stanford: Stanford University Press, 2001), 11–12.

6. Jacques Derrida, "Hostipitality," trans. Barry Stocker and Forbes Morlock. *Angelaki* 5.3 (December 2000): 6.

7. In contrast to the modern tendency to view Southern hospitality as a natural and essential cultural attribute of the South, Southern claims to hospitality were openly assailed during the sectional crisis leading up to the Civil War. Narrative accounts and images of Southern hospitality

routinely appeared in travel narratives, almanacs, pamphlets, and fiction. While Southerners and sympathetic Northerners typically portrayed Southern hospitality as evidence of gracious civility and natural refinement, abolitionists vigorously questioned whether Southern social practices contingent upon slave labor could be called "hospitality" at all. For representative examples of sympathetic treatments (and attacks on Northern lack of hospitality), see Nehemiah Adams, D.D., *A South-Side View of Slavery; or, Three Months at the South, in 1854* (Boston: T. R. Marvin, 1855), 7–19, 44–53, 118–37; Rev. H. Cowles Atwater, A.M., *Incidents of a Southern Tour: or The South, as Seen with Northern Eyes* (Boston: J. P. Magee, 1857), 74–89, 116–20; David Brown, *The Planter: or, Thirteen Years in the South. By a Northern Man* (Philadelphia: H. Hooker, 1853), 32–35, 58–61, 116–17, 176–97, 198–206, 216; and Martha Haines Butt, *Antifanaticism* (Philadelphia: Lippincott, Grambo, 1853), especially the preface and the first chapter, "Southern Hospitality," 13–24. For representative attacks on Southern hospitality, see James Redpath, *The Roving Editor: or, Talks with Slaves in the Southern States* (New York: A. B. Burdick, 1859), 68–70, 107–13, 133–47, 179–84; Rev. Philo Tower, *Slavery Unmasked: Being a Truthful Narrative of a Three Years' Residence and Journeying in Eleven Southern States: To Which Is Added The Invasion of Kansas, Including the Last Chapter of Her Wrongs* (Rochester: E. Darrow & Brother, 1856), 398–417; and Francis Colburn Adams, *Manuel Pereira, or, The Sovereign Rule of South Carolina, With Views of Southern Laws, Life, and Hospitality* (Washington: Buell & Blanchard, 1853) and *Our World, or, The Slaveholder's Daughter* (Auburn, NY: Miller, Orton & Mulligan, 1855).

    8. Edward A. Pollard, *The Virginia Tourist: Sketches of the Springs and Mountains of Virginia* (Philadelphia: J. B. Lippincott, 1870). Further references will be cited parenthetically in the text. Pollard's travel guide was also serialized in *Lippincott's Magazine of Literature, Science and Education* that same year. The Lippincott publishing house had strong ties to Southern markets both before and after the war and published many pro-Southern titles; for discussions of the Lippincott house, see James Cephas Derby, *Fifty Years Among Authors, Books and Publishers* (New York: G. W. Carleton, 1884), 381–89; and Frank Luther Mott, *A History of American Magazines* (Cambridge, MA: Harvard University Press, 1957), III: 396–401.

    9. Nina Silber, *The Romance of Reunion: Northerners and the South, 1865–1900* (Chapel Hill: University of North Carolina Press, 1993), 92.

    10. Edward A. Pollard, *The Lost Cause Regained* (New York: G. W. Carleton, 1868), 155.

    11. Frederick B. Goddard, *Where to Emigrate and Why* (New York: Frederick B. Goddard, 1869), 336. Further references will be cited parenthetically in the text.

    12. Also see Charles F. Atkinson and Francis William Loring, *Cotton Culture and the South with Reference to Emigration* (Boston: A. Williams, 1869). In contrast to Pollard, some letters from Southern officials in these two emigration texts warn upper-class Northerners that they will not be well received in the South (see Goddard, *Where to Emigrate and Why*, 420–21, for example). For a series of widely conflicting impressions on the reception of Northerners in the South, see Atkinson and Loring, *Cotton Culture*, 67–84.

    13. David W. Blight, *Race and Reunion: The Civil War in American Memory* (Cambridge, MA: Harvard University Press, 2001), 260. Also see Jack P. Maddex Jr., *The Reconstruction of Edward A. Pollard: A Rebel's Conversion to Postbellum Unionism* (Chapel Hill: University of North Carolina Press, 1974). Maddex describes Pollard's remarkable evolution from Old South secessionist to New South unionist; but even as Pollard moved away from his Southern nationalist ideology, he remained committed to the doctrine of white supremacy and the social separation of the races.

    14. *Oxford English Dictionary* http://www.oed.com/.

    15. Silber, *The Romance of Reunion*, 69.

    16. For evidence of Woolson's shrewd nostalgia, which quietly incorporated white Northerners of a certain class, see her travel sketch of Charleston, "Up the Ashley and Cooper," *Harper's Monthly*

(December 1875): 1–24. Woolson seems to celebrate the class distinctions implicit in the discourse of Southern hospitality; she also reminds her readers that the original Charlestonians included "the only *bona fide* United States nobility of which we have record" (3), and she goes on to paint a romantic picture of the "great magnificence" and "lavishness" of the planter lifestyle. There is little mention of the war or slavery and no hint of the complicated politics of reconstruction. Instead, Woolson's narrative, like much of the period literature described by Silber, seems "directed to the potential tourist" (73). Her travel account opens with a detailed picture of Charleston from the aerial view of St. Michael's Church spire, where it is possible to make out the Battery, Fort Sumter, Morris Island, and "the old ridge of Battery Wagner," though Woolson does not elaborate. Instead, after briefly describing the "picturesque" qualities of the city streets and architecture, her narrative moves "up the two rivers to search out the old manors, with their legends and history, now almost forgotten, of colonial times and of the Revolution" (4). Published on the eve of the nation's centennial year, "Up the Ashley and Cooper" turns away from the present—from the fresh memories of the Civil War and the stubborn political uncertainties of reconstruction—and back toward the shared mythology of the colonial era and the Revolutionary War, when Northerners and Southerners stood united against the British.

17. Wyatt-Brown, *Southern Honor*, 337.

18. Constance Fenimore Woolson, *Rodman the Keeper: Southern Sketches* (New York: Appleton, 1880), 106. The discussion of both "Old Gardiston" and "Rodman the Keeper" is based on the stories as they appeared in this collection, which will be cited parenthetically in the text.

19. Greenberg, *Honor and Slavery*, 70.

20. Wyatt-Brown, *Southern Honor*, 339.

21. Woolson elsewhere shows that this sentiment is not limited to Southerners. In "King David," the main character David King, a Northern teacher working with the freedmen, invites two of his students to dine in his home, yet he refrains from eating with them, going so far as to fix an entirely new supper after they depart. The racist representations of African Americans in this text stand in sharp contrast to this Memorial Day scene from "Rodman the Keeper." It is fair to say that Woolson's writings contain conflicting representations of race, and it can be difficult to locate her position precisely among the views articulated by her characters and her narrators.

22. Amy Kaplan, "Manifest Domesticity," *No More Separate Spheres! A New Wave American Studies Reader*, ed. Cathy N. Davidson and Jessamyn Hatcher (Durham, NC: Duke University Press, 2002), 185.

23. A brief survey of topics covered in chapter 11 of Julia McNair Wright's *The Complete Home* (Philadelphia: J. C. McCurdy, 1879) suggests the sometimes contradictory conceptions of hospitality in the nineteenth century. Titled "Hospitality in the Home," the chapter refers to hospitality as "the queen of social virtues" and lists more than thirty subheadings, including the following: "Ostentatious hospitality—Spasmodic—Nervous— . . . Common-sense hospitality—Hospitality without apology—Biblical hospitality—Selfish hospitality—Excessive hospitality—Elegant hospitality—The right kind of hospitality—Bible instances—Plainness in hospitality . . . Abuse of hospitality—Good Samaritan deeds—The poor— . . . Decrease of hospitality—Old-time manners— . . . Choicest form of rural hospitality" (ix). It is worth noting that Wright also published a reconstruction novel titled *The Cabin in the Brush* (Philadelphia: J. P. Skelly, 1870), which focuses on the plight of refugees in the aftermath of the war. The biblical imperative of hospitality is the novel's recurring message.

Imagining Sites of Memory in the Post–Civil War South

The National Cemetery in Woolson's "Rodman the Keeper"

—Martin T. Buinicki

In a call for the establishment of national cemeteries at the end of the Civil War, a contributor to *Harper's New Monthly Magazine* writes, "We go for closing up the war now, and ending it fitly and nobly."[1] Such a conclusion, the author argues, could only come once the "scattered dead of the Union army, whether white or black" were gathered into state-sanctioned resting places (321). Rather than bringing closure, however, the writer suggests that these cemeteries might serve an educational function: "This would give a national cemetery to every state affected by the war, on the field of our greatest victory or at place of most importance, to stand as a monument forever to the South, and to us all, of the crime and folly of Secession" (321). Such seemingly contradictory ends—marking the cessation of hostilities while at the same time forever invoking their cause—call into question exactly what function these national cemeteries would serve for the nation's recovery, and what memories would be preserved. How would national cemeteries, admitting only Union dead, promote reconciliation in the South, and how would this effort to memorialize those lost in battle reconcile the postwar present with the Confederate past?

It is precisely this question that Constance Fenimore Woolson takes up in her 1877 story "Rodman the Keeper." Set in the Reconstruction-era South, the story critiques any effort to evade the legacy of the war through the embrace of antebellum history and significantly complicates the notion that romantic union can signify the healing of national division. Whatever reconciliation that emerges comes as characters confront the gaping chasm between an irretrievably lost past and an uncertain future, leaving them struggling for meaning in an ambiguous and restless present. In a nation where, as Woolson laments, "the closely ranged graves [...] seem already a part of the past, that near past which in our hurrying American life is even now so far away" (127), Southerners and Northerners alike find themselves longing for those places and people that once defined them.[2] In "Rodman the Keeper" Woolson depicts how this longing aids in the creation of what the critic Pierre Nora terms *lieux de mémoire*, "sites of memory" that serve as symbolic representations of a collective "will to remember" offering some hope of reunion without denying the difficulties of either the past or present.

When Woolson's story was published in the collection *Rodman the Keeper: Southern Sketches*, a critic for the *Atlantic Monthly* noted, "[Woolson] has at least pointed out a region where much can be done, and where she can herself do good work if she will keep 'closer to the record.'"[3] In criticizing the "realism" of Woolson's heroines, who "read like what one finds oftener in poor novels than in real life,"[4] the reviewer draws attention to the problem of historically accurate representations that Nora sees underlying the collapse of memory into history. "Memory," Nora argues, "is a perpetually actual phenomenon, a bond tying us to the eternal present; history is a representation of the past. [...] Memory installs remembrance within the sacred; history, always prosaic, releases it again"; for Nora, "History's goal and ambition is not to exalt but to annihilate what has in reality taken place."[5] Woolson strays from "the record," and, in doing so, reveals the present-day conflict her characters face in the postwar South; as Leonardo Buonomo notes of Woolson's Civil War stories, "salvaged from oblivion and the omissions of historiography are for the most part, not surprisingly, the bitter memories, resentment, the struggle for survival and sacrifices of southern women."[6] Even more than some form of missing content, however, "Rodman the Keeper" renders visible the rapidly expanding division between history and memory, representation and lived experience, a historicized past and the brutal realities of the present. In Woolson's story, the national cemetery at its center and the rituals surrounding Memorial Day not only capture something otherwise lost in Reconstruction-era history but also hold out the possibility for citizens to make peace both with the past and with one another.

In the decade after the war, Americans, particularly in the North, were confronting the question not only of what to do with the scattered war dead, but also of how to honor their sacrifice and commemorate their deeds as a new generation was rising with little personal memory of war and the years that preceded it. As an author for *Harper's Monthly* noted in 1876, "The name of 'Mason and Dixon's Line' is one that to the rising generation is fast losing its significance and power, though for the first half of the century it was in every one's mouth [...] as the watch-word and battle-cry of slavery on the one hand and freedom on the other."[7] A local clergyman preparing a history of the soldiers from Norwich, Connecticut, lamented, "So many years have elapsed since the war closed, that the remembrance of many facts and incidents that should have been preserved, has faded away."[8] This lament about the vast expanse of time separating the historian from his subject was published in 1873.

The national cemetery in "Rodman the Keeper" depicts the creation of a site of memory that will preserve the past in the present, a space dedicated to the work of remembering, making the act of memory a lived experience somehow different from simple textual study. The story begins with an epigraph, selections from a poem by Thomas Bailey Aldrich. In the first stanza, the speaker suggests that the events of the past are fleeting, only to reverse course and insist that the graves of the fallen will always bring the Civil War to mind:

> The long years come and go,
> And the Past,
> The sorrowful, splendid Past,
> With its glory and its woe,
> Seems never to have been.
> —Seems never to have been?
> O somber days and grand,
> How ye crowd back once more,
> Seeing our heroes' graves are green
> By the Potomac and the Cumberland,
> And in the valley of the Shenandoah! (124)

And yet if funereal reminders are scattered across the landscape, their effect seems less than salutary. Woolson crops the poem considerably to include this much-later stanza:

> When we remember how they died,—
> In dark ravine and on the mountainside,
> In leaguered fort and fire-encircled town,
> And where the iron ships went down,
> How their dear lives were spent
> In the weary hospital-tent
> In the cockpit's crowded hive,
> —it seems
> Ignoble to be alive! (125)

So, in the story's opening epigraph, grave sites can invoke the past, but the result of such memory appears to be a wish to obliterate the present, or at least to deny it.[9] This is our troubling introduction to the story of John Rodman, a Union veteran and keeper of a government cemetery located on the grounds of a former Confederate prison. Rodman's life is consumed by the process of trying to record the names of the dead. Even though his quarters include a "loud-ticking clock on the wall" (125), Rodman seems in a world where time has literally stood still: "The small town, a mile distant, stood turning its back on the cemetery; but the keeper could see the pleasant, rambling old mansions, each with its rose garden and neglected outlying fields, the empty Negro quarters falling into ruin, and everything just as it stood when on that April morning the first gun was fired on Sumter" (125). The narrator does not acknowledge the contradiction between these last two statements—clearly everything is not as it stood at the firing on Sumter—instead emphasizing a South that has turned its back on the cemetery in an apparent effort to deny the present and this tangible reminder of the Union victory. In this apparent stasis, Rodman spends his time logging the names of the buried, even though the graves themselves do not seem to fulfill the memorial duty suggested in the story's epigraph: "it was the keeper's habit to walk slowly up and down the path until the shadows veiled the mounds on each side [...]. 'So time will efface our little lives and sorrows,' he mused, 'and we shall be as nothing in the indistinguishable past'" (127). As the narrative begins, then, the cemetery appears to be a precarious site of memory at best.

The uncertain signification of the burial mounds is highlighted by the grave that preoccupies Rodman the most, that of "Blank Rodman, Company A, One Hundred and Sixth New York." Because of the blank, Rodman is left to imagine both a memory of and an attachment to this other Rodman: "I remember that regiment; it came from the extreme northern part of the State. Blank Rodman must have melted down here, coming as he did from the half-arctic region along the St. Lawrence. [...] I am convinced that Blank is a relative,' he said to himself; 'distant, perhaps, but still a kinsman'" (128–29). The grave markers can only point to the past, yielding memories that are strangely divorced from actual people and events, like Rodman's unnamed relative.

Rodman's inevitable confrontation with the post–Civil War present is itself oddly mediated by memory. One day he goes in search of a spring on a neighboring plantation, thinking to himself, "If it could only be like the spring down under the rocks where I used to drink when I was a boy!" (129). Of course, his New England past is as foreclosed to him as his irreclaimable kinship with Blank Rodman, and what he discovers instead is a dying Confederate veteran. This is the vision that continually wipes away his other memories. One night there is a storm, and "Memory brought back the steep New England hillsides shedding their rain into the brooks, which grew in a night to torrents and filled the rivers so that they overflowed their banks; then, suddenly, an old house in a sunken corner of a waste rose before his eyes, and he seemed to see the rain dropping from a moldy ceiling on the straw where a white face lay" (133). His life before the war is barred from his recollection, not by the war itself but by the present human representative of both its cost and its aftermath.

In addition to the dying Confederate, the story also features a young woman, Bettina Ward, the man's cousin. She is not quite old enough to have truly understood the hardships of the war years, but she is haunted by memories of *others'* reactions to it: "I was but a child; yet I remember the tears of my mother, and the grief of all around us" (145). These impressionistic memories are supplemented by texts; her reading includes "a life of General Lee and three or four shabby little volumes printed at the South during the war" (138). She is haunted by a past she is unable to recall directly, and her relationship to the Civil War—the defining event of her life as it brought ruin and death to her family, leaving her to struggle in the aftermath—is in part mediated by books. For Bettina, then, memory as a lived and ongoing experience is continually at risk of lapsing into history, archival traces embodied in external sources. It teeters on the brink of becoming what Nora calls "indirect"—that is, "memory transformed by its passage through history."[10]

And yet the South that Bettina now inhabits is not simply formed by its antebellum history and stories of the war itself; the national cemetery that features so prominently in the narrative is a physical site dedicated not to the former glory of the South but to the ongoing memory of the war's costs. With its government sanction and Union groundskeeper, it is ultimately representative of the present struggles of Reconstruction. Woolson writes,

> One morning in May the keeper was working near the flagstaff, when his eyes fell upon a procession coming down the road which led from the town and turning toward the cemetery. No one ever came that way: what could it mean? It drew near, entered the gate, and showed itself to be Negroes walking two and two [. . .] not one was without a badge of mourning. All carried flowers, common blossoms from the little gardens behind the cabins that stretched around the town on the outskirts—the new forlorn cabins with their chimneys of piled stones and ragged patches of corn; each little darkey had his bouquet and marched solemnly along, rolling his eyes around, but without even the beginning of a smile, while the elders moved forward with gravity, the bubbling, irrepressible gayety of the Negro subdued by the newborn dignity of the freedman.
> "Memorial Day," thought the keeper; "I had forgotten it." (140)

The irony of Rodman's forgetfulness is of course unmistakable, and it indicates the dilemma in which Woolson's characters find themselves. Memories of life in the pre–Civil War United States are denied by youth, or, in Rodman's case, by the demands of the present, or they are mediated through crumbling estates and textual traces. The nature of Civil War memories has yet to be determined, but those too seem oddly inaccessible to these characters. Rodman, a veteran, forgets

Memorial Day; for all of his tallying in the ledger, there is still the "Blank" Rodman, and he himself is not John Rodman, veteran, but "the Keeper." How the traumatic events of the war will ultimately be remembered is left uncertain, yet, in her invocation of Memorial Day, Woolson suggests how acts of commemoration can create sites of memory like this unnamed national cemetery that will serve to integrate the past into the troubled present. We see this integration in the freedmen's flowers, marking remembrance of the past and serving as reminders of the "new forlorn cabins" and the realities of life during Reconstruction.

Woolson's portrayal of Memorial Day raises some significant questions regarding the exact setting of the story, in terms of both time and place. Although Woolson does not name the cemetery, Karen Weekes has asserted that it is most likely Andersonville and that, contrary to Woolson's description, the cemetery was visited by both Northerners and Southerners, at least on July 4, 1879.[11] While it is true that by the 1870s there was significantly more shared celebration and commemoration of the Civil War, sectional tensions nonetheless persisted. The historian William A. Blair refers to the period as "The Era of Mixed Feelings," and argues that the centennial of national independence, for instance, became an important moment for Southerners to show their patriotism and re-solidify traditional power structures as Reconstruction came to an end:

> Former Confederates did show a greater willingness to make peace with the North during the mid 1870s, but the literature of reunion, with rare exception, has overlooked the political reasons behind this stand. Ex-Confederates reached across the bloody chasm to protect their hold on regional power, adopting accommodations so authorities would not have reason to intervene in southern affairs and would let the best white men govern. [...] With the centennial in 1876, white southerners began to celebrate July Fourth once again, but it was not because they had become converted nationalists. They used the anniversary to bolster regional instead of national importance.[12]

It is unclear exactly why Woolson omits Southerners from the Memorial Day remembrance in her story. The move certainly works to deny any appearance of inevitable reconciliation, even a politically motivated and, for a Northerner, suspect one. Weekes suggests that to depict Southern participation would have diluted the sectional tensions that the author explores in the story: "If Woolson had represented the cemetery as visited by both sides [...], she would have removed some of Rodman's isolation and diminished the theme of dichotomy and resentment between the North and South."[13] This may indeed be the case, as we are told that Rodman "lived and moved in a vacuum; wherever he went there was presently no one save himself; the very shopkeeper who sold him sugar seemed turned into a man of wood" (126). Rodman's isolation at the beginning of the story highlights his interactions with Ward, the Confederate veteran, implying that it is on the level of soldiers that reconciliation can be found, as Rodman imagines the spirit of his dead kinsman Blank Rodman remarking, "We do not object to the brave soldier who honestly fought for his cause, even though he fought on the other side" (134). Including a white Southern citizenry would certainly have diluted the exchange between Rodman and Ward.

Still, readings such as these are premised on the assumption that the cemetery is indeed Andersonville in the late 1870s. While scholarly research has provided a geographic location, Woolson's story refuses to offer a specific setting. Rodman's lament that "not a white face" had attended the Memorial Day ceremony suggests that the reunion rhetoric and cross-sectional observations becoming more prominent in the late 1870s had not yet emerged, a suggestion underlined by Rodman's own perception of the holiday:

> Now, the keeper had not much sympathy with the strewing of flowers, North or South; he had seen the beautiful ceremony more than once turned into a political demonstration. Here, however, in this small, isolated, interior town, there was nothing of that kind; the whole population of white faces laid their roses and wept true tears on the graves of their lost ones in the village churchyard when the Southern Memorial Day came round, and just as naturally the whole population of black faces went out to the national cemetery with their flowers on the day when, throughout the North, spring blossoms were laid on the graves of the soldiers. (140)

Elizabethada Wright argues, "The differences in Southern and Northern passions can be seen in Memorial Day celebrations. [. . .] The South's Confederate Memorial Days outdid (and still outdo) the North's in speeches, flowers, parades, and attendance . . . The keeper of a Confederate cemetery could never forget Memorial Day."[14] This may be true, but here Rodman seems explicitly to reject Memorial Day, not from a lack of passion (as he clearly respects "true tears") but precisely because of invidious comparisons and unspoken political agendas. Rodman's sentiments on the holiday suggest that the story is set earlier in Reconstruction, when tensions remained quite high.

As early as 1869, writers for both the *New York Times* and the *Richmond (Va.) State Journal* lamented "this war of the roses," which seemed only to continue the past conflict. While the writer for the *Times* attacked both North and South in a piece entitled "Shall the Hatchet Ever be Buried?" [sic], the writer for the *Richmond State Journal* is particularly harsh regarding the Confederate Memorial Day, partly in response to an erroneous report in another paper that misrepresented the *Times* piece as critiquing solely the North:

> Your ladies began it two years before the Grand Army of the Republic resorted to it as a measure of retaliation. They had no precedent in this or any other country for it. The soldiers who had fallen in all the previous wars in America, had been permitted to sleep their last sleep on the fields where they fell, and the ground was hallowed by their dust. [...] Not so, however, with our civil strife. Its rancors must not be permitted to die out; but each year the ghosts of the dead must be invoked to renew the slumbering animosities of sectional hate, to keep open the wounds of war, and teach their little children that vengeance is a holy duty, which they must study to accomplish. It is unfortunate that this "battle of the flowers" should have begun; but the ladies of the South are responsible.[15]

Rodman's lament about "political demonstrations" hearkens back to this criticism, and further evidence pointing to an earlier period during Reconstruction can be found in the freedman's statement that "we's kep' de day now two years, sah, befo' you came, sah, an we's teachin' de chil'en to keep it, sah" (141). This would seem to suggest the time period to be around 1870 or 1871, since the first Union "Decoration Day" celebration was in 1868.[16]

Still, Rodman's comment regarding the racial make-up of the mourners suggests a later date; even in 1871 there was controversy about allowing the public to decorate Confederate graves in Arlington National Cemetery.[17] Rodman could hardly regret a lack of white participation in the South if such participation was at least suspect, if not barred. The story seems to conflate the increased openness in memorial celebrations of the later 1870s (in keeping with the time of the story's publication) with the sectional attitudes of the early part of the decade.[18] Rodman's attitudes about the "politics" in such celebrations might offer an explanation and an insight into Woolson's own views. The story calls for an "authentic" act of commemoration, memory divorced from the political aspects of the post-Reconstruction United States.[19]

Troublingly, the narrator devalues the participation of African Americans in such a project: "They knew dimly that the men who lay beneath those mounds had done something wonderful for them and for their children; and so they came bringing their blossoms, with little intelligence but with much love" (141). Despite the patronizing tone, this loving connection between the freedmen and the fallen plays a crucial role in rendering the cemetery a site of memory. Nora notes, "Memory takes root in the concrete, in spaces, gestures, images, and objects; history binds itself strictly to temporal continuities, to progressions and to relations between things."[20] The act of bringing flowers, of the unrepresented sense of "something wonderful," grants the actions of the African-American celebrants a particular weight, locating true memory in their gestures near the graves rather than in the prosaic descriptions of historical progress.

While there are compelling possibilities in the portrayal of this freedmen's Memorial Day, Woolson ultimately emphasizes white participation as the most important; "Rodman the Keeper" embodies hope for the creation of an authentic site of memory in the unreconstructed Bettina Ward. Near the end of the story, she comes to the cemetery late at night to kneel at the graves. When Rodman confronts her, they have the following exchange:

> "I wished to come here once, and I did not wish to meet you."
>
> "Why did you wish to come?"
>
> "Because Ward was here—and because—because—never mind. It is enough that I wished to walk once among those mounds."
>
> "And pray there?"
>
> "Well—and if I did!" said the girl defiantly.
>
> Rodman stood facing her, with his arms folded; his eyes rested on her face; he said nothing.
>
> "I am going away tomorrow," began Miss Ward again [...] "I have sold the place, and I shall never return, I think; I am going far away."
>
> "Where?"
>
> "To Tennessee."
>
> "That is not so very far," said the keeper, smiling.
>
> "There I shall begin a new existence," pursued the voice, ignoring the comment.
>
> "You have scarcely begun the old; you are hardly more than a child, now."
>
> (144)

The text implies that Bettina cannot simply flee: as she contemplates her new existence, her identity seems threatened. She becomes "the voice" as she tells Rodman that she has "sold the place." Bettina seems further removed from both herself and us as she leaves her home to begin again. It is only when a new existence can be at peace with the old, Woolson suggests, when both the freedmen and the survivors North and South can commemorate and mourn the dead, that these characters come to terms with the rapidly changing world around them.

The physical location and the emotional investment of the prayerful gesture ground the characters and grant the cemetery its significance. However, while Bettina's walk in the cemetery seems to help solidify it as a site of memory, a moment later she refuses a request to take part in another ritual, one that highlights the tenuous separation between memory and history:

> The keeper had not moved from the doorstep. Now he turned his face. "Before you go—go away for ever from this place—will you write your name in my register," he said— "the visitors' register? The Government had it prepared for the throngs who would visit these graves; but with the exception of the blacks, who can not write, no one has come, and the register is empty. Will you write your name? Yet do not write it unless you can think gently of the men who lie there under the grass. I believe you do think gently of them, else why have you come of your own accord to stand by the side of their graves?" [...]
> "I can not! Shall I, Bettina Ward, set my name down in black and white as a visitor to this cemetery, where lie fourteen thousand of the soldiers who killed my father, my three brothers, my cousins; who brought desolation upon all our house, and ruin upon all our neighborhood, all our State, and all our country?—for the South *is* our country, and not your North. Shall I forget these things? Never!" (145)

By signing the log, Bettina would become part of the historical record, a trace of past events. To become part of this history, she suggests, would mean denying her own memories of the Confederacy and the war; ironically, the historical preservation of her visit would come at the cost of her forgetting all that her family and "country" have suffered. At the same time, signing the visitors' log is part of the ritual of visiting the cemetery, one that continues in many places to this day.[21] Bettina has conspicuously refused to take part, backing away precisely at that locus where memory and history meet in the archive.

The other important aspect of this passage is the indication of how the freed African-Americans who visit the cemetery are denied a place in the historical record. Their attendance to Memorial Day is integral to transforming the geographic place into a "site of memory," but their contribution, it is suggested, will be invisible to history, for "the register is empty" (145). Even while the participation of both the white Southern belle and the freed slaves constitutes what Nora describes as a "symbolic action" that will "block the work of forgetting," their unwillingness or inability to sign the visitors' log leaves their action both incomplete and outside the grasp of history.[22] Without this written record, we are forced to turn back to the site itself, which is, Nora argues, precisely its function: "Contrary to historical objects, however, *lieux de mémoire* have no referent in reality: or, rather, they are their own referent: pure, exclusively self-referential signs. That is not to say that they are without content, physical presence, or history; it is to suggest that what makes them *lieux de mémoire* is precisely that by which they escape from history."[23]

While Bettina's refusal to sign the log suggests the pessimism that some critics see as a defining feature of "Rodman the Keeper," it is also the act that helps to confirm the national cemetery as a site of memory holding out hope for possible reconciliation. As Wright puts it, "Bettina offers an alternative memory, one not told in the national cemetery, a memory that makes clear that the South is its own country and that rejects the claim that the North has become the entire country."[24] While it is true that Bettina's refusal signifies her continued sectional animosity, that does not negate her earlier gesture, her prayers among the graves, where hope in the story might be found and where memory is finally preserved.

If Woolson offers the national cemetery as a site of memory, it is worth asking what is to be forgotten. Such a question may reveal what Weekes describes as "northern bias" in this Southern tale. When the Confederate veteran dies, he is not interred in the national cemetery, regardless of his newfound rapprochement with Rodman: "The keeper watched the small procession as it passed his gate on its way to the churchyard in the village" (143). His burial in the town churchyard recalls the restrictions imposed upon the government cemetery, and so do the muttered comments of the helpless doctor who visits Ward before his death: "the old gentleman mounted his horse and rode away, his first and last visit to a national cemetery. 'National!' he said to himself—'national!'" (138). His remark reflects the anger felt by many white Southerners as the national cemeteries were created. An editor for the *Richmond Daily Examiner* wrote, "'The Nation's Dead,' as our stricken opponents are called, are abundantly cared for by their Government. We, it is true, poor and needy, have to contribute to the magnificent mausoleums that enshrine their crumbling relicks [sic]. The nation contemns [sic] our dead. They are left in deserted places to rot into oblivion."[25] While the legislation creating the national cemetery system contained no such overt condemnation, it did spell out clearly who was to be allowed burial. By 1870, this language had acquired a striking specificity in a bill allowing for the burial of veterans in the cemeteries: "That the body of any one who served as an officer or a soldier of any of the armies of the United States during the war for the suppression of the rebellion, and was honorably discharged from such service, who may hereafter die [. . .] may be buried in any one of the national cemeteries established by acts of Congress."[26] Confederate soldiers were simply not part of the equation in the early establishment of the cemeteries, leaving them "out of sight" and outside of the national sites of memory.[27]

While the Confederate is denied his place in the cemetery, Woolson ends "Rodman the Keeper" with an inclusive gesture and at least a suggestion of voluntary reunion. If Bettina's prayers in the cemetery represent her recognition of what has been lost, a transitory action that evades the signifying practices of history, then Rodman's final action also demonstrates a subtle attempt to preserve a memory of

Southern struggles. A week after Bettina departs, Rodman returns to the family's estate, which has been purchased by a newcomer from New England:

> "Pulling down the old house, are you?" said the keeper, leaning idly on the gate, which was already flanked by a new fence.
> "Yes," replied the Maine man, pausing; "it was only an old shell, just ready to tumble on our heads. You're the keeper over yonder, an't you?" (He already knew everybody within a circle of five miles.)
> "Yes. I think I should like those vines if you have no use for them," said Rodman, pointing to the uprooted greenery that once screened the old piazza.
> "Wuth about twenty-five cents, I guess," said the Maine man, handing them over. (146)

The vines in question had been planted by Bettina earlier in the story: "It was a woman's pathetic effort to cover up what can not be covered—poverty" (138). The vines, then, evoke Bettina and her pride, as well the present destitution suffered by Southerners during Reconstruction. For the "Maine man," however, they simply signify monetary value. His ignorance regarding the pathos embodied in the vines is highlighted by Woolson's repeated reference to his place of origin. The "Maine man" may have moved to the South, but, for all of his knowledge of his neighbors, Woolson clearly does not view him as becoming a part of the community or helping to forward the cause of reunion. As isolated as Rodman is from the townspeople, he has similarly been separated from his Northern roots, and his interactions with Bettina and her cousin have clearly had an impact. When contrasted with the exploitative and geographically identified "Maine man" and his preferences, Rodman's decision to take the vines suggests a gesture of true memory, its meaning—beyond a desire not to forget what has occurred—left undefined, transitory but real.

In her discussion of the scene, Wright notes,

> [T]he keeper of the national cemetery—the one with material resources to create national memory of the North's story but filled with this new passion for the South's—attempts to save a piece of Bettina's memory, purchasing from the Northerner for twenty-five cents the vines that Bettina had planted to cover her postbellum poverty. It is this memory as well as memories of the De Rossetts' absent grandeur that haunt the reader and Rodman at the end of this story. Absence is more potent than Rodman's very present national cemetery.[28]

As Wright points out, Rodman's actions in the final scene are an attempt at preserving memory; however, such an act is not in opposition to the "material" national cemetery. Rather, just as Bettina's prayers mark an emotional gesture that coincides with the physical presence of the cemetery, Rodman's purchase of the vines binds him to the De Rossett estate. The two actions are parallel and both work to render the geographic spaces something more—sites of memory that point to the possibility of reconciliation through a mutual act of remembering.

Of course, as Wright observes, the present-day Andersonville site in Georgia on which this story is likely based may not have succeeded in maintaining the memory of those who are buried there, as even the sculpture at the entrance of the cemetery is dedicated not to Union soldiers but to all prisoners of war. "Like Rodman who forgot Memorial Day," Wright notes, "many seem to forget the prisoners of Andersonville as well as what they fought for."[29] And yet in spite of the absence of memory at a given geographic site, Woolson's nameless cemetery and its stoic keeper remain. Nora writes, "[M]emory has never known more than two forms of legitimacy: historical and literary. These have run parallel to each other but until now always separately. At present the boundary between the two is blurring."[30] Woolson's under-appreciated story "Rodman the Keeper" illustrates the literary power of memory after the Civil War, when national cemeteries first required "keepers." For Woolson, the site of memory emerges from the bond formed when the freed slaves pay their respects, when Bettina bows her head in prayer among the graves, and when Rodman preserves the simple vines symbolic of her pride and perseverance. Finally, a continual return to stories like Woolson's ensures that a memory of the Civil War and its aftermath survives beyond the steady march of history.

Notes

1. James F. Russling, "National Cemeteries," *Harper's Monthly* (August 1866): 321. *Making of America*, Cornell University Library, May 6, 2007, http://cdl.library.cornell.edu/moa/. I am grateful to my research assistant, Johanna Brinkley, for her assistance in locating this and other historical documents.

2. Constance Fenimore Woolson, "Rodman the Keeper," *Constance Fenimore Woolson: Selected Stories and Travel Narratives*, ed. Victoria Brehm and Sharon Dean (Knoxville: University of Tennessee Press, 2004), 127. Further references will be cited parenthetically in the text.

3. Thomas Sergeant Perry, "Some Recent Novels," *Atlantic Monthly* (July 1880): 125. *Making of America*, Cornell University Library, May 6, 2007, http://cdl.library.cornell.edu/cgi-bin/moa/.

4. Perry, "Some Recent Novels," 125.

5. Pierre Nora, "Between Memory and History: Les Lieux de Mémoire," trans. Marc Roudebush, *History and Memory in African-American Culture*, ed. Geneviève Fabre and Robert O'Meally (New York: Oxford University Press, 1994), 285, 286.

6. Leonardo Buonomo, "The Other Face of History in Constance Fenimore Woolson's Southern Stories," *Canadian Review of American Studies* 28.3 (1998): 15. Where Buonomo sees "Rodman the Keeper" as a "pessimistic counterpart" to Woolson's "Old Gardiston" (24), however, I argue that any hope in either of these stories is ultimately found in "Rodman the Keeper."

7. Rev. Tryon Edwards, "Mason and Dixon's Line," *Harper's Monthly* (September 1876): 549. *Making of America*, Cornell University Library. May 6, 2007, http://cdl.library.cornell.edu/cgi-bin/moa/.

8. Malcolm McGregor Dana, *The Norwich memorial; the annals of Norwich, New London country, Connecticut, in the great rebellion of 1861–65* (Norwich, CT: J. J. Jewett, 1873): iii–iv. *Making of America*, University of Michigan. May 6, 2007, http://name.umdl.umich.edu/acl1756.0001.001.

9. Elizabethada A. Wright argues that Woolson employs the poem to "alert her readers not to trust Roman's credibility" (37): "In verses not included by Woolson at the beginning of 'Rodman,' Aldrich's narrator bemoans that 'Never sweetheart, or friend, / Wan pale mother, or bride, / Over these mounds shall bend,' concluding by asking the South to 'learn to hold [the Union dead] dear' (643). Both Woolson and her audience would have known that Aldrich's request would most likely be heeded because there were stories of Southern women caring for the Union dead" (36–37). See Wright, "Keeping Memory: The Cemetery and Rhetorical Memory in Woolson's 'Rodman the Keeper,'" *Studies in the Literary Imagination* 39.1 (2006): 29–54. It is difficult to address exactly what Woolson or her contemporaries might have known or thought about Southern women caring for Union graves, particularly in light of the continuing tensions that lay just under the surface of memorial celebrations and the existence of national cemeteries. Wright does not address the stanzas that Woolson does choose to include as her epigraph, stanzas that seem much more preoccupied with the grave as a repository of memory and a provocation to the living.

10. Nora, "Between Memory and History," 290, 289.

11. Karen Weekes, "Northern Bias in Constance Fenimore Woolson's *Rodman the Keeper: Southern Sketches*," *Southern Literary Journal* 32.2 (2000): 113–14.

12. William A. Blair, *Cities of the Dead: Contesting the Memory of the Civil War in the South, 1865–1914* (Chapel Hill: University of North Carolina Press, 2004), 107.

13. Weekes, "Northern Bias in Constance Fenimore Woolson's *Rodman the Keeper: Southern Sketches*," 114.

14. Wright, "Keeping Memory," 45.

15. "The Origin of Decoration Day. From *The Richmond (Va.) State Journal*," *New York Times*, June 14, 1869, 1. See also "Shall the Hatchet Ever be Buried?" [sic], *New York Times*, June 3, 1869, 4.

16. Blair, *Cities of the Dead*, 71.

17. Blair, *Cities of the Dead*, 74.

18. This is not to say that sectional animosity regarding Decoration Day had completely dissipated by mid-decade. A writer for the *New York Times* noted in 1875, "We presume it will be found on examination, that Decoration Day is to the great majority of those who take part in it a patriotic demonstration, awakening a spirit which is not consistent with paying the same honors to the dead of both sides." See "Decoration Day," *New York Times*, May 25, 1875, 6. Still, the author writes, "If there are those who prefer to decorate all graves alike, let them do so without criticism or opposition. Those who do not share the disposition will concede that it is a kindly one, which may bear good fruit" (6). This conciliatory tone is certainly different from what prevailed during the late 1860s and early 1870s.

19. Such nonpartisan celebrations may have been hard to come by during this period. A dispatch to the *New York Times* provided this description of Memorial Day at the national cemetery in Wilmington, North Carolina, in 1876: "Several ex-Confederate soldiers were present and laid flowers on several graves. The cemetery is in splendid condition. Each grave had a small United States flag planted above it. [...] The public offices were closed, the bells were tolled, and the stores were closed when the Confederate dead were decorated; but not so to-day; all stores were kept open; and the bells were not tolled. There were fully ten thousand people inside the cemetery." See "Memorial Day Elsewhere," *New York Times*, May 31, 1876, 2. This seems a good example of what Blair refers to as the "mixed feelings" of this period.

20. Nora, "Between Memory and History," 286.

21. The Cambridge American Cemetery and Memorial for U.S. soldiers outside of Cambridge, England, has just such a registry. When I visited with a historian friend, she urged me to sign the book because, she asserted, historians relied upon just these documents to conduct their work.

22. Nora, "Between Memory and History," 295, 295–96.

23. Nora, "Between Memory and History," 300.

24. Wright, "Keeping Memory," 38.

25. Quoted in Blair, *Cities of the Dead*, 53.

26. U.S. Congress, A Bill to provide for the burial of deceased ex-officers and soldiers of the United States Army in the national cemeteries, H.R. 1296, 41st Cong., 2nd sess., Washington: GPO, 1870.

27. Even given the passion for the "Lost Cause," Confederate fears may not have been wholly unfounded. In 1903, the Civil War veteran and author Ambrose Bierce wrote a short piece entitled "A Bivouac of the Dead," contrasting the "beautiful national cemetery at Grafton, duly registered" with the "forgotten graves" of Confederate soldiers nearby on a hillside. "So neglected and obscure is this *campo santo*," Bierce observed, "that only he whose farm it is [. . .] appears to know about it." See *Ambrose Bierce's Civil War*, ed. William McCann (Washington, DC: Regnery Gateway, 1956), 71, 72. My colleague David M. Owens has traveled to the site and found it still very much as Bierce described it, save that the current landowner has had to remove the last remaining tombstones to a shed to protect them from thieves and vandals. See his essay "Visiting 'A Bivouac of the Dead,'" *The Ambrose Bierce Project Journal* 1.1 (2005), http://www.ambrosebierce.org/journal.html.

28. Wright, "Keeping Memory," 40.

29. Wright, "Keeping Memory," 45–46.

30. Nora, "Between Memory and History," 300.

Poking King David in His Imperial Eye/"I"

Woolson Takes On the White Man's Burden in the Postbellum United States

—Carolyn Hall

> "Freedmen! Yes; a glorious idea! But how will it work its way out into practical life? What are you going to do with tens of thousands of ignorant, childish, irresponsible souls thrown suddenly upon your hands; souls that will not long stay childish, and that have in them also all the capacities for evil that you yourselves have . . . ?"
> —Constance Fenimore Woolson, "King David"

Early in "King David" (1878, 1880), David King contemplates what he will do in the South as a teacher in a new freedom school. Not surprisingly, his words reveal this white man's enduring prejudice as well as his abolitionism. More important, his comment reveals the way in which Northerners capitalized on the freedpeople's situation and lingering sectional distinctions to assume for themselves superior subject positions. David rhetorically acknowledges the common humanity between himself and his black students, but his paternalistic attitude, fueled by the belief that Union victory indicated divine endorsement of Northern progress, keeps him from recognizing that black and white Americans share more than a "capacity for evil." Through this failing and others, Woolson directs her readers' critical attention toward the Reconstruction that had only recently concluded when "King David" went to press.

First published in New York's *Scribner's Monthly* (April 1878), "King David" appeared in a magazine known for adopting the sentiment of national reconciliation that had found its way into many postwar periodicals. This fact may have contributed to the critical reading of Woolson's story as an attempt, in Anne E. Rowe's words, to "salve the conscience of the nation." While "King David" indeed responds to the (white) nation's apparent weariness with Reconstruction and particularly the continuing problems associated with the freedpeople, Woolson's story satirizes those Americans who placed self-interest and self-aggrandizement above true (re)incorporation of all the nation's citizens. Primarily by criticizing the protagonist's faulty and often hypocritical thinking, "King David" targets specifically its postbellum Northern readership. David King casts himself as deliverer of both former slavemaster and former slave; he is the Northern bringer of light to a darkened region. In order for King to fulfill this self-designated role, Southerners must require deliverance. Meanwhile, a persistent European equation of property ownership with full citizenship promoted a presumed Northern superiority. In response to such willful blindness, "King David" slyly reveals the sometimes hidden operations of empire: in this case, the Northern imperial gaze across the postwar South, an aggrandizing gaze that impeded genuine Reconstruction.[1]

Situating Woolson's story in the context of New World studies opens the door to this more complex reading. According to Jon Smith and Deborah Cohn, the U.S. South is a "locus of literally disciplined bodies in a (largely) postplantation realm still dealing with the legacy of race slavery." Likeminded scholars have recently linked the South with other postcolonial sites in order to understand better what Smith and Cohn describe as the struggle between the "dominant and subdominant within the 'native' culture itself." To establish the South as a postcolonial site, critics like Dewey W. Grantham have explained how the ex-Confederacy can be seen as a "colonial appendage" of the North/nation, and George Handley has declared that the South "essentially was the first colony of U.S. imperial expansion." Specifically relevant to Woolson's "King David" is Jamie Winders's investigation of how Northern travel writers after the Civil War employed a "discourse of imperialism that translated a North-South regional binary into a colonizer-colonized distinction and framed the South as an imperial holding of the U.S." Examining this discourse within "King David" ultimately provides a reading notably different from those belonging to scholars like Peter Schmidt, who believes that the "primary cultural work of Woolson's story was to reassure the guilty conscience of her readers" with a tale that asserted Reconstruction's ideals might still be achieved "with the plantation master as the best teacher for blacks" (53–54).[2]

The former slavemaster that readers discover is, in fact, racist to a degree well beyond Woolson's custom. Advocating violence suggestive of the Ku Klux Klan, Harnett Ammerton does not offer a Reconstruction in any way tenable for the freedpeople. Neither does the Captain, a crass Yankee materialist who has adopted a false title to engender undeserved trust. He advocates reconstructing the recently defeated South via commercial and political exploitation, especially of the racial Other, for personal gain. Unlike these two men in that he truly wants to help the freedpeople, David King still approaches the postwar South with his self-interest (albeit unacknowledged) at the fore. David ranks his Northern prejudices above those of the white Southerners he meets, and he sees himself in a position permanently superior to the ex-slaves. Ultimately subverting white racist commentary and innuendo, Woolson's story underlines for readers the role their Northern bias played in Reconstruction's failure.[3]

On a "civilizing" mission nonetheless, David King approaches the South and its various inhabitants as assets: the people are to be (re)educated and their land (re)appropriated. Through the flowers David has transplanted from the North, the narrator compares him to "English ladies in India."[4] Although this comparison indicates that the New Hampshire man is out of place in his new Southern home, the reference to the British colonization of India also suggests something about David's attitude toward the region and its people. Like "the best ye breed" in Rudyard Kipling's later poem "The White Man's Burden," David has assumed a burden that involves a self-imposed exile in the South, where he attempts to coach both former slavemasters and freedpeople, again to borrow from Kipling, "(Ah, slowly!) toward the light."[5] While viewing the South like a colony proves corruptive, David's good intentions are not stripped of their merit. Instead, Woolson offers in 1878 a story about a reconstructing impulse that has become contorted. Her tale, then, urges readers toward a different kind of light: reconciliation without the elimination of sectional and, more important, racial biases is hardly *re*-construction.

This particular criticism of a failed social project emerges through Woolson's repeated narrative gestures to a Northern cum "national" imperialism, beginning with her invocation of the empire's "call to go" in the first two paragraphs of "King David" (781). Closely following the Civil War, Woolson's protagonist uses these very words to describe his desire to leave his Northern home and bring his version of the light to the ex-slaves in an African American settlement called Jubilee-town, located "far down in the South." Acting upon what he deems the North's "first duty" toward the freedpeople, David King believes their education is "work fitted to his hand"; thus, he approaches this "responsibility" with high hopes (781). The presumptuous Northerner is, however, disabused. His students never meet his professed expectations, and most of them gradually stop coming to his freedom school. Having learned what he terms "the lesson of a failure" (789), King finally quits his teaching position and returns to the North.

While the reader can attribute part of David's failure to the disruptive influence of the Captain, who has come South to find fortune and power irrespective of who gets hurt, some blame must fall on David's (mis)perception of his African American pupils. Despite his apparent concern, David consistently sees them as "the other race" (783). He calls them "ignorant, childish, irresponsible souls" (781). Rather than live among them, he sets up house "a little distance from the settlement"; in his view, he has "allowed himself that grace" (782). He willingly attends religious services with his students, but he does so "for the sake of example" (783). Particularly telling is the moment when David offers two of his black pupils, who have dropped by his home unexpectedly, the dinner he has just prepared for himself. He does not eat with them; furthermore, he not only washes their dishes after they leave, but he also throws away "every atom" of the food already prepared and begins a new meal (783). King must repeat to himself that "it *is* right" that Pompey, Cassius, and Caesar should be free because, unlike the freed slaves belonging to the "ancients" whom these names recall, the skin color of David's students distinguishes them from their fellow "citizens" (784–85).

This physical indicator, which clearly supersedes any other observation by Woolson's protagonist, signified to white Americans like David an inferior social position inextricable from past practice and belief. The institution of slavery had turned African Americans into property themselves, barring them, in many cases, from legally claiming anything of their own. Even where the law allowed slaves to accumulate property, their masters still owned them and thereby reduced that accumulation to an informal arrangement. In a discussion of American imperialism, traced from European practices before the colonization of North America to present-day U.S. imperialism, Eric Cheyfitz explains how the European/Western understanding of property has been used to rationalize Euro-American perspectives on the Other, particularly when white characters like David desire to possess something. Cheyfitz cites, for example, the likening of seventeenth-century Native Americans to animals since, from a European perspective, both merely roamed and foraged the land they occupied. "Not to have 'propertie,' then," Cheyfitz explains, "is to lose, from a European perspective, a significant part of one's humanness." While the ex-slaves in "King David" are no longer someone else's property, they have been free for only a short time, and they possess very little of their own. To David, they are different from their prewar counterparts in name only.[6]

Despite a firm belief in the freedom school, David continues to connect his students with an inferiority that even their new legal status cannot surmount. Following the war, the influence of over two hundred years of slavery could not simply be erased, at least not with mere proclamations. Garrison Frazier, one of the black religious leaders whose intercession resulted in the property directives of General Sherman's Special Field Order 15, recognized the connection between property ownership and freedom. He explained, "The way we can best take care of ourselves is to have land." While Frazier was in part being practical, acknowledging that ex-slaves needed to find means to support themselves, he also understood that *owning* property, specifically real estate rather than personal property, would go a long way toward distancing the freedpeople from their former position *as* property. Unfortunately, the former slaves' antebellum status and postbellum difficulties with unsympathetic whites conspired to perpetuate pre-emancipation views. As Alexis de Tocqueville explained in his early examination of race relations in the United

States, "an imaginary inequality that has its roots in mores always follows upon the real inequality that fortune or law produces." Consequently, de Tocqueville rightly asserted, "the remembrance of slavery dishonors the race, and race perpetuates the remembrance of slavery." Former slaves were "dishonored" since their skin color relegated them to inescapable positions of inferiority.[7]

David King's hypocritical behavior reveals how his pedagogy is colored by such associations. Since David interprets the Freedmen's Bureau "call" as a project of deliverance, his students must need someone to deliver them. The ex-slaves have to remain in a position of dependence or David risks losing his desired identity as bringer of civilization, specifically in the form of education as well as social and economic reform. This process of (re)defining is what Cheyfitz calls "translation": "the other is translated into the terms of the self in order to be alienated from those terms." While David is "thrift[y]" and instructs his students "carefully" and "[p]atiently" (784, 783), he views the former slaves as "improvident" (782). For months they attend classes from early morning to night, yet David calls them "idle and shiftless" (784). He is knowledgeable while they are "ignorant" (781), and he never seems to notice that "keen sharp eyes me[e]t the master's" (783). Although David ostensibly wants to "raise" the freedpeople to his level of citizenship, he has translated them into permanent dependents unable to govern themselves.[8]

Similar assumptions about African American dependence recurred in 1860s rhetoric regarding what Woolson's narrator calls "the emancipation problem" (781). Even after the Civil War, writers for Southern periodicals likened former slaves to children in order to explain the postwar role their inability required of whites. In an article for *DeBow's Review* (June 1866), for example, one writer admonished his fellow white Americans to treat the freedpeople as "mere grown-up children, entitled like children, or apprentices, to the protection of guardians or masters, and bound to obey those put above them, in place of parents, just as children are so bound."[9] Articles in Northern periodicals, too, cast former slaves as dependants. In the *New York Times*, an article on the future of the freedmen explained that observations of the "negro character" had left the "impression that [the freedman] is a child, with a child's faults and a child's virtues."[10] Even Northern African Americans claimed that the freedpeople required guidance. According to the *Christian Recorder*, the official organ of the African Methodist Episcopal Church, "so destitute are the freedmen within our bounds of practical information, so accustomed to being led, so childish and hopeless in every respect, that the providence of God imperatively, though informally, constitutes us their guardians." Likewise, in one of many letters of advice printed in the *Recorder*, the editor Elisha Weaver told his newly free readers, "we counsel you just as we would if you were our own children." In fact, David King's advice to his students in Woolson's story echoes Weaver's when he admonishes ex-slaves not to drink or steal but to be thrifty and diligent.[11]

Like Woolson's protagonist, these writers were not just characterizing the freedpeople. They, too, "translated." The writer for *DeBow's Review* described a familiar social arrangement that made former slavemasters once again "guardians or masters" over African Americans. The *New York Times* writer began his article by illustrating how "Northern charity" was responsible to "train the freemen to walk alone." The writers for the *Christian Recorder* offered a clear picture of who the free African Americans were via their postbellum relationship to those more recently enslaved. While presuming to concern themselves with the freedpeople, these articles function as depictions of those who clearly distinguish themselves from that Other. Particularly for the country's free blacks, claiming a position superior to that of the former slaves established a connection with white Americans who likewise separated themselves from the ex-slaves. Just as men and women became in domestic rhetoric, according to Amy Kaplan, "national allies against the alien," distinguishing capable adult citizens from childlike freedpeople offered a way to negotiate sectional and racial boundaries.[12]

The desire to cross the sectional divide in search of subscribers led some editors of Northern publications to advocate postbellum reconciliation early on. Dr. Josiah Gilbert Holland of New York's *Scribner's Monthly*, for example, understood that a national market was necessary to achieve the large readership he and the magazine's other founders desired. Consequently, *Scribner's Monthly* specifically courted Southern readers and writers, as well as those sympathetic to the South. Designed as a family periodical to rival the likes of *Harper's Monthly* and the *Atlantic Monthly*, Holland's magazine printed fiction by well-known American authors like Rebecca Harding Davis, Bret Harte, and George Washington Cable. By the time Woolson began publishing in its pages, the magazine had achieved a circulation of over 100,000, was addressing the controversial issues other contemporary periodicals avoided, and was providing its readers with what Holland called a "vital connection" to "current topics of thought." This "Illustrated Magazine / For the People," as the magazine's title page asserted, employed innovative wood-engraving techniques that enhanced the magazine's popularity by appealing to illiterate as well as literate consumers with what has been called "the finest workmanship of the age."[13]

Particularly reliant upon these illustrations were travel writers whose work was, according to Arthur John, a "dependable feature of family entertainment" in midcentury American monthlies.[14] Though foreign locales were sometimes favored, travel writing after the Civil War increasingly focused on the United States itself; given the magazine's conciliatory agenda, stories and essays about the South coincided with the effort to redefine a national landscape. Because discovery necessarily preceded progress, writers visited American locales on behalf of their less-traveled brethren and thereby enabled a cultural expansion into territories already technically part of the national landscape, an activity made all the more poignant by the recent separations of war. Stories like "King David," then, offered readers both North and South a re-legitimization and redefinition of the people and places located within the reincorporated South.

One of *Scribner's Monthly*'s most successful examples of travel writing was Edward King's *The Great South*, which appeared in installments from November 1873 to December 1874. Four years prior to publishing Woolson's "King David," *Scribner's* devoted around 450 pages to fifteen different illustrated articles about the South, as the series surveyed the various Southern states King visited and offered more than 430 engravings of illustrations by J. Wells Champney. "There can be no doubt," Frank Luther Mott has asserted, "that King's series was an effective factor in sectional reconciliation." Despite Holland's clear desire to increase the magazine's readership throughout the country, he frequently denounced racist practices; in June 1880, for example, he wrote, "It cannot be disputed that the great obstacle that stands to-day in the way of the negro is the white man, North and South." If Northern readers could nonetheless see what promise lay in cultivating the South, and Southern readers could take pride in the section's potential, as revealed in the prose and pictures of *The Great South*, the two regions could unite under a common and mutually beneficial goal: the civilizing mission of social and economic "progress." According to Robert Scholnick, with *The Great South* "King and Champney defined a South now ripe for commercial development."[15]

Recognizing the imperial project within Edward King's series, Jennifer Rae Greeson has linked King's chronicle to Henry Morton Stanley's account of his travel through Africa and his discovery there of the missionary David Livingstone. Greeson claims that Holland arranged for a "parallel 'expedition'" via King's journey through the South, territory "recently subdued in war, currently occupied by the U.S. military, and in the midst of a civilizing process called Reconstruction." Greeson calls the series a "usurpation of the most popular form of British imperial travel writing in the 1860s and 1870s: the interior Africa exploration narrative." Even Holland's choice of King as traveler/writer conjures colonial Africa because King had worked a few years earlier as Stanley's "last press corps companion before the latter's secret departure for Africa." King had gone on to write about Stanley's exploits in two articles for *Scribner's Monthly*. Having herself contributed several pieces to *Scribner's*, Woolson would undoubtedly have been familiar with Edward King's expansive series; consequently, the reader can see "King David" as a response, in part, to blatant images of American empire that capitalized on the South as the next logical extension of the nation's civilizing mission. Woolson's choice of David's last name, in fact, recalls the series' author as much as the topics Woolson discusses in her story.[16]

Like Woolson's "King David," Edward King's series translates reconstructing the South into an imperial venture. In his study of Louisiana, the opening for both the magazine series and the eventual book, King's first words suggest that, despite the war's recent devastation, the South holds unbounded potential: "Louisiana to-day is Paradise Lost. In twenty years it may be Paradise Regained." King then recalls the state's colonial history, noting how it was "sought" as a prize by "those great colonizers of America."[17] Since Louisiana had long been part of the United States, this reference likens the country to Europe's imperial nations and Louisiana to a reclaimed prize. From the outset, King casts the United States, specifically the North, as another great colonizer. After briefly tracing Louisiana's path to statehood, he describes the increasing business activities and opportunities for profit that the region offers forward-thinking white Americans.

Edward King repeats this economically oriented gaze across the Southern states he visits, regularly using terms like "capital," "commerce," and "wealth." More than once he reveals to his readers the want of Northern capital in the South: King relates the story of a Louisiana native, for example, who has "written repeatedly, urging people at the North to invest, but they would not." In contrast to white Americans ready to profit from the region is the racial Other, who either opposes or fails to recognize the region's potential wealth. King speaks, for instance, of Native Americans among white "roughs" of a savage West, where they stand in the way of the nation's vast economic potential because "the Indian jealously refuses to allow the white man to make [the land] blossom as the rose." In Alabama, King observes a "great congregation of idle negroes in the market square"; to his dismay no one is "at work." Despite his concern that black laborers are not capitalizing on the opportunities provided by the sharecropping system, he does find the plantation picturesque and the cotton gin impressive.[18]

Woolson's Northern protagonist likewise casts an imperial eye toward the Southern plantation. In addition to his desire to deliver the "childish" inhabitants of Jubilee-town, this King aspires to own land; even to an abolitionist, property matters. Despite the charitable nature of his "call to go," David subscribes to the romantic myth of the antebellum South: to him "a cotton field represent[s] the South—a cotton field in the hot sunshine, with a gang of slaves toiling under the lash of an overseer" (782). David's "fancy" is to acquire his own plantation and get the local African Americans to work it for him. However benevolent his desire to provide paying work for his students so they may "lay up something for the winter" (784), David truly hopes that, by becoming a planter and master over these men, he can gain for himself the aristocratic status he associates with men like the former planter and slavemaster Harnett Ammerton. David sees Ammerton as a "born patrician"; in this man's presence, the teacher feels "homely" and "awkward" (784). Although David believes slavery, and thus Ammerton as slavemaster, to be wrong, his vision places him (almost) in Ammerton's shoes. Woolson even refers to David as "the master" on several occasions. While he is a *school*master, the reader cannot fail to recall the term's more oppressive and racially charged echo.[19]

Given his personal stake in partly assuming Ammerton's former role, David tips his hand to canny readers in the North. He further reveals that he does not operate from a position of genuine interest in helping the freedpeople integrate into contemporary American society when he extends the "call to go" to the African Americans themselves. Rather, David exhibits what Sharon Dean has called the "ultimate colonialism, aimed at educating the vanquished to serve as ambassadors to what he conceives as an even more primitive culture." To make the freedpeople "noble" in his mind, David "speak[s] to them often of their wonderful lot as the emancipated teachers and helpers of their race; laying before them their mission in the future, which was to go over to Africa, and wake out of their long sloth and slumber the thousands of souls there" (781). Since David's characterization of the former slaves here is analogous to how he sees himself, the narrator's observation that the freedmen have "only a mythic idea of Africa" is also true of David (781): he does not understand the people he intends to save. Besides jabbing here at colonizationists, Woolson criticizes the self-centered nature of much white American involvement with the fate of the freedpeople. David's "[e]xtreme near-sightedness" is not merely literal (781).[20]

When this Northerner fails to see the paradox resulting from his desire to "elevate" the freedpeople while remaining their "master," he illustrates another feature of translation. Cheyfitz expands the term to include a repressive element: "For [American] imperialism historically has functioned (and continues to function) by substituting for the difficult politics of translation another politics of translation that represses these difficulties."[21] In his view, imperialism in the United States is fraught with problems because its defenders make presumptions insupportable in practice. To maintain their imagined superiority, American imperialists must "translate" yet again: they must "forget" inconvenient evidence to the contrary. Because David sees in his male students potential "danger"—a lack of knowledge and control that will become a problem should he fail in his "duty" to teach them right from wrong—he would give "years of his life for the power to restrict the suffrage" (781-82). Simultaneously, however, he recognizes that years of instruction have not eradicated such dangers from white society. David thinks to himself that the freedpeople possess "all the capacities for evil that you yourselves have—you with your safeguards of generations of conscious responsibility and self-government, and yet—so many lapses!" (781). Despite this realization and a later revelation of prejudice toward "poor whites" with their "ignorance and dense self-conceit" (783), he never considers restricting white freedom or suffrage.

His latent desire to appropriate the former slavemaster's claim to a kind of aristocracy notwithstanding, the Northern David comes to ex-master as well as ex-slave from a position of authority because he believes himself superior to Southern whites and blacks alike. As Eric Foner has asserted, "'free-labor ideology' affirmed the superiority of Northern society to the 'backward' slave South." The egalitarian sentiments permeating American rhetoric since the Revolution had, according to Robert J. Steinfeld, led to "new attitudes" about the "relationship between employee and employer"; workers had long insisted that, despite an absence of property, "they were the equals of their employers." In the decades prior to David King's trip South, this belief and other tenets of the "ideology of free labor" were "vigorously disseminated throughout the country as part of an emotional campaign against slavery." Consequently, David extends the rhetoric of free labor into his personal answer to the "emancipation problem" (781). Unlike slavemaster Ammerton, whose vision of the freedpeople avers that they "must be taken care of, worked, and fed" as he and other whites like him "work and feed [their] horses," David intends to remedy "generations of servitude and ignorance" by hiring the freedmen to work for "fair wages" (784). He sees himself as the enlightened Northerner, the conqueror and thus bringer of modern civilization to Southern whites as well as Southern blacks. Though the schoolmaster and slavemaster are of the same race, David intends to school the slavemaster: he will impose his Northern superiority, usurp the master's role, and claim both political and economic ascendance in the reconstructed South.[22]

Woolson's choice to link David to the Freedmen's Bureau thus becomes significant. As Foner has explained, "unifying the Bureau's activities was the endeavor to lay the foundation for a free labor society—one in which blacks labored voluntarily, having internalized the values of the marketplace, while planters and civil authorities accorded them the rights and treatment enjoyed by Northern workers." Although certain elements of this aim are laudable, it too rings of translation. The freedpeople will become consumers of Northern goods and the whites around them will become guardians of their rights. Unfortunately, the Bureau's aims in practice fell far short of their racially uplifting promise. According to Stephen Steinberg, despite the fact that the agency was "established ostensibly to promote the welfare of emancipated slaves," the Freedmen's Bureau was the "chief instrument for organizing a system of contract labor that reduced the black population of the South to a state of virtual peonage." Nevertheless, David sticks to his Bureau's exhortation. Even when he sees that his efforts among the freedpeople have fallen short, he maintains that adopting his model of Northern culture is key to "civilizing" the former slaves (781).[23]

Ammerton, the planter, also describes what he believes freedom should look like for the ex-slaves. He tells David that, in response to African American attempts at greater mobility and refusal to work as before emancipation, he and the other planters have formed "an association for [their] own protection"; they claim that they are ready to "shoot down anyone found upon [their] premises" (787). Unquestionably reminiscent of the often violent and unlawful behavior of organizations like the Ku Klux Klan, his declaration illustrates how some Southern whites were predictably translating black liberty to define their own postwar positions. Stripped of his status as master, Ammerton requires a new sign of his (supposed) superiority; thus, he returns to skin color. In some ways fending off the regional suppositions of an interloper like David King, the Southerner claims kinship with the Northerner based on their whiteness. As Alfred J. López explains, "whiteness" is "both the tool and self-reproducing product of empire."[24] This move then requires that nonwhites be inferior and unable to improve their condition or they will upset the re-imposed hierarchy. They cannot be integrated into a national identity; they must remain irretrievably foreign.

Unfortunately, Woolson's Captain does not offer the freedpeople a more viable version of citizenship. Like the stereotypic carpetbagger—and not the majority of those who went south like David to teach former slaves—he has come to the region to make money and garner votes. To achieve his goals, the Captain exploits the freedmen distrustful of their former masters and looking to exercise their newfound power of choice. He is not above using alcohol and propaganda, both of which undermine David's efforts and prove detrimental to the African American women who suffer the abuse and neglect that their drunken men inflict. The Captain, of course, does not care about these women or their men; lasting social change is not his mission. He explains to David, "Now's the time for smart chaps like us—'transition,' you know. The old Southerners are mad, and won't come forward, so we'll just sail in and have a few years of it. When they're ready to come back—why, we'll give 'em up the place again, of course, if our pockets are well lined" (785). Woolson's portrayal of this profiteer indicts those Northerners who viewed the defeated South primarily as an opportunity for personal gain, which Edward King's series invited.

Like the Captain, David is concerned with his own postwar status; consequently, Woolson makes him a parody. She may thereby have been responding to the conversation among prominent Northern magazines, including *Scribner's*, which attempted to define national character in New England terms. Nancy Glazener explains that, to the editors of such periodicals as the *Atlantic Monthly*, the "North's victory in the Civil War meant that the national influence of New England culture was dramatically confirmed." As a "narrow-chested" man with a "delicacy of constitution" (781), David hardly fits the image of the manly, self-governing, and individualistic Yankee that Northern writers asserted as the ideal American immediately after the war. Woolson's own later headnote, a poem by Richard Watson Gilder, pokes fun at David for taking himself so seriously and for following the doctrines of "empty air" and "unseen book[s]." Further undermining his authority and integrity is his claim that he has "no right to judge" (783), yet he judges constantly.[25]

Even David King's name becomes a parody. Recognizing a hint of it from the Bible, his students call him King David, a gesture that is itself an act of translation. The freedpeople have re-figured David in their own terms. For Northern readers, this re-figuring of the "master" by his students reflects the difficulties of translation: neither the freedpeople nor David understand each other. For this very reason, Woolson's King David is ironically unlike his biblical namesake, who united the Northern and Southern nations of Israel under his rule and expanded his kingdom by conquering new nations. And yet the biblical example implies that a divine mandate informs the Northerner's "call," if not his flawed response. Despite his selfish and anachronistic beliefs, David King still offers freedmen their likeliest chance at social change, their best hope for a better life as the economic and social conditions of the South improve.

Since David is the wrong man for the right job, Woolson quietly suggests someone who might be the right man. Although she does not offer much in "King David" regarding black agency after the war, she opens the door through Uncle Scipio, an older student who is briefly given a voice. Following David's announcement that he is leaving Jubilee-town and will solicit an African American replacement, Uncle Scipio explains, "a color'd man will unnerstan us, 'specially ef he hab lib'd at de Souf; we don't want no Nordern free niggahs hyar" (789). Predictably, Uncle Scipio does not advocate returning power to Southern Redeemers, as ex-Confederates began returning to Southern statehouses. But he also questions whether a free black person from the North would view the freedpeople any differently. Uncle Scipio effectively argues that former slaves can and should take an active role in shaping their own futures. His words also highlight the fact that former plantation masters are not the only "Southerners"; the definitions ascribed by David *and* Ammerton are too narrow. Just as Southerners would argue against what Smith and Cohn call "monolithic formulations of Americanness" as imagined by a "rich, imperial white Northeast," so Woolson asserts that there is no one "Southerner," no one "black," and no one "Northerner" for that matter. By this point her Northern readers, who already suspect they should not want to be Ammerton, ultimately do not want to be the Captain or David either, as the story of Reconstruction continues.[26]

The final words of Woolson's story belong to yet another Northerner, this one living in David's New Hampshire town. Having noticed that King has abandoned his Southern efforts and returned to teach in a local school, a village gossip murmurs, "Didn't find the blacks what he expected, I guess" (789). While the line certainly conjures David's inability to relate to his black pupils, it reflects once again Cheyfitz's notion of translation: David invented a version of the freedpeople so he could provide their "light." When his pupils did not play the parts he had scripted, he could not prevail as the superior Northerner, let alone the biblical King David as Christ figure that he envisioned himself to be. Thus, David's experiences in

Jubilee-town reveal what Deborah Cohn has called the "interdependence of notions of blackness and whiteness."[27] Whether in the freedom school or in the figurative classroom David attempts to create on the plantation, he requires that both whites and blacks, both plantation masters and "ignorant" pupils, acquiesce to a latter-day errand into the wilderness and a proffered light in the face(s) of darkness. Fittingly, the village gossip at the end of the story reveals his own blindness as well. Believing that he and his neighbors have already sacrificed enough, he too has translated black Southerners in order to relieve himself of further responsibility.

David's ultimate failure in Jubilee-town illustrates the problem with the Northern view of the postwar South as at once foreign and domestic. The beginning of what Schmidt calls "Jim Crow colonialism," this perspective clouded many Northern perceptions of the former slaves and interfered with any lasting progress regarding the postbellum status of the freedpeople, who remained alien, irreducibly "other." As George Handley explains, the "Union's attempt to integrate the New South after the Civil War fortified on an international scale the very plantation structures the North had decried." Reconstruction failed because many Northern whites extended a victorious manifest destiny at the expense of black Americans, who were no longer slaves but still were more foreign than fellow citizens.[28]

"King David" had a lesson for its Northern white readers: Radical Reconstruction depended upon a very different reconstruction of the readers themselves. In theory, the postwar nation might have achieved a sectional and racial reconciliation that reflected true social progress; in reality, a belief in commercial and cultural superiority impeded the progress thought to have been achieved by reunification and three Constitutional amendments. While David's attempts to help evaporate, his goals remain laudable since they aim for social change in a recuperating nation. Particularly in his deflated return north, David illustrates what Woolson's Northern readers could still learn: that they had yet to change their views of Northerners as well as Southerners, white and black, despite the changed postwar environment. In Woolson's hands, David King could finally enlighten someone.

Notes

1. For Rowe's observation, see "Constance Woolson and Southern Local Color," *Critical Essays on Constance Fenimore Woolson*, ed. Cheryl B. Torsney (New York: G. K. Hall, 1992), 149. For reconciliatory sentiment in *Scribner's/The Century*, see Arthur John, *The Best Years of the Century: Richard Watson Gilder, Scribner's Monthly, and the Century Magazine, 1870–1909* (Urbana: University of Illinois Press, 1981), 41; "The Century Magazine 1870–1924," *Pan American Magazine* 37 (July 1924): 344; L. Frank Tooker, *The Joys and Tribulations of an Editor* (New York: Century, 1924), 40–41; and Timothy P. Caron, "'How Changeable Are the Events of War': National Reconciliation in the *Century Magazine*'s 'Battles and Leaders of the Civil War,'" *American Periodicals* 16 (2006): 151–71.

2. See Jon Smith and Deborah Cohn, Introduction, *Look Away! The U.S. South in New World Studies*, ed. Jon Smith and Deborah Cohn (Durham, NC: Duke University Press, 2004), 6, 5. Grantham's phrase appears in *The South in Modern America: A Region at Odds* (Fayetteville: University of Arkansas Press, 2001), xvi; and George Handley's in *Postslavery Literatures in the Americas: Family Portraits in Black and White* (Charlottesville: University Press of Virginia, 2000), 20. Jamie Winders examines the "discourse of imperialism" in "Imperfectly Imperial: Northern Travel Writers in the Postbellum U.S. South, 1865–1880," *Annals of the Association of American Geographers* 95 (2005): 391–410; and Peter Schmidt discusses Woolson's story in *Sitting in Darkness: New South Fiction, Education, and the Rise of Jim Crow Colonialism, 1865–1920* (Jackson: University Press of Mississippi, 2008), 53–54.

For postcolonial criticism applied to Southern fiction, see also *South to a New Place: Region, Literature, Culture*, ed. Suzanne W. Jones and Sharon Monteith (Baton Rouge: Louisiana State University Press, 2002); *Bridging Southern Cultures: An Interdisciplinary Approach*, ed. John Lowe (Baton Rouge: Louisiana State University Press, 2005); and John T. Matthews, "Globalizing the U.S. South: Modernity and Modernism," *American Literature* 78 (2006): 719–22.

For arguments that U.S. imperialism began before the Civil War, see Michael Paul Rogin, *Fathers and Children: Andrew Jackson and the Subjugation of the American Indian* (New York: Knopf, 1975), 167; Richard Drinnon, *Facing West: The Metaphysics of Indian-Hating and Empire-Building* (Minneapolis: University of Minnesota Press, 1980); and John Carlos Rowe, *Literary Culture and U.S. Imperialism: From the Revolution to WWII* (New York: Oxford University Press, 2000), where Rowe calls Captain David Porter's attempt to "annex" the Marquesas Islands in 1812 "arguably the first formal act of U.S. imperialism" (9).

3. The disagreement regarding readings of Woolson's "King David" because of a racist rhetoric notably atypical for her writing recalls the much-debated *Adventures of Huckleberry Finn*. In her discussion of that novel, Christine MacLeod observes that Mark Twain had to find a way to criticize the very people he relied on for a living; see "Telling the Truth in a Tight Place: *Huckleberry Finn* and the Reconstruction Era," *Southern Quarterly* 34.1 (1995): 6. Similarly, Sharon Kennedy-Nolle has noted Woolson's awareness of the contradictory pressures of conscience and market by linking Woolson's "qualified endorsement of the freedpeople" with "the postwar market demand for stories that would increasingly emphasize conciliatory sectional relations"; see "'We Are Most of Us Dead Down Here': Constance Fenimore Woolson's Travel Writing and the Reconstruction of Florida," *Constance Fenimore Woolson's Nineteenth Century: Essays*, ed. Victoria Brehm (Detroit: Wayne State University Press, 2001), 145.

Regarding postwar problems treated in "King David," see Edoarda Grego, "Down South: 'Southern Races' and Southern Questions in Woolson's Fiction," *Prospero* 9 (2002): 71–85. For Reconstruction's problems more generally, see Eric Foner, *Reconstruction: America's Unfinished Revolution, 1863–1877* (New York: Harper and Row, 1988); and Michael W. Fitzgerald, *Splendid Failure: Postwar Reconstruction in the American South* (Chicago: Ivan R. Dee, 2007).

4. Constance Fenimore Woolson, "King David," *Scribner's Monthly* (April 1878): 782. All future references will be to this initial publication of Woolson's story and noted parenthetically in the text.

5. "The White Man's Burden," *McClure's* (February 1899): 4, 5.

6. See Eric Cheyfitz, *The Poetics of Imperialism: Translation and Colonization from The Tempest to Tarzan* (New York: Oxford University Press, 1991), 59. For examples of such property and how slaves exercised their ownership, see Dylan C. Penningroth, *The Claims of Kinfolk: African American Property and Community in the Nineteenth-Century South* (Chapel Hill: University of North Carolina Press, 2003), 45–109.

7. For Frazier's remarks, see "The Freedmen in Georgia," *Christian Recorder* (February 18, 1865): 2. On January 11, 1865, Frazier and other African American community leaders in Savannah, Georgia, met with Secretary of War Edwin Stanton and General William T. Sherman. On January 15, Special Field Order 15 designated 400,000 acres of confiscated Confederate plantations, including the Carolina Sea Islands and the strip of land running thirty miles inland and between the Ashley and St. John Rivers along the Carolina coast, for division and possession by 40,000 former slaves. This order is the likely source of the "40 acres and a mule" rumored to have been promised to each ex-slave after the war. While records and acknowledgments of property ownership among slaves did exist, they were not very visible, especially to Northerners viewing the freedpeople after emancipation—thus, the significance of landownership recognized by the federal government. For de Tocqueville's antebellum observation, see *Democracy in America*, ed. Harvey C. Mansfield and Delba Winthrop (1835; Chicago: University of Chicago Press, 2000), 327.

8. Cheyfitz, *The Poetics of Imperialism*, 15. Toni Morrison has explained that, since "[n]othing highlighted freedom—if it did not in fact create it—like slavery," postwar whites substituted sectional affiliation and complexion for the institution that provided them with Morrison's "projection of the not-me." This "not-me" is the result of translation. See *Playing in the Dark: Whiteness and the Literary Imagination* (New York: Vintage, 1992), 38.

9. "What's to Be Done with the Negroes?" *DeBow's Review* (June 1866): 578. James Dunwoody Bronson DeBow began this New Orleans monthly in 1846. As the war approached, the journal became increasingly pro-slavery and pro-secession. For examples of similar rhetoric regarding the freedpeople, see "The Negro Race in America," *Index* (August 5, 1865): 489–90; and "Mr. Goldwin Smith and the Question of Slavery," *Index* (May 26, 1864): 331. Edited by Henry Hotze, a strong defender of slavery, the *Index* in London was the only uninterrupted Southern journal during the war years, when Hotze sought to encourage international recognition of the Confederacy by influencing public opinion in England and France.

10. See "The Freedmen, Their Capabilities and Prospects," *New York Times*, August 27, 1865, 2; a similar example appears in "The Points to Be Secured Before Reconstruction," *New York Times*, May 5, 1865, 4. Begun in 1851 by Henry Jarvis Raymond, an active Republican, the newspaper sought to occupy a kind of middle ground among other publications circulating during the war. A pro-Union bias is clear, however, since the periodical's articles often figure the South as "Other."

11. "The Freedmen's Conference in Philadelphia," *Christian Recorder*, October 21, 1865, 1; and Elisha Weaver, "Advice from the Editor of this Paper," *Christian Recorder*, December 16, 1865, 198. The *Christian Recorder* began in earnest in 1861 as a vehicle for the Northern black elite to reach out to and "lift up" the African American masses. Edited by Weaver, the *Recorder* reported events specifically relevant to black Americans throughout the nation; its distribution in the South originated with African American Union soldiers.

12. See "What's to Be Done," 578; and "The Freedmen," 2. For Kaplan's shrewd phrase, see "Manifest Domesticity," *No More Separate Spheres! A Next Wave American Studies Reader*, ed. Cathy N. Davidson and Jessamyn Hatcher (Durham, NC: Duke University Press, 2002), 184. While Kaplan explains that antebellum domestic rhetoric shifted the "demarcations of otherness" from gender to race, white Northern and Southern writers made a similar move shortly after the war, replacing section with race. A similar act of translation among African American writers was less successful in the long run, as the increasing popularity of plantation fiction in the 1880s would attest.

13. Holland's observation about the magazine's vitality appeared in "Topics of the Time," *Scribner's Monthly* (November 1880): 151. For the high opinion of the magazine's illustrations, especially after *Scribner's* became the *Century* in 1881, see "The Century Magazine 1870–1924," *Pan American Magazine*

37 (July 1924): 342. Begun in 1870, *Scribner's Monthly* addressed, according to Frank Luther Mott, "morals and manners, politics, religion, current events, and popular tendencies," but the magazine's mainstay was its fiction. When Holland died in 1881, Richard Watson Gilder became editor. See *A History of American Magazines* (Cambridge, MA: Harvard University Press, 1970), III: 459, 6.

14. See John, *The Best Years of the Century*, 17.

15. For Mott's assessment of *The Great South*, see III: 465. For King's observation, see "The Shadow of the Negro," *Scribner's Monthly* (June 1880): 304. For Scholnick's claim, see "*Scribner's Monthly* and 'The Pictorial Representation of Life and Truth' in Post–Civil War America," *American Periodicals* 1 (1991): 61.

16. For Greeson's evaluation of *The Great South*, see "Expropriating *The Great South* and Exporting 'Local Color': Global and Hemispheric Imaginaries of the First Reconstruction," *American Literary History* 18 (2006): 498, 497, 499. Greeson argues that King's descriptions of the South's resources appear simultaneously with extensive criticism of the lazy or degenerate nature of various Southern populations. "Taken together," Greeson writes, "the two organizing elements of King's 'exhaustive' text create a moral imperative for the U.S. occupation and administration of a populated and resistant territory—an imperative ideally suited to the postbellum needs of a national audience beginning to imagine the U.S. as a modern imperial power on the European model yet ambivalent about the prospect" (505). For a discussion of the series and its place in *Scribner's*, see Paul H. Buck, *The Road to Reunion 1865–1900* (Boston: Little, Brown, 1937), 130–32, 222. For King on Stanley, see "An Expedition with Stanley," *Scribner's Monthly* (November 1872): 105–12; and "How Stanley Found Livingstone," *Scribner's Monthly* (January 1873): 298–315.

17. Edward King, "The Great South: Old and New Louisiana," *Scribner's Monthly* (November 1873): 1, 2.

18. King revised his periodical installments when they were collected. See *The Great South: A Record of Journeys in Louisiana, Texas, the Indian Territory, Missouri, Arkansas, Mississippi, Alabama, Georgia, Florida, South Carolina, North Carolina, Kentucky, Tennessee, Virginia, West Virginia, and Maryland* (Hartford: American Publishing, 1875) 32, 197, 334. Such views reflect what Cheyfitz explains regarding translation, Native Americans, and property; see 59–82.

19. For discussion of the plantation myth in literature, see John Lowe, "Re-creating a Public for the Plantation: Reconstruction Myths of the Biracial Southern 'Family,'" *Bridging Southern Cultures*, 221–53. In "The Other Face of History in Constance Fenimore Woolson's Southern Stories," Leonardo Buonomo argues that David's "aspiration to possess a portion of 'representative' Southern soil betrays, [...] a streak of Yankee arrogance and acquisitiveness (the cotton field is a synecdoche for the entire South, a picturesque South in miniature)"; see *Canadian Review of American Studies* 28.1 (1998): 20. While Buonomo cites this and other passages to illustrate what he calls "the tendency of the winning side—the triumphant North—to impose its values on the South," he softens Woolson's satire by adding that the Northerners she critiques "patronize" or "exploit" the South without "making an effort to understand it" (20). Significantly, he does not go on to explain how these problematic views and consequent failings implicate the story's readers.

20. For Dean's colonialist view, see *Constance Fenimore Woolson: Homeward Bound* (Knoxville: University of Tennessee Press, 1995), 64. The two places on the globe that David and his students examine at this moment in the story are the "Soudan" and "Kong" (781), notable because, when Woolson wrote this story, Anglo-Egyptian forces were attempting to colonize Southern Sudan; Northern Sudan was already an Egyptian colony; and Belgium was colonizing the Congo. Furthermore, in 1878, the year "King David" appeared, Henry Morton Stanley published *Through the Dark Continent*, while working in Africa for King Leopold II of Belgium.

21. Cheyfitz, *The Poetics of Imperialism*, xvi.

22. Foner's observation appears in "Slavery, the Civil War, and Reconstruction," *The New American History, Revised and Expanded Edition*, ed. Eric Foner (Philadelphia: Temple University Press, 1997), 91; more broadly, see Foner, *Reconstruction*, especially his discussion of land, labor, and the freedmen, 346–409. For Steinfeld's claims, see *The Invention of Free Labor: The Employment Relation in English and American Law and Culture, 1350–1870* (Chapel Hill: University of North Carolina Press, 1991), 122, 123, 177. Regarding the real inequalities of free labor prior to the war, see Bruce Levine, *Half Slave and Half Free: The Roots of Civil War* (New York: Hill and Wang, 1992), 46–70.

23. Foner, *Reconstruction*, 143–44; Stephen Steinberg, *The Ethnic Myth: Race, Ethnicity, and Class in America* (Boston: Beacon, 2001), 192. For more on the Freedmen's Bureau, see Paul A. Cimbala and Randall M. Miller, *The Freedmen's Bureau and Reconstruction: Reconsiderations* (New York: Fordham University Press, 1999); and W. E. B. Du Bois, *The Souls of Black Folk* (1903; New York: Modern Library, 1996), 15–42.

24. Alfred J. López, "Dressing for Success in the New Global U.S. South; Or, the Rediscovery of the New World," *American Literature* 78 (2006): 703.

25. For Glazener's assessment, see *Reading for Realism: The History of a U.S. Literary Institution, 1850–1910* (Durham, NC: Duke University Press, 1997), 27. The *Atlantic Monthly* was first published in 1857; although its founders intended to reflect a broad American sensibility, the magazine revealed in its early years a clear New England bias. Woolson added Gilder's poem when she collected "King David" in *Rodman the Keeper: Southern Sketches* (New York: D. Appleton, 1880), 254.

26. Smith and Cohn, *Look Away*, 1. Concerning the active role African Americans played in Reconstruction, see W. E. B. Du Bois, *Black Reconstruction in America: An Essay Toward a History of the Part Which Black Folk Played in the Attempt to Reconstruct Democracy in America, 1860–1880*, ed. Henry Louis Gates Jr. (New York: Oxford University Press, 2007), 13–24, 149–94.

27. Deborah Cohn, "U.S. Southern Studies and Latin American Studies: Windows onto Postcolonial Studies," *American Literature* 78 (2006): 704.

28. Schmidt, *Sitting in Darkness*, 14; Handley, *Postslavery Literatures in the Americas*, 20.

Cypresses, Chameleons, and Snakes

Displacement in Woolson's "The South Devil"

—Kathleen Diffley

Shortly after the sun-drenched opening of "'The South Devil" (1880), Woolson's story of a Florida swamp by that name, musician Carl Brenner takes a plummeting fall. Despite the warning of his stepbrother at work in the nearby orange grove, he has been trying to catch the elusive spirit of the swamp that he hears as song, particularly after climbing to the forest's treetop canopy and a riotous beauty that the steady Mark Deal never sees. Carl and Mark are happenstance brothers: their widowed parents have just married in Pennsylvania and Mark has taken in hand the consumptive Carl, an itinerant musician whose health is as broken as Mark's heart. They both need to recuperate. When Mark first proposed to Carl's cousin and was rejected, he went north on an expedition to the Arctic; upon his return, he proposed again, was again rejected, and took Carl south to Florida and an abandoned postwar plantation. Woolson's story opens as Mark tries to reconstruct the home he hankered for in the company of the invalid Carl, whose face carries the recollection of his cousin Leeza. But while Mark labors among the oranges, Carl is haunted by the South Devil's unwritten song and he climbs a ladder of vines to the lofty canopy, where he falls asleep.

His is what Fred Lewis Pattee has called the "lotos eaters' Florida," where the cypress swamp becomes the site of beauty's lure.[1] Up among the "great red blossoms swinging in the air" (178), Carl hears the recurring song because he has the "divine gift" of tracing harmonies, what Woolson calls "the gift which is the nearest to heaven" (187). While Mark spends hours tending his investment, Carl gives way to miasmic summons, an aesthetic surrender that David Miller describes in *Dark Eden* as "a dangerous but also an exhilarating and self-renewing experience."[2] For Woolson, as Sharon Dean has observed, the swamp's appeal lies in what only Carl recognizes: "the aloneness and mystery and threat that is the lot of the artist."[3] Of course the South that seduces him also puts him to sleep, and the ethereal heights he reaches can then be guessed by the distance he falls. If "The South Devil" is Carl Brenner's story, as most scholars believe, it is because he burns (as his German name suggests) with a consumptive's fever that becomes an artist's transcendent joy.

But his rude fall leaves Carl stranded, a Northern interloper unable to move until he is rescued by his prosaic stepbrother. From Mark Deal's perspective, the swamp is less Edenic than evil, its red blossoms not semi-tropical blue gentians but screens for venomous predators. The first thing he does upon finding Carl is to kill a snake, the beginning of a very different reading of the Southern swamp as historically charged. The swollen cypresses Mark sees initially suggest the postwar logging opportunities in northern Florida, where he has come to plant orange seedlings at an abandoned sugar and indigo plantation. Like him, other Northerners would shortly arrive in growing numbers—some to recover their health, others to linger in winter warmth, and still others to speculate in the Florida futures that Mark works to ensure. From the story's opening on December 23, he stands in for Northern vigor, what Karen Weekes glosses as the "thrift, industry, and pragmatism" that will rescue the "indigent" South.[4] For such sojourners, postwar Florida was not an airy preserve but a place in flux, mobile and regenerative, like the ancient cypresses that wear their roots as exotic "knees." If "The South Devil" is Mark Deal's story, as I propose, it is because he is his stepbrother's keeper and he deals with the aftermath of Carl's fall into time and place, specifically into the Florida swamp as a postlapsarian world of opportunity and trespass.

Significantly, Woolson's swamp can be traced to a part of the South that was simultaneously ancient and heterogenous. As Victoria Brehm and Sharon Dean have observed, "The South Devil" is almost certainly set in the swampy terrain south of St. Augustine.[5] Founded in 1565 and thus the oldest continuous European settlement in North America, the city already traced a history under the Spanish, the British, and the Americans that had left behind remarkably mixed populations. Where other parts of the South were socially stratified and politically conservative, northern Florida was at once steeped in the past like the rooted cypresses and yet chameleonic, home to Woolson's "dead hidalgos," Seminole fugitives, recent freedpeople, imported Minorcans, and mixed-blood hunters. In "The South Devil," I argue, the paradox of roots afloat and of age in the midst of social change, of cypresses and chameleons, proves expensive for self-absorbed interlopers, which a recently arrived musician and an industrious planter will soon find out. What is more, Northerners who have moved into someone else's home like Mark are wary of a third swamp thing: water moccasins, which in Woolson's story let loose both the horror and the power of postwar itinerancy as well as the South's imagined venom for Northern intruders.

And yet Carl's venture into the swamp's maze and his subsequent fall prove fortunate, which Woolson would underline by adding a headnote to her story when she collected "The South Devil" with her other Southern sketches. Pausing on those lines and on her deliberate tinkering with the assumed invitation of the picturesque, whose recognizable visual codes drew armchair tourists so easily to the defeated South and draw Carl so effortlessly to the exotic swamp, reveals an unsuspected and alternative model for a reconstructing nation. As Woolson's readers eventually discover in the canoe that carries Mark back to Leeza and a Northern reunion, which Carl arranges before his consumption proves fatal, Florida's unusual terrain frustrates imposed progress along ready paths but insinuates an equally unusual social substitute. When Mark makes his way with his brother's body through the dark beauty he has disdained, his canoe repeatedly bumps against aquatic plants that migrate, plants that carry their snaky roots with them in clumps. More than the seedlings that Mark abandons or Carl's harmonies that slip away, those clumps metaphorically dislodge the zeal of imperial trespass and substitute the opportunity for mobile congregation, just when displaced Northerners were beginning to clog Southern channels and to suggest a newly disparate social order. Starting with Mark's devotion to Southern dirt and Carl's appreciation of Southern color, then, "The South Devil" investigates differing paradigms for national reform and multiple postwar ways of seeing, especially seeing what is literally beneath the surface.

What neither Mark nor Carl generally sees, strikingly, is Southerners. In this particular story of Reconstruction, every principal character arrives from the North. Mark comes to make his fortune in Florida oranges, as he tries to warm a frozen heart. Carl hopes to regain his health in the Florida sun and to write at last the music he hears again in the swamp's "fairy-land" (178). Carl's friend Schwartz simply follows the migrating Northerners and their money, a card sharp's main game. While Carl may be intent on harmonies, what he actually delivers in "The South Devil" is this slippery friend, who fills him with liquor and steals all the hidden money a diligent Mark has saved. As Woolson puts it, the villainous Schwartz was "borne southward on the tide of winter travel to Florida" (184), and it is Northern travelers who become his chief focus and Woolson's own. In this story, it is not an adaptable South that interests Woolson so much as an adaptable North, whose regional practices are tied to covert theft as well as industrious thrift.

For that reason, it is a matter of some moment that "The South Devil" was published in Boston's *Atlantic Monthly* and then collected in Woolson's *Rodman the Keeper: Southern Sketches* (1880) after Reconstruction officially ended. By then, northern Florida was fast becoming what Steven Noll has called both "tourist attraction" and "resource to be exploited."[6] But the story is set, as Woolson explains, some fifty years after the First Seminole War (1816–1818) and thus closer to the late 1860s and a different national crossroads. During the years immediately following the Civil War, the *Atlantic Monthly*'s title page carried an engraving of Old Glory adorned with a liberty cap, which was meant to recall the periodical's antislavery origins in 1857 and the "Yankee humanism" that Ellery Sedgwick has seen successive editors purveying.[7] The late 1860s also witnessed concerted debate, in periodicals as well as in Congress, about three Constitutional amendments that would permanently abolish slavery and extend the civil rights that the *Atlantic Monthly* had long championed. "The fundamental and unanswerable argument in favor of the enfranchisement of the negro is found in the undisputed fact of his manhood," wrote Frederick Douglass in the magazine's pages during 1867.[8] Situating "The South Devil" in the midst of radical amendments, which occupied and reconstructing states like Florida would need to ratify, meant choosing a moment in which a new social order was beginning to coalesce.

For the *Atlantic Monthly* and its fellow travelers, casting the postwar South and especially Florida as the staging ground for Northern projects was not unusual, as Woolson had already discovered. In 1873, the year she arrived in St. Augustine, Harriet Beecher Stowe published a collection of Florida sketches from New York's *Christian Union* as *Palmetto-Leaves*, a book steeped in the "glorious, bewildering impropriety" of a front-yard swamp but engaged in turning that sense of liberation to the historic advantage of freedpeople.[9] As John T. Foster and Sarah Whitmer Foster have pointed out, the aim of Stowe and her extended family during their own protracted Florida sojourn between 1867 and 1884 was considerably more ambitious than the multiracial church, school, and orphanage they built near Stowe's home in Mandarin. "At the heart of Harriet Beecher Stowe's thoughts about living in the South," the Fosters write, "lay a desire to participate in its transformation into a progressive place."[10] To that end, her letters to the *Christian Union* during the early 1870s were strategically designed, the Fosters argue, to promote travel, encourage emigration, and tilt the state's voting majority on behalf of newly free citizens. Stowe's political agenda failed as Reconstruction waned, but her willingness to imagine Florida as a Northern borderland circulated as purposefully in genteel periodicals as Northern capital (and Northern card sharps) circulated up and down the Southern state.

Woolson provides a hint of social difference and Stowe's larger Reconstructive projects in the only Southerners her story includes: Scipio, the black cook who "knew every inch of the swamp" (188); a "mongrel" hunter "having probably Spanish, African, and Seminole blood" (187) who moves into Mark Deal's house when the brothers depart; even the Aztec tomb that Carl frequents and the cathedral nuns (silver lamps, tapers, the madonna) who pray over him after he dies. But in the story Woolson tells, they have almost nothing to say and seem instead to be part of the "*voicelessness* of the conquered and reconstructed South" that Henry James would remark upon when he described Woolson and her work for *Harper's Weekly*.[11] Rather than pursue their comparative inertia, "The South Devil" examines the Northern preoccupation with exotic refuge, particularly the come-hither that picturesque conventions had made familiar and that spreading regionalism would ensconce. The story of Mark Deal and Carl Brenner quietly probes Yankee humanism as a way of seeing and casts postwar liberty as the drama of an itinerant family without roots. For readers of the *Atlantic Monthly* in particular, Woolson's fictional compass pointed north, though self-reflectively and by way of newfound brothers who would bring the Florida swamp closer to subscriber front yards.

As though to underline a focus on Northern desire rather than Southern development, Woolson added a curious headnote when she collected "The South Devil" in her volume of Southern sketches. Taken from Joaquin Miller's *Songs of the Sun-Lands* (1873), the epigraph introduces three stanzas from "Isles of the Amazons," a long poem about the dismay of a war-weary Spanish knight who leaves Europe for a shimmering peace up the Amazon and among the militant women whose queen falls in love. Like Woolson's description of the swamp Carl enters, Miller's lines further saturate the story's opening pages with tropical color, particularly when she recalls Miller's phantasmagoria in "the trees that lean'd" and the cockatoo that moved "in plumes of gold and array'd in red" as the battered knight begins to sing.[12] Another Aeneas on the banks of the Tiber, Miller's knight turns out to be on the verge of a new empire; the "tall brown Queen" is so undone by love for him that she accepts the end of Amazon rule and crowns the knight king. But the stanzas Woolson selected and rearranged conclude with a disquieting serpent that fondles the white limb of a sycamore. In Miller's next stanza, which Woolson did not reprint, the knight falters, his song ends, and the serpent opens its "iron jaws."[13] For readers of *Rodman the Keeper*, especially those familiar with the sensational Miller and the *Sun-Lands* song his reviewers most often noticed, the appeal of faraway beauty was unmistakable, even before the story's cypresses with their fitful music, but so were Woolson's doubts about a frontier Eden.

Lounging on the sand when "The South Devil" opens, Carl Brenner nonetheless thinks he knows the territory, at least as well as Miller's beloved knight knew the Amazon. Carl can still spot the tall chimneys of the old plantation house, with its occasional outbuildings and the radiating paths that lead, among other places, to the swamp. Of course, the chimneys are ruined, the mansion is a sorry pile of stones thanks to Seminole attack, and the plantation paths have been overrun by jessamine vines. But Mark has restored a usable outbuilding (new board roof, new wooden shutters, new steps, red cotton curtain) and, besides, Carl is as adaptable as the "old green chameleon" that climbs onto his outstretched coat and turns brown. He is also willing to adapt what he finds to his own purposes. For Carl, the black cook Scipio is "Africanus," the Spanish live oak is a sunshade, and the Spirit of the Swamp is a dark "languorous" woman. From the story's first scene, he is a newcomer who "basked," like Woolson's readers, in the fetching pleasures of white sand, dancing butterflies, and enough "soft, balmy, fragrant air" (174–75) to send the thermometer to 88° on Christmas Day. Thanks to Mark's industry, he has already discovered that it is a short, cleared, and inviting walk to the swamp.

All the more reason to wonder about the exotic tug of the picturesque and the cultural agendas its postwar use could serve, even if Carl eventually chooses not to notice them aloft in the cypresses. For Stowe, book chapters on "A Flowery January in Florida," "Picnicking up Julington," and "Swamps and Orange-Trees" were ultimately meant to turn the invitation of paradisial warmth into a heaven on earth for black Americans, and she was not alone in describing Florida's Reconstructive possibilities, various as they were already proving to be. William Cullen Bryant, who reported on an 1873 visit in three letters to the *New York Evening Post*, was also preoccupied with "the effects of Freedom on the Negro," but his political concerns lapsed in the colorful face of alligators, king-fishers, and water-turkeys, as well as Northern invalids and "idlers," the very consumers of the picturesque that Sidney Lanier, in his turn, hoped to encourage.[14] Lanier was commissioned in 1875 by the Atlantic Coast Line Railway to assemble a Florida guidebook, which appeared as *Florida: Its Scenery, Climate, and History* (1875, 1876, 1877, 1881). Lanier reported that he was asked to write "at once a literary attraction and a statistical thesaurus," a portable and appealing guide for the tourist trade the railroad wanted to promote.[15] What he noticed on his own trip to Florida during the spring of 1875 would have more than a little in common with Carl's wayward artistry and Woolson's unsettling pictures.

Like Stowe's leaves and Bryant's letters, Lanier's volume was a sketchbook of sorts and bound to familiar pictorial conventions that railroad travelers would recognize. But his tack as a Southern poet and an accomplished musician—indeed, principal flute with Baltimore's Peabody Orchestra—was to modulate picturesque directives, as Carl would, with an idiosyncratic impulse. "Lanier's Florida," writes Anthony Wilson, "is a place of infinite possibility: emphatically not the economic possibility that industrialists and developers were beginning to perceive and seize but spiritual possibility as an ameliorative to that very drive."[16] With the same kind of imaginative play that draws Carl into Woolson's swamp, Lanier opens his guidebook by comparing the moment just before particles crystallize, what he calls "the moment of molecular indecisions," to the contemporary state of popular curiosity about Florida, "which by its very peninsular curve whimsically terminates the United States in an interrogation-point."[17] Where Stowe translated picturesque advertisement into political program and Bryant favored journalistic observation that slid into colorful pitch, Lanier substituted the flash of artistic whimsy that curved the picturesque and thus conventional ways of seeing.

Woolson also understood the magic of verbal pictures well before she paused on the play of color in Florida's swamps. As early as "The Haunted Lake," a descriptive sketch of the lake district near Cooperstown that helped inaugurate her career

Fig. 1, Leatherstocking Falls.
Constance Fenimore Woolson,
"The Haunted Lake."
Harper's Monthly (December 1871): 23.

Fig. 2, View in Charleston, South Carolina, Showing St. Michael's Church.
Constance Fenimore Woolson, "Up the Ashley and Cooper."
Harper's Monthly (December 1875): 2.

at *Harper's Monthly* (December 1871), she also discovered how readily art departments turned verbal pictures into fetching wood engravings, how quickly a studied description of "Leatherstocking Falls" became a consumable scene (Fig. 1). The transformation could prove infectious, particularly for a young writer seeking a livelihood in illustrated magazines. Several years later, Woolson's "Up the Ashley and Cooper" introduced readers of *Harper's Monthly* (December 1875) to Charleston as "the picturesque city of the Southern Atlantic coast," which the magazine's art department cast as a streetscape with St. Michael's church (Fig. 2). In the opening paragraphs of her sketch, Woolson organized the scene as a moonlit vista from St. Michael's spire: first the city's streets with their "broad verandahs" and "hidden gardens" and then the harbor with Battery Wagner and Fort Sumter "frowning" in the distance, before such islands led to the "shimmering" streams of the Ashley and the Cooper running inland.[18] Here and later with the river front at Drayton Hall, the gardens at Magnolia, and the ruins of Middleton Place, Woolson recalled what the magazine's readers could literally see: South Carolina's Revolutionary past and its earlier colonial settlement, its hereditary estates.

But from her sketch's opening paragraphs, there was also a surreptitious ease of appropriation, a schematic framing of scene after scene as her tourist eye and then the Harper art department found a spire, a river, a path, as readily as Carl found his way to the swamp. In the travel narrative that Woolson constructed along South Carolina's waterways, the most surreptitious reckoning actually concerned armchair tourists rather than eighteenth-century relics, the gazers for whom such prospects were assembled rather than the archeological detritus of historical ruins. "The picturesque scene," writes John Conron, "arranges its constituent forms in groupings and sequences, situates the spectator in relation to these arrangements and lights, and frames them in signifying ways."[19] What Ann Bermingham has called the "scopic dominion" of the "Picturesque eye" was inevitably at work in the North's illustrated magazines, even at "Leatherstocking Falls," but it was inevitably suspect when Northern travelers, travel writers, and musicians ventured south.[20]

Like Lanier, however, Woolson was also restless with picturesque conventions and already examining their familiar hermeneutics before "The South Devil" revealed the swamp's summons and threat. In the midst of parlaying Southern scenes into Northern sketches, her revisionist correctives were also welcome in illustrated magazines, which were more given to bricolage than ideological purity. Intent on the complications of traveling witness together with the ample self-indulgence of traveling conventions, exactly what Carl Brenner does not see, Woolson's comic "In Search of the Picturesque" was published by *Harper's Monthly* (July 1872) just as her travel sketches began to appear and even before she arrived in Florida. In the earlier travelogue's instructive plot, two young cousins and their grandfather leave the city's pavements for "Arcadia" and what looks like picturesque travel's customary

Fig. 3, "How Pure Is This Atmosphere!"
Constance Fenimore Woolson, "In Search of the Picturesque."
Harper's Monthly (July 1872): 161.

master narrative, which Conron reads as a version of divine errand: I came, I saw, I conquered in print. But Woolson's travelers are immediately overwhelmed by dust on the road, by scorching heat, and by corduroy log construction full of chuckholes, as well as too many hills, torrents of rain, and flies in the hotel dining room. Unlike Carl, they cannot bask; unlike Mark, they cannot simply labor. Not only are they on the road, but they do not understand at first that the road is traveled both ways, especially as a commercial thoroughfare. The eggs, honey, buttermilk, and cider they stop to purchase, for instance, have already been sold to meet metropolitan demand, while the country women they encounter want news of city fashions and the coming circus. It is as though the produce from Mark Deal's orange groves were already moving through commercial channels, winter commodities that might prompt audiences for Carl's song.

Rather than limn rural prospects as grace-notes or Lanier's interrogation points, however, Woolson keeps her eye on her benighted travelers (Fig. 3), whose dusty progress the Harper art department also illustrated. Instead of framing a vista, the magazine's engraving frames the wooden supports of the moving carriage, which frame in turn the travelers themselves. Instead of detailing an imperial progress via what Albert Boime has called a "magisterial gaze," this illustration details carriage wheels and clouds of dirt, the watchful strain of managing the horses, and the motion of a vehicle so beset by Woolson's rattling peddler's wagon on the road ahead that the passing scenery has disappeared. "We jolted, slipped, and dragged along," her fretful narrator observes, "until the carriage, clogged with earth, creaked like a great caravan, and the original color of the horses was lost in mud."[21] Here the tourist "I" becomes at once subject and scene in an "atmosphere" that is "pure" only in its gentle mocking, as though a prosaic Mark took Carl's vision to task.

Comic pokes did not keep Woolson from framing picturesque scenes for further *Harper's Monthly* sketches. In "The Oklawaha" (January 1876), she observed with the picturesque's conventional allure: "As the sun sank low in the west the red glow, which we could not see in the sky above through the dense umbrella-like tops of the cypresses, penetrated the open spaces below, and rested on the claret-colored water, as though the sun had stooped and shot under the trees, determined that the dark river, which he could not reach through the day with all his shining, should yet feel his power ere he stepped below the horizon."[22] But her early self-reflective "search" demonstrates that familiar tropes could be dismantled and a visual calculus undone. In "The South Devil," she would again insinuate an ironic slant on narrative omnipotence in Carl's fall, and she would remove the picturesque frame as well as the easy path of waterfall or city street to pause in the swamp on Carl's danger and Mark's dismay.

The result for her Northern stepbrothers at odds would be a damaged landscape that resists a unifying imperial field, a loosening picture with multiple perspectives that would complicate the view from distant armchairs or a convenient church spire. As Kim Ian Michasiw has put it in parsing the broad principle of multiple picturesque perspectives, "The beholder's position in front of the canvas is devalued as there is no place before the canvas from which the various elements in the scene can be unified, even harmonized. If there is to be a privileged prospect, the one seeking it must abandon spectatorship and enter the plane of representation."[23] For Woolson's Northerners and her story's Northern readers, in other words, the South Devil could only be seen at different moments from different perspectives and then only along uneven ground and through a swampy quagmire of Southern mud.

More specifically, Woolson's story of Florida's peculiar topography, what wetlands historian Christopher Meindl has termed "Florida's liquid landscape,"[24] countered the kind of picture conjured by Edward King in his continuing series on *The Great South* for New York's *Scribner's Monthly*, which included "Pictures from Florida" in 1874. Attentive to the state's recuperative climate, its winter temperatures, and its investment opportunities, King paused on the fecund appeal of "nature run riot," where "the very irregularity is delightful, the decay, charming, the

Fig. 4, "A Florida Swamp."
Thomas Bangs Thorpe, "*Picturesque America*: The St. John's and Ocklawaha Rivers, Florida." *Appletons' Journal* (November 12, 1870): 580.

solitude, picturesque."[25] He thereby epitomized Florida's alien appeal during the 1870s while echoing the very first installment of *Picturesque America* in New York's *Appletons' Journal*: Thomas Bangs Thorpe's "The St. John's and Ocklawaha Rivers, Florida," which appeared in 1870 with Harry Fenn's engraving of "A Florida Swamp" (Fig. 4). Like those after him, including Woolson, Thorpe described and Fenn drew the strange cypress "knees" as emblematic roots for the deracinated, an extravagant nature for travelers whose lives were ever more routinized by the emerging consumer economy of the North.[26] Woolson's endorsement of that cypress logic lies in Carl's heavy-lidded appreciation; but from Mark's perspective the fall into time was almost literally a fall into Fenn's writhing snakes.

So the layered stories of "The South Devil" prove metaphoric and revelatory. When Carl goes missing on Christmas Eve, it is the exhausted Mark who follows the light of his torch and the trail of Carl's footprints into the swamp, a trail that leads him across "sharp cypress-knees standing sullenly in the claret-colored water" (177). They serve as a regenerative hint of Mark's further reason for taking Carl on, even beyond his resemblance to the girl Mark has loved and apparently lost. Mark Deal confesses that he came to Florida to work the land and to get warm, after his brutal exposure to "the numbing ice, the killing ice" (183) of an Arctic expedition that recalls a similar and widely reported venture during the 1850s under Elisha Kent Kane. As Woolson's first readers would have remembered, almost all of Kane's crewmen returned from their desperate trek of eight hundred miles across the polar icecap. But Woolson changed the expedition story to one of dwindling resources and wrenching farewells, a tale of stranded comrades as the ice field breaks up and they drift apart on "ice-islands" (184). While Mark survives, everyone else dies frozen in his own block of ice, each drifting "in the slow eddy, each solemnly staring, one foot advanced, as if still keeping up the poor cramped steps with which he had fought off death" (184). That stranded separateness in the very posture of imperial adventure drives Mark south and eventually across the cypress knees that take him to the spot where Carl has fallen. Even the subsequent loss of his savings or, for that matter, the narrative theft of his story when Carl shares it with Schwartz do not separate him from the brother he has found and, significantly, their connection develops in Florida rather than Pennsylvania, in the land of winter heat rather than winter cold.

But if Florida was a Southern refuge for both brothers, it was a refuge with a difference—in fact, several of them. Historically, Spanish Florida had welcomed runaway slaves from British Georgia, just as the plantation on which Woolson's story seems to be set had introduced Minorcan laborers who then sought sanctuary in St. Augustine. The swamps, in their turn, had served as a refuge for the Seminoles escaping Andrew Jackson and federal removal. Woolson's figure for such absorption and adaptability is the chameleon, which Harry Fenn also alluded to with his lizard on a limb in picturesque Florida and which "The South Devil" invokes for its mutable hide as well as its tenacious claws. Adapting in the opening scene to the color of Carl's brown sack-coat, the chameleon is later seen weathering trouble against the side of a house and in some numbers. "'In a storm,'" Carl tells Schwartz, "'they will come and hang themselves by one paw on our windows, and the wind will blow them out like dead leaves, and rattle them about, and they'll never move'" (183). Like the state's Seminoles, Minorcans, and fugitive slaves, chameleons bespeak adjustment to change, a peculiar Florida past confirmed in the flaring colors of Woolson's antimodern swamp.

But in "The South Devil," the chameleons languidly catching flies never come near the recollected Indians, the mongrel hunter, or the black cook. It is Carl's coat that the "old green chameleon" first clings to, and Schwartz the "visitor" who notices a chameleon on the wall. In the story's opening paragraph, Carl lounges in the December sun "like a chameleon," and Schwartz later works the Esmeralda Parlors in San Miguel before escaping in a flash of disappearing color on a moonlit smuggler's boat. Yet it is not illegal shipping or, for that matter, Klan violence that Woolson's story follows. While Woolson dubbed herself "a red hot abolitionist, Republican and hard-money advocate" in an 1876 letter to Paul Hamilton Hayne,[27] her preoccupation in "The South Devil" does not seem to be the radical politics that other Northerners would seek to impose but the damage that Florida's visitors were likely to bring with them. Where Woolson's recurring chameleons could have signaled Florida's changing colors and social relations, they suggest instead the sticky tongues and sleepy self-satisfaction of indolent Northerners, like the footloose Schwartz and the lounging Carl.

It is in the swamp's murky waters that the South takes its revenge and offers its alternative, at least the South that Mark Deal imagines—and here Woolson departs somewhat from the simple domesticity of Harry Fenn's snaky mother with her brood. Upon discovering Carl at night, when the predators begin to surface, Mark stakes out a dry spot with burning torches at its four corners and begins to pace "the little knoll fort" he has created "like a picket walking his beat" (178). To keep himself awake, he sings "Gaily the Troubadour" repeatedly and brings the troubadour home from Palestine over and over again, a sojourner who returns from the "sun-lands." Although Mark can endure the centipedes, scorpions, and spiders that swarm the nighttime cypresses, he fears the moccasins that gather at the watery edge of his imposed domestic makeshift. "After a while," Woolson writes, "they began to rise to the surface; he could distinguish portions of their bodies in waving lines, moving noiselessly hither and thither, appearing and disappearing suddenly, until the pools around seemed alive with them" (179). What Mark sees in this nightmarish vision actually looks like the "waving lines" of his own abandoned roots, the venomous return of what he has repressed first for the frozen North and then for the steamy South.

Just as arresting and improbable, like the Arctic's ice-islands and the swamp's matted canopy, is what happens during the hour before dawn. An enormous snake appears and Mark, who has been singing all night of the troubadour's lady love, imagines it to be the hideous "queen of the moccasins" come to challenge his claim, much as Joaquin Miller's Spanish knight encounters the brown Queen of the Amazons. But Mark, another singer of songs, has none of the knight's weary patience. Shooting the snake, he kills the fatal reminder of his own crusade, the rootless search for glory far from home. As though to confirm the point, Mark later finds himself on a second swampy knoll in a second nightmarish vision of five thousand moccasins "coiling and gliding over the roots of the cypresses" (189). It is as though Harry Fenn's mother snake were striking back—or rather, since this is Mark's phantasmic vision, as though the Northern hunger for Southern roots were suddenly alive with venom.

The measure of Mark's displacement and his troubadour longing for home is revealed in "The South Devil" by what he finally chooses and what he throws away. Part of that is Carl's doing: although the musician's quest lapses and with it Mark's danger, Carl replaces the song he can not quite catch with the cousin he has no trouble reaching hundreds of miles away. Even after his death, the network of postal lines between northern Florida and eastern Pennsylvania, as elaborate as the swamp that Mark must navigate with Carl's body, delivers a letter from Leeza, a letter that turns Florida's picturesque terrain into "a ghastly mockery" (193). With a "sudden repugnance," Mark kicks aside the veinous oranges and their "rich, pulpy decay" (193) as he remembers apples and the hearty roots of a Pennsylvania orchard. Instead of snakes in the water and a new imperial adventure in the orange industry, Mark opts for the "cool brown rocks" of a Northern spring that will banish at last the "hot steaming air" (193) of the swamp. With his gun and Carl's violin, at once Miller's knight and Palestine's troubadour, he heads "Northward," Woolson's inevitable redirection and her story's final word.

But Mark Deal's abrupt departure is not Woolson's most instructive reckoning, even in "The South Devil." If waving lines in the water suggest that an invaded land could rise up as Mark self-consciously fears, Woolson's Florida also provides an alternative trope for postwar migrations, one that could encompass her own itinerancy and what Peter Caccavari has called her "traveling regionalism."[28] The swamp's channel, which ultimately carries Mark and the dead Carl to San Miguel, is clogged by "matted water vines" that slow Mark's progress and catch at his boat "like hundreds of hands" (190). In noticing the "great lily leaves," Woolson seems to be alluding to the "floating islands" of *Pistia spathulata*, the water lettuce she describes more fully in "The Oklawaha." Water lettuce, she notes there, is "a singular aquatic plant, associating in large communities or islands, sometimes several miles in length and a quarter of a mile in breadth, on large rivers or bays. These islands are nourished and kept in place by long fibrous roots, and are often alive with alligators, snakes, frogs, otters, heron, and curlew, until they seem like communities." As her travel account goes on to add, "in storms and high water they are driven from their moorings, and float about until they secure a footing again, when they flourish and spread themselves until again broken up and dispersed."[29] While Mark's vines in the water like Carl's vines in the air come and go quickly in "The South Devil," Woolson's pause elsewhere on island "communities" always on the move reveals a Florida alternative to the cypresses Mark envies, the chameleons Carl imitates, and the snakes that rise up to threaten them both, before Carl's transcendent artistry collapses.

Neglected by the airy Carl and ignored by the purposeful Mark, the oxymoronic island "communities" that Woolson describes at length quietly suggest the postwar makings of a new and heterogenous social order. Forever on the move, the clumps of water lettuce seem like cypress knees that drift and disperse, chameleons that let go rather than cling, snakes that play well with others. In their unpicturesque displacements, these storm-driven clumps reveal Woolson's final challenge to handy visual codes and the postwar tourists they invited. In place of picturesque summons, whether to Southern dirt or to Southern color, water lettuce communities with their "long, fibrous roots" dangling beneath the surface embody the difference between seeing there and being there, the difference between church spire preeminence and riverbank observation. As recuperative as miniature arks, Woolson's migrating clumps suggest Northern social makeshifts on swampy Southern waterways and, in "The South Devil," a fortunate fall into dealing with national Reconstruction.

Notes

1. Fred Lewis Pattee, "Constance Fenimore Woolson and the South," *South Atlantic Quarterly* 38.2 (April 1939): 136. "The South Devil" originally appeared in the *Atlantic Monthly* (February 1880): 173–93, where the "dark, languorous, mystical" swamp was first described (181). Unless otherwise indicated, all future references to Woolson's story will be to this early version and will be noted parenthetically in the text.

2. David C. Miller, *Dark Eden: The Swamp in Nineteenth-Century American Culture* (New York: Cambridge University Press, 1989), 3.

3. Sharon L. Dean, "Constance Woolson's Southern Sketches," *Southern Studies* 25.3 (Fall 1986): 280.

4. Karen Weekes, "Northern Bias in Constance Fenimore Woolson's *Rodman the Keeper: Southern Sketches*," *Southern Literary Journal* 32.2 (Spring 2000): 104.

5. *Constance Fenimore Woolson: Selected Stories & Travel Narratives*, ed. Victoria Brehm and Sharon L. Dean (Knoxville: University of Tennessee Press, 2004), 173.

6. Steven Noll, "Steamboats, Cypresses, and Tourism: An Ecological History of the Ocklawaha Valley in the Late Nineteenth Century," *Florida Historical Quarterly* 83.1 (Summer 2004): 7. For a keener sense of the "grand balls and parties" that the winter season in Jacksonville had already made familiar, see Floyd and Marion Rinhart, *Victorian Florida: America's Last Frontier* (Atlanta, GA: Peachtree Publishers, 1986), 45. As the Rinharts point out, newspapers in the mid-1870s were already testifying to the "gambling dens, thieves, and bunko artists" that Northern visitors were attracting (48). In "The South Devil," Carl points to such urban bedevilment when he shrugs off Mark's fear of the swamp. "'The prince of darkness never lives in the places called by his name,'" Carl observes; "'he likes baptized cities better'" (176).

7. Ellery Sedgwick, *The Atlantic Monthly, 1857–1909: Yankee Humanism at High Tide and Ebb* (Amherst: University of Massachusetts Press, 1994). For an illuminating overview of the magazine under William Dean Howells, who was committed to a tradition of "socially engaged literature" and "liberal Republican politics" (132), see ch. 4, "William Dean Howells (1871–1881): Editorial Realist," 112–59.

8. Frederick Douglass, "An Appeal to Congress for Impartial Suffrage," *Atlantic Monthly* (January 1867): 112.

9. Harriet Beecher Stowe, *Palmetto Leaves* (1873; Gainesville: University Press of Florida, 1999), 138.

10. John T. Foster Jr. and Sarah Whitmer Foster, *Beechers, Stowes, and Yankee Strangers: The Transformation of Florida* (Gainesville: University Press of Florida, 1999), 1.

11. Henry James, "Miss Constance Fenimore Woolson," *Harper's Weekly* (February 12, 1887): 114. James later reprinted his comments in *Partial Portraits* (London: Macmillan, 1888), 177–92.

12. Constance Fenimore Woolson, *Rodman the Keeper: Southern Sketches* (New York: D. Appleton, 1880), 139. Here are the unconsecutive stanzas that Woolson added from Miller's poem as a headnote:

> The trees that lean'd in their love unto trees,
>   That lock'd in their loves, and were made so strong,
> Stronger than armies; ay, stronger than seas
>   That rush from their caves in a storm of song.
>
> The cockatoo swung in the vines below,
>   And muttering hung on a golden thread,
> Or moved on the moss'd bough to and fro,
>   In plumes of gold and array'd in red.
>
> The serpent that hung from the sycamore bough,
>   And sway'd his head in a crescent above,
> Had folded his head to the white limb now,
>   And fondled it close like a great black love.

13. Joaquin Miller, *Songs of the Sun-Lands* (London: Longmans, 1873), 109. Miller's second volume of "songs" capitalized on his success in London, where British literary society dubbed him the "Byron of the Rockies" when he arrived from the American West in sombrero, spurs, and bearskin cape. As Nathaniel Lewis observes, Miller turned local color into spectator sport by "inventing himself as 'picturesque.'" See *Unsettling the Literary West: Authenticity and Authorship* (Lincoln: University of Nebraska Press, 2003), 83. Benjamin S. Lawson points as well to Miller's widely memorized poem "Columbus" (1896), with its repeated command to "Sail on!" See "Joaquin Miller," *Updating the Literary*

West, sponsored by the Western Literature Association (Fort Worth: Texas Christian University Press, 1997), 207. By reorganizing selected stanzas from "Isles of the Amazons," Woolson quietly trumped cockatoo with serpent and thus plumbed color with sudden threat, as she perforated Miller's imperial fantasy.

14. See Charles I. Glicksberg, "Letters of William Cullen Bryant from Florida," *Florida Historical Society Quarterly* 14.4 (April 1936): 255–74, where observations about "the Negro" (263–67), river fauna (268–70), and a "northern invasion" (272–74) can all be found. Bryant's letters appeared in the *New York Evening Post*, which he edited, on March 24, 1873, April 3, 1873, and April 15, 1873.

15. See Edd Winfield Parks, *Sidney Lanier: The Man, the Poet, The Critic* (Athens: University of Georgia Press, 1968), 28. Aubrey Harrison Starke has pointed out that two chapters on northern Florida, excerpted in *Lippincott's* during October and November 1875, were Lanier's first appearance in the Northern press as a writer of prose. See *Sidney Lanier: A Biographical and Critical Study* (Chapel Hill: University of North Carolina Press, 1933), 224. *Florida* appeared shortly thereafter, in time for winter travel. Jane S. Gabin has noted the book's "financial success," and she pauses on the chapter "For Consumptives," whose disease Lanier shared. See *A Living Minstrelsy: The Poetry and Music of Sidney Lanier* (Macon, GA: Mercer University Press, 1985), 80–81. Gabin also considers the long poem that Lanier completed before departing for Florida. In that work, titled *The Symphony* (1875), Lanier urges Art over Trade, and his poem concludes with a line that Carl Brenner could have written: "Music is Love in search of a word." For Gabin's further discussion, see 81–84.

16. Anthony Wilson, *Shadow and Shelter: The Swamp in Southern Culture* (Jackson: University Press of Mississippi, 2006), 99.

17. Sidney Lanier, Florida *and Miscellaneous Prose, Centennial Edition of the Works of Sidney Lanier*, VI, ed. Philip Graham (Baltimore: Johns Hopkins University Press, 1945), 9.

18. Constance Fenimore Woolson, "Up the Ashley and Cooper," *Harper's Monthly* (December 1875): 1–2.

19. John Conron, *American Picturesque* (University Park: Pennsylvania State University Press, 2000), 8–9.

20. Ann Bermingham, "The Picturesque and Ready-to-Wear Femininity," *The Politics of the Picturesque: Literature, Landscape and Aesthetics since 1770*, ed. Stephen Copley and Peter Garside (New York: Cambridge University Press, 1994), 93. For the political implications of such staged vision, which was especially tempting and troubling after the Civil War, see "Imperial Landscape" and W. J. T. Mitchell's unsettling observation: "Landscape might be seen more profitably as something like the 'dreamwork' of imperialism, unfolding its own movement in time and space from a central point of origin and folding back on itself to disclose both utopian fantasies of the perfected imperial prospect and fractured images of unresolved ambivalence and unsuppressed resistance." *Landscape and Power*, ed. W. J. T. Mitchell (Chicago: University of Chicago Press, 1994), 10. Lynn Murray finds "a pattern of political and aesthetic colonization" in the images of illustrated magazines like *Harper's Monthly*, while Jeffrey Auerbach traces in the framework of the picturesque "a much more comprehensive trope than Orientalism." See Murray, "'A Newly Discovered Country': The Post-Bellum South and the Picturesque Ruin," *Nineteenth Century Prose* 29.2 (Fall 2002): 105; and Auerbach, "The Picturesque and the Homogenisation of Empire," *British Art Journal* 5.1 (Spring/Summer 2004): 52.

21. Constance Fenimore Woolson, "In Search of the Picturesque," *Harper's Monthly* (July 1872): 166. For a full-scale demonstration of the organizing trope Woolson counters, see Albert Boime, *The Magisterial Gaze: Manifest Destiny and American Landscape Painting c. 1830–1865* (Washington, DC: Smithsonian Institution Press, 1991).

22. Constance Fenimore Woolson, "The Oklawaha," *Harper's Monthly* (January 1876): 165.

23. Kim Ian Michasiw, "Nine Revisionist Theses on the Picturesque," *Representations* 38.1 (Spring 1992): 86.

24. Christopher F. Meindl, "Water, Water Everywhere," *Paradise Lost?: The Environmental History of Florida*, ed. Jack E. Davis and Raymond Arsenault (Gainesville: University Press of Florida, 2005), 123.

25. Edward King, "*The Great South*: Pictures from Florida," *Scribner's Monthly* (November 1874): 8.

26. Thomas Bangs Thorpe, "*Picturesque America*: The St. John's and Ocklawaha Rivers, Florida," *Appletons' Journal* (November 12, 1870): 582. The South, as Edward Ayres observes, has long been "the American place where modern life has not fully arrived, for good and for ill." See "What We Talk about When We Talk about the South," *All Over the Map: Rethinking American Regions*, ed. Edward L. Ayres et al. (Baltimore: Johns Hopkins University Press, 1996), 65. After the Civil War, the South became what Nina Silber has called "an antimodern refuge" for growing numbers of Northern travelers who were "haunted by standardization." See *The Romance of Reunion: Northerners and the South, 1865–1900* (Chapel Hill: University of North Carolina Press, 1993), 69. As Woolson was learning, Florida soon became the South's principal tourist draw.

27. Constance Fenimore Woolson to Paul Hamilton Hayne, April 17, 1876, Paul Hamilton Hayne Papers, Rare Book, Manuscript, and Special Collections Library, Duke University, Durham, North Carolina. Note that Woolson's letter is marked "Easter Monday," which puts it a day after April 16, 1876, the date scholars have used for years. Warm thanks to Orion A. Teal at Duke University for pointing this out and for adding that the archival copy of this letter has been annotated in pencil with the correct date.

28. Peter Caccavari, "Exile, Depatriation, and Constance Fenimore Woolson's Traveling Regionalism," *Women, America, and Movement: Narratives of Relocation*, ed. Susan L. Roberson (Columbia: University of Missouri Press, 1998), 19–37. Caccavari sees Woolson modeling postwar identity on the very mobility Mark Deal dismisses. "Woolson took the rootlessness to be a part of her contemporary condition," he writes. "She saw it as an opportunity for self-reconstruction" (23). Identity in perpetual movement made Woolson what Caccavari calls "a *polylocalized* soul," which he describes as "someone who is in some sense 'native' to a number of places, not by birth or even duration of habitation, but by observation and imagination" (24). As it happens, Woolson also found in swamp botany a trope for what Caccavari astutely posits as reconstructive paradigm.

29. Woolson, "The Oklawaha," 174. The observations come from Woolson's fictional naturalist, who has been reading William Bartram's *Travels* (1791) and specifically Bartram's description of the St. Johns River.

"Burned into Us as by a Red-Hot Fire"
Novels of the South

The moment I take up my pen, the old home scenes are all I ever see; I see them so vividly that I can see nothing else. I have a theory, too, that those of us who remember the war,—who were old enough to be stirred by it, yet, at the same time, young enough to have it the first great event of our lives,—we, of that generation, are the most deeply-dyed "Americans" that exist. We cannot help it. Our "country," and all that means,—patriotism in its warmest form, was burned into us as by a red-hot fire, and the results are ineffaceable.
—*Constance Fenimore Woolson to Hamilton Mabie*

The Portrait of a Southern Lady in Woolson's For the Major

—Janet Gabler-Hover

> Her great art is the lie.
> —Friedrich Nietzsche, *Beyond Good and Evil*

Traveling South during the 1870s, Constance Fenimore Woolson provided Southern travel sketches, short stories, and novels to popular Northern magazines including *Harper's Monthly* and *Appletons' Journal*. These were lucrative: Northern readers were insatiably curious about the postwar South. Woolson's motives were more complicated, however. In her Southern novel *For the Major* (1882–83), for example, Woolson turns the table on Northerners, subtly indicting them for appropriative perspectives on the South during the post–Civil War period. Woolson's novel dramatizes types of Northern exploitation of the postbellum South described to a certain extent by Kevin O'Donnell in a recent anthology of Appalachian travel writing.[1] In *For the Major*, characters inflected as Northern fantasize the post–Civil War South to be a mythical *tabula rasa* on which to play out and resolve their own fantasies and anxieties: a psychological landscape of Southern chivalry and romance, and, in particular, of the Southern "lady." The antebellum South was being re-packaged by Northerners experiencing the South as psychologically exploitable.

For the Major explores one of the South's most potent myths—that of the Southern lady. This novel, on a literal level, depicts the Southern Belle archetype in Woolson's character Madam Carroll, only to dispel it. She does this not to condemn the Southern lady, but to expose her Northern characters' narcissistic investment in fantasizing Southern womanhood. Woolson plays with stereotypical aspects of the Southern archetype to suggest that a complex and paradoxical sexual dynamics underwrites the myth of the antebellum Southern woman. Various Southern feminist critics have explained that the Southern lady was perceived by Southern men as both sexually innocent and flirtatiously decorative; she was commodified as an object of desire with no agency of her own.[2] Thought both chaste and innocent, sexually and emotionally, she was, in Freudian terms, an ideal receptor for male needs; the object of desire who could not desire back, nor in any way threaten the fragility of the male ego by asserting her own identity. Woolson parodies this in *For the Major*, unveiling, through the course of the plot, a Southern heroine who is anything but innocent. Although Madam Carroll fails the Southern litmus test, I would argue that when she chooses to disclose who she really is she draws back the curtain on potential disguises familiar to many Southern women of the time. Woolson wants to show the regional inscription on Southern women who were compelled (more than Northern women) to sacrifice or veil their own constitutive power or agency for the sake of Southern men and the South in general, through to Reconstruction, in some cases. Through her heroine, Woolson speaks on behalf of Southern women who fulfilled this role.

Readers of Woolson's Northern fiction might be surprised at Woolson's sympathetic portrayal of the Southern lady in *For the Major*. Typically, Woolson indicts her deceptive women characters, using an actress metaphor to target her female villains. Along with other authors of her time, Woolson tended to equate duplicitous women with unethical behavior through the metaphor of the actress. However, Woolson also had an ideal of female heroism, which turned her typical appraisal of the deceptive woman inside out.

While unethical women in Woolson's fiction use their wiles for personal gain, female heroes in Woolson's work reluctantly accept duplicitous roles in order to protect men from men's narcissistic weaknesses. This kind of sacrificial duplicity came with an emotional cost to the women themselves, since in truth they longed to be sincere. It is this motivation—the voluntary sacrifice of a woman's emotional center for the sake of a man—that makes her self-immolating actress heroines so heroic in Woolson's eyes.

Woolson's Duplicitous Women, North

Before considering Woolson's treatment of the Southern lady in *For the Major*, one need understand that Woolson saw American women *regionally*. In *Anne*, a male protagonist remarks "'You can tell a New York girl at a glance when you meet her in the West or South,' and "I can tell a difference between the people of Massachusetts and the people of South Carolina . . . ."[3] In particular, Woolson reads regional difference into her depiction of duplicitous women. This treatment contains contradictions in Northern fiction, but the *Southern* woman seems exaggeratedly duplicitous in comparison to Woolson's Northern heroines. In *Anne*, serialized immediately before *For the Major* in *Harper's Monthly* (December 1880 through May 1882), Woolson shared with other Northern authors the depiction of the deceptive woman through the metaphor of the actress. In her influential book on nineteenth-century American drawing room society, Karen Halttunen argues that Americans were increasingly cynical about the existence of any true identity beyond the mask of social façade.[4] However, that does not jive with such authors as Henry James and Edith Wharton applying the epithet of the actress to cast doubt on the moral reliability of female characters; therefore, by extension, suggesting that there is indeed a *genuine* female self beyond the female surface. As an example, in James's *The Bostonians*, characters judge feminist orator Verena Tarrant on the basis of her personal authenticity, and they fret at the conundrum that "if [Verena] is theatrical, she was naturally theatrical." The stoic Dr. Prance bluntly dismisses Verena as "a deceiver," while the besotted Basil Ransom determines that Verena has "an air of artless enthusiasm, of personal purity."[5]

The period's authors, including Woolson, were enthralled with the theater. Theater fascinated Woolson; Edith Wharton's engagement can be shown even in the theatrical layout of *The House of Mirth*. Henry James wrote for the theater, including for the actress Ada Rehan; he was also a close friend of former actress Fanny Kemble, whom James called "'the first woman in London,'" and "'one of the consolations of my life!'"

Nevertheless, admiring the theater does not necessarily mean banishing ambivalence. Leon Edel notes that James responded negatively to actresses' seductive nature: "as a rule James did not like actresses and the 'mountebank' side of their art."[6]

James's mountebank evaluation was typical of the time. Theater critic Kim Marra notes that late nineteenth-century "critics and audiences [were] anxious about female sincerity," finding actresses, in particular, "at once threatening and appealing," paradoxically: "flagrantly defying bourgeois canons of feminine purity, piety, dependency, and modesty," they did so with a "seeming lack of guile."[7] Woolson's actress/gender drama is nuanced psychoanalytically, in terms reminiscent of Sigmund Freud's work on male identity formation, especially Freud's envisioning male identity as threatened in infancy by the Oedipal, or castration, complex. Freud's former student, Jacques Lacan, focuses in particular on the castration complex as it relates to the son and his mother. While on the one hand the son fears that his father will castrate him because of the son's desire for his mother, the son is even more threatened by his mother, so that his relationship to the mother is more formational. In the Freudian drama, after the son discovers his mother's radical otherness—that she has no phallus—he imagines and fears that his mother wants his, a desire which, if acted upon, will result in his own castration. Equally, however, the son yearns back to his time of the Pre-Oedipal bliss, tied to the mother's Pre-Oedipal role as a giver of unconditional love. Freudian theorist Madelon Sprengnether explains that in the early Pre-Oedipal stage, *mother* "represents a fantasy of plenitude, an Edenic state of oneness with the body of the mother." This essay argues that these Freudian dynamics are at work in Woolson's fiction, given their fullest expression in Woolson's Southern heroine in *For the Major*.

There are two kinds of actresses in Woolson's work: the "innocent" and the dangerously "guileful." One unselfishly lies to protect a male protagonist; feigning a lack of agency (desire), serving as gatekeepers of the male ego. The guileful woman is propelled by her own self-interest. Taking advantage of a man's willing credulity and emotional narcissism, she becomes, for men in Woolson's fiction, Freud's feared "hidden face of the mother as death."[8] Woolson's actress retains the perilous status she was perceived to have on the actual stage during Woolson's time.

Woolson's Northern novel *Anne* is, according to Cheryl B. Torsney, the "first of [Woolson's] strong woman narratives"[9] in which Woolson identifies with the novel's eponymous heroine. In the novel, Anne is principally admired for her truthfulness and her inability to "act." Anne "told the truth exactly on all occasions" (62:371, 723); she is "truthfulness itself" (62:372, 856). The novel, which moves from an old military base on Mackinac Island, Michigan, to New York City high society, establishes an ethical hierarchy of women; those who fall short are marked with the metaphor of actress. An early example is Anne's scheming younger sister, Tita, who cunningly steals Anne's first beau Erastus Pronando, an event foreshadowed by her early presence at a military ball in a "tableau dress." A military wife scoffs, "'See the puss now!'" and derides, "'See the child—how theatrical!'" (62:377, 44–45). Woolson also criticizes New York society widow Helen Lorrington, who steals Ward Heathcote away from Anne through the presentation of a false report that Anne is already engaged: "It was a lie direct. But Heathcote did not know it" (64:380, 195). Put to the same test, Anne strives to keep secret her affections for Heathcote because she knows her friend Helen loves him, failing, however, because she was "so inefficient an actress that she trembled as she spoke . . . return[ing] his gaze through a mist of tears" (63:375, 388). By contrast, the text reveals that Helen set up her life as "a drama" in which "she performed her own part brilliantly" (62:372, 847).

The detrimental effect Helen's deceit has on Heathcote reveals Woolson's continual intimation that American men are invariably weak, reliant for their ego identity on women. Women's lies, suggests Friedrich Nietzsche, are dangerous to men. The Freudian theorist Mary Ann Doane explains that, for Nietzsche, it is the *illusion* of depth in women that makes women the provider of men's sense of plenitude—"the notion," as Doane describes it, "of a truth *beyond* appearance," which is the center of man's existence.[10] However, for Nietzsche, a woman is conniving because although she suggests she "'conceals an essence of a reality beneath appearances,'" "she has no essence and would only like to make us think that she does. Her 'essence' is to appear."[11] In *Anne*, her hero Heathcote covets Anne's "sincerity, combined with the peculiar intensity of feeling beneath the surface" (407). On the one hand, the Southern antebellum lady would seem a perfect manifestation of Nietzsche's indictment. On the other, explains the historian Anne Firor Scott, the Southern "lady" offered by one antebellum Southern magazine writer notes that Southern girls are "marked with a delicate sense of propriety, happily mingled with an artless innocence." On the other hand, the Southern lady was also a Belle; this first image was paired with the Southern woman's place in "the mythology [that] assured every young woman that she was a Belle, endowed with magic powers to attract men and bend them to her will"[12]—in other words, Woolson's consummate actress *and* her female heroine. Woolson inflects this dichotomy along both gender and regional lines in *For the Major*: men in the novel are soothed by her ornamental abilities, but Madam Carroll's Northernized stepdaughter is dismissive and angry, viewing her as a Belle.

Woolson's Duplicitous Women, Turned South

Woolson's early knowledge of Southern antebellum women is suggested in her novel *Anne*, when the heroine's attendance at a boarding school run by a Madame Moreau is an allusion to the New York boarding school Woolson attended in New York under the guidance of Madame Chegaray, graduating at age eighteen in 1858. Anne and her schoolmate refer affectionately to Madame Moreau as "Tante." Anne's "Tante" is Woolson's "Tante," spoken of affectionately as "Tante" in the memoirs of the former student and prominent New York socialite Marion Gouverneur. Her narrative indicates that Woolson would have been acquainted with young Southern women early in her life. Gouverneur profiles the Southern women that Woolson would have met. She recalls the Southern young ladies' fervent attachment to the antebellum South and its traditions:

> When I entered Madame Chegaray's school . . . a large number . . . were from the Southern States. How well I remember the extreme loyalty of the Southern girls to their native soil! I can close my eyes and read the opening sentence of a composition written by one of my comrades, Elodie Toutant, a sister of General Pierre G.T. Beauregard of the Confederate Army—"The South, the South, the beautiful South, the garden spot of the United States." This chivalric devotion to the soil whence they sprang apparently was literally breathed into my Southern school companions from the very beginning of their lives. Their loyalty possessed a fascination for me, and although I was born, reared,

and educated in a Northern State, I had a tender feeling for the South, which still lingers with me.[13]

Woolson expresses her own love of the South in her Southern travel reminiscences. Her early biographer, John Dwight Kern, notes Woolson's travelogues during this period "give us a much more intimate picture of her personal life in the South than exists for any previous period," adding that "her love of the South is clearly indicated" by the number of books she set in the region.[14] It is the Southern woman's love for the South—and her willingness to sacrifice for it—that Woolson will find heroic in *For the Major*, serialized in *Harper's Monthly* from November 1882 to April 1883. Unlike the roaming construction of place in *Anne*, *For the Major* focuses on one scene—a Southern home in the Appalachians. In particular, the novel's focus on the image of the antebellum lady as a specific site of fantasy for the novel's characters comes from a Northern perspective. This is shown as different from the view of the Southern man, who sees the lady as a stabilizing force against the loss of the antebellum South.

For the Major opens with one of the more salient historical facts of the Southern Reconstruction period: displaced aristocratic plantation-owning Southerners moved to rural areas where they took refuge from their losses.[15] The novel opens onto a rural domestic scene in the North Carolina Appalachians, with the arrival of Northern-educated Sara Carroll to the diminished dwelling of her elderly Civil War hero father, Major Carroll, and his younger wife, Sara's stepmother Marion, or Madam, Carroll. The opening irony in the novel is that although Sara is New England raised, she is invested in the idea of the South as her home, and in her image of her father as an exalted Civil War hero. However, Sara responds as a Northern woman in her judgment of her stepmother as an inferior, judging the South a- historically with the fixity of an outsider's imposed position. Upon her arrival, Sara is assessed by villagers in the hamlet of Far Edgerley as "rather distant, reserved" by virtue of her longtime residence in New England with her uncle, a "cold New Englander." There she lived in "one of those villages of New England with still, elm-shaded, conscientious streets, white silent houses, the green blinds all closed across their broad fronts."[16] Her conscientiousness extends to her Puritan rigor of taste, of which she is proud: "All my gowns are black, of course. There is one I call best, but that is severely plain" (65:390, 909–10). Dress has a moral nuance—implicitly anything but black is frivolous—and she uses this integer of taste to condemn her more decorative stepmother.

An index of the New England woman's stereotypical view of the Southern lady's immoral frivolity appears in Harriet Beecher Stowe's *Uncle Tom's Cabin* in the character of Marie St. Augustine, an indolent, racist Southern wife fueled by her hedonism and obsession with appearance: "From her infancy, she had been surrounded with servants, who lived only to study her caprices; the idea that they had feelings or rights had never dawned upon her."[17] Marie's influence is countered by her husband's Yankee aunt Miss Ophelia, who indignantly and briskly sets the house to rights.

Woolson actually inflects onto Sara the Northerner's appropriative view of Southern landscapes described by Kevin O'Donnell as the Northern tourist's "Arcadian longing" for the lost rural Arcadia of the now industrialized North, "for [the] stability that found its image in the landscape of the mountain South, even as industrialism [imported by Northerners] was beginning to transform that landscape forever." Travel prints "can be read as a desire to possess the landscape of the South."[18] Although she has never *been* to the Appalachians, Sara romanticizes them and invests in them a nostalgic longing for *home*. Arriving in the crepuscular light of the late afternoon, Sara insists she be allowed to see the mountains, "to be sure that I am really *home* at last; that this is Chillawassee, that the Black Range is opposite, and that there in the West the long line of Lonely Mountain is rising against the sky" [italics mine]. Her stepmother responds wryly to this desire, "'As it is dark, perhaps you could see them as well from a comfortable chair in the library,'" but Sara counters, "'By no means. They will reveal themselves to me; you will see. I know just where they all ought to be; I made a map from the descriptions in your letters'" (65:390, 909). This romantic mapping of the Reconstruction Appalachians can be contrasted with Madam Carroll's sense of an Appalachian road: "This road was red because it ran through red clay; and a hopelessly sticky road it was, too, at most seasons, as the horses of the Tuloa stage line knew to their cost" (65:390, 908).

Sara's longing for her Confederate war hero father and her Southern "home" corresponds to her view of her stepmother as a rival and Southern Belle, at the worst, or Southern lady, at the least. Seen through Sara's eyes, the accounts Sara adds up suggest this is true. Right away, Madam Carroll refuses to let Sara see her "very tired" father when Sara first arrives at Far Edgerley. Sara's response that "'It is little past ten. He must still be awake. Could I not just slip in for a moment, just to speak to him?'" (65:390, 909) seems justified. So does her frustrated response when her request to take up her father's breakfast the following morning is denied. In response, "a high flush rose in Sara's face.... She looked hurt and angry. 'Pray, who does take his breakfast then?' she asked.... 'I take it,' replied Madam Carroll, gently." Sara seems at wit's end: "'Very well, mamma; I will not begin by being jealous of you!'" (65:390, 912). Sara perceives herself in competition with her father's wife, but she insinuates as well that she sees her stepmother as actively engaged in trumping her.

Examples stack up. Sara is dismissed from her father's study when she wishes to read to him. The reader learns Madam Carroll was responsible for the father's original separation from his daughter, sending her east to boarding school. For

Sara, this is a Southern Belle's machinations, and the Belle has won. Upon Sara's removal, the Major's "wife had gained what her daughter had lost" (66:39, 98). Sara notes her stepmother's contrivance of a "youthful, almost childlike, aspect" and her ornamental role as the Major's "pretty little wife" (65:390, 910). She views with contempt how her stepmother enhances her "young-old" attire by "the arrangement of *the* hair" [italics mine] (65:390, 910). How should one take "the" as opposed to "her" in this description of Madam Carroll's hair? It has the effect of disembodying the woman and turning her into an object. Sara bases much of her contempt for her stepmother on what she judges to be her stepmother's shallow obsession with fashion. With her typical blind narcissism, Sara fails to acknowledge the effortful nature of what her stepmother has done to protect her stepdaughter's illusions: "Left alone, Sara Carroll looked round her room. As much had been done to make it bright as woman's hands, with but a small purse to draw upon, could accomplish. The toilet table, the curtains, the low lounge, with its great, cool, chintz-covered pillows, the hanging shelves, the easy chair, the writing table—all these were miracles of prettiness and ingenuity. *But the person for whom this had been done saw it but vaguely. She was thinking of only one thing— her father*" [italics mine] (65:390, 912).

Woolson sets up strategic plot reversals that undermine this simplistic view of Madam Carroll as a Southern Belle, finally rendering her status as a Southern lady problematic as well. To protect her husband, Madam Carroll's first reversal is to draw back the curtain on the illusion of her father as a vigorous Confederate hero frozen in time. This is what the Major needs to think about himself in order to retain his honor. But with his demanding daughter, the Major's actions become effortful, threatening to shatter his own myth of his continuing virility. The narrator has earlier noted that with Sara, the Major had "to take himself more vigorously at hand, as it were." Although "his hand . . . had the shriveled appearance, with the veins prominent on the back, which more than anything else betrays the first feebleness of age," the narrator notes that "the instance he recognized [his daughter] his manner, attitude, even his whole appearance, changed, as if by magic; his spectacles were off; he had straightened himself, and risen" (66:391, 95). As we see in her portrait of the Major, Woolson shows her awareness of the Reconstruction plight of the fallen and demoralized Reconstruction Southern soldiers. The Major is one such soldier, who, loathe to admit his own diminished status, depends entirely upon his wife to sustain his illusions. As Woolson writes, Madam Carroll has been producing the illusion that "there was no change [since the Civil War], that everything was precisely as it had been" (66:391, 98). This is something Sara does not know, and in puzzlement, finally, she turns to her stepmother.

Given Woolson's early focus on Sara and later on other characters to the exception of Madam Carroll, it is extremely significant to note that all plot reversals, and all plot solutions, come from Madam Carroll, who bears the burden of all the sad knowledge she has to hide. As a typical avatar of Woolson's female heroism, freedom comes for Madam Carroll during her discursive plot reversals, when, to protect her husband, she has no choice but to tell parts of the truth and to express her own emotions. Madam Carroll leads Sara to understand her father's aging debilities, his demoralized position due to the downfall of the Southern cause, and his need to retain his delusion of former grandeur, which has been the foundation of his ego identity. Sara is stunned by her realization that everything her stepmother has done functions to sustain this illusion; her dress, her diminishment of her own role as an economic force in the household, her little manipulations to shield her husband by moving up the time of their social hour as if it were *she* who was tired, the sustained illusion of her own youth and reliance on her husband's chivalry—all these produce the desired reaction: "For the Major depended more and more each day upon his little wife.... he liked to look at her; her bright little gowns and sunny curls pleased him, and made him feel young again.... He had come, too, to have a great pride in her ... He had always been a proud man, and now his pride had centered itself in her" (66:392, 243).

Sara finds she must take part in en*acting* this illusion against her pride in her own New England straightness. There is a wry moment when Madam Carroll tells her stepdaughter that Sara will find it hard to drop "so fully upon a lower plane" (66:391, 99) in order to *act* on behalf of her father. Although Sara is forced to respect the skill and love exerted in her stepmother's "never-failing touch of the mistress's hand upon the household helm," habitually "the daughter would unconsciously fall back into her old opinion of her" [Madam Carroll] (66:392, 245).

What Sara perceives as merely decoration Woolson wants the reader to see as woman's *work*. This was not only *emotional* work but physical work. Recently, historians of the South—Anne Firor Scott, Drew Gilpin Faust, Catherine Clinton— have emphasized a broader recognition of Southern white women's material labor on the plantation.[19] One of the most important responsibilities for the Southern matron was her important textile work; this relation to textiles became more profoundly taxing during and after the Civil War, due to the Northern blockade and the increasing impoverishment of Southern families. Increasingly, the actual weaving itself was being done by Southern matrons instead of slaves. Drew Gilpin Faust notes the alarm men felt with this increasing manifestation of their wives' labor, one Southern husband writing home that "'I do not like the idea of your weaving. It is mortifying to me. I wish you not to do it,'" and another dictating "'I do not want you to do anything ... I did not espouse for you for no such purposes. I done [sic] so for my high esteem of your intrinsic worth; also that you might remain handsome; also for the love I had for you[r] soft and pliant hands and loving face. I do not wish the latter to be furrowed by physical labor.'"[20]

Woolson depicts the fallen position of this plantation family through the mistress's vexed efforts to work wonders with her needle. The "Farms" is not a romantic getaway, but a hard, cold necessity that Woolson must have recognized through her travels. The Carrolls have removed to North Carolinian Appalachia from somewhere else, probably from South Carolina, since their relatives are "Sea Island Carrolls" (260). These impoverished relatives have given the Appalachian Carrolls their carriage since they "had not even mules to draw it." Such dire conditions ring historically true. Just as Faust notes that during the war, women moved place to place "in dilapidated wagons, or even aside intractable mules,"[21] the carriage carrying Sara to Far Edgerley is "drawn by mules" (65:390, 908). Similarly, Madam Carroll's textile work waged against insurmountable odds, along with those of her fellow townswomen, is an accurate depiction of Southern women's "make-do" efforts during and after the Civil War. Madam Carroll tells her stepdaughter wryly that women's dress in Far Edgerley has suffered from a "superabundance of trimming," and that "the finest skill will not take the place of a little fresh trimming merely; there comes a time when the finest skill will not take the place of a little fresh material.... The Greers, for instance, have made over their green poplins twice a year ... but they are still the same green poplins," and "Miss Corinna Rendlesham, too, and her sisters have accomplished wonders with different combinations of narrow black velvet ribbons and fringe on their black silks—so much so, indeed, that the material is now quite riddled with the old lines of needle-holes where trimmings formerly ran" (65:390, 910). Madam Carroll knows that such makeshift work presents a pantomime of lingering prosperity.

For the Major demonstrates an active resistance to the New South Reconstruction world of marketplace economics, where women were beginning to pursue needlework as well as other professions outside the home including nursing, teaching, newspaper editing, factory work, and stenography. In the postwar South of lingering aristocratic codes, men would have been even more threatened than in the North by women transgressing the bounds of their proscribed role as agent-less foils for their husband's hypermasculinity. Staunchly resisting this New South world, "Far" Edgerley is a defiant remove from even lower Edgerley, which has "two thousand inhabitants, cheese factories, sawmills, and a stage line across Black Mountain to Tuloa, where connection [could be] made with a second line, which went eastward to the railway.... so far at least, the Spirit of Progress had not climbed Chilawassee Mountain, and thus Far Edgerley was left to its prejudiced creed."

Even more threatening in the South than other women workers, one would imagine, was the early manifestation in the Civil War South of women holding benefit performances, often with *tableaux vivants*. Faust writes that this "participation in benefit dramas and tableaux marked a significant departure from woman's customary place," one "soldier signing himself 'Hope' wr[iting] to the *Confederate*

Union to ask the papers' readers, "'Is it right for young ladies to appear in public on the stage?'" Southern women on stage had to have been threatening, since "wartime theatricals, in particular the widely popular tableaux, encouraged respectable women to don costumes and for the first time venture onto a stage . . . where roles and identities could be invented and changed." The theatrical image of a Southern woman playing a role would trigger a Southern man's deepest concerns. Anne Scott continues to elaborate on how likely it was that Southern men unconsciously feared a duplicity underlying women's piety and submissiveness, for "despite the vigor of [Southern men's accolades to women], there is some evidence that Southern men did not feel altogether secure in their self-proclaimed position of lord and master of the whole patriarchy. Fear lay beneath the surface of the flowery praise of woman and the insistence that God had made them that way."[22]

What Woolson clearly knows and shows in *For the Major* is the illusion of *non-*performativity the Southern lady had to sustain in order to preserve her husband's sense of active agency. This was the *real* work, one might argue, of the antebellum Southern lady. Southworth exposes this irony in her second and third major plot reversals. Madam Carroll's artifice is intensified through the course of further plot developments. Only the Major never actually *sees* her artifice. Ironically, the Major is blinded before he dies at the end of the novel. This fact serves to make Madam Carroll's actions seem heroic instead of meaningless. Madam Carroll's deceptions are not turned against her, for she has been acting "like" a Southern lady *for* the Major.

The last two plot reversals of expectations/assumptions in the novel are catalyzed by Woolson's midnovel introduction of a seductive and exotic stranger into the comfortable world of Madam Carroll's drawing room and into the mythologized antebellum idyll of Far Edgerley. The person most disturbed by this is the Reverend Frederick Owen, a recent arrival to Far Edgerley who serves as a complement to Sara Carroll in their symbolic roles as Northerner inflected characters who respond narcissistically to the South. Sara responds to her father, and fatherland, as a lost site of unconditional love, and Frederick responds narcissistically to the myth of the Southern lady (Madam Carroll) as the archetypal unconditional mother in a Freudian sense.

From the opening of the novel, Frederick Owen stands in the metaphorical space of Northern regionalism. It is unclear why Woolson does not present unambiguous Northern characters; instead, she represents a pastiche of Northern inflected points of view. Like Sara, Owen is an outsider come to Far Edgerley who is linked to New England through his defense of New England against the charge of Puritanism: "'I do not think there is now as much of—of the [Puritan] atmosphere you mention, as there once was,' said the rector, smiling" (65:390, 915). The smile secretly acknowledges his superior awareness. His connection with the North is also suggested by his outsider response to Madam Carroll as if she were an extraordinary and unusual woman. Madam Carroll is the type of lady that a Southern gentleman would have expected to encounter. He is reminiscent of a Northern character in Woolson's earlier "Up in the Blue Ridge" (1874),[23] Stephen Wainwright, who becomes obsessed with the religious piety and purity he finds in a Southern young woman during his Appalachian tour. Hidden from her view, he scrutinizes her praying, covering every physical part of her body with his appraising gaze and reveling in her submissive posture.

Jennifer Fleissner theorizes that due to the "New Woman" prototype in turn-of-the-century America, "the deepest repositories of sentimental, therapeutic, indeed nostalgic culture in the 1890s may have belonged to the era's manly men" who responded with a "nostalgic masculinity."[24] Frederick Owen finds in the archetype of the Southern lady the site for his manly man-ness, necessarily bolstered by a woman he perceives as having unconditional maternal love that provides a sense of male plenitude. If the Carroll drawing room is *For the Major's mise en scène*, Owen is its most perfect spectator. Owen watches Madam Carroll obsessively, admiring her innocence, her child-like manner, her attention to dress. Woolson characterizes Owen's obsession as narcissistically involved:

> His liking for the little mistress of the house was strong and sincere. He thought her very sweet and winning. He found there, too, *an atmosphere in which he did not have to mount guard over himself and his possessions—an atmosphere of pleasant welcome and pleasant words, but both of them unaccompanied by what might have been called, perhaps, the acquisitiveness which prevailed elsewhere. No one at the Farms wanted him or anything that was his, that is, wanted it with any tenacity.* [italics mine] (66:392, 247)

The height of Owen's maternal fantasy occurs in a deathbed scene witnessed by Owen in which he sees Madam Carroll ministering to a dying child. The word "mother" is obsessively repeated in Owen's head, as the narrator describes his thoughts. It is deliberate that the poor Appalachian mother can't be easily discerned from Madam Carroll's own role as mother in this text: Witness to Madam Carroll and the child's Appalachian mother nursing the "poor crippled boy [Appalachian boy who] had just breathed his last breath of pain, [Owen] had been much touched by the sweet, comprehending sisterly tenderness of the mother who was a lady to the mother who was so ignorant, rough-spoken, almost rough-hearted as well. But, though rough-hearted, she had loved her poor child as dearly as that other mother loved" (66:392, 247). This is a fantastical male dream of the "Mother."

Ironically, Owen's fantasies about Madam Carroll are harshly disturbed by the arrival in town of a "stranger" midway through Woolson's novel. This plot element of the stranger named DuPont introduces a disquieting element out of touch with the other plot events in the novel. Not coincidentally, it is the arrival of this stranger that catalyzes the remaining plot revelations in the text. This is an evocative point, since it seems that Woolson interjects this stranger, DuPont, as the symbolic representative of a number of dissonant Southern global voices. These voices threaten to disrupt the Reconstruction echo of the antebellum South with pieces of history making the South part of a larger global South conversation. The second major plot disclosure reveals that DuPont is Madam Carroll's son from an earlier marriage, whom she believed dead. DuPont, therefore, poses a direct threat to the Major's reliance on his wife and her Southern lady image. Just as much as the frozen-in-adolescence son, *Scar*, shared by the Major and Madam Carroll, DuPont is a wounded son of the South linked more largely to the West Indies by his long residence there, particularly in Martinique. Woolson's references to DuPont's love of flowers suggests Martinique's fame still today as "The Island of Flowers," a term allegedly inaugurated by Columbus calling the island "Martinica," or Island of Flowers. Columbus marks the beginning of an imperialism that resulted in the virtual extermination of Martinique's Amerindians, and the seventeenth-century's mass importation of slaves from the African coast, slaves who revolted successfully to bring about abolition in 1848, is a temblor of slave revolt taking place simultaneously with the antebellum slavery South.

DuPont, with his "slender brown fingers" (66:392, 250) and "brown face" (66:393, 408), writes songs that echo "the wild plaintive cadences of the Indian women of tribes long gone ... of the first African slaves polling their flat boats along the Southern rivers" (66:392, 250). This could be about Martinique as well as the United States South. Woolson deliberately adds this echo of global imperialism, one promptly dismissed by a Far Edgerley townswoman: "I call all the West Indies very foreign ... They don't seem to me civilized. They are principally inhabited by blacks." (66: 394, 570). DuPont provides dissonance, too, that disturbs Owen's platonic idyll of the Southern lady, Madam Carroll, whom he believes has become sexually involved with DuPont. When Owen thinks DuPont is finally leaving, he cheers, "'Hangman's day!'" (66:393, 405). An odd response, this, coming from a minister (especially one Northernized). It evokes the Reconstruction and post-Reconstruction lynching of black men accused of sexually accosting Southern women. DuPont's ominous presence provides the undertone to antebellum Southern mythology, the witness voice to Southern imperialism, extending from the imperialism of the Mexican-American War (one town resident's husband died at Chapultepec) to the global Southern reaches of slavery. Just as the Major's stunted son, as a frieze of the antebellum South, never grows up and never gets larger, DuPont dies of lingering illness.

Owen's eyes are opening to Madam Carroll's erotic agency as he imagines her coupling with an exotic "Other." Destroying his fantasy of Madam Carroll as the unconditional mother, Owen is re-routed to "the vicissitudes of desire via the Oedipus and [the] castration complex . . . the split encoded in Western Christianity between woman as asexual mother (Mary) and as erotic object (Eve)." The Freudian critic Madelon Sprengnether explains that "the third and most terrifying aspect of the preoedipal (m)other, the autonomy of her desire [is] perceived by the [male] infant as the threat of death" as opposed to "the fantasy of mother as the source of unconditional love and a focus of nostalgic longing."[25] Faced with this desiring mother, Owen is "struck into silence. This little, gentle, gentle-haired lady . . . was this she? . . . It seemed to him as if some evil spirit had suddenly taken up his abode in her" (66:393, 412).

The second reversal of plot expectations involves Owen's discovery that his assumptions are mistaken; Madam Carroll explains that Dupont is not her lover, but her son, which she is forced to admit in confidence to Sara, and, then, to Owen, in order to shield this disclosure from her husband. Closely following this is Madam Carroll's third reversal of plot assumptions. Adding to Owen's horror and disillusion, he is told that in terms of its most basic component—blood—she is *not* a member of Southern aristocracy. Madam Carroll has only been *acting* the Southern lady; she discloses that she comes from the mixed stock of a con artist Baptist minister and the daughter of a Vermont farmer. In addition, she had been previously married to an infamous scoundrel with whom she had two children, one of them DuPont. To Owen's increased dismay, he discovers that she is not as young as she had suggested; she hid her advanced age from her future husband; her pretension to youthful beauty, then, another performative façade. She is the ironic obverse of the Southern motto that Major Carroll has his young (stunted) son spell out in blocks from his book of heraldic maxims: "Good-blood-can-not-lie" (66:391, 94).

It is Sara, however, to whom Owen applies the epithet of actress; he misapprehends her motives in keeping secret meetings with DuPont to protect her stepmother, sees both women as colluding, and thus sweeps both in his condemnation of either: "'She is acting. . . . She does it well.'" This thought gives rise to an expressed scorn "fixed full upon [Sara] over the little mother's head" (66:393, 412).

In her earlier *Anne*, Woolson unambiguously condemned women with an aptitude for acting. However, the actress epithet in *For the Major* is aimed toward the South and Southern women. The Southern lady, *For the Major* implies, is in thrall to the requirements of male narcissism. Woolson's habitual use of the actress metaphor manifests in *For the Major* in support of Southern women and in resistance to the Northern postcolonial imagination of the postwar South encoded in the Southern lady archetype. The psychoanalytical critic Mary Ann Doane notes that, for Nietzsche, women had to be "veiled" in order to make "truth [for men] profound, to ensure that there is a depth that lurks behind the surface of things" (118–19). For the nihilist Nietzsche, not only is the burden of truth-bearing on women, but their depth is an illusion; hence, the unveiled woman metastasizes death in her image. In a kindred manner in *For the Major*, impending death haunts Owen's discovery that Madam Carroll has hidden her age through "her veil of curls" (265) which, when parted after the Major goes blind, shows Owen a "veil of golden hair, no longer curled ... put blankly back ... [so that] the blue eyes he had always thought so pretty, looked tired and sunken and dim with crow's-feet at the corners." For Owen, the veil is lifted; the "nothing" men fear to see signified in "the old withered look of her small wrists and hands" (355).

Readers, however, are not supposed to see Madam Carroll—or the Southern lady—in Owen's light. Woolson offers her portrait of the Southern lady by providing an *ersatz* Southern lady whose successful mimetic reproduction of the type intimates that *all* Southern ladies were similarly compelled to be mimetic reproductions. The heroism in this female archetype, for Woolson, was the selflessness of the performance. Woolson shows the great emotional relief that Madam Carroll feels in her own un-cloaking when she knows it will no longer hurt her husband; her relief that the back story of her life can be revealed, with its griefs and its sufferings, and her great bodily relief as well that she will no longer have to keep up the pretense of youthful appearance: "'You think me about thirty-five, don't you? I am forty-eight. I was thirty-five when I married the Major. All this golden hair would be heavily streaked with gray if I should let it alone. . . . I prefer that you should know; and it is also a relief to me to tell'" (66:395, 730). Reviewing *For the Major*, Henry James wrote "*For the Major* has an idea, a little fantastic perhaps, but eminently definite. This idea is the secret effort of an elderly woman to appear really as young to her husband as (owing to peculiar circumstances) he believed her to be when he married her. Nature helps her . . . and art helps nature, and her husband's illusions. . . . help them both, so that she is able to keep on the mask till his death, when she pulls it off with a passionate cry of relief—ventures at last, gives herself the luxury, to be old."[26] James understood Woolson's intention for her heroine in *For the Major* perfectly, although he misses the regional nuance in Woolson's portrait of the Southern lady—the actress of the South.

Notes

1. See Kevin O'Donnell, "Introduction," *Seekers of Scenery: Travel Writers from Southern Appalachia*, ed. Helen Hollingsworth and Kevin O'Donnell (Knoxville: University of Tennessee Press, 2004), 1–39.

2. This image of Southern womanhood is noted by critics including Anne Firor Scott, *The Southern Lady from Pedestal to Politics, 1830–1930* (Chicago: University of Chicago Press, 1995), and

Anne Goodwyn Jones, *Tomorrow's Another Day: The Woman Writer in the South, 1859–1936* (Baton Rouge: Louisiana State University Press, 1981).

3. Constance Fenimore Woolson, *Anne*, Harper's Monthly (May 1881), 859. *Anne* ran serially from December 1880 through May 1882. Future references are noted in the text by volume, date, and page according to the following key: 62:367 (December 1880), 62:370 (March 1881), 62: 371 (April 1881), 62: 372 (May 1881), 63:375 (August 1881), 64: 380 (January 1882).

4. Karen Halttunen, *Confidence Men and Painted Women: A Study of Middle-Class Culture in America* (New Haven, CT: Yale University Press, 1982).

5. Henry James, *Henry James Novels, 1881–1886: Washington Square, The Portrait of a Lady, The Bostonians* (New York: Library of America, 1985), 848, 854, 848.

6. Clare Benedict notes that Woolson "had an intense love ... of fine acting." See *Constance Fenimore Woolson, Five Generations (1785–1923)*, ed. Clare Benedict (London: Ellis, 1930), II: xiv. This is the type of conundrum critics face when examining such authors' pejorative use of the actress metaphor in their writing. For information on Edith Wharton's many connections to the theater, see Cynthia Griffin Wolff, "Lily Bart and the Drama of Femininity," *American Literary History* 6 (Spring 1994): 71–87. The quotation from James is taken from Leon Edel, *Henry James: A Life* (New York: Harper & Row, 1985), 230.

7. Kim Marra, *Strange Duets: Impresarios & Actresses in the American Theatre, 1865–1914* (Iowa City: University of Iowa Press, 2006), 11.

8. Madelon Sprengnether, "(M)other Eve: Some Revisions of the Fall in Fiction by Contemporary Writers," *Feminism and Psychoanalysis*, ed. Richard Feldstein and Judith Roof (Ithaca, NY: Cornell University Press, 1989), 300, 303.

9. In "The Traditions of Gender: Constance Fenimore Woolson and Henry James," Cheryl B. Torsney writes that "Anne Douglas and Constance Fenimore Woolson share interests and backgrounds." See *Critical Essays on Constance Fenimore Woolson*, ed. Cheryl B. Torsney (New York: G. K. Hall, 1992), 165. In the same collection, see also Sharon L. Dean, "Women as Daughters; Women as Mothers in the Fiction of Constance Woolson," 192.

10. Mary Ann Doane, "Veiling Over Desire: Close-ups of the Woman," *Feminism and Psychoanalysis*, 120–21.

11. Eric Blondel, qtd. in Doane, "Veiling Over Desire," 120–21.

12. Scott, *The Southern Lady from Pedestal to Politics*, 7, 23.

13. Marion Gouverneur, *As I Remember; Recollections of American Society during the Nineteenth Century* (New York: D. Appleton, 1911), 50, 307. Rayburn S. Moore, *Constance Fenimore Woolson* (New York: Twayne, 1963) notes the resemblance between the fictional Tante in *Anne* and Woolson's own life; see 145 n. 14. Sharon L. Dean notes that Madame Chegaray's school was "a fashionable New York academy attended mostly by Southern women." See *Constance Fenimore Woolson: Homeward Bound* (Knoxville: University of Tennessee Press, 1985), 3.

14. John Dwight Kern, *Constance Fenimore Woolson, Literary Pioneer* (Philadelphia: University of Pennsylvania Press, 1934), 48, 80.

15. See Drew Gilpin Faust, *Mothers of Invention: Women of the Slaveholding South in the American Civil War* (Chapel Hill: University of North Carolina Press, 1966), 40–42.

16. Constance Fenimore Woolson, *For the Major*, Harper's Monthly (November 1882): 915. *For the Major* ran serially from November 1882 through April 1883. Future references are noted in the text by volume, issue, and page using the following key: 65:390 (November 1882), 66:391 (December 1882), 66:392 (January 1883), 66: 393 (February 1883), 66:395 (April 1883).

17. Harriet Beecher Stowe, *Uncle Tom's Cabin* (New York: W. W. Norton, 1994), 134.

18. O'Donnell, "Introduction," 4, 14.

19. See, for instance, Catherine Clinton, *The Plantation Mistress: Woman's World in the Old South* (New York: Pantheon, 1982), 18.

20. Faust, *Mothers of Invention*, 47, 260.

21. Faust, *Mothers of Invention*, 43.

22. Scott, *The Southern Lady from Pedestal to Politics*, 105–33; Faust, *Mothers of Invention*, 27, 227; Scott, *The Southern Lady from Pedestal to Politics*, 18.

23. Constance Fenimore Woolson, "Up in the Blue Ridge," *Appletons' Journal* (August 1878): 104–25.

24. Jennifer Fleissner, *Women, Compulsion, Modernity: The Moment of American Naturalism* (Chicago: University of Chicago Press, 2004), 17.

25. Sprengnether, "(M)other Eve," 304–5.

26. Henry James, "Miss Woolson," *Literary Criticism: Essays on Literature, American, English Writers* (New York: Library of America, 1984), 642.

Northeast Angels

Henry James in Woolson's Florida

—Geraldine Murphy

While working on *The Master*, Colm Tóibín visited Lamb House for inspiration. He found what he was looking for on James's mantelpieces: in the dining room, a bust by Hendrik Andersen and in the front reception room, a piece of needlework by Constance Fenimore Woolson—salvaged by James, presumably, from her apartment in Venice after her suicide. Noting "the same pride of place" given to these artifacts, Tóibín recognized that Woolson was as important to James as the handsome young sculptor to whom he wrote his most impassioned letters.[1] While Woolson scholars would not dispute James and Woolson's intimacy, they might be struck by the disparities of representation at Lamb House rather than the equivalences. Woolson was not enshrined in memory by her novels, as Andersen was by his sculpture, but by a traditionally feminine craft. James's letters to Andersen survive, but James silenced Woolson by destroying both sides of their correspondence. By suppressing her words and displaying her needlework, the Master preserved his own fiction of the "essentially conservative" woman he described in "Miss Woolson" (1887), the essay he wrote for *Harper's Weekly*.

James's silencing propensities, however, are but one aspect of his friendship with Woolson: if he dampened (to resort to Jamesian metaphor) he also fertilized, sometimes unwittingly. By the same token, Woolson and her fiction inspired James as well. In *A Private Life of Henry James*, Lyndall Gordon has recently analyzed the relationship of Woolson and James and the intertextuality of their short stories. "The full force of their friction," she says, "was unleashed in their works, which debate the issue of dominance with a fury that was a counterpoint to mutual graciousness."[2] The rich literary relay between these two writers can hardly be described in the traditional sense of influence. It is more a force field, erotically charged, to be sure, magnetized by the dynamics of affection and competition, flattery and candor, romantic possibility and renunciation.

My project here is to pursue a line of inquiry—admirably opened by Gordon and other feminist scholars—over the broader terrain of Woolson's *East Angels*, a novel serialized in *Harper's New Monthly Magazine* from January 1885 to May 1886 and published in book form by Harper & Brothers in 1886. Set in the sleepy little coastal city of Gracias-a-Dios (St. Augustine), *East Angels* traces the encounters between a group of transplanted northerners and the local Floridians: the impoverished gentry, the African American house servants and field hands, and the poor whites of the region. This long, intricately plotted novel is a lapidary comedy of North/South manners in the era of Reconstruction, but the local-color aspect of *East Angels*, rich as it is, is subordinated to the tragic love story of two northerners, the unhappily married Margaret Harold and Evert Winthrop, her husband's cousin. In these characters, Woolson draws fictional portraits of herself and James and dramatizes several facets of their relationship, both intellectual and emotional. Developing views she had no doubt expressed in person as well as in letters and reviews, she comments on James's fiction and carries out the various debates between them on nationalism and expatriation, regionalism and cosmopolitanism. The thwarted passions of Margaret and Evert represent a truth about her relationship to James that Woolson could not otherwise express. The love "triangle" (never actually a triangle because Margaret and her husband did not love each other) is the vehicle by which Woolson ruthlessly exposes Victorian patriarchal ideologies of love and marriage sparing no one, least of all her heroine. Although Margaret is associated with the revolutionary heritage of Madame de Staël and Margaret Fuller, she is "a Corinne mute, a Margaret dumb." *East Angels* could hardly be called an autobiographical novel, yet it enacts contradictory emotions of desire and anger all too familiar to its author.

Approaching *East Angels* through the lens of Woolson and James's relationship raises a host of critical and theoretical questions that should be acknowledged. Biographical criticism has been in disrepute since the formalists held sway, and women novelists in particular have been admonished for failing to distance themselves from the raw material of experience and transform it into autonomous works of art. The insights of poststructural and postmodern theoretical discourses have further problematized bourgeois subjectivity, authority, and authorship, with the death of the author presaging the more recent deaths (or erasures) of race, gender, and sexuality. Anglo-American feminist criticism reached a crisis of confidence in the 1990s when the biographical criticism that validated women's lives, experiences, voices, and traditions encountered these theoretical paradigms. The larger question, then, is how to attend to the biographical in the current critical and theoretical climate—how to employ, in Alison Booth's words, "a more wary kind of biographical criticism" attentive to the insights of contemporary theory and yet sympathetic to the emancipatory political impulses that energized feminist criticism in the United States.[3] The more immediate question is how to return to Woolson and James's intimacy without overlooking the important revisionist perspectives on it that recent Woolson scholars have provided and without resurrecting the tragicomic stereotype of a spinster in love with a confirmed bachelor.[4]

Biographical criticism has been particularly unkind to Woolson. The James revival of the twentieth century fulfilled Woolson's prophesy of her friend's greatness, yet it kept her own work alive as a literary-historical footnote to the Master's. Leon Edel disparaged Woolson's writing as second-rate regionalism and wondered why James devoted any critical attention to it. In his detailed account of Woolson's death, Edel raises the question as to whether "frustrated love for Henry" contributed to her suicide.[5] Since the late 1980s, Woolson scholars have challenged Edel's characterization of Woolson, her work, and her relationship to James; they have interpreted Woolson's pursuit of James as professional and strategic rather romantic and pathetic, and they have detailed the tendency toward acute depression that ran in the Woolson family.[6] In the dialectic of Woolson criticism, however, this is a good moment to return to Woolson's relationship with James, for, challenging as it may have been for her, it was a galvanizing force in her fiction.[7] Woolson's "Henry James" inhabits every page of what many critics consider her finest novel.

Evert Winthrop as Henry James

Evert Winthrop is a wealthy northerner who comes south, as he says in the first line of the novel, seeking "blue sky." Evert's formidable Aunt Katrina joins him in Florida, accompanied by the estranged wife of his cousin, Lansing Harold. The beautiful, high-minded Margaret "immolates herself," says James, ". . . deliberately, completely, and repeatedly, to a husband whose behavior may as distinctly be held to have absolved her."[8] Lanse has abandoned his wife for a European *femme du monde*. After several years' absence he returns, crippled, and expects his wife to resume the outward form of their marriage. Evert initially dislikes and misjudges Margaret. He assumes, for example, that it is she who has left Lanse, because she is too prim and judgmental to appreciate the carefree manliness of her husband. Eventually, however, Evert falls deeply in love with Margaret and urges her to divorce his cousin, who deserts her again in the course of the novel and comes back a physical wreck. To Evert's pain and outrage, Margaret will not consider divorce, but he can see that the contest between love and duty is destroying her, so he reluctantly withdraws from the field. Like James's Isabel Archer, Margaret stays in her empty marriage.

While James gave no sign that he recognized himself in Evert Winthrop, there is abundant textual evidence that Woolson modeled her character on James. In a letter, Woolson had described James at thirty-six as having "a beautiful regular profile, brown beard and hair, large light grey eyes from which he banishes all expression, and a very quiet, almost cold manner." While he is "unpretending and unobtrusive," she notes that she "wouldn't like to be the person who should think from his unpretending quietness that he could not be incisive when he chose!"[9] The thirty-five-year-old Evert Winthrop also has light gray eyes, "with, for the most part, a calm expression. But they easily became keen, and they could, upon occasion, become stern." He has "a short, thick, brown beard . . . and thick, straight hair, closely cut, of the true American brown . . ."[10] In manner and temperament, too, Winthrop resembles James: he "possessed observation in abundance"; he was "prudent and cool," "a good son," and "a good nephew" (*EA* 67, 120). (His Aunt Katrina, in name at least, recalls James's Aunt Kate.) Bland and amiable on the surface, he keeps his social presentation in "strict control." His friends accuse him of wearing "a mask" (*EA* 57–58). In her letters to James (of which only four from 1882 to 1883 survive), Woolson teased him about his own buttoned-down demeanor, yet she also praised her friend for his "incorruptible, and dignified, and reasonable modesty."[11] Similarly, Winthrop "was essentially modest at heart," and despite his urbanity he "had his ideal of what the best of life should be, and he kept it like a Madonna in its shrine" (*EA* 121)—a simile evocative of James's own short story, "The Madonna of the Future" (1873) and its theme of artistic idealism. When the Civil War broke out, Winthrop was abroad, "indulging that love for pictures which he was rather astonished to find that he possessed" (*EA* 128)—a love that James, too, possessed.

There are many details of James and Winthrop's lives that do not coincide, that indeed suggest a mirror opposition between them. The household James grew up in, for example, was crowded, noisy, peripatetic, and idiosyncratic, with a transcendentalist seeker at the helm; Winthrop, however, was an only child whose mother died after his birth. He was raised in an empty, old New England house, systematically and rigorously trained by a Puritan father who regarded science as the new revelation. Winthrop inherited the family iron foundry and a considerable fortune, yet by acquiring iron mines and other businesses, he became a Gilded-Age industrialist and quadrupled his wealth. During the war, he returned from Europe and served as a captain in the Union forces, a step the elder James brothers famously did not take. These contrasts between family, upbringing, and education, between businessman and artist, warrior and civilian, man of action and man of contemplation provide a convenient cover to throw readers off the scent; James hated publicity and would not have appreciated an obvious fictional portrait. Nevertheless, Woolson's representation of Winthrop masculinizes the James figure in a way that would have flattered the original. As an American artist, James fretted about being "uptown" in the domestic sphere rather than "downtown" in the masculine world of business. When Evert tells his cousin "I'm a manufacturer myself" (*EA* 411), it is hard not to read his comment as a double-entendre.

Florida as Italy

Woolson makes Evert Winthrop a descendent of Puritan Boston on his father's side and Dutch New York on his mother's, thus identifying him with James's American residences as well as the cultural hegemony of the northeast and its cultural myopia toward the rest of the country. One theme of her epistolary discourse with James was his ignorance of the United States. When Woolson emphatically tells him, "No—you do not love your native land," and declares herself "an American of the interior of New Hampshire (my birthplace), an American of the Western Reserve of Ohio," she is figuratively donning a coonskin cap, claiming allegiance to mythic American figures like Daniel Boone, Davy Crockett, and Natty Bumppo, her great-uncle Fenimore Cooper's literary creation (HJL III 527). Her comic patriotism was no doubt more diverting than conversations with his family on the subject of his expatriation or the chauvinism of American reviewers who criticized *Daisy Miller* (1878) and *Hawthorne* (1879). Yet she had a serious perspective to offer on regional and national identity, and she dramatized it in Winthrop's experience of Florida:

> Like most New-Englanders, he had unconsciously cherished the belief that all there was of historical importance, of historical picturesqueness, even, in the beginnings of the republic, was associated with the Puritans from whom he was on his father's side descended.... And if, with liberality, he should stretch the lines a little to include the old Dutch land-holders of Manhattan Island, and the river up which the *Half-moon* had sailed, that had seemed to him all that could possibly be necessary; there was, indeed, nothing else to include. But here was a life, an atmosphere, to whose contemporary and even preceding existence on their own continent neither Puritan nor Patroon had paid heed. (*EA* 15)

Winthrop tells Dr. Kirby he is "ashamed of [him]self" for describing everything he sees like a tourist in a foreign country, when Florida "ought to be as much a part of me, and I of it, as though it were Massachusetts Bay." Dr. Kirby, who feels no "sympathetic ownership" in Winthrop's native region, marvels inwardly at such "singular views" but concludes they are harmless enough: "Florida would remain Florida, in spite of northern hallucinations" (*EA* 83). Formerly unacquainted with the South, Winthrop now annexes it in a benevolent yet nonetheless imperial act of imagination, while Dr. Kirby, even after the Civil War, is still staunchly anticolonial. Thinking nationally, Woolson implies, involves thinking regionally, or at least recognizing there are those who do.

Woolson also figures Florida as a foreign country, but not in the way Dr. Kirby does. As she repatriates the James figure and enriches his understanding of American identity, she internationalizes Florida, making it a domestic Italy. The striking physical resemblances between the two semi-tropical peninsulas are often observed: "the blue above the silver beaches of Florida melts as languorously as that above Capri's enchanted shore" (*EA* 53). More important, Florida is associated with Italy because of its significance for Woolson and James. "It was in Italy that they had met, Italy had been a party to their first impressions of each other, and Italy should be a party to their happiness."[12] This observation is from *The Portrait of a Lady* rather than *East Angels* and refers to Osmond and Isabel Archer, but it speaks to Woolson's expectations as well. She and James had first met in Florence in 1880. Woolson had never been abroad before, and James became her guide to the treasures of the Old World. He was "a delightful companion," she wrote to more than one relative. "He has been so much in Italy that he knows the pictures as well as I know Florida."[13] Over the next two years, James spent several months in the United States. "You are never in Italy," Woolson complained to him from Venice in 1883, "but always in America; just going; or there; or just returned" (*HJL* III 557). The following year, she began to write *East Angels*.

The "beautiful peninsula" that awakens Winthrop's appreciation for his own country echoes the "divine peninsula" that James described in his travel writing on Italy. Significantly, Winthrop begins to reevaluate his conception of national identity and to appreciate the relative antiquity of Floridian civilization from the upper story of East Angels; his elevated vantage point opens literal and figurative vistas that condense Winthrop and James, Florida and Italy, the Spanish conquest of the new world and the Italian Renaissance:

> When Raphael was putting into the backgrounds of his pictures those prim, slenderly foliaged trees which he had seen from Perugino's windows in his youth, the Spaniards were exploring this very Florida shore; yet when he, Evert Winthrop, had discovered the same tall, thin trees . . . from the overhanging balcony of the little inn at Assisi—it had seemed to overhang all Umbria—did he not think of Raphael's day as far back in the past . . . ? (*EA* 16)

Perugia, James had observed in "A Chain of Cities" (1873), ought to be known not only "as the city of Raphael's master" but also "as the little City of the infinite View"; due to its centrality, "you all but span the divine peninsula from sea to sea."[14] Through the figure of Evert Winthrop, who rides horseback on the pine barrens of Florida the way James rode on the Italian *campagna*, Woolson masculinizes her friend and makes him textually available for heterosexual romance. She repatriates the cosmopolite and schools him in the ways of his native land. At the same time, she "Europeanizes" Florida by superimposing Italy upon it, conflating the "beautiful peninsula" and the "divine peninsula," post–Civil War Florida and post-*Risorgimento* Italy.

James did not visit the American South until late in life, but he, too, found Italy in Florida. In the concluding chapter of *The American Scene* (1907), he ironically invokes Byron's anticipation of Italy when he reaches balmy Jacksonville and finds himself capable of being "Byronically foolish" about the St. Johns River serving as his Mincio. These rich associations cannot be sustained, however; aside from its natural beauty, Florida is as prosaic as the rest of the United States. Spanish St. Augustine, the Gracias-a-Dios of *East Angels*, provides kitsch, not antiquity. Illustrators, novelists, and genealogists conspire to create a romantic past, says James, and the public "goes upon its knees to be humbuggingly humbugged."[15] Whether he ruthlessly demythologizes Florida to defy the script which Woolson had written him into we cannot know. But his concession to a "pleasing" but "consciously and confessedly weak" Florida so feminizes the state, and is so characteristic of the incapacitating tributes that Woolson received from James, that it prompts the question. Speaking for the state that cannot speak for itself, he observes "that it really knew itself unequal to any extravagance of demand upon it, but that (if it might so plead to one's tenderness) it would always do its gentle best." To James, "the Florida of that particular tone was a Florida adorable."[16] A Florida abashed and inarticulate evokes uncomfortable parallels with Woolson and her female protagonists. Patriarchal silencing is a motif of her corpus, and it is highly elaborated in *East Angels*. The novel ends—as does her better-known short story, "At the Château of Corinne"—with a coercive husband having the last, patronizing word, unaware of its import to his sensitive spouse.

The Portrait of a Lady

Woolson also pays homage in *East Angels* to two of James's fictions set in Italy, *Daisy Miller* and *The Portrait of a Lady* (1881). Garda Thorne is remarkably beautiful like Daisy, as well as frank and natural. Winthrop finds her "the most natural young girl he had ever met" (*EA* 9). She tries to provoke Winthrop/Winterbourne, the gentleman who is too "stiff," who has "lived too long in foreign parts" (in this case, the North). In a carriage on the pine barrens, for example, she urges Winthrop to cross a stream that looks too deep to him in order to see him "excited." Her caprice recalls the whim Daisy suddenly has for a ride in a rowboat or her more provocative flirtation with Giovanelli. Thanks to Garda's willfulness, she and Winthrop spend the night together stranded on the barrens. They are intrigued enough with each other to become engaged, although to Dr. Kirby's consternation, his young charge treats her commitment as lightly as Daisy Miller does. Garda is something of a romantic decoy in *East Angels*, however, for Winthrop's true object of affection is a more mature, sensitive, and profound woman. In character and situation, Margaret Harold bears a much closer resemblance to Isabel Archer Osmond.

Georgia Kreiger has accurately called *East Angels* a rewriting of *The Portrait of a Lady*.[17] It is no accident that portrait imagery abounds in Woolson's novel. After Winthrop meets Garda he realizes that he is thinking about her a good deal, "but was it not natural—coming unexpectedly upon so much beauty, set in so unfamiliar a frame? It was a new portrait, and he was fond of portraits; in picture-galleries he always looked more at the portraits than at anything else" (*EA* 24). The man Garda eventually marries, Lucien Spenser, is an amateur painter who begins with landscapes and ends up painting Garda's portrait. Winthrop, too, takes up sketching in Florida. Margaret's husband, Lanse, is a large, genial, proto-Hemingwayesque outdoorsman who on the surface is nothing like Gilbert Osmond, yet both are selfish egoists who marry idealistic women and then aestheticize and objectify them. To accommodate Lanse, Margaret gives up her simple dress and "Quakerish" hairstyle and wears expensive finery, jewels, and a more elaborate coiffure. "[Y]ou might very well dress to please me," he reasons, "since I regard you as a charming picture, keeping my hands off." As she sits knitting one evening, Lanse insists on rearranging the composition she makes. "It's only that I want my picture more complete—that's all" (*EA* 439, 442). With her husband's arrival, Margaret is transformed into a figure very much like Isabel—not the vibrant girl of Gardencourt, but rather the Roman Isabel on display Thursday evenings at the Palazzo Roccanera: coiffed, brocaded, bejeweled, and miserable.

The parallel between Margaret and Isabel (and through Isabel to the goddess Diana) is underlined in the remarkable midnight scene in the swamp. When Margaret and Winthrop journey into a Floridian heart of darkness by torchlight, she is wearing a small gold arrow pin, a piece of jewelry that helps her save Winthrop. (To prevent him from succumbing to swamp gas, Margaret soaks her lace scarf and fastens it around his forehead with the pin.) Woolson admired *Portrait* and wrote to James that it was his best novel to date; her only substantive criticism was that James never made it clear "whether Isabel really loved Osmond." If she did not, then "the absence of heart-breaking, insupportable, killing griefs in her heart and life ... is quite natural." If she did love him, her "following agony" ought to be represented (*HJL* III 535). The grief and agony that may be wanting in *Portrait* are amply furnished in *East Angels*. Woolson details Margaret's suffering within the marriage, as James did Isabel's, but she makes it clear that Margaret never loved Lanse. The literally killing griefs that Margaret endures are caused by her renunciation of her deep, passionate love for Winthrop.

The Portrait of a Gentleman

"How did you ever dare write a portrait of a lady?" Woolson asks James in the same letter. "Fancy any woman's attempting a portrait of a gentleman! Would'nt [sic] there be a storm of ridicule!" (*HJL* III 535). She deprecates her own creative powers in that quarter, yet she attempts such a portrait in *East Angels*. Many contemporary reviewers of the novel found Margaret too good to be true, but they did not question the verisimilitude of the principal male characters, Lanse and Evert. The preoccupation with Margaret may have diverted attention from Woolson's remarkable analysis of patriarchal ideology and her detailed, and devastating, portrait of sexual politics.

Lanse, the Osmond figure, wounds Margaret with impunity—repeatedly, guilelessly, and remorselessly. Their marital history is not the stuff of broken crockery or sentimental tears, however, but a *haute bourgeois* nightmare of propriety, a domestic space in which no one can hear Margaret scream. Woolson's representation of a bad match is calculated to inflict maximum emotional damage upon the woman and minimum social opprobrium upon the man. Well into the novel, on a foray into the Monnlungs swamp, the returned prodigal takes Evert into his confidence regarding his desertions and infidelities, about which he had advised Margaret "to treat such things as a lady should," with a discretion born of powerlessness to protect *his* good name as well as her own. Having no close relatives to go to, Margaret spends eight years enduring uncharitable constructions on Lanse's desertion by his own doting aunt and judgmental cousin. Aunt Katrina has become dependent on Margaret, but Lanse confidently tells Evert that Mrs. Rutherford "would give her up to me" (*EA* 414–18). Like Isabel, Margaret is merely a tool for her husband's convenience. Where Gilbert Osmond is deliberately sadistic, however, Lanse is unconsciously selfish—or, as Woolson implies, simply exercising patriarchal privilege:

> his principle ... appeared to have been to allow himself ... the most radical liberty of action, while at the same time in speech, in tastes, in general manner, he remained firmly, even aggressively, a conservative; Lanse's "manner" had been much admired. Always, so he would have said, he behaved "as a gentleman should." (*EA* 432)

No "serpent in a bank of flowers" (*PL* 461), Lanse is a good storyteller, amusing, fair, and generous by his own lights. He may be less frightening to his wife than Osmond but he is certainly as galling. Because he is incapable of sounding the depths of her character or understanding her true nature, Lanse's well-meant compliments to his wife act as salt in the wound. At the end of the novel, he complains that Evert never visits them, then observes, "Do you know that you've grown old, Madge, before your time?" She acknowledges that she has and Lanse's often-quoted final comment closes *East Angels*: "Well—you're a good woman" (*EA* 591). Fear and loathing may be the proper response to Osmond; to Lanse it is despair.

Evert Winthrop is not Lanse. To begin with, he's more "American" than his cousin, who, finding the education of a virginal young bride tiresome, muses about a "paradise" in which a girl of seventeen knows as much as a woman of thirty. "Don't talk your French to me," Winthrop growls, "I don't admire it" (*EA* 413). When he hears about Lanse's past behavior and his intention to get Margaret back, Evert is disgusted. Blunt and honest, he is a man of deep feeling, capable of an enduring love and faithfulness. Garda discovers Margaret's secret, and she urges her friend to leave Lanse for Evert. "Such a love as his would be! . . . [H]ow *can* you refuse it?" "He is like you, with him it is once" (*EA* 578, 579). Nevertheless, like Lanse, Evert is sexist almost to the point of misogyny. To apply the yardstick of *The Portrait of a Lady* once again, the James figure in *East Angels* is not Ralph Touchett with sound lungs but Caspar Goodwood revisited.

Evert's passion for Margaret is profound and unshakable, yet, obtuse about her feelings and contemptuous of her principles, he bullies and exhausts her. He's furious when she thinks and acts independently of him: when she insists on the midnight search in the swamp for Lanse, for example, or—after Lanse's second desertion—she keeps Evert at arm's length. In the isolated house on the St. Johns River, he considers breaking into her bedroom. Although he realizes that this is going "too far," he descends the stairs "with a momentary revival in his breast all the same of the old despotic feeling, the masculine feeling, that a woman should not be allowed to dictate to a man what he should say or not say, do or not do; in refusing to see him even for one moment, Margaret was dictating" (*EA* 488). After he declares his love, late in the novel, he says he will always keep Margaret in his sights: "Do you suppose I should obey your rules—even your wishes? Not the least in the world!" (*EA* 541). Only a fear of his presence makes her declare her love for him, so that he understands why he must stay away. Even so, he comes back: "Have you I will!" he cries, and holds her wrists "with a grasp like iron" (*EA* 550). A series of encounters is engineered by Winthrop, who keeps advancing arguments to bring them together. "And must I always be the one?" she asks, meaning the one principled enough to leave (*EA* 590).

Corinne, or Florida

The parallels between Margaret Harold and Woolson are as striking as those between Evert Winthrop and James. Like Woolson, Margaret hails from New Hampshire; she is nomadic, with no real home of her own; she is enervated by perfumes and floral scents; she collects ferns; she is in Florida accompanying an ailing, elderly relative (in Woolson's case, her mother). Like Anne, the heroine of

Woolson's previous novel, Margaret is unappreciated and misunderstood by those around her because of her sagacity, intelligence, emotional depth, and refinement. Woolson emphasizes the common lot of women who write and women who do not when she associates Margaret with Madame de Staël and Margaret Fuller. It is Mrs. Thorne, the quaint relic of New England transcendentalism, who points out the resemblance:

> "Do you know, Mr. Winthrop, that Mrs. Harold quite fills my idea of a combination of our own Margaret Fuller and Madame de Staël."
> "Yet she can hardly be called talkative, can she?" said Winthrop, smiling.
> "It is her face, the language of her eye, that gives me my impression. Her silence seems to me but a fullness of intellect, a fullness at times almost throbbing; she is a Corinne mute, a Margaret dumb."
> "Were they ever mute, those two?" asked Winthrop.
> Mrs. Thorne glanced at him. "I see you do not admire lady conversationalists," she murmured, relaxing into her guarded little smile. (*EA* 100)

A wealth of meaning is coded in this exchange. Woolson and James differed on de Staël and Fuller, and, like nationalism and expatriation, this subject may have been a topic of their discourse that found its way into fiction. Today, *Corinne, or Italy* (1807) is rarely read outside of graduate programs, yet de Staël's novel was an important influence on nineteenth-century women writers, Woolson among them. The female version of the Byronic hero, Corinne is an *improvisatrice* whose divinely inspired poetry enthralls her native Italy. She first appears en route to the Capitol to be crowned with a laurel wreath in the tradition of Petrarch and Tasso. Sensitive to the attention of handsome Lord Nelvil, Corinne turns back quickly to glance at him and her crown slips from her hair, ominously foreshadowing her fatal love for the conventional Northern aristocrat and the loss of her artistic independence. Margaret Fuller, who identified with de Staël, was dubbed "the Yankee Corinna." Her story, "Mariana," is a version of the Corinne narrative, and the figure she cut during the fabled "Conversations" she held for Boston women in the early 1840s further echo de Staël's flair for the dramatic, her sybilline knowledge, and her conversational brilliance. Similarly, Fuller achieved fulfillment in Italy through her love for Ossoli and the birth of their son as well as in her involvement with the Italian revolution. Both authors wrote their heroines as versions of themselves, especially de Staël, who sat for her portrait turbaned like Domenichino's Sybil.[18]

James's and Woolson's heroines, one in post-*Risorgimento* Italy and the other in post–Civil War Florida, allude, if only by contrast, to literary foremothers for whom Italy represented creative inspiration, liberation, and personal fulfillment. When in *The Portrait of a Lady* the Countess Gemini, Osmond's sister, tells Isabel that their mother was called "the American Corinne," she acknowledges that they are "dreadfully fallen, I think, and perhaps you'll pick us up" (384). Isabel, in other words, might revivify them with a purer spirit of transcendentalism. But Isabel cannot turn the clock back to the antebellum age; romantic idealism gives way to realism in the post-revolutionary era, and she is, as Ralph exclaims, "ground in the very mill of the conventional!" (612). Neither can Margaret Harold escape to the North from the slavery of a loveless marriage; Lanse's second return extinguishes that dream. Isabel reconciles herself to Rome as "the place where people had suffered" (551), just as Margaret resigns herself to the American South, another place where people had suffered.

In the thousands of pages of literary criticism that James published in his long career, there are few references to Madame de Staël. He dutifully observes that she "discovered Germany" for the French and—in the introduction to "Miss Woolson"—that de Staël was one of France's "three female writers of the first rank," but he clearly found her estate, Coppet, more charming than its mistress.[19] The playful tone of a 1903 letter does not mask the aggression of his desire to kick "that big yellow-satin *derrière* of Mme de Staël" (HJL IV 265). His reservations about Fuller are better known; in *Hawthorne*, James observes that despite her commanding presence in transcendentalist circles, the Yankee Corinna "left nothing behind her but the memory of a memory.... [S]he was a talker, she was *the* talker, she was the genius of talk." Her "strange history" and "strange destiny" eclipsed her writing. Fuller's presence—the "Margaret-ghost" as James later called it—inhabits his fictions, especially *Portrait* and *The Bostonians* (1886).[20]

Woolson explores masculine hostility toward the *improvisatrice* in "At the Château of Corinne," (1887) a story that has provocative similarities to *East Angels* and sheds additional light on the themes under discussion. John Ford, a character modeled on James, plays Nelvil to Katharine Winthrop's Corinne. Ford dismisses Katharine's volume of poetry and the very notion of a woman writing. "Every honest man feels like going to her, poor mistaken sibyl that she is, closing her lips with gentle hand, and leading her away to some far spot among the quiet fields, where she can learn her error, and begin her life anew," he tells Katharine. He urges her to take his attack "as a true woman should," echoing Lanse's advice regarding a husband's infidelity.[21] Among the most striking parallels between this story and *East Angels* are the courtships conducted by the James figures. Both are struggles for dominance that require the progressive humbling of the beloved. "You would keep women down with an iron hand," Katharine tells Ford (244), recalling Evert Winthrop's iron foundry and his iron grip. The silencing of Katharine and Margaret is also immediately evident, particularly in contrast to their literary antecedents, de Staël and Fuller. Katharine relinquishes her pen to be a "true woman," the angel of John Ford's house back in New York. Margaret (whose maiden name, Cruger, echoes Fuller's name) is neither an *improvisatrice* nor a revolutionary; to be either was to open oneself to the masculine ridicule to which both de Staël and Fuller were subjected—the kind of ridicule James was eminently capable of employing. Feminized in other arenas, he exercised male privilege most fiercely in the literary marketplace; many women writers dreaded him as a reviewer. It is not surprising that Margaret, like Katharine, is silenced, nor that Woolson, a "ladylike" woman writer who subscribed to the dictates of "true womanhood" and deferred to James personally and professionally, would feel acutely the contradictions that Katharine and Margaret embody.

Less obvious, but equally intriguing, are the historical implications of the name "Winthrop" in Woolson's novel and short story. Evert Winthrop's Puritan lineage from the Massachusetts Bay colony is clear enough in *East Angels*. His ancestor John Winthrop, the first governor of the colony, was hostile to intellectual women and banned the famous Antinomian *improvisatrice*, Anne Hutchinson, in order to silence her. Napoleon had similarly exiled Madame de Staël to Coppet because he saw her as a threat to the imperial order of post-revolutionary France. In "At the Château of Corinne," Woolson also hints at an American tradition of patriarchal control: Katharine first married a Winthrop (when she was seventeen and he fifty-two), and Ford's proposal to her—at Coppet—is presided over by "Benjamin Franklin," a caretaker who holds the keys to Corinne's estate. The conclusion of Ford's sardonic toast to the portraits of Corinne/de Staël and her circle—that they never step from their canvases into the present—represents a late-nineteenth-century determination to suppress revolutionary possibilities, especially as they pertain to women. Ford's success is apparent in the last paragraphs of the story. Corinne is safely contained in *his* library, where a painting of Coppet hangs above the collected works of Madame de Staël. Her writings no longer inspire a wife who has put down her pen but serve as a trophy of his rapacious courtship.

Woolson and James

At the same time chapters of *East Angels* were appearing in *Harper's New Monthly Magazine*, *The Bostonians* was coming out in *The Century* (February 1885–February 1886). In *his* novel, James is probably teasing Woolson when he refers to another domestic peninsula with "low horizons," "mild air," and "summer haze"—Cape Cod—as "the Italy, so to speak, of Massachusetts."[22] A private joke of the same order, directed at James, occurs in *East Angels*: on the foray with Margaret into the swamp at midnight, Evert ironically predicts that they'll never survive. "They'll write our biographies," he tells Margaret, and opines that the only literature "so completely composed of falsehoods, owing to half being kept back, as biographies... [are] autobiographies" (*EA* 470). Although James eventually wrote his autobiography (and kept more than half back), he feared public exposure and made life difficult for his future biographer.[23] Serial publication was ideal for this kind of literary backchat, and it is likely that Woolson and James scattered subtle references in their fiction for each other's appreciation.

More significant, however, are the similarities between *East Angels* and *The Bostonians* in subject and theme. Both are set in the post–Civil War United States and address questions of nationalism and regionalism, sexual politics and patriarchy, love and renunciation. Upon hearing Verena Tarrant's inspired public speaking, Basil Ransom remembers "the *improvisatrice* of Italy, and this was a chastened, modern American version of the type, a New England Corinna, with a mission instead of a lyre" (*Bostonians* 270). The references to Fuller in the characterizations of Olive Chancellor and Verena are richer and more explicit than in *The Portrait of a Lady*, and the domestic progeny of antebellum transcendentalists are more "dreadfully fallen" than the expatriate Osmonds, from the glory days of abolitionism to the quackeries of reform. Yet compliant, good-natured Verena is even less prepared than Isabel to pick them up. Ransom is as uncompromising as John Ford and as relentless as Evert Winthrop in making her choose love over work, him over Olive. The feminist *improvisatrice* must trade public speaking for pillow talk. "You won't sing in the Music Hall," Ransom tells Verena, "but you will sing to me" (402). In the conclusion, he carries her off wrapped in a cloak "to conceal her face and her identity," and leaves the Music Hall in "complete, tremendous silence" (464). Clearly, James had been attentive to *East Angels*. Possibly he was influenced in his topic by Woolson's raillery about his ignorance of America. In an 1883 notebook entry, he describes the new novel as "an attempt to show that I *can* write an American story."[24]

It is easy to forgive Woolson for playing the America card with gusto, for it was the only advantage she enjoyed. Socially and professionally she was more vulnerable than James, and emotionally and psychologically, she was vulnerable *to* him. When Margaret tells Winthrop "I adore you" and yet refuses to divorce his cousin, we can read this as an erotically charged articulation of love and rage, a bold declaration that is simultaneously a rejection. Married, Margaret is doubly inviolate: to her husband because of his crippled body and to Winthrop because she has a husband. Romantic love hardly leveled the playing field for Victorian men and women, yet the man who is enthralled is at least momentarily powerless. In "At the Château of Corinne," a smitten John Ford declares to Katharine, "Do with me as you please: I must bear it" (241). When there is no hope of fulfillment, however, the lover experiences something of the abjection usually reserved for women. If Garda is right—"with him it is once"—then in renouncing Winthrop, Margaret imposes renunciation, suffering, and a blighted life upon him as well. Indeed, she announces her love only to make it clear that he can never see her again.

East Angels is Woolson's richest engagement with the heart and mind of Henry James. His appearance, demeanor, and regional affiliations are identical to those of Evert Winthrop, and the divergent points of the portrait—Winthrop's military service as a Union officer, his career as a successful industrialist and businessman—masculinize James in a manner he would have appreciated. James and Woolson were never in the United States together once they became intimates, so she could never introduce him to the places she loved. She brings Winthrop to Florida, however, to appreciate his own country and to reflect upon his sense of national identity—to learn, in short, the lessons she wanted James to learn. At the same time, she cosmopolitanizes Florida by identifying it with James's Italy. These two mild peninsulas rich in history and natural beauty symbolize the fragility of national unity in the aftermath of revolution and civil war in Europe and the United States. Woolson's novel also revises *The Portrait of a Lady* from a woman's perspective. Margaret is a sister to Isabel Osmond, motivated by the highest principles in marrying yet trapped in an unbearable union, while Lanse and Osmond are brothers under the skin: both control and display their wives and use them as tools for their own convenience. Evert Winthrop is a better man than Lanse, but he, too, wants to dominate the woman he loves. Woolson draws on the heritage of European and American romanticism and echoes James in *Portrait* by representing Margaret as a fallen, silenced version of earlier nineteenth-century *improvisatrices*. In the Reconstruction South she dreams of achieving freedom but is instead re-enslaved.

While *East Angels* allowed Woolson to carry on intellectual and literary debates with James and even to reinvent him and his fiction, it also afforded the more radical possibilities of performing ambivalent passions toward the Master of ambiguity: to avow without avowing, to control without controlling, to spurn and humble for life. Thwarted love equalizes Margaret and Evert; a mutual anguish is the only alternative to submission and dominance. No one is likely in this critical climate to lose sight of the fact that Margaret is a fictional construction, but neither do I want to sever entirely the relationship between the performative text and the historical author. Just as a feminism that ironizes "women" will have a dubious grassroots appeal, so too a literary criticism that kills the author will have unfortunate consequences for women writers. Margaret may be "a Corinne mute, a Margaret dumb," but there is no reason for her creator to share that fate.

Notes

1. Colm Tóibín, "The Haunting," March 14, 2004, www.telegraph.co.uk, 1–2.
2. Lyndall Gordon, *A Private Life of Henry James: Two Women and His Art* (New York: Norton, 1998), 172.
3. One of the few recent texts on this topic is William H. Epstein, ed., *Contesting the Subject: Essays in the Postmodern Theory and Practice of Biography and Biographical Criticism* (West Lafayette, IN: Purdue University Press, 1991), "Introduction," 1–7. Alison Booth, "Biographical Criticism and the 'Great' Woman of Letters: The Example of George Eliot and Virginia Woolf," *Contesting the Subject*, 86. On the crisis in Anglo-American feminist criticism, see Susan Gubar, "What Ails Feminist Criticism?" *Critical Inquiry* 24 (1998): 878–902.
4. Interestingly, fiction has rushed in where criticism has feared to tread. James and Woolson's relationship has been the subject of four recent novels: Emma Tennant, *Felony* (2002; New York: Vintage, 2003); David Lodge, *Author, Author* (New York: Viking, 2004); Colm Tóibín, *The Master: A Novel* (New York: Scribners, 2004); and Elizabeth Maguire, *The Open Door* (New York: Other Press, 2008).
5. Leon Edel, *Henry James: The Middle Years, 1882–1895* (Philadelphia: J. B. Lippincott-Avon Books, 1962), 203–4, 363.
6. Cheryl B. Torsney, "The Traditions of Gender: Constance Fenimore Woolson and Henry James," and Joan Myers Weimer, "The 'Admiring Aunt' and the 'Proud Salmon of the Pond': Constance Fenimore Woolson's Struggle with Henry James," *Critical Essays on Constance Fenimore Woolson*, ed. Cheryl B. Torsney (New York: G. K. Hall, 1992), 152–71, 203–16; Sharon L. Dean, *Constance Fenimore Woolson: Homeward Bound* (Knoxville: University of Tennessee Press, 1995), 82–98.
7. Gordon's study inaugurates such a move. See also Victoria Coulson, *Henry James, Women, and Realism* (Cambridge: Cambridge University Press, 2007), 96–140, especially 132–35. With subtlety and theoretical sophistication, Coulson interprets the social/fictional engagement of these authors as "a collaborative game" that acts out each player's accommodation and resistance to heteronormativity.
8. Henry James, "Miss Woolson," *The American Essays of Henry James*, ed. Leon Edel (1956; Princeton, NJ: Princeton University Press, 1990), 171.
9. Clare Benedict, *Constance Fenimore Woolson* (London: Ellis, 1930), 185n.
10. Constance Fenimore Woolson, *East Angels* (New York: Harper's, 1886), 41. Subsequent references will be cited in the text as EA.
11. Leon Edel, ed., *Henry James Letters*, 4 vols. (Cambridge, MA: Harvard University Press, 1974–1984), III, 526, 543. Subsequent references will be cited in the text as HJL I–IV.
12. Henry James, *The Portrait of a Lady*, ed. Nicola Bradbury (New York: Oxford University Press, 1995), 380. Subsequent references will be cited in the text.
13. Benedict, *Constance Fenimore Woolson*, 192.
14. Henry James, "A Chain of Cities," *Collected Travel Writings: The Continent*, ed. Leon Edel (New York: Library of America, 1993), 504.
15. Henry James, *The American Scene* (1907; London: Granville, 1987), 312–13, 329–30.
16. James, *The American Scene*, 331–32.
17. Georgia Kreiger, "*East Angels*: Constance Fenimore Woolson's Revision of Henry James's *The Portrait of a Lady*," *Legacy* 22.1 (2005): 18–29.
18. Ellen Moers's discussion of the influence of the Corinne myth on Anglo-American women writers is still the most comprehensive. *Literary Women* (New York: Doubleday, 1976), 173–210. Woolson was introduced to *Corinne, or Italy* by her teacher at the Cleveland Female Seminary, Miss Guilford (Gordon, *Private Life*, 23). On de Staël's importance to Fuller, see Paula Blanchard, "*Corinne*

and 'the Yankee Corinna': Madame de Staël and Margaret Fuller," *Woman as Mediatrix: Essays on Nineteenth-Century European Women Writers*, ed. Avriel H. Goldberger (Westport, CT: Greenwood Press, 1987), 39–46.

19. Henry James, *Literary Criticism*, ed. Leon Edel, 2 vols. (New York: Library of America, 1984): "discovering Germany" qtd. in II, *French Writers, Other European Writers, The Prefaces to the New York Edition*, 28. James, "Miss Woolson," 163. James mentions Sainte-Beuve's reservations about "the 'romantic' life" that went on at Coppet (II: 686) and notes "the full complement of malice" that de Staël, Madame Récamier, and their ilk possessed. *Literary Criticism* I, *Essays on Literature, American Writers, English Writers*, 200.

20. Henry James, *Hawthorne*, Intro. Tony Tanner (London: Macmillan/St. Martins, 1967), 83. Katherine Swett asserts that Corinne "shadows Woolson's novel as she does James's [*Portrait*]" but does not analyze how, focusing instead on travel and scene. "Corinne Silenced: Improper Places in the Narrative Form of Constance Fenimore Woolson's *East Angels*," *Constance Fenimore Woolson's Nineteenth Century: Essays*, ed. Victoria Brehm (Detroit: Wayne State University Press, 2001), 163. See Joel Porte for a brief but cogent consideration of Isabel's debt to Corinne, "Introduction: *The Portrait of a Lady* and 'Felt Life,'" *New Essays on "The Portrait of a Lady*," ed. Joel Porte (Cambridge: Cambridge University Press, 1990), 12–14. More critics have observed the influence of Fuller on *Portrait*. Kathleen Lawrence's analysis is astute (although she finds James more sympathetic to Fuller than I do). "Osmond's Complaint: Gilbert Osmond's Mother and the Cultural Context of James's *The Portrait of a Lady*," *Henry James Review* 26 (2005): 52–67. See also John Carlos Rowe, *The Other Henry James* (Durham, NC: Duke University Press, 1998), 39–42, and Paul John Eakin, "Margaret Fuller, Hawthorne, James, and Sexual Politics," *South Atlantic Quarterly* 75 (1976): 331–38. In 1884, as Woolson was beginning to write *East Angels* and James *The Bostonians*, Julian Hawthorne created a stir in northeastern literary circles when he published in *Nathaniel Hawthorne and His Wife* a hostile reflection on Margaret Fuller previously omitted from his father's *Italian Notebooks*.

21. Constance Fenimore Woolson, "At the Château of Corinne," *Women Artists, Women Exiles: "Miss Grief" and Other Stories: Constance Fenimore Woolson*, ed. Joan Myers Weimer (New Brunswick, NJ: Rutgers University Press, 1988), 233–34. Subsequent references will be cited in the text.

22. Henry James, *The Bostonians*, Intro. Irving Howe (New York: Modern Library, 1956), 356. Subsequent references will be cited in the text.

23. Leon Edel, *Literary Biography: The Alexander Lectures*, 1955–56 (Toronto: University of Toronto Press, 1957), 26.

24. James, *The Complete Notebooks of Henry James*, ed. Leon Edel and Lyall H. Powers (New York: Oxford University Press, 1987), 19.

The Merits of Transit

Woolson's Return to Reconstruction in *Jupiter Lights*

—Sharon Kennedy-Nolle

In a memorable scene from the late novel *Jupiter Lights* (1889), the heroine Eve Bruce encounters her sister-in-law Cicely Abercrombie. Luring Eve to the Southern mansion's "disused" ballroom, Cicely compels Eve to dance as she "put her arms round her waist and forced her forward"; she then "seized Eve's comb," undoing Eve's hair.[1] The eerie, sensual scene predates the domestic violence that will follow when Cicely's absent husband returns and tries to murder the family. Critics like Caroline Gebhard have thus read this erotic moment of homosocial alliance as an alternative to the violence inherent in heterosexual unions.[2] But what is especially striking is Cicely's song for the dance. In a "silvery voice" she chants she is "niggerless, niggerless, nig-ig-ig-gerless," always ending with "a wild little courtesy" (40). Repeated elsewhere, the song makes clear that the novel's preoccupation with domestic violence integrates the postwar roles of domestic workers. Woolson suggests through her resolution of household trauma that no true sectional healing can begin without considering the place of freedpeople in the reconstructed family.

Although her concern with both the configuration of the postwar national family and the role of freedpeople as citizens was longstanding, *Jupiter Lights* remains unique as a novel of the Redemption era, which nominally began with the Compromise of 1877. Thereafter, Southern conservatives increasingly returned to power on the strength of repudiating Reconstruction, a stance which *Jupiter Lights* challenges. Serialized in *Harper's Monthly* from January to June 1889, the novel warrants renewed critical attention for its backward glance to earlier postwar years. Like other American novelists, notably Thomas Nelson Page, Woolson profitably returned decades after the Civil War to this period of widespread resistance. Unlike Page, however, Woolson refused to capitalize on the rising tide of reactionary backlash. Instead, *Jupiter Lights* fosters a retrospective engagement in order to question the nation's increasingly conservative drift toward segregation as national policy, culminating in the 1896 landmark case of *Plessy v. Ferguson*. With the Supreme Court's sanction, "separate but equal" would try to keep African Americans "in their place" until the policy was finally overturned in 1954's *Brown v. Board of Education*. Anticipating the Court's revisionist sentiment by some sixty years, Woolson's novel ventures bold claims on behalf of freedpeople by dramatizing the benefits of civil rights for all Americans.

Insistently, *Jupiter Lights* argues against keeping anyone in confined places and constricting roles by celebrating the freedom available in movement. Mobility of mind and body becomes a strategy for resisting the hardening stasis of Jim Crow. After moving to Europe, Woolson portrays postwar Americans ironically united by a common displacement from home and a shared tendency toward transitional identities as a means of economic and social empowerment. Woolson shows how restless transit especially promotes opportunity for black Americans transitioning to the new freedoms of citizenship. Specifically, she showcases scenes of racially integrated travel, and she dramatizes the dangers to African Americans of remaining immobile. Fixed to one place, they become easy targets for accusations of murder. Similarly, Woolson demonstrates how white women also are at risk when they enter the confinement of abusive marriages. Woolson's novel highlights the shared vulnerability of white married women and freedpeople to white masters, while protesting against vigilante violence directed toward African Americans.

Jupiter Lights begins with the arrival of the Northern maiden aunt, Eve Bruce, on a Georgia barrier island to take unwelcome charge of her nephew Jack, son of her deceased brother, a Union soldier. Indeed, as her last name suggests, Eve takes a kind of husbandly command of the disrupted household that consists of her sister-in-law, Cicely; Cicely's grandfather, Judge Abercrombie; Sabrina, a maiden aunt; and several loyal servants. Upon learning that Cicely has been remarried to a man who physically abuses her and Jack, Eve resolves to rescue them from Ferdie Morrison. The novel's page-turning drama climaxes when Eve shoots Ferdie in self-defense, before they all flee to the North and Ferdie's half-brother, Paul Tennant. For chapters, they remain on the move, endlessly seeking distractions from family turmoil. The story shifts to Eve and Paul's developing romance, which is hindered by Eve's guilt over shooting Ferdie. After he dies (the result of his many Savannah "sprees"), the family eventually returns home, while Eve escapes to an Italian convent. There Paul forcefully overcomes her hesitation to marry, and the reader is left far from the formidable challenges of the postwar South.

The ending of *Jupiter Lights* does not call for a return to the radical political and social agendas of Reconstruction. Instead, Woolson draws her own color and gender line to dramatize the limitations of remaining in transit and assuming a transitional identity. Social equality is resisted while gender conventions are ultimately reinforced. The novel's final turn toward conservatism may also have reflected Woolson's ex-patriot situation. Like James, she was far from the troubled South and more concerned about writerly competition in an increasingly professionalized field, competition for publishers that made the bottom line paramount.[3] Given Woolson's savvy awareness of her readership, her conventional ending is unsurprising, and her book sold well upon publication.[4]

While it may have pleased readers, the novel's ambivalent melodrama confused and exasperated critics, a reaction that persists to this day. Contemporary reviewers such as the *Atlantic Monthly*'s Horace Scudder found the story "somewhat disturbing" in its "fictitious pathology," while an anonymous reviewer for the *Critic* complained of its "tendency toward the morbid." The *Literary World* began by declaring this latest novel "will add little, if anything, to her reputation," while the *Nation* concluded that Woolson must have been "possessed" by "an evil spirit" to write such "high-flown romance," a judgment Woolson feared might have reflected the views of William Dean Howells.[5] Yet nearly all reviewers concurred with the writer for the *Critic*, who singled out Woolson's delineations of minor regional characters for praise; indeed, it is with the portrayals of servants that her most radical claims were ventured.[6] As a revisionist novel, *Jupiter Lights* probes opportunities for African Americans in 1889 while also generating book sales. Through its contradictory thematic rhythms, the novel captures the complex dynamics of postwar politics that were played out in Georgia.

Historians have noted how short-lived Reconstruction was in Georgia, where the election of Democrat James Smith to the governorship meant that Redeemers reclaimed the statehouse in 1872, five years before Reconstruction officially ended. As Russell Duncan has observed, Georgia experienced three phases of Reconstruction: "first in 1865, under moderate Andrew Johnson's presidential plan which restored lands to planters and denied black franchisement; then in 1868, under congressional Reconstruction [which prompted the election of black legislators whom white office-holders promptly expelled]; and finally in 1870, after the reseating of expelled legislators and ratification of the Fifteenth Amendment."[7] In analyzing the trajectory of Georgia's Reconstruction, historians have noted that the state did not produce aggressive black leadership. The apparent conservatism, fatalism, and forgiving trust of former slaves in former slaveholders was readily exploited by their white Democratic colleagues, who soon mobilized what Edmund L. Drago has called "one of the largest, best-disciplined, and most effective Ku Klux Klan's in the South."[8] In *Jupiter Lights*, Woolson registers the Klan's power in the long shadows cast over the fates of those who defy the will of "the higher race" (226).

Although Georgia's Reconstruction was contested, the historian John Inscoe has found evidence of "experimentation, opportunism, and idealism" as freedpeople tried to realize their citizenship. Recent scholarship has demonstrated that there were "cracks in the armor of Jim Crow" through which black and white Georgians could challenge white supremacy.[9] Such challenges show that the patterns of interracial relations were intricate and nuanced, as well as dependent upon locale, community, and time period.[10] This was particularly true of Sapelo Island, which John Kern has identified as the 1869 setting for *Jupiter Lights*.[11]

Located about seventy miles south of Savannah, this Georgia barrier island was an ideal place for Woolson to put bold ideas into play because it boasted a large, stable community of freedpeople, whose descendants still live there today.[12] Sapelo's residents were among the most assertive Georgians in claiming their entitled home when the island was carved up for settlement in the spring of 1865. They quickly translated freedom into the rights and privileges of citizenship as they established an integrated school in June 1865, founded a still active black Baptist church in 1866, and started voting in 1867 until their 1906 disfranchisement. Moreover, they prevented implementation of the sharecropping and gang-labor practices that defeated black Southerners elsewhere.[13] Their success was due, in part, to the unusual legacy of slavery on Sapelo, which would help credit characters in *Jupiter Lights* like the drayman and Porley.

Indeed, the antebellum patterns of slavery in the coastal counties of Chatham, Liberty, and McIntosh, which includes Sapelo, offered the best prospects for Woolson to stage Reconstruction's possibilities. Unlike other colonies, Georgia had enjoyed a prohibition on slavery until 1751; the legislative imposition of slavery not only changed the landscape toward the cultivation of large cash-crop plantations but also established the pattern of interracial relations created there, especially among new bondspeople who had a recent knowledge of freedom in Africa. In this regard, historians such as Betty Wood have asserted that the "sheer novelty" of the slavery system "cannot be overemphasized."[14] Moreover, the introduction of a task system of labor from South Carolina to the Georgia lowcountry ensured that African American slaves owned some time for themselves, which they used to great advantage in creating market gardens, hiring themselves out, forging a trade network, and even accumulating property. All of their efforts, however contested by elite whites, contributed to a vibrant informal slave economy that encouraged not only material gain but, more important, an autonomy that Woolson recognized.[15] Through a series of encounters between white characters and freedpeople, she revises condescending stereotypes to recast former slaves as neither "a novelty" nor a "poor, poor people" who are "scattered and astray with no one to advise them" (49). In *Jupiter Lights*, they are dynamically self-sufficient.

This independent spirit had been particularly evident on Sapelo Island. There the bondspeople grew rice, sugar, and Sea Island cotton under a distinctive slave regime run by the planter Thomas Spalding.[16] His Sapelo plantation was conventional in size and crop but singular in its indoctrination into slavery. Newly arrived Africans were placed under the tutelage of established slaves for several months until their abilities could be assessed. They were then settled into black-overseen, gender-segregated "units" in which they progressed from manual labor to the work best suited to their skills and personality.[17] Beginning with his first land acquisition in 1802, Spalding and his bondspeople, estimated at three hundred by the 1850s, left a lasting legacy on Sapelo, a unique freedpeople's community that Woolson acknowledges in her novel. After encountering a hostile freedman on the mainland, Cicely quickly reminds her grandfather, Judge Abercrombie, that "this isn't the island; this is South Carolina" in order to subdue his violent reaction (63). Throughout the novel, Woolson remains attentive to the realities of this peculiar locale, where regional differences had important consequences.

In describing the greater postwar landscape, however, Woolson registers the ubiquity of decay. Wherever Eve goes on or off the island, she finds nothing but ruins, some caused by Sherman's marauding march.[18] After the war, rice cultivation collapsed on Sapelo and other Sea Islands, mainly because planters could not find a profitable alternative to slave labor. Indeed, the Carolina and Georgia Sea Islanders never could restore rice cultivation to prewar levels.[19] As late as 1869, Eve Bruce encounters only ongoing deterioration as "much of the land was now worthless, disintegrated and overgrown with lespedezza" (61). Moreover, the Southerners she meets seem too paralyzed to clear the weeds and repair the damage.

Inside the plantation household, there is further disarray as tawdriness mixes with the leftovers from recent plunder. Eve discovers that "the dinner service" was "a mixture of old Canton blue and the commonest, thickest white plates; coarse dull goblets and cut-glass wine glasses; the knives were in the last stage of decrepitude, and there was no silver at all [. . .]; it had been replaced by cheaply plated spoons and forks, from which the plate was already half gone" (84–85). The mingling of cheap and fine housewares reflects the uneasy coexistence of different classes and races now come into an equalizing proximity.[20] Some postwar women such as the Abercrombies' neighbors, the Misses Polly and Leontine, have learned to become self-sufficient. As "mothers of invention," to borrow the historian Drew Faust's useful phrase, they are now in the kitchen themselves, baking in order to gain a living.[21] Overwhelmed by the region's violent history and present decay, Eve despairs, "Oh, if only I could get away from this hideous country—this whole horrible South!" (80). Woolson suggests that the postwar family cannot heal and build anew, nor can postwar citizens such as Eve reconcile themselves to help in rebuilding the nation.

But if the South in ruins is a failure, the North with all the destructive energy of hasty beginnings is hardly better. Woolson dramatizes converging sectional plights as Eve and her family flee north to escape Ferdie. At Cicely's insistence, they travel to a small town on Lake Superior to seek paradoxical refuge with Paul Tennant, whose name itself suggests impermanence. As their boat docks in Cleveland, the weary travelers see a "yellow river, greasy with petroleum from the refineries higher up" (115). The narrator describes Port aux Pins, the family's final destination, as "simply hideous," "scarred," "deplumed," and finally "hateful" (139–40). Called "Potterpins" by the locals, the mispronunciation reveals how shabbily the roughshod region has maintained its Continental promise. Given its "roadways half laid out, with shanties and wandering pigs, discarded tin cans, and other refuse, and everywhere stumps, stumps," Potterpins is an environmental nightmare created solely out of Yankee greed (139). This pollution is the byproduct of "mud, talk, and ambition, the sort of place which the Yankees produced wherever they went, and which they loved" (139). In this "early in the morning, ten minutes ago place," even the Northern misfit Kit Hollis struggles in his auction shop to capitalize on constant turnover, an effort the beleaguered Southerners cannot begin to muster (141).

Far from the romance of reunion, which Nina Silber sees characterizing the postwar literary scene, this novel indulges the romance of disunion.[22] If Eve cannot tolerate the "hideous" South, neither can the judge withstand the "ugly" Potterpins of the North (139). Judge Abercrombie can still declare "God bless my country!" but has a notion of "country" that is severely "limited": it narrowly remains "the territory which lies between the Saint Mary's River and the Savannah" (306). Even the boundlessly optimistic shopowner Hollis concedes that the judge is doomed if he remains, and he protests to Paul, "if you keep him on here long he won't stand it—he'll mizzle out. He'll simply die of Potterpins" (141). In comparing the South to the North, Woolson's narrator glumly concludes: "It might have been said, perhaps, that between houses and a society uncomfortable from age, falling to pieces from want of repairs, and houses and a society uncomfortable with youth, unfurnished, and encumbered with scaffolding, there was not much to choose" (140). Woolson thereby suggests that sectional reconciliation is unlikely, not only because of lingering bitterness about the war but also because of an ongoing estrangement from the landscape.

In such a quandary, the only solution for the characters—in both the North and the South—is to flee from these alien territories, although both sections share the titular beacons of Jupiter Lights. Even read as metaphors for Eve's relationship with Paul, her Northern analogue in loneliness and pride, the lighthouses underscore each character's dark isolation. Although Eve relies on them as compelling guides in her travels and, at one point, even fills in desultorily as lighthouse keeper for an afternoon at the Northern Jupiter Light, they do not provide her with clear moral compass nor anchor her to a home (298).

Indeed, much of the novel revolves around perpetual travel for all its characters. En route to Cleveland, Eve wonders if "they should never arrive, as if they should journey forever" (121). Eve's reaction is understandable for no sooner have they docked than Cicely impetuously announces she wants to get back to Ferdie that minute. The solution for Cicely's madness, Ferdie's dementia, the judge's health, Eve's lovesickness, Hollis's unrequited love, and every other ailment is to keep moving. The apparent inability of postwar white Americans to find themselves a home bodes darkly for the Reconstruction agendas of Northern occupation, Southern relocation, and sectional reunion.

But what spelled despair for white Southerners and Northerners spelled opportunity for African Americans of both regions, as advances in transportation networks kept everyone on the move. Indeed, the strength of the Sea Island communities may have been their ability to tolerate the upheaval of shifting refugee populations after the Union navy descended in 1861.[23] *Jupiter Lights* suggests that remaining in a state of flux may be the best alternative freedpeople have for avoiding Jim Crow stagnation. Woolson capitalized on the booming development of transportation networks during the 1880s, when the South took the national lead in constructing the railroads and streetcars that encouraged Southern urban development. After the Southern Railway and Steamship Association was organized in 1875, the national increase in mileage during the 1880s was 79 percent, while ten Southern states alone, including Georgia, increased their railroad networks by 98 percent.[24] Streetcars, a mark of urban maturity as Howard Rabinowitz has noted, were the "most significant franchised operation of the closing twenty years of the century."[25]

Tempering this newfound mobility during the 1880s was the introduction of segregation laws, which, some scholars have argued, was hardly coincidental; rather, it was a response to the proliferation of railroads as well as the newfound prosperity of African Americans who made gains in literacy, landowning, wealth, and businesses.[26] Although Woolson does not foreground prosperity for any Americans, neither does she portray the segregated travel that was hardly clear cut or inevitable. As Edward Ayers, following C. Vann Woodward, has argued, the 1880s were a time of "much uncertainty and much bargaining, many forays and retreats."[27] The enforcement of segregation policy was partly a function of practical matters like a shortage of cars. Since the 1850s, African Americans had mounted legal challenges to racially exclusionary practices on railroad cars, an effort that intensified during the late nineteenth century.[28] Within Georgia, black legislators like Sapelo's Tunis Campbell, forced to ride a steamer in the open with freight rather than white passengers, protested against unequal treatment on public conveyances.[29] When the first separate-but-equal streetcar laws were passed in Georgia during 1891, just two years after *Jupiter Lights* appeared, it was despite a history of African American resistance against separate *and* unequal treatment; in 1872, black Savannahians objected to unequal accommodations for which they were charged the same as white passengers. Their protest ended in a riot that temporarily forced the suspension of Jim Crow policies.[30]

This postwar flux, which inspired Woolson, can be seen in *Jupiter Lights* when a black driver does not yield the road or when a hurrying mulatto ship waiter so jostles the judge off the sidewalk that he is left "spattered" with "mud from shoulder to shoe" by a speeding buggy (143). Where plantation fiction catered to nostalgic

Northerners, Woolson's novel captures the contemporary clash between white expectations and black resentment, especially in transit. Just when Judge Abercrombie smugly wonders, "Where can a gentleman travel now, with the element of the unexpected as a companion?" he and the Abercrombie ladies encounter an "insolent" drayman (62). In response to the judge's repeated demand to "turn out, boy!" the drayman "planted himself" by sticking his hands in his pockets and retorting with "a turn out yourself" (62–63). Anxious to avoid a fight, the outraged elderly judge is forced to move his wagon first. Woolson stages this interracial confrontation to challenge the nearly automatic tendency of former white masters to retaliate against mobile African Americans.[31] Reminding the judge that the drayman is "a good deal stronger than you are" and will be "alone" with the women after he has "struck down" his antagonist, Cicely breaks the Southern habit of violence in "the turbulent old despot" by teaching him to "curb" himself (623). Cicely raises the stereotypical fear of assault in order to *dissuade* rather than incite the apoplectic judge. The jarring episode teaches him as well as Woolson's readers that times have indeed changed but that changes, however unpleasant, do not necessitate segregation.

On the contrary, Woolson champions the benefits of integrated travel for all Americans. It is in scenes of transit that she affirms interracial cooperation by showing the sustained, reciprocated value of African Americans to white families, while de-emphasizing traditionally subservient roles. In contrast to the novel's humorous portraits of incompetent white servants such as Meadows or Miss Mile there is Porley, the black chambermaid who endears herself to her charges despite her inefficiency. Whereas Miss Mile, that "clean, broad-faced, turn-out-your-toes, do-your-duty-old relict," is quickly dismissed, Porley endures (262). Because of her familial care for a whole bevy of young passengers heading for Cleveland, she lands a job caring for Cicely's baby, Jack, as they travel on together (114). Beloved by both black and white children, Porley promotes interracial reunion because she can empathize with fellow travelers, even those who are white.

The mutual benefits that empathy inspires appear in another travel scene. On the next boat, a black singer croons in a way that reflects the loneliness of the displaced Abercrombies. Watching him, a distraught Eve finds herself lulled into reverie as she hears "one of the sweetest voices in the world" (120). As seductive counterpart to Cicely's "niggerless" song, his blues affirm the integral presence and cultural value of black Americans to the nation. His alienation as he is "roaming alone *through* / This world's wilderness" is something Eve can readily share (120). A cross-racial bond is achieved, if briefly, as a transfixed Eve "looked at him" and then at the spellbound audience. Such scenarios ask readers to reconsider the separate paths they might be tempted to take.

The novel's perpetual transit also reflects the transitive state of freedpeople as they evolve from contraband to citizens. References to the ex-slaves as "nigroes" recall that time of uncertainty when they exercised new options (36). While Cicely's family repeatedly laments that "It's niggers that are lacking," Woolson's cast of characters shows that freedpeople have hardly disappeared; they are simply working and relaxing alongside whites (35). Woolson shows that it is really a question of fully integrating former slaves into the free labor force. Even before the war, an unmistakable biracial community centered around Savannah had already arisen from an informal lowcountry economy in which encounters between non-slaveholding whites and enslaved blacks were common, mutually beneficial, and complex.[32] The postwar collapse of rice cultivation prompted further innovative trade networks. With the development of Savannah as a port, the entire landscape was changed as plantations were broken up into a patchwork of small farms and expanded market gardens tended by freedpeople who shipped vegetables and fruit to Northern consumers.[33]

Sapelo's freedpeople, along with other black Sea Islanders, had responded enthusiastically to General Sherman's Field Order #15, which redistributed "forty acres and a mule" in January 1865.[34] When their hopes for landownership began to dim, Sea Islanders were sustained by the counsel of local black politicians and fiercely resisted the imposition of labor contracts. In December 1866, the bureau agent Tunis Campbell drew upon his own funds to purchase Belle Ville plantation, a 1,250-acre mainland plantation, as a rent-to-own cooperative for freedpeople, and he soon organized a Farmer's Association that operated like a city government. Ignited by Campbell's activist zeal, Sapelo's freedpeople vigorously asserted their right to set their own work hours, to plant crops of their choice, and to dispose of their harvests as they saw fit, even though they were jailed for their recalcitrance.[35] After Northern entrepreneurs moved quickly to lease plantations, freedpeople who held independent grants totaling some 550 acres hired other freedmen to assist them, much to the pain of white planters.[36] Their resistance to contract labor all but ruined the crop that year and the white planters were gone by January 1867, but the freedpeople remained.[37] When Woolson pauses on her portraits of the island's freedpeople, she reveals their diversity and their spirited embrace of the freedom they claimed.

Specifically, Woolson highlights how postwar black Georgians could adopt transitional identities in order to make a living. Eve encounters an "elderly negro," whose job is to keep the mail (if not himself) moving even though he cannot read (70). As soon as the postmaster's illiteracy is discovered, his defiant wife intervenes; she hangs on to his job by claiming his eyesight is poor and "officiously" shows Eve the door. Like many other African American women after emancipation, the postmaster's wife is determined to translate freedom into a hard-won economic self-sufficiency and political authority.[38] The dissemblance of this "little yellow woman" echoes that of many Georgian free women of color, whom Adele Alexander has characterized as "elusive" (70). Legally, socially, and economically marginal, often racially hybrid, and illiterate in many cases, they concealed parts of their lives when necessary.[39] Soon Woolson's postmaster reappears as a "dignified gentleman," dressed up "in his best black coat, with a silk hat, the blue goggles and a tasselled cane" to deliver a letter personally so that Eve will not betray him by revealing his illiteracy (77). "At the top of his voice," Woolson writes, Mister Cotesworth "declaimed the addresses" in a manner akin to the way other minor, white characters easily perform different identities with great patriotic pageantry for a local Fourth of July parade (201–4). Of more serious consequence, the postmaster's performance of a costumed reading and his wife's performance of a lie reveal the ambitions of black Georgians to prosper and prevail.[40]

As the story's domestic nightmare unfolds, Woolson shows that it is former masters who pose the greatest threat to the survival of freedpeople and white married women. By highlighting their shared fear of white men like Ferdie, Woolson explodes the myth that it is black men whom white women most fear. The novel reflects the reality that, despite Georgia's postwar antimiscegenation laws, interracial sexual contact including long-term monogamous relationships continued to occur.[41] Even before the provocative encounter with the drayman, *Jupiter Lights* tackles contemporary notions about interracial contact between black men and white women. In the opening scene Woolson uses humor to defamiliarize the appearance of interracial assault as Meadows, the white English maid, defends herself against a black servant's endeavor to carry her luggage (5). After misunderstanding Uncle Abram's courteous persistence, Meadows finally uses her bag "as a missile over the side of his head" until he runs off (5–6). Defusing the scene, a "laughing" Cicely exclaims, "I didn't expect anything half so funny" (6). From the novel's opening pages, Woolson assures her readers that such encounters leave white women safe and even entertained; the deadly encounters involve Cicely's demented husband, whose murderous rage always erupts within the walls of a presumed domestic sanctuary.

In highlighting how white wives remain most at risk when at home, Woolson dramatizes the real danger to immobile freedpeople: that they will be caught up in the domestic violence at the novel's center. Woolson shows that blaming former slaves for postwar violence comes conveniently to white Southerners like the judge, who rationalizes, "Niggers are constitutionally timid, and they always have pistols nowadays" (135). All that is needed is a "theory" that is "probable enough" to blame two black men for Ferdie's shooting (134–35). Their arrest becomes a thin excuse to retreat from Reconstruction. Planters frame Ferdie's death as a "sacrifice to the present miserable conditions of our poor State, where the blacks, our servants [...] are put over us [...] are entrusted with dangerous weapons" (226). They insist that Ferdie's death be "held up as a marked warning to the entire North" when they demand that "this tale should be told everywhere, on the steps of courthouses and in churches, and the question should be solemnly asked, Shall things continue? — Shall the servant rule his lord?"

(226). Worth little more than their value as scapegoats, these two nameless men face prison, if not death. Even after Eve confesses that she pulled the trigger, there is no mention of anyone informing the authorities that the jailed men are innocent. Their fate seems dangerously irrelevant.

If Woolson's white Southerners turn Ferdie's shooting into an excuse for stifling upstart African Americans, Woolson's novel also signals the risks of *immobility*, especially as the threat of segregation increases. With biting humor Eve discredits white comfort in a segregated heaven that "is not like the Declaration of Independence" (320). As she puts it, "'I mean that all men "are created equal"; your heaven has an outside colony for negroes, and once or twice a week white angels go over there, I suppose, ring the Sunday-school bell, and hold meetings for their improvement'" (320). Lampooning smug confidence in a segregated afterlife, Eve mocks both the segregated solutions of the South and the paternalistic interventions of the North.

Woolson balances her revisionist agenda by dramatizing the dangers of assuming that transitional roles and identities can last. Eve may flout familiar postures and conventional roles, but her marriage to Paul is ominous, especially since his behavior borders on the abusive as critics have noted.[42] When she begs to be "of use" in the more conventional spinsterish roles of family "nurse," "housekeeper; anything," Paul asserts that she is no longer "needed down there" because the Abercrombies "have plenty of people."[43] Free black labor ultimately eases Eve out of her caregiver responsibilities and into the confinement of Paul's arms and his promise that "from this moment I take charge of you" (321). Similarly, Ferdie's murderous capacity derives from his ability to "change so unconsciously into a savage" while so misrecognizing others that he obliterates their identities (94). His desire to kill is based upon his perception, as Cicely explains, "that I am some one else, a woman who is going to attack his wife; and he thinks that Jack is some other child, who has just injured *his* Jack" (100). Serving as both potential perpetrator and eventual target, the family becomes the site of punishment for those who transgress beyond its reconstructed bounds.

Moreover, Woolson suggests through her representation of Native Americans that assuming transitional identities and adopting transitive lifestyles can backfire. *Jupiter Lights* showcases the Indians as an ethnic group decimated by perpetual relocation and contact with Anglo-American social custom and culture. No longer a fearsome force inspiring "sudden alarms and the musket laid ready to hand," they have declined to "few in number, harmless" while they wait in "temporary" villages to be shifted yet further west (139, 170). Wearing their "ready made coats and trousers" as well as their "beaded moccasins," they exist at stalled transitions as "amusing" diversions to tourists Eve and Paul (151, 170). The judge considers them "another species of nigger" (139); they chauffeur and tend to the needs of the family on their camping trip just like black servants. Moreover, when the Indians become drunk and disorderly, Paul and his band of vigilantes eliminate them through violent intimidation and arrest, a tactic familiar to African Americans in the unreconstructed South. Left "abject and terrified," they are "dismissed" and replaced by immigrant Irish laborers (256–57). Their transitional status ends with their seemingly inevitable elimination.

At the close of the story, the keeper of the convent that shelters Eve flatly declares that "Americans are limited" (344). It would seem Woolson shares that view given how far she is willing to risk her readership in her revision of Reconstruction's possibilities. Yet Eve's opening gambit about the "extraordinary navigation" required to steer between the Sea Islands' treacherous channels of "apparent aimlessness" and the open sea of "terrific inequalities" applies to Woolson's literary project as well (1–2). In a novel obsessed with exploring the merits of transit, she must practice an "extraordinary navigation" to keep Reconstruction's promise afloat. Challenging her readers for being so "umped-up" on the prevailing Jim Crow penchant for fixed identities and confined positions, Woolson returns to the promise inherent in those earlier treacherous years while trying to avoid the open sea of postwar inequality (2). Through her measured endorsement of transit and transitional identity, Woolson kept herself one step ahead of her readers while always seeking to avoid the darker shallows of retrenchment, disfranchisement, and despair. Itself a beacon, *Jupiter Lights* tries to illuminate how segregation would stymie *all* American citizens who let themselves drift.

Notes

1. Constance Fenimore Woolson, *Jupiter Lights: A Novel* (1889; New York: AMS Press, 1971), 40. Hereafter cited parenthetically in the text.

2. Caroline Gebhard, "Romantic Love and Wife-Battering in Constance Fenimore Woolson's *Jupiter Lights*," *Constance Fenimore Woolson's Nineteenth Century: Essays*, ed. Victoria Brehm (Detroit: Wayne State University Press, 2001), 83–96.

3. See Christopher P. Wilson, *The Labor of Words: Literary Professionalism in the Progressive Era* (Athens: University of Georgia Press, 1985), 40–91; and Susan Coultrap-McQuin, *Doing Literary Business: American Women Writers in the Nineteenth Century* (Chapel Hill: University of North Carolina Press, 1990), 105–99.

4. In *Constance Fenimore Woolson* (New York: Twayne, 1963), Rayburn S. Moore cites Harper and Bros. figures of 6,000 copies sold, making *Jupiter Lights* her third best-selling novel, following *Anne* and *East Angels*, published by the firm (159).

5. Moore, *Constance Fenimore Woolson*, 106.

6. Horace Scudder, "Recent American Fiction," *Atlantic Monthly* (January 1890): 1268; "Review of Jupiter Lights," *The Critic* (February 1, 1890): 51; *Literary World* (January 4, 1890): 41; the *Nation* (March 13, 1890): 224–55, which is a reprint from the *New York Evening Post*. The anonymous

reviewer for the *New York Times* ("A Southern Romance," December 29, 1889, 11) and George Saintsbury, writing for *The Academy* (February 1, 1890): 77, praised Woolson's portrayal of the South. More recently, John Kern finds the novel "so far-fetched as to challenge belief"; see *Constance Fenimore Woolson, Literary Pioneer* (Philadelphia: University of Pennsylvania Press, 1934), 176. Meanwhile Alexander Cowie declares it "her least valuable novel" in *The Rise of the American Novel* (1951), reprinted in *Critical Essays of Constance Fenimore Woolson*, ed. Cheryl B. Torsney (New York: G. K. Hall, 1992), 113. Rayburn Moore judges the book "not entirely a failure" (108), while Caroline Gebhard categorizes it as "strange" in its defiance of conventional genres (83).

7. *Freedom's Shore: Tunis Campbell and the Georgia Freedmen* (Athens: University of Georgia Press, 1986), 9. Also see Alan Conway, *The Reconstruction of Georgia* (Minneapolis: University of Minnesota Press, 1966), the first cautiously revisionist scholarship on Georgian Reconstruction since C. Mildred Thompson's *Reconstruction in Georgia: Economic, Social, Political, 1865–1872* (New York: Columbia University Press, 1915). Book-length studies continue to be scarce. For a general overview, see Numan V. Bartley, *The Creation of Modern Georgia* (Athens: University of Georgia Press, 1983), 45–102; and Peter Wallenstein, *From Slave South to New South: Public Policy in Nineteenth-Century Georgia* (Chapel Hill: University of North Carolina Press, 1987), 131–207. The following biographies are also helpful: William Warren Rogers, *A Scalawag in Georgia: Richard Whiteley and the Politics of Reconstruction* (Urbana: University of Illinois Press, 2007), 80–169; Russell Duncan, *Entrepreneur for Equality: Governor Rufus Bullock, Commerce, and Race in Post–Civil War Georgia* (Athens: University of Georgia Press, 1994), 39–147; and Ruth Currie-McDaniel, *Carpetbagger of Conscience: A Biography of John Emory Bryant* (New York: Fordham University Press, 1999), 42–154. Also see Lewis Nicholas Wynne, *The Continuity of Cotton* (Macon, GA: Mercer University Press, 1986), especially 29–86, 105–17, for analysis of longtime planter dominance in politics.

8. *Black Politicians and Reconstruction in Georgia: A Splendid Failure* (Baton Rouge: Louisiana State University Press, 1982), 162. Many of Georgia's black leaders were ministers, inexperienced in law and government as well as humble in education and material resources. See Drago, 160–63; Joseph P. Reidy, "Aaron A. Bradley: Voice of Black Labor in the Georgia Lowcountry," *Southern Black Leaders of the Reconstruction Era*, ed. Howard N. Rabinowitz (Urbana: University of Illinois Press, 1982), 281–308; and James M. Russell and Jerry Thornberry, "William Finch of Atlanta: The Black Politician as Civic Leader," *Southern Black Leaders of the Reconstruction Era*, 309–34.

9. John C. Inscoe, *Georgia in Black and White: Explorations in the Race Relations of a Southern State, 1865–1950* (Athens: University of Georgia Press, 1994), 4, 2. On white Georgian resistance to Reconstruction policies, see Mark V. Wetherington, *Plain Folk's Fight: The Civil War and Reconstruction in Piney Woods Georgia* (Chapel Hill: University of North Carolina Press, 2005), 261–93; Rogers, *A Scalawag in Georgia*, 34–79; Drago, *Black Politicians and Reconstruction in Georgia*, 141–59; Jonathan M. Bryant, "'We Have No Chance of Justice Before the Courts': The Freedmen's Struggle for Power in Greene County, Georgia, 1865–1874," Inscoe, *Georgia in Black and White*, 13–37; and Russell Duncan, "A Georgia Governor Battles Racism: Rufus Bullock and the Fight for Black Legislators," Inscoe, *Georgia in Black and White*, 38–64. For firsthand accounts, see House, *Conditions of Affairs in Georgia*, 40th Cong., 3rd sess., 1869, pt. 1, Misc. Doc. 52, 1–48, and Documentary Evidence, 48–139.

10. See Daniel W. Stowell, "'The Negroes Cannot Navigate Alone': Religious Scalawags and the Biracial Methodist Episcopal Church in Georgia, 1866–1876," Inscoe, *Georgia in Black and White*, 65–90; Jennifer Lund Smith, "The Ties That Bind: Educated African-American Women in Post-Emancipation Atlanta," Inscoe, *Georgia in Black and White*, 91–105; Glenn T. Eskew, "Black Elitism and the Failure of Paternalism in Postbellum Georgia: The Case of Bishop Lucius Henry Holsey," Inscoe, *Georgia in Black and White*, 106–40; Adele Logan Alexander, *Ambiguous Lives: Free Women of Color in Rural Georgia, 1789–1879* (Fayetteville: University of Arkansas Press, 1991), 142–202; and

Drago, *Black Politicians and Reconstruction in Georgia*, 35–140. On black laborers' resistance to white planters, see Paul A Cimbala, *Under the Guardianship of the Nation: The Freedmen's Bureau and the Reconstruction of Georgia, 1865–1870* (Athens: University of Georgia Press, 1997), 193–216; and Charles L. Flynn, *White Land, Black Labor: Caste and Class in Late-Nineteenth Century Georgia* (Baton Rouge: Louisiana State University Press, 1983), 57–149.

11. Kern, *Constance Fenimore Woolson*, 91.

12. As of 1994, Sapelo had just sixty-seven residents, mostly elderly. See William S. McFeely, *Sapelo's People: A Long Walk into Freedom* (New York: Norton, 1994), 14, 33. For firsthand WPA interviews of Sea Island ex-slaves, including those of Sapelo residents, see *Drums and Shadows: Survival Studies among the Georgia Coastal Negroes*. Savannah Unit, Georgia Writers' Project, Work Projects Administration, 2nd ed. (Athens: University of Georgia Press, 1986), 158–72.

13. McFeely, *Sapelo's People*, 82–128. Also see Paul A. Cimbala, "The Freedmen's Bureau, the Freedmen, and Sherman's Grant in Reconstruction Georgia, 1865–1867," *Journal of Southern History* 55 (November 1989): 597–632. Sometime after the *Brown v. Board of Education* decision in 1954, Sapelo's school closed, and island children were sent to integrating schools on the mainland, as McFeely notes (*Sapelo's People*, 112).

14. Betty Wood, "Some Aspects of Female Resistance to Chattel Slavery in Lowcountry Georgia, 1763–1815," *Historical Journal* 30 (1987): 606. Also see Wood's monograph, *Slavery in Colonial Georgia, 1730–1775* (Athens: University of Georgia Press, 1984).

15. For a discussion of Sea Island agricultural development and the social life that ensued from settlement to the Civil War, see Mart A. Stewart, *"What Nature Suffers to Groe": Land, Labor, and Landscape on the Georgia Coast, 1680–1920* (Athens: University of Georgia Press, 1996), especially 1–192; Timothy James Lockley, *Lines in the Sand: Race and Class in Lowcountry Georgia, 1750–1860* (Athens: University of Georgia Press, 2001); and Betty Wood, *Women's Work, Men's Work: The Informal Slave Economies of Lowcountry Georgia* (Athens: University of Georgia, 1995). For a comparative study, see Philip D. Morgan, *Slave Counterpoint: Black Culture in the Eighteenth Century Chesapeake and Lowcountry* (Chapel Hill: University of North Carolina Press, 1998). On the task system, see Thomas F. Armstrong, "From Task Labor to Free Labor: The Transition along Georgia's Rice Coast, 1820–1880," *Georgia Historical Quarterly* 64 (1980): 432–47; and Philip D. Morgan, "Work and Culture: The Task System and the World of Lowcountry Blacks, 1700–1880," *William and Mary Quarterly* 39 (1982): 563–99.

16. A leading tidewater planter as well as politician, amateur architect, shrewd businessmen, and prominent citizen of McIntosh County, Thomas Spalding (1774–1851) was also an innovative agriculturist. At the height of his influence in 1850, Spalding was elected chairman of the statewide Committee of Thirty-Three that met to decide the issue of secession. See E. Merton Coulter, *Thomas Spalding of Sapelo* (Baton Rouge: Louisiana State University Press, 1940), 264–66. For biographies of other rice planters, see James E. Bagwell, *Rice Gold: James Hamilton Couper and Plantation Life on the Georgia Coast* (Macon, GA: Mercer University Press, 2000); and William Dusinberre, *Them Dark Days: Slavery in the American Rice Swamps* (New York: Oxford University Press, 1996).

17. As McFeely makes clear, early accounts of a nearly benign form of slavery must be viewed skeptically. Spalding did contend with runaways and even the attempt to establish a maroon (*Sapelo's People*, 54–55).

18. While Savannah was spared destruction after the city surrendered in December 1864, the area was still desolate from the effects of Sherman's occupation and from a conflagration in January 1865. See Alexander A. Lawrence, *A Present for Mr. Lincoln: The Story of Savannah from Secession to Sherman* (Macon, GA: Ardivan Press, 1961), 198–246; and Anne J. Bailey, *War and Ruin: William T. Sherman and the Savannah Campaign* (Wilmington: Scholarly Resources, 2003), 1–16, 103–28.

19. On the collapse of coastal rice culture, see James M. Clifton, "Twilight Comes to the Rice Kingdom: Postbellum Rice Culture on the South Atlantic Coast," *Georgia Historical Quarterly* 62 (1978): 146–54. On the fate of rice culture as well as that of cotton and tobacco from the 1880s through the 1980s, see Pete Daniel, *Breaking the Land: The Transformation of Cotton, Tobacco, and Rice Cultures since 1880* (Urbana: University of Illinois Press, 1985).

20. On the strained, often violent, nature of interracial and gendered contacts within postwar households, see Marek Steedman, "Gender and the Politics of the Household in Reconstruction Louisiana, 1865–1878," *Gender and Slave Emancipation in the Atlantic World*, ed. Pamela Scully and Diane Paton (Durham, NC: Duke University Press, 2005), 310–27; Laura F. Edwards, *Scarlett Doesn't Live Here Anymore: Southern Women in the Civil War Era* (Urbana: University of Illinois Press, 2000), 118–89; *Gendered Strife and Confusion: The Political Culture of Reconstruction* (Urbana: University of Illinois Press, 1997), 66–183; Jacqueline Jones, "Encounters, Likely and Unlikely, between Black and Poor White Women in the Rural South, 1865–1940," *Georgia Historical Quarterly* 76 (1992): 333–53. For an excellent primary source, see Sea Islander Frances A. Butler Leigh, *Ten Years on a Georgia Plantation* (1883; rpt. with an introduction by Dana D. Nelson, in *Principles and Privilege: Two Women's Lives on a Georgia Plantation* [Ann Arbor: University of Michigan Press, 1995]).

21. Drew Gilpin Faust, *Mothers of Invention: Women of the Slaveholding South in the American Civil War* (Chapel Hill: University of North Carolina Press, 1996), 7.

22. Nina Silber, *The Romance of Reunion: Northerners and the South, 1865–1900* (Chapel Hill: University of North Carolina Press, 1993), 39–65.

23. For the Spalding family, a pattern of migration was created as chattel were taken inland to Milledgeville while the Sea Islands became a haven for slave refugees. Many were picked up by gunboats and joined the army. See McFeely, *Sapelo's People*, 63–81. When the Spaldings returned, over six hundred refugees were expelled from the island and were thus in exodus again. See McFeely, *Sapelo's People*, 137.

24. Howard N. Rabinowitz, "Continuity and Change: Southern Urban Development, 1860–1900," *The City in Southern History: The Growth of Urban Civilization in the South*, ed. Blaine A. Brownell and David R. Goldfield (New York: Kennikat Press, 1977), 105. Also see Howard N. Rabinowitz, *The First New South, 1865–1920* (Illinois: Harlan Davidson, 1992), 29–71; and Duncan, *Entrepreneur*, 98–121.

25. Rabinowitz, "Continuity and Change," 113.

26. Edward L. Ayers, *The Promise of the New South: Life after Reconstruction* (New York: Oxford University Press, 1992), 140–41.

27. Ayers, *Promise of the New South*, 137.

28. See Barbara Young Welke, *Recasting American Liberty: Gender, Race, Law, and the Railroad Revolution, 1865–1920* (New York: Cambridge University Press, 2001), 280–375; and Janice Sumler-Edmond, "The Quest for Justice: African American Women Litigants, 1867–1890," *African American Women and the Vote, 1837–1965*, ed. Ann D. Gordon (Amherst: University of Massachusetts Press, 1997), 100–119.

29. Duncan, *Freedom's Shore*, 48–49.

30. Drago, *Black Politicians and Reconstruction in Georgia*, 98–100.

31. See Scott Nelson, "Livestock, Boundaries, and Public Space in Spartanburg: African American Men, Elite White Women, and the Spectacle of Conjugal Relations," *Sex, Love, Race*, ed. Martha Hodes (New York: New York University Press, 1999), 313–27.

32. See Betty Wood, *Women's Work*, especially 101–21, and Timothy Lockley, *Lines*, 29–97, for discussion of the biracial complexity of the informal slave economy. Also see Whittington B. Johnson, *Black Savannah: 1788–1864* (Fayetteville: University of Arkansas Press, 1996), 85–132; Timothy J. Lockley, "Spheres of Influence: Working White and Black Women in Antebellum Savannah," *Neither*

Lady Nor Slave: Working Women of the Old South, ed. Susanna Delfino and Michele Gillespie (Chapel Hill: University of North Carolina Press, 2002), 102–20; and Dennis Rousey, "From Whence They Came to Savannah: The Origins of an Urban Population in the Old South," *Georgia Historical Quarterly* 79 (1995): 305–36.

33. Within the Savannah area, market gardens had existed since the colony's founding. See Wood, *Women's Work*, 80–100. In the 1870s, slave and free gardeners, who had farmed since the 1850s, filed claims with the federal government for property confiscated by Union troops. In Liberty County, adjacent to Sapelo, forty African Americans filed successfully with the Southern Claims Commission, as the county tax rolls for the 1870s and 1880s reveal. See Philip D. Morgan, "The Ownership of Property by Slaves in the Mid-Nineteenth Century Low Country," *Journal of Southern History* 49 (August 1983): 399–420; Morgan, "Work and Culture," 587–99; and Loren Schweninger, *Black Property Owners in the South, 1790–1915* (Urbana: University of Illinois Press, 1990), 143–232.

34. Later rescinded by President Johnson, Sherman's order helped create entitlement expectations that were difficult to undo. See Cimbala, *Under the Guardianship*, 166–92; and Claude F. Oubre, *Forty Acres and a Mule: The Freedmen's Bureau and Black Landownership* (Baton Rouge: Louisiana State University Press, 1978). For a firsthand account, see J. T. Trowbridge, *The South: A Tour of Its Battlefields and Ruined Cities* (Hartford: L. Stebbins, 1866), 532–36.

35. See Cimbala, "The Freedmen's Bureau," and *Under the Guardianship*, 131–65; Reidy, "Aaron A. Bradley: Voice of Black Labor in the Georgia Lowcountry"; and Russell Duncan, *Freedom's Shore*, especially 12–75. A New Jersey free man and veteran of the Port Royal "Experiment," Reverend Tunis Campbell tried to settle the freedpeople permanently on the land as voting freehold farmers. A bureau agent, justice of the peace, and state senator, Campbell worked unstintingly for black civil rights to the ire of many whites. He was the only local agent fired for political reasons in 1867, when he was replaced by a Spalding relative. See McFeely, *Sapelo's People*, 138. Elected as a state senator in 1868 and later expelled, Campbell was eventually run out of Georgia after being put in a work gang. This was the second occasion in which he was unfairly convicted of malpractice in office for the false imprisonment of a white man. For his own account, see *Sufferings of the Rev. T. G. Campbell and His Family in Georgia* (Washington: Enterprise, 1877).

36. Cimbala, "Freedmen's Bureau," 616.

37. Cimbala, "Freedmen's Bureau," 621. During the Reconstruction years, Sapelo's freedpeople turned to other enterprising ventures with some success. By 1880, sixteen Sapelo Islanders owned land. Their money was earned by their work in the newly emergent cash-paying timber and turpentine industries as well as the later resort and tourist boom, which drew black workers away from the fields. Other Sapelo freedpeople engaged in subsistence agriculture as well as timbering and oyster harvesting ventures in the Duplin River estuary. While individual enterprises on Sapelo eventually folded, an influx of capital came to the greater area of the Sea Islands. See McFeely, *Sapelo's People*, 143, as well as Stewart, "What Nature Suffers to Groe," 193–242. For a case study of the nearby resort built and served largely by a black and immigrant workforce, see William Barton McCash and June Hall McCash, *The Jekyll Island Club: Southern Haven for America's Millionaires* (Athens: University of Georgia Press, 1989), 1–53. Woolson captures the freedpeople's resilient and improvisational natures as they carved new opportunities for themselves out of upheaval.

38. See Leslie A. Schwalm, *A Hard Fight for We: Women's Transition from Slavery to Freedom in South Carolina* (Urbana: University of Illinois Press, 1997), 147–268; Tera W. Hunter, *To 'Joy My Freedom: Southern Black Women's Lives and Labors after the Civil War* (Cambridge, MA: Harvard University Press, 1997), 21–97; Noralee Frankel, *Freedom's Women: Black Women and Families in Civil War Era Mississippi* (Bloomington: Indiana University Press, 1999), 56–180; and Elsa Barkley Brown, "Negotiating and Transforming the Public Sphere: African American Political Life in the Transition

from Slavery to Freedom," *Jumpin' Jim Crow: Southern Politics from the Civil War to Civil Rights*, ed. Jane Dailey, Glenda Gilmore, and Bryant Simon (Princeton, NJ: Princeton University Press, 2000), 28–66; and Martha S. Jones, *All Bound Up Together: The Woman Question in African American Public Culture, 1830–1890* (Chapel Hill: University of North Carolina Press, 2007), 119–208.

39. Alexander, *Ambiguous Lives*, 7. See also Elizabeth Regosin, *Freedom's Promise: Ex-Slave Families and Citizenship in the Age of Emancipation* (Charlottesville: University Press of Virginia, 2002), 41–53.

40. On the historically influential and charged value of the postmaster position, see Richard R. John, *Spreading the News: The American Postal System from Franklin to Morse* (Cambridge, MA: Harvard University Press, 1995), 112–68; within the context of postwar Georgia patronage systems, see Rogers, *A Scalawag in Georgia*, 111–13, 125–27.

41. For Georgia, see Mark Schultz, "Interracial Kinship Ties and the Emergence of a Black Middle Class, Hancock, Georgia, 1865–1920," *Georgia in Black and White*, 141–72. Also see Hannah Rosen, *Terror in the Heart of Freedom* (Chapel Hill: University of North Carolina Press, 2009), 133–75; Martha Hodes, *White Women, Black Men: Illicit Sex in the Nineteenth-Century South* (New Haven, CT: Yale University Press, 1997), especially 147–75; Peter W. Bardaglio, *Reconstructing the Household: Families, Sex, and the Law in the Nineteenth-Century South* (Chapel Hill: University of North Carolina Press, 1995), 176–213; Victoria E. Bynum, "Misshapen Identity: Memory, Folklore and the Legend of Rachel Knight," *Sex, Love, Race*, 237–53; and Laura Edwards, "The Disappearance of Susan Daniel and Henderson Cooper: Gender and Narratives of Political Conflict in the Reconstruction-Era U.S. South," *Sex, Love, Race*, 294–312.

42. See Gebhard, "Romantic Love and Wife-Battering," 85; and Sharon L. Dean, *Constance Fenimore Woolson: Homeward Bound* (Knoxville: University of Tennessee Press, 1995), 128–32.

43. Although apparently not an option for Cicely, nearby Savannah traditionally offered single women social networks and the chance of benevolent work long before the war multiplied such opportunities. See Christine Jacobson Carter, *Southern Single Blessedness* (Urbana: University of Illinois Press, 2006), 13–40, 95–149.

"*Pioneers of Spoliation*"

Woolson's *Horace Chase* and the Role of Magazine Writing in the Gilded-Age Development of the South

—Kevin E. O'Donnell

Constance Fenimore Woolson wrote and published her last novel, *Horace Chase*, at the end of the Gilded Age.[1] *Harper's Monthly* circulated the first chapter in January 1893, and the serial ran for ten months during what would turn out to be Woolson's last year on earth. Each month that year, as successive installments of the novel appeared on newsstands in railroad stations, the U.S. economy—and, indeed, the global economy—looked more and more precarious. The Panic of 1893 marked the end of the Gilded Age as well as the end of Woolson's life; she died the next January, probably suicide. *Horace Chase: A Novel* first appeared in book form in the spring of 1894, a few months after the author had been laid to rest. Woolson wrote the novel in the rented rooms where she spent the last few years of her life—in Oxford, England, and in Florence, Italy. During this period, when she also traveled to other parts of Europe and to North Africa, she often wrote on hotel stationary, using hotel pens. At the time she wrote the book, Woolson had not seen America in almost fifteen years.

Horace Chase is set in the early 1870s, some twenty years prior to its composition and an ocean away from the European rooms where it was penned. The novel takes place in the American southeast, particularly in two subregions: the coastal southeast—including the Carolinas and the Atlantic coast of northern Florida, around St. Augustine—and the mountain South, around Asheville, in western North Carolina.

Woolson had traveled and stayed in those regions during the first part of her writing career, after her father died in 1869. During the 1870s, Constance—Connie, her friends and family called her—wintered with her mother in St. Augustine and traveled to the mountains during warmer months. The pair lived an itinerant existence, traveling throughout the South so that Woolson could write about a region that was poised for development following the carnage and chaos and economic stagnation of the Civil War. When her mother died in 1879, Woolson left the country, never to return.

By the time she wrote *Horace Chase*, however, the regions of the American South where the book is set had been altered dramatically. As Reconstruction drew to its ignominious end, enormous commercial energies were unleashed. Over the next two decades, the quiet, historic southeastern coastal towns of Woolson's memory were transformed into bustling tourist destinations for Northerners. At the same time, the ancient, old-growth deciduous forests of the mountain South were clear-cut by industrial logging on an unprecedented scale as the Gilded Age gathered steam. Set at the beginning, and written toward the conclusion, of this era, *Horace Chase* provides gilded bookends of a sort. In particular, Woolson links the industrial and commercial exploitation of the region with her contributions to illustrated magazines. By connecting periodical writing with Gilded-Age commercial development, the novel thus provides an oblique commentary on Woolson's own avocation and livelihood, even as her pages offer an elegy for the lost landscapes of the South.

The Gilded-Age Colonization of the South

Historians often use the term "Gilded Age" to refer to the twenty-year period from the middle of Reconstruction to the Panic of 1893, a period that corresponds almost exactly to Woolson's writing career. Just as she began to make a living from her pen, the first modern corporation or "holding company" was formed in New York, specifically as a vehicle for building the Southern Railway.[2] Between 1870, the year Woolson first sold an essay to *Harper's Monthly*, and the last years of the century, manufacturing output in the United States increased sevenfold, though the country's population increased only about two and a half times.[3] Woolson's career as a magazine contributor thus coincided with this age of economic development.

In 1873, a few years after Woolson began writing professionally, Mark Twain and Charles Dudley Warner published a novel called *The Gilded Age: A Tale of Today*, the book that subsequently gave its name to the era.[4] Twain and Warner were Connecticut neighbors at the Nook Farm enclave in Hartford along with Harriet Beecher Stowe, whose backyard adjoined the yards of their homes. Twain and Warner wrote *The Gilded Age* mostly in tag-team fashion, each passing the manuscript over the backyard fence after he had completed a section. The manuscript thus went back and forth during the late winter and early spring of 1873—as it happens, the very time when the fictional events of *Horace Chase* commence. That year saw the end of Ulysses S. Grant's first term, though he would go on that fall to win reelection. Twain's and Warner's book is, in part, a satire of the greedy mismanagement under Grant's postwar administration, during a period of heavy federal spending on railroads and reconstruction.

In *The Gilded Age*, one of the main characters becomes a lobbyist in Washington, DC, where she attempts to persuade Congress to purchase Tennessee land owned by her adoptive family. Such schemes involving similarly "unimproved" Southern land, railroads, and federal money became all too familiar in real-life public affairs of the period. By the end of Grant's second term, his name had become synonymous with graft. The novel's events reflect such developments; even its "sterling" hero finds real wealth when he discovers coal on Southern lands purchased by the parents of his beloved. For him as for others, the economic relationship between the North and the South was essentially colonial: Northern urban centers provided capital, technology, and administration, while the South provided natural resources and cheap labor. The resulting industries were largely extractive. Raw or lightly refined resources were shipped to the North or to England, where factories would then create the real wealth. The South received comparatively little economic benefit. By the 1890s, however, Southerners were left to face the resulting environmental damage: "worn-out soil, cut-over timberlands, and worked-out mines," as the historian C. Vann Woodward has written.[5]

Travel Writing in Illustrated Monthly Magazines

Much of the money that flowed through capital markets to finance Southern investments came through New York City and was managed by firms on Wall Street in lower Manhattan. Less than half a mile away were the publishing offices of Harper and Brothers, located at Franklin Square in a landmark building with a cast-iron façade that had been constructed on Pearl Street in 1854. In 1850, the Harpers had founded *Harper's New Monthly Magazine*, which was by 1873 arguably the most widely circulating of the American monthlies. Filled with wood engravings as the *Atlantic Monthly* was not, the illustrated monthlies that saw their heyday during the latter half of the nineteenth century included *Appletons' Journal*, *Lippincott's Magazine*, the *Galaxy*, and *Scribner's Monthly*, later to become the *Century*. These magazines often competed for the same contributors; Woolson published pieces in all six at one time or another, before opting to write exclusively for *Harper's Monthly* beginning in 1884.

Even in the 1870s, when Woolson first began writing, *Harper's Monthly* was already a venerable institution. At first an "eclectic" that reprinted mainly English authors with original wood engravings, the magazine had by 1853 begun to pay American writers for original articles about American locales. Circulation rose from 7,500 in 1850 to more than 100,000 in less than three years. When the Civil

War began in 1861, the magazine's monthly circulation was nearly 200,000. Four years later, circulation rose again, and the success of *Harper's Monthly* inspired competitors. By the mid-1870s, *Scribner's Monthly* and *Appletons' Journal* had ushered in the era of the illustrated monthlies, magazines that generally reached the peak of their influence and circulation in the 1880s.[6]

Travel writing was their premier genre and was so popular as the Gilded Age unfolded that some volumes of *Harper's Monthly*, for example, were at least half full of armchair itinerancy. During the 1870s and 1880s, a period of great industrial development and territorial expansion, readers were curious about distant places, and travel articles provided glimpses of far-flung locations, combined with plenty of information about transportation routes as well as business opportunities. Travelogues in Northern periodicals oriented in turn the course of investment and development.

The historian Alan Trachtenberg in his classic 1982 study, *The Incorporation of America: Culture and Society in the Gilded Age*, describes how the "tightening systems of transport and communication, the spread of a market economy into all regions" fueled the postwar economic boom. The spread of transportation technologies then gave rise to new economic relationships and social arrangements, "the remaking of cultural perceptions," and "new hierarchies of control."[7] As Trachtenberg would have it, the ascendancy of American illustrated monthlies was inextricably linked to the growth of these technologies, especially the railroad. Trains distributed monthly magazines, courtesy of the U.S. Postal Service, and often in remote locations. Additionally, railway station newsstands were an important distribution point for single issues, and railway stations as well as passenger trains themselves became important sites of reading. Business travelers, in particular, would peruse magazines in the station and on the train, often while traveling on business related to development spurred by the railroad and, in turn, promoted by magazines.

Just as Woolson's career followed the arc of the Gilded-Age economy, her fortunes likewise rode the rising postwar wave of illustrated monthlies. It is not surprising, then, that travel writing was Woolson's bread and butter; she and her mother lived an itinerant existence during the 1870s so that Woolson could write about the areas she visited and thereby support them both. She lived to travel and traveled to live, particularly when the pay for travel articles was much better than the pay for fiction. Woolson's magazine travel pieces produced her primary income, and they also provided her with raw material that she would later transform into stories and then novels. As a purveyor of travel writing, Woolson therefore played a role in the commercial and industrial development of the postbellum South. Along with others who wrote about the region, she affected the commercial development of two particular locales that would also be featured in her last novel.

Early Travel Essays: The Seaside and the Mountains in the South

Woolson's travel piece about St. Augustine, Florida, as "The Ancient City" appeared in *Harper's Monthly* in December 1874 and January 1875.[8] The story is a creative mix of fiction and travel writing that features a fictionalized ensemble of genteel Northerners visiting the city. The dramatic tension centers around romance: Which man will gain the favor of the pretty young woman? Will the twenty-eight-year-old Sara, on the verge of spinsterhood, find love before it is too late? Amid the unfolding drama, the article presents readers with travel information about St. Augustine and surrounding areas along the Atlantic coast.

Woolson was far from the first national magazine writer to describe northern Florida after the Civil War. Indeed, Woolson's essays about the area were part of the considerable publicity and national attention that hit the area at that time. Harriet Beecher Stowe, for one, had bought land in Mandarin, not far from St. Augustine, and had begun spending winters there with family members in the late 1860s. Her series of articles about life along the rivers and swamps near Mandarin began appearing during 1870 in the *Christian Union*, a New York-based newspaper that was edited by her brother, Henry Ward Beecher. Around the same period, T. B. Thorpe penned a piece for *Appletons' Journal* entitled "St. John's and the Ocklawaha Rivers, Florida," which featured the region around St. Augustine and was illustrated by the ever-popular Harry Fenn. The article then served as the first installment in *Picturesque America*, a popular illustrated travel series also published by the Appletons and sold by subscription beginning in 1872. Four years later, the same firm brought out Sidney Lanier's *Florida*, a travel book that appeared in 1876.

Clearly, Woolson was not a pioneer in the Sunshine State. In 1873, the year she began wintering in St. Augustine with her mother, 14,000 tourists visited the state of Florida, according to Harriet Beecher Stowe.[9] Nonetheless, Woolson *was* what more recent marketers would call an "early adopter." Among other writers and travelers, she discovered Florida ahead of the main wave of development and the full-scale Northern invasion of the region, which magazine writing helped to promote. Even as she was writing, Woolson was aware of what would happen as Northerners began arriving in greater numbers. At one point her narrator quotes "a lady friend, a new arrival," who "had visited the Ancient City forty years before, in the days of the *ancien régime*":

> These modern houses springing up every where have altered the whole aspect of the town. I am glad I came back while there is still something left of the old time. Another five years and the last old wall will be torn down for a horrible paling fence.[10]

Her articles about St. Augustine are tinged with sadness and impending loss.

Three years later, the industrialist Henry Flagler, half owner of Standard Oil, arrived in the city with his invalid wife to escape Northern winters. The trip in 1878 marked the beginning of Flagler's fascination with Florida; he would soon divest himself of his Standard Oil interests in order to develop a great hotel in St. Augustine, the Ponce de Leon. He would also begin commercial development of the state as a tourist mecca, with St. Augustine as the main railroad / steamboat connection. So immediate was his success that David Chandler describes Flagler in his biography's subtitle as "The Visionary Robber Baron Who Founded Florida."[11] By the mid-1890s, Flagler's development efforts had spread south to Miami and beyond, and by that time Florida had acquired associations with land speculation that the state retains to this day.

Woolson's career was noticeably different, not least in leaving Florida behind. Not long after she wrote "The Ancient City," Woolson wrote about the mountains of western North Carolina in "The French Broad."[12] Like "The Ancient City," this account is a mix of fiction and travelogue that features an ensemble of genteel travelers, some of which were already familiar to Woolson's readers. The title of this second travel piece comes from the name of a high mountain river, the French Broad, which cuts a dramatic gorge through what was then the last major undeveloped break in the high ridges of the southern Appalachians. Railroad maps from the period show a large, railroad-free area centered around the wide mountain stream.[13] Woolson knew that a line through the gorge would connect railroads on the eastern seaboard with those in the Tennessee and Ohio River valleys. The French Broad River country was, in that sense, virgin territory that was ripe for exploitation.

As with Florida, Woolson was far from the first to write about the mountains of western North Carolina for a national audience. Indeed, another article entitled "The French Broad," written by F. G. De Fontaine and illustrated (like the T. B. Thorpe piece about northern Florida) by Harry Fenn, also appeared in the first volume of *Picturesque America*. Numerous other travel pieces about the mountain South appeared in national periodicals in the early 1870s. What is more, when Woolson's article was published in *Harper's Monthly* for April 1875, her account was soon competing with a serial by Frances Fisher Tiernan (a.k.a. Christian Reid) entitled "'The Land of the Sky;' or, Adventures in Mountain By-Ways," a novel whose installments ran in *Appletons' Journal* beginning in September. Much like Woolson's article, Reid's novel features a traveling party with much to say.

Once again, Woolson was not a pioneer in the strict sense of that term. But in "The French Broad," she was again an early adopter. At the time she traveled in and wrote about the mountainous region near Asheville, the area was already popular among Southern vacationers seeking to escape the heat of the lowland summers. For the most part, however, Northern tourists had not yet discovered the Appalachians.[14] That made Woolson's work part of another literary land-grab, a wave of publicity that preceded, by a few years, the large-scale commercial development of a Southern region's resources. Less than four years after "The French Broad" appeared, the Swannanoa tunnel would be completed in 1879 and would bring the Western North Carolina railroad from the east into Buncombe County and, the following year, into Asheville. Four years after that, the trunk line would be completed through the French Broad gorge and would connect the eastern seaboard with the Tennessee River Valley to form the last major link in the eastern railroad system. The last southern mountain tracks would thereby be opened to loggers, and the reckless cutting of the area's forests would begin in earnest.

Horace Chase as Environmental Elegy

Almost twenty years after writing "The Ancient City," about St. Augustine, and "The French Broad," about the mountain South, Woolson set her last novel in the same two locales. When she sat down in Europe's rented rooms to write *Horace Chase*, most of the virgin forest around Asheville was already gone, and both Florida and Appalachia had been transformed forever. Perhaps for that reason, Woolson's book does not emphasize place as much as an earlier novel like *Anne* (1882), which evokes its Great Lakes setting in rich and tender detail. Instead, Woolson focuses on a love story and emphasizes the psychology, motivations, and relationships of her characters. Nevertheless, *Horace Chase* reflects a deep concern with the way Northern capitalists altered Southern landscapes.

The book's title character is, in fact, a capitalist who arrives in Asheville on a spring day in 1873. At thirty-eight, he is a self-made robber baron who has already accumulated four separate fortunes. He has come to the mountains to convalesce, though he has a perennial eye toward investment opportunities. As one local resident remarks, "He has not been well, I believe ... and he was advised to try mountain air. In addition, he is said to be looking into the railroad project" (16). His arrival in Asheville causes a stir, especially among members of the Franklin family—a mother and her three children, one son and two daughters. They are Northerners who have moved south after the death of the paterfamilias. The Franklin daughters include Dolly, the firstborn and an invalid, plus Ruth, at eighteen the baby who is pretty, footloose, and marriageable.

Chase soon strikes up a romance with the lovely young Ruth. Before long the two get married and the family's fortunes improve, despite the concern of various parties. But over the course of the next three years, several tragedies occur. The novel's primary conflict comes about when young Ruth later falls in love with Walter Willoughby, an otherwise minor character who is the scoundrel son of Chase's business partner. Chase himself is often preoccupied and distant, as readers might expect from a capitalist busy building his fifth fortune. Ultimately, Chase forgives

Ruth's indiscretions and welcomes her back. His contrition, warmth, and forgiveness restore to the Franklins the promise of order.

By the novel's final pages, Chase appears to be Woolson's hero—if her book can be said to have a hero at all when the title character remains oddly remote and inscrutable. More disconcertingly, he appears at first to be a villain, at least to the Asheville residents who worry about what the Northern capitalist might do to their beautiful mountain town. Early on, for example, before Chase has made an appearance, Mrs. Franklin mentions that her family is planning to dine with Mr. Chase. Her friend, Commodore Anthony Etheridge, responds with indignation:

> "Horace Chase; I knew he was here. I should like to kick him out!"
> "Why so fierce?" said Mrs. Franklin . . .
> "Of course I am fierce. We don't want fellows of that sort here; he will upset the whole place!" (16)

Later in the conversation, Etheridge continues:

> "The one solace I got out of the war was the check it gave to the advance of those horrible rails westward; I have been in hopes that the locomotives would not get beyond Old Fort [North Carolina—twenty miles East of Asheville] in my time, at any rate. Why, Dora [Etheridge here addresses Mrs. Franklin], this strip of mountain country is the most splendid bit of natural forest, of nature undraped, which exists to-day between the Atlantic Ocean and the Rockies." (16)

To this outburst Mrs. Franklin responds, "'I am afraid I don't care for nature undraped so much as you do, commodore; I think I like draperies'" (16).

Etheridge replies in turn with what appears to be a full-blown environmental jeremiad. Here he contrasts the magnificent wild forests of the United States with the fenced landscapes of Britain and Europe:

> "Of course you do! But when you—and by you I mean the nation at large—when you perceive that your last acre of primitive forest is forever gone, then you will repent. And you will begin to cultivate wildness as they do abroad, poor creatures—plant forests and guard 'em with stone walls and keepers, by Jove!" (17)

Thus, in this early chapter, the novel strikes a note of concern for the "primitive forest," a theme that Woolson's novel will sustain.

Before considering how southern Appalachia is portrayed, it is worth reviewing what actually happened to the region's forests during the twenty years between the time of the novel's setting and the time of its composition. Due to a long growing season and high rainfall, the mountains around Asheville in the 1870s had the most magnificent—and the most commercially valuable—forests on the North American continent. With predictable Gilded-Age hubris, those forests were logged after Northern and international "syndicates" or holding companies purchased large tracts of land. Using new technologies like narrow-gauge railways, steam-powered cable skidders, and splash dams, the companies cut so relentlessly that mechanized logging operations could reduce a virgin deciduous forest to an eroded hillside within a matter of months. Slash was left where it fell, usually to dry and catch in fires that would sometimes last for years, as the earth burned down to mineral soil and bare rock. Within three decades, more than 90 percent of the trees in the southern mountains were cut.[15]

The industrial logging of southern Appalachia was, as Wallace Stegner has written, without precedent. And since the nineteenth century, such destructiveness has been matched in scale only by the current logging of the Amazon rainforest.[16]

The Meaning of Mr. Bubble: Coding in Woolson's Novel

According to literary scholars Victoria Brehm and Sharon Dean, Woolson did not feel free to explore contested subjects or to express unguarded opinions as she wrote. In the introduction to their 2004 collection of Woolson's short stories and travel narratives, Brehm and Dean cite a letter Woolson wrote to a colleague after meeting in 1876 with a *Harper's Monthly* editor who warned about broaching a certain controversial topic. "I thought he meant that and was abashed and fearful," Woolson wrote to her friend. "I am glad to hear he did not entirely cross off my name from his list."[17]

Those remarks suggest how much Woolson depended upon the Harpers for her livelihood; the mere thought of an editor's displeasure made her "abashed and fearful." Brehm and Dean claim that Woolson's meeting with that editor "was to affect her fiction the rest of her life."[18] Rather than risk her income by courting controversy, Woolson went on to develop "a method of subtextually encoding her opinions" that Brehm and Dean describe at length:

> She used names, dates, places, quotations of songs and poems to create a secondary reality—a subterranean text underneath what might appear to be a romance or story of society—which would then convey her opinions on slavery and Reconstruction, on the growing tendency of the United States to try to forget the Civil War, and later, after she moved to Europe, on her role as an art-

ist and on international politics. It was a clever method developed by a gifted, frustrated artist forced to write for the entertainment market.[19]

To be sure, Brehm and Dean do not test their provocative thesis, but they do indicate places here and there in Woolson's fiction where a kind of encoding seems to be at work.

In *Horace Chase*, the subtextual possibilities are intriguing. There are, for example, the further remarks of Commodore Etheridge, the nature lover who worries about the damage that Horace Chase could inflict on the "primitive forest" around Asheville. After he laments the forest's impending demise, Etheridge speculates about the source of the Northerner's wealth:

> "Horace Chase appears here as the pioneer of spoliation. He may not mean it; he does not come with an axe on his shoulder exactly; he comes, in fact, with baking-powder; but that's how it will end. Haven't you heard that it was baking-powder? At least you have heard of the powder itself—the Bubble? I thought so. Well, that's where he made his first money—the Bubble Baking-Powder; and he made a lot of it, too! Now he is in no end of other things. One of them is steamships . . ." (17–18)

After cashing in on "Bubble Baking Powder" for his initial fortune, Chase makes his second from silver, his third from lumber, and his fourth from steamships. Only baking powder was not the sort of raw material or transportation industry that typically created Gilded-Age barons. Yet Chase's connection to Bubble Baking Powder is repeated elsewhere in Woolson's novel; Etheridge even takes to calling the Northerner "Mr. Bubble," and he refers to Chase as a "bubbling capitalist" (20).

In a history of American advertising that was written in the 1920s, Frank Presbrey observes that Royal Baking Powder undertook systematic advertising campaigns as far back as the 1870s, one of the first American companies to do so.[20] Ellen Gruber Garvey further observes that, when national magazines began developing advertising revenue in the 1870s, their two biggest advertisers were Pear's Soap and Royal Baking Powder.[21] Not surprisingly, the Royal company's steady ads by the 1890s provided a significant source of revenue for all the prominent monthlies (Fig. 1). The fact that Chase's fortune began with baking powder thus suggests that he is in some ways connected with the magazines; at the very least, Woolson's subtext becomes a kind of inside joke. In *Horace Chase*, the baking powder nod serves as a metonymic reminder of newly emerging ads, of the magazines in which they appeared, and of the travel writing industry that had made Woolson financially solvent.

276   Kevin E. O'Donnell

ROYAL BAKING POWDER
Absolutely Pure.

This powder never varies. A marvel of purity, strength and wholesomeness. More economical than the ordinary kinds and cannot be sold in competition with the multitude of low tests, short-weight alum or phosphate powers. Sold only in cans. ROYAL BAKING POWDER CO., 106 Wall street, New York.   oc4,3taw&S1y

Fig. 1, Advertisement for Royal Baking Powder.
Atlantic Monthly (December 1891): 880.

Also worth noting is the brand name for Chase's baking powder: Bubble. The word "bubble" in the nineteenth century was associated with economic speculation, and Woolson's novel begins in 1873, the year a financial panic was precipitated by Jay Cooke's overspeculation and the collapse of his banking firm. Twenty years later, when Woolson's novel was serialized, another financial panic hit. The timing scarcely seems coincidental: the country's later financial panic was set in motion during 1891 by the collapse of London's Baring Bros. Bank. In Europe, at the very time Woolson was writing her chapters and before the 1893 panic had actually begun, there was much discussion of the American speculative bubble that was about to burst.

Spoliation

When Etheridge refers to Chase as a "pioneer of spoliation," armed not with an axe but with baking powder, the phrase arguably refers not only to Horace Chase, the fictional capitalist, but also and more obliquely to Woolson herself. After her death in 1894, critics came to associate Woolson with the word "pioneer." Fred Lewis Pattee in 1917 called Woolson a "pioneer of literary realism."[22] John Dwight Kern, who authored the first full-length Woolson biography in 1934, titled his book *Constance Fenimore Woolson: Literary Pioneer*.[23] In 2004, Anne Boyd remarked in *Writing for Immortality* upon this tendency of literary scholars. Boyd observed that, by calling her a "pioneer," critics were in fact dismissing Woolson, in a back-handed way, as an author who broke ground as a postwar realist but never achieved her full potential.[24] An additional possibility, which Boyd does not mention, is that critics may have connected Woolson to the word "pioneer" by association with her famous great-uncle, James Fenimore Cooper, whose best-known work is *The Pioneers* (1823). Woolson was known to play up her association with Cooper to further her professional career. In a letter to Samuel Mather, sometime during the 1880s, she wrote: "I am still sailing on my middle name—as I have done ever since I came abroad."[25] At the time, she had been living and traveling in Europe for several years.

The connection between Woolson and the identity of the pioneer might seem tenuous when considered only in the light of this association with her great-uncle. But Woolson herself was, in fact, a kind of pioneer—not only of literary realism (as critics would later have it), but also and more directly as a kind of literary travel pioneer, one of the *de facto* scouts for Gilded-Age capitalists who sought investment opportunities during the 1870s and 1880s. Woolson had a knack for finding places in the South just before Northern capitalists began large-scale development. In both St. Augustine and Asheville, she was in that sense a pioneer for the railroads. Both regions saw a frenzy of development shortly after she wrote about them.

Furthermore, it is worth considering the historical model for Cooper's own literary hero. Natty Bumppo, the main character of the Leatherstocking books, was based on the real-life Daniel Boone, who was still alive and already famous when *The Pioneers* was published. As the Boone biographer John Mack Faragher has written, the similarities between the fictional character and the real-life Boone were "lost on few" when *The Pioneers* appeared during the 1820s.[26] Among other things, there was the echo of the names—Nathaniel Bumppo, Daniel Boone. Additionally, both characters inhabited relatively undeveloped areas; when the developers moved in, they moved on.

In that respect, in her relationship with developers and capitalists, Woolson also has parallels with Daniel Boone, who had not actually settled the wilderness any more than she would. Boone was not the first white man to go through the Cumberland Gap, nor was he the first white man to settle in the Kentucky bluegrass region around what would become Boonesboro. Many nameless pioneers had preceded him in both those endeavors. Boone's main service was to survey Kentucky for the wealthy land-developer Richard Henderson.[27] Like magazine writers in the South during the early 1870s, Boone never "discovered" any new regions for himself. Instead, he helped to publicize what others had found, and the capitalists followed on his heels. What's more, Boone, like Woolson, was itinerant throughout his life. When the capitalists moved in and exploited a region, Boone, like Woolson, moved on.

If Horace Chase then recalls Woolson as a "pioneer of spoliation," a defense of Chase should follow Etheridge's jeremiad. In fact, not too many chapters later Commodore Etheridge and Horace Chase have a chance to talk. By this time, Etheridge is losing his memory. He is older than he appears; he is not a man of means. Woolson's narrator observes that Chase "recognized in Etheridge a man who would never have denied himself luxury unless forced to do it, a man who would never have been at Asheville if he could have afforded Newport; the talk about 'nature undraped' was simply an excuse" (85). As further details emerge, Etheridge's credentials as a nature lover become tarnished.

Chase does not have the last word, however. From Asheville, he takes the Franklins along on a carriage excursion into the Great Smoky Mountains. The traveling party includes young Ruth, whom Chase is surreptitiously courting. On the border between Tennessee and North Carolina, the party stops to take in the view:

> Up here at the top of the pass there were no clearings visible; for long miles in every direction the forest held unbroken sway, filling the gorges like a leafy ocean, and sweeping up to the surrounding summits in the darker tints of the black balsams. The air was filled with delicate wild odors, a fragrance which is like no other—the breath of a virgin forest.
>
> "And you want to put a railroad here?" broke out Dolly, suddenly. (109)

Dolly Franklin, the invalid older daughter, is in some ways the moral commentator of the book, and her outburst here carries real weight. Considering that Chase's "third fortune" has come from lumber and that, throughout the book, the narrator refers to the region's "magnificent forest," this passage certainly sounds like a rebuke.

In one of Woolson's last letters, written more than twenty years after her father had died, more than ten after her mother had passed, and not long before her own death in Venice, she wrote of herself, "I often think that though I stay abroad, I *remember* better than anyone else."[28] At the time, Woolson had lived abroad for more than fourteen years and was finishing *Horace Chase*. When she wrote the passage about the high pass, from memory, in a crowded European city, she almost certainly knew that the forest she was describing was already gone forever. Indeed, between the time Woolson left the United States for Europe and the time she wrote *Horace Chase*, public awareness of conservation issues had grown dramatically. What was then termed "the Nature Movement" had begun to influence American letters and politics alike. In 1890, for example, the *Century* featured John Muir's articles promoting the conservation of California's Yosemite Valley as a national park, articles that helped move a bill through Congress to establish the park that very year. By 1891, Congress had acted to regulate logging practices after growing public outcry, though legislation would prove to be too little, too late, for the Appalachian forest already destroyed.

Woolson surely knew about these developments. Nevertheless, her novel refuses to condemn its title character. As the book draws to a close, Chase generates excitement among a group of Asheville residents with his plans to make the town a destination for Northern tourists. Chase "surveys a valley" near Asheville "with critical eyes," describing how he would like to see the area transformed into a European style resort, with illuminated waterfalls, Tyrolean architecture, and children dressed in peasant costumes (350). Woolson's description of a tourist development here could be considered prophetic: Chase's vision in this passage resembles nothing so much as modern-day Helen, a tourist town in the north Georgia mountains built around a Bavarian theme, a town less than two hours from Asheville that was first developed in the 1960s.

In describing his vision of a mountain resort for Northerners, Chase says he will paint the town's churches and buildings to make them look good for the tourists. He wants to "boom" the buildings, he says, using a slang word that at the time meant, roughly, "to prepare for gaudy development." As Woolson's novel puts it:

> "All right; we'll boom them all," said Chase, liberally. "There might be a statue of Daniel Boom in the park, near the casino," he went on, in a considering tone; "he lived near here for some time. Though, come to think of it, his name was Boone, wasn't it?—just missed being appropriate!" (352)

Chase's reference to Boone as "boom" is more than just a slip of the tongue. His ear helps to connect the coded themes of the book. The postwar capitalist on the move and linked metonymically with the magazine profession is further connected with Natty Bumppo and, however obliquely, with Woolson herself.

Many readers of late would like to see Chase laid flat. He fits current notions of the Gilded-Age villain—the monopoly capitalist from the North, exploiter of the environment, builder of tacky tourist developments, figure of excess. But Woolson refuses to reduce his stature. In fact, she claimed, in a letter to *Harper's Monthly* editor Henry Mills Alden, that she intended Chase to be the "principal personage" in the novel. "The man is intended to be more important than the woman," she wrote, and she confided that the book represented her effort to "describe the masculine mind."[29] Yet to many reviewers during Woolson's time—and to readers today—her title character remains oddly blank, remote, distant. Arguably, Chase embodies Woolson's own unresolved conflicts. After all, from the trees he would log came the paper for her book, and from his expansionist impulse came her continuing circulation. So, too, the illustrated monthlies that provided Woolson with her income and independence were inextricably, perhaps irresolvably, intertwined with both the economic production and the reckless destruction of the Gilded Age that Chase comes to embody.

Notes

For their generous help in tracing nineteenth-century advertising still extant, the author would like to thank Jessica R. Olin at Hiram College; Nancy Story, Gary Ginther, and Diana Nichols at Ohio University Libraries; and Amber Paranick at the Library of Congress.

1. Constance Fenimore Woolson, *Horace Chase: A Novel* (New York: Harper and Brothers, 1894). All subsequent references will be to this edition and will be made parenthetically in the text.

2. Scott Reynolds Nelson, *Iron Confederacies: Southern Railways, Klan Violence, and Reconstruction* (Chapel Hill: University of North Carolina Press, 1999), 7.

3. Gerald Gunderson, *A New Economic History of America* (New York: McGraw-Hill, 1976), 305.

4. Mark Twain and Charles Dudley Warner, *The Gilded Age: A Tale of To-Day* (Hartford: American Publishing Co., 1873).

5. C. Vann Woodward, *Origins of the New South* (Baton Rouge: Louisiana State University Press, 1951), 320. See also *Origins of the New South Fifty Years Later: The Continuing Influence of a Historical Classic*, ed. John B. Boles and Bethany L. Johnson (Baton Rouge: Louisiana State University Press, 2003).

6. Frank Luther Mott, *A History of American Magazines*, II: *1850–1865*, III: *1865–1885* (Cambridge, MA: Harvard University Press, 1967).

7. Alan Trachtenberg, *The Incorporation of America: Culture and Society in the Gilded Age* (1982; New York: Hill and Wang, 2007), 3–4.

8. Constance Fenimore Woolson, "The Ancient City, Part I," *Harper's Monthly* (December 1874): 1–25; and "The Ancient City, Part II," *Harper's Monthly* (January 1875): 165–85.

9. Mary B. Graff, "The Author," introduction to *Palmetto Leaves*, a facsimile reproduction of the first edition by Osgood (1873; Gainesville: University Press of Florida, 1968), xvi.

10. Woolson, "The Ancient City, Part II," 171.

11. David Leon Chandler, *Henry Flagler: The Astonishing Life and Times of the Visionary Robber Baron Who Founded Florida* (New York: Macmillan, 1986).

12. Constance Fenimore Woolson, "The French Broad," *Harper's Monthly* (April 1875): 617–36.

13. Edward L. Ayers, *The Promise of the New South: Life After Reconstruction* (New York: Oxford University Press, 1992), 10–11.

14. S. Kent Schwarzkopf, *A History of Mt. Mitchell and the Black Mountains: Exploration, Development, and Preservation* (Raleigh: North Carolina Division of Archives and History, 1985), 35, 81.

15. Ronald D. Eller, *Miners, Millhands, and Mountaineers: The Industrialization of the Appalachian South* (Knoxville: University of Tennessee Press, 1982), especially ch. 3, for a definitive account of this process.

16. Wallace Stegner, "A Capsule History of Conservation," *Where the Bluebird Sings to the Lemonade Springs: Living and Writing in the West* (New York: Random House, 1992), 124.

17. Quoted by Victoria Brehm and Sharon L. Dean, "Introduction," *Constance Fenimore Woolson: Selected Stories and Travel Narratives*, ed. Brehm and Dean (Knoxville: University of Tennessee Press, 2004), xvi–xvii.

18. Brehm and Dean, "Introduction," xvi.

19. Brehm and Dean, "Introduction," xvii.

20. Frank Presbrey, *The History and Development of Advertising* (Garden City, NY: Doubleday, Doran, 1929), 252.

21. Ellen Gruber Garvey, *The Adman in the Parlor: Magazines and the Gendering of Consumer Culture, 1880s to 1910s* (New York: Oxford University Press, 1996), 86. Garvey devotes much of ch. 3 to an extended discussion of Royal Baking Powder and its importance to the magazine industry. Predictably, magazine covers from single issues are hard to find thanks to the common archival practice of stripping them before binding.

22. Fred Lewis Pattee, *A History of American Literature since 1870* (New York: Century, 1917), 317–18.

23. John Dwight Kern, *Constance Fenimore Woolson, Literary Pioneer* (Philadelphia: University of Pennsylvania Press, 1934).

24. Anne E. Boyd, *Writing for Immortality: Women and the Emergence of High Literary Culture in America* (Baltimore: Johns Hopkins University Press, 2004), 238.

25. The letter, from a collection in the Princeton University Library, is quoted in Boyd, 204 n. 67.

26. John Mack Faragher, *Daniel Boone: The Life and Legend of an American Pioneer* (New York: Holt, 1992), 331.

27. Faragher, *Daniel Boone*, 98–140.

28. Clare Benedict, *Five Generations, 1785–1923*, II: *Constance Fenimore Woolson* (London: Ellis, 1929), xii.

29. Cited in Kern, *Constance Fenimore Woolson*, 93.

"Shimmering Inlets"
Remembering Back, Looking Forward

Do you remember the pine-barrens of Florida, starred with those little flowers? There were "lagoons" there too; & shimmering inlets; & channels; & beaches. Some day I shall come back; & live in St. Augustine—perhaps!
—*Constance Fenimore Woolson to Edmund Clarence Stedman*

"A Modern and a Model Pioneer"

Civilizing the Frontier in Woolson's "A Pink Villa"

—Annamaria Formichella Elsden

Fanny Churchill's pink villa, alluded to in the title of Constance Fenimore Woolson's 1888 short story, has an almost mystical beauty. Called a "delicious nest" by a visiting Englishman, the villa "crown[s] one of the perpendicular cliffs of Sorrento, its rosy façade overlooking what is perhaps the most beautiful expanse of water in the world—the Bay of Naples."[1] A central rendezvous point for a circle of British and American expatriates in Italy, the terrace is described as "an enchanting place for lounging, attached as it was to a pink-faced villa that overlooked the sea" (839). Indeed, the villa virtually becomes a character in the story—it is given a face and said to "witness the wedding" of Eva Churchill and David Rod that culminates the narrative. Yet, despite its warm appeal, her mother's pink villa is precisely what the main character leaves behind in favor of a new habitation depicted as far less cozy. Eva forsakes Europe and her mother for David Rod's plantation in Florida, which boasts "a creaking saw-mill," a "groaning dredge," and "two hideously ugly new school-houses, set staring among the stumps" (846). In contrast to the leisurely spaces and rarefied atmosphere in which Eva has been raised, Rod's New World home suggests rugged, anti-aesthetic functionality.

What should we make of the fact that Eva can be lured away from this pink villa, with its clearly feminized valence, by the masculine Florida plantation? How do we read her defection from this maternal space and her return to what is emphatically the fatherland? At first glance the ending appears to be serene, as critics have pointed out. Robert White notes that "[t]he story ends happily with the departure of the wedded lovers for Florida"[2] and Peter Caccavari observes, "With Eva's marriage to David, it seems that Woolson will break down boundaries, will free her heroine from the house that keeps her from the outside world and from herself."[3] Yet aspects of the story menace this narrative resolution. Not surprisingly, the contrast between the pretty pink villa and the remote Florida plantation invokes other binarisms familiar to readers of nineteenth-century international fiction: Old World/New World, culture/nature, and indulgence/industry. But any traditional interpretation of these dualities must be qualified by the issues of gender and colonialism raised in the story. The question of whether Eva makes the right choice is a thorny one indeed.

Unfortunately, critics often comment too simplistically on Woolson's work in general and this story in particular, tending to overlook the national implications of her fiction. Surprisingly, one particularly harsh critic indirectly points up the larger issues functioning beneath the surface of Woolson's stories: "Simply because her tales are so mediocre and lacking in individual luster, they can all the more properly be viewed as an index to the culture which produced and ingested them."[4] In the process of undercutting Woolson's literary talents, this critic at least acknowledges the cultural resonances of her work, and these resonances are what concern me here. My reading raises these questions: what index to America does Woolson's story provide? When Horace Bartholomew calls David Rod "a modern and a model pioneer," casting him as the symbolic repository of his nation's ideals, how confident should we be in the notion of American "progress"? In allowing New World practicality to win Eva's young heart, "A Pink Villa" would seem to champion American industry and the men who embraced it. It is my purpose, however, to explore how other concerns complicate the plot's romantic resolution and undermine what might too easily seem a defense of American pragmatism and masculine enterprise. I want to suggest that the feminine values emphasized in the story's title articulate Woolson's ambivalence about Eva's fate in Florida and the masculine project of America.

With a name like David Rod, there can be no doubt that the suitor who wins Eva's hand is intended as a definitively masculine character. The work he does falls within the domain of what nineteenth-century Americans considered manly, especially in contrast to the idle lifestyle enjoyed by Eva's mother (Fanny Churchill) and her circle of expatriate friends. Explaining the allure of her villa, Fanny observes of her guests, "They come to see the view . . . to sit in the shade and talk. I give very good dinners too" (843). Rod, on the other hand, spends his time hard at work. The consummate entrepreneur, he has built a plantation in the wild southern fringes of Florida, has cleared the land, operated the sawmill, "grubbed up stumps," and confronted bears in the process, all with his own large, capable hands. Horace Bartholomew, a close acquaintance of both Fanny and David Rod and the liaison who brings them together, articulates a profound respect for such enterprise: "If I admire Rod, with his constant driving action, his indomitable pluck, his simple but tremendous belief in the importance of what he has undertaken to do, that's my own affair" (846). David Rod can shoot with extraordinary accuracy, sail a ship like a professional mariner, and generally overcome the many frontier obstacles that arise in his path. The story's characterizations all conspire to construct David Rod as hypermasculine in a distinctively American way, his strength and self-reliance clearly representing the frontier spirit so often celebrated in patriotic rhetoric.

David Rod's "constant driving action" is so impressive that it causes some of the Pink Villa's loungers to scrutinize the way they spend their time. Unlike the expatriate community in Italy, David Rod is "no talker at all; he says very little at any time; he's a doer—David is; he *does* things" (846). Bartholomew emphasizes "does" and goes on to say, "I declare it used to make me sick of myself to see how much that fellow accomplished every day of his life" (846). Rod's excessive masculine activity makes Bartholomew question his own worth, and has a similar effect on Eva. Though at the story's beginning Eva is well on her way to marriage with a Belgian nobleman and a life of aristocratic ease, David Rod's mesmerizing masculinity seems to cast a spell over Eva and cause her to relinquish all her previous ties. She tells her mother, "I have never seen any one like him," and then echoes the self-loathing expressed by Bartholomew earlier in the story: "Didn't I tell you that he cares nothing for me? I think he despises me—I am so useless!" (851). On the surface, the story seems to posit a dichotomy between the aristocratic socializing that occurs in Sorrento and the productive labor Rod pursues in Puntas Palmas, Florida. Those who know better—namely, Bartholomew and Eva—recognize the superiority of gainful employment over idle enjoyment.

But the choice is not so clear-cut. Although idealized by Bartholomew and Eva, Rod's masculinity has a dark side that the story exposes. What he does in the service of enterprise can be seen as more than opportunistic, indeed as downright exploitative. He explains to Eva's mother, "[M]y plantation isn't old and it isn't Spanish; it's a farm and quite new. I am over here now to get hands for it . . . laborers—Italians. They work very well in Florida" (840). David Rod has traveled to Italy not as the typical American sightseer, but rather as a plantation owner looking for cheap labor. David the doer becomes David the master, much to the admiration of Horace Bartholomew, who praises him for his "Italian colonization scheme" and exclaims that Rod has developed his plantation in Puntas Palmas to such an extent that "In ten years more . . . he will have civilized that entire neighborhood" (845–46). Rod's workers, in Bartholomew's estimation, benefit from the opportunity to participate in his plantation economy, but this opinion is clearly informed by Bartholomew's hopeless devotion to his friend. In comparison, an 1878 editorial titled "The Chinese Must Go" and published in New York's *Labor Standard* suggests the deplorable treatment of imported laborers. "We have certainly a right to protect and use every available means against the capitalistic combinations through which thousands of poor and ill-fed beings are imported to this country from China, Italy and elsewhere," wrote the Irish-born socialist Joseph McDonnell. "Let us use our organized power against the capitalistic combinations which carry on a slave trade between this country and China and elsewhere, by importing thousands for the purpose of reducing wages in America. Let our first stand be against those rich and intelligent thieves who strive to perpetuate and establish a system of overwork and starvation pay."[5]

By raising the specter of Florida, Woolson conjures up a particularly vexed nexus of economic relations more closely tied to exploitation than to a humanitarian agenda. Beginning in the eighteenth century, Florida landowners engaged in the practice of importing laborers from the Mediterranean countries of Spain, Greece, and Italy. American capitalists such as Andrew Turnbull saw the Mediterranean people as well suited for the hot climate and brutal labor expected in Florida, although when the indentured laborers arrived, the conditions they found were deplorable. Patricia C. Griffin describes a representative encounter at Turnbull's eastern Florida plantation: "In early August of 1768, ships carrying a large contingent of the Italian and Greek recruits arrived at [Andrew Turnbull's] plantation to find appalling living conditions. Lacking sufficient housing, many of the earlier arrivals had built themselves rude, palm-thatched huts (*casas de guano*)—dirt floored, leaky in the rain, and rife with insects. People were dying at an alarming rate."[6] Turnbull, who might have served as a prototype for the industrious and indomitable David Rod, traveled himself to Europe to recruit Italians and other Mediterranean laborers. History shows him to be a brutal taskmaster whose ill-advised policies—all based on a refusal to consider the native cultures of the workers he had "imported"—ultimately resulted in discontent, demoralization, and death for many of his hands. Jane Quinn, in her study of Minorcans in Florida, describes Turnbull's New Smyrna plantation in terms that suggest a military compound: "After the rebellion that cost the lives of two Italian settlers, the British governor set up a permanent guard of ten soldiers to prevent future uprisings. No attempt, apparently, was made to provide schooling for the children of the settlers. . . . Watched by the British guards, brutalized by heartless overseers, whatever education they received was vocational."[7] The historical treatment of Mediterranean workers in Florida certainly complicates our understanding of Rod's "civilizing" influence on them.

What, exactly, the word "civilized" means in Woolson's usage is open for debate—it's a slippery term. In the heart of the Victorian Era and at the height of British expansion and colonialism, civilizing had much to do with xenophobia and ethnocentrism. Turning colonies into smaller versions of bourgeois Britain was seen as a benevolent and appropriate civilizing mission. The intentions of the American government in regard to Native Americans were much the same, as evidenced by the Dawes General Allotment Act, passed in 1887 just a year before the publication of Woolson's story. The act sought to assimilate American Indians into white culture by breaking up tribal lands and parceling out allotments. The results were devastating, with Native Americans losing millions of acres and population numbers reaching a new low by the start of the twentieth century. From a contemporary vantage point, these practices are clearly oppressive, and the nuances of Woolson's story reveal her similarly critical stance on such civilizing measures. David Rod's name itself suggests an authoritarian role/rule and punitive consequences for disobedient subservients. His desire to "civilize" his plantation workers seems to be completely self-serving; the only justification given for his transatlantic labor trade is the observation that "[t]hey [Italians] work very well in Florida" (840). His motives are hardly depicted as humanitarian. Further, the concept of civilizing the frontier by civilizing an already "civilized" people brought to an American plantation and forced to work sugarcane seems somewhat ludicrous. The irony of the term can't have been lost on Woolson and is not lost on her readers.

It's worth noting that Rod's appropriation of Italy runs counter to conventional ways of subordinating Italy in comparison to America. In much nineteenth-century travel literature, Italy is represented as a locus of genteel culture and vilified accordingly for its femininity. In David Rod's revision of this familiar dichotomy, Italy becomes colonizable precisely because it offers a kind of untapped masculine labor pool, a repository of brute strength. The end result of this reconfigured perspective, however, is a reinscription of a familiar power dynamic, as Italy is physically, rather than psychologically and culturally, subordinated to the American masculine agenda. The masculinity that made the Italians worth pursuing as workers would have no doubt unsettled the American men who indentured them, and perhaps it was this anxiety that inspired a brutal and brutalizing plantation system designed to keep the hands from becoming too strong.

Woolson's story suggests that while "civilized" has historically denoted values or practices (art, education, courtesy, socioeconomic privilege) apart from brute strength, the civilizing potential of David Rod actually adheres in his physical power. At the moment when Eva makes it clear to her mother that she has chosen Rod, he is at the height of his masculinity: "But though he was sorry, he was resolute, he was even stern; in his dark beauty, his height and strength, he looked indeed, as Bartholomew had said, a man" (855). Eva falls victim to his manly power, as the land in Florida, the indigenous laborers, and the Italian workers do as well. This more brutal aspect of "civilizing" is a dark cornerstone of the story that, I would argue, unsettles the apparently happy ending.

It seems also worth noting the intertextual reference that occurs at the moment when Bartholomew praises Rod as "a modern and a model pioneer" (845)—ostensibly "modern" because he "civilizes" his field hands. In response, an Englishman named Gordon-Gray murmurs, "Pioneers! Oh, pioneers!" (845). Ironically, as the story points out, not one of the Americans present recognizes the quotation from Walt Whitman's *Leaves of Grass*. The poem "Pioneers! O Pioneers!" is a provocative allusion for Woolson to include, given Whitman's often-controversial status. More provocative still is the poem's first stanza, in which the poet urges, "Come, my tan-faced children / Follow well in order, get your weapons ready; / Have you your pistols? have you your sharp-edged axes?"[8] The invocation of Whitman's verse occurs during a discussion of Rod's remarkable industry and "colonization scheme." Read in the context of Rod's intention to "import" Italian laborers, Whitman's exhortation to tan-faced children to take up their weapons registers more powerfully as an appeal to the Italians, the darker people, rather than to fair-skinned plantation owners like Rod. In keeping with the spirit of the poem, it seems more appropriate to cast the Italian workers in the role of pioneers, to call to them as the poem does, "We take up the task eternal, and the burden, and the lesson" (229). The Italian servants seem to be more ideologically aligned with Whitman's theme than David Rod in his carefully chosen Tampa-made clothing. Certainly, at the very least, the reference raises questions about who, exactly, merits pioneer status and ironizes Bartholomew's lofty praise of David Rod and his civilizing potential.

Taking into account the issues of gender and motherhood epitomized in the image of the pink villa, I would propose that the story offers an alternative definition of "civilized," one that champions maternal values. The theme of mothers seems crucial, given that Fanny Churchill's perspective opens *and* closes the story *and* dominates much of the action. Further, Whitman's "Pioneers! O Pioneers!" contains two stanzas that celebrate motherhood and the bonds between women. In this poem, Whitman challenges his readers to "Raise the mighty mother mistress" (230) and later calls out, "O you young and elder daughters! O you mothers and you wives! Never must you be divided . . ." (232). Clearly Whitman's vision of the pioneer spirit includes a lofty place for mothers and demands solidarity between mothers and daughters in order to support the project of "civilizing" the nation.

The details of Woolson's story further emphasize the maternal. Devoted as a mother and also devoted to the concept of motherhood, Fanny Churchill takes what she calls her "business" very seriously: "From the girl's babyhood the mother had had her small white-curtained couch placed close beside her own. She could not have slept unless able at any moment to stretch out her hand and touch her sleeping child" (849). Eva's union with David Rod threatens to sever this bond, a possibility that devastates Fanny: "At this Fanny broke down again, and completely. For it was only too true; it would depend upon that stranger, that farmer, that unknown David Rod, whether she, the mother, should or should not be with her own child" (854). In contrast, as Fanny points out earlier in the story, European cultures and specifically France hold the mother in higher esteem: "in France the mother is and remains the most important person in the family. . . . Not only will they never wish to separate me from Eva . . . but such a thought would never enter their minds; they think it an honor and a pleasure to have me with them" (839). Through Fanny's role as mother, Woolson presents an alternative form of civilized behavior, one that privileges family relationships between women rather than profit and conquest.

Indeed, the individualist values of the New World to which Eva is drawn contrast sharply with the nurturing environment in which she has been raised, a disparity that casts a shadow on Eva's future. When Fanny's relationship with her daughter is interrupted by David Rod's enterprise, she can only gaze forlornly at her sleeping child and wonder about her fate: "What will her life be now? What must she go through, perhaps—what pain, privation—my darling, my own little child!" (856). The mother's anguish, presented in a lengthy passage just before the concluding wedding ceremony, qualifies the reader's certainty regarding Eva's marital bliss. This discomfort is heightened, rather than allayed, by Bartholomew's comments to Fanny: "[Rod's] whole heart is in that farm, that colony he has built up down there.... It's all he knows, and he thinks it the most important thing in life; I was going to say it's all he cares for, but of course now he has added Eva" (856). Rather than foregrounding Eva's centrality in Rod's life, Bartholomew's syntax appends Eva to the plantation as an obvious afterthought.

In addition to a husband whose true passion lies in his business, Eva is also burdened with a background that makes her entirely unfitted for life in the States. As Fanny remarks at the beginning of the story, "Eva is different; she has been brought up over here entirely .... The very qualities that are admired here would be a drawback to her there" (838). Later, on realizing Eva's intentions with Rod, Fanny fears for the safety of her only child: "How much good will her perfect French and Italian, her German, Spanish, and even Russian, do her down in that barbarous wilderness?" (854). Even late into the nineteenth century, Florida was associated in the American imagination with savagery, as Edward Williamson observes: "Until long after the Civil War, to most Northerners and Europeans Florida was a forbidden land. Associated in the common imagination with the dark Everglades and the bloody Seminole wars, the state's name evoked thoughts of swamps, marshes, canebrakes, and alligators."[9] Notably, Woolson's fictional Puntas Palmas is located on the southern coast, at the farthest fringe of the North American continent, perhaps based on the city of Palm Point which lies at the eastern edge of the Mangrove Swamp in the Everglades, a far cry from the secure domesticity of fashionable Sorrento. Fanny's observation is astute: the Rod plantation is likely to be barbarous, in more ways than one.

With lingering misgivings about David Rod's aggressive profiteering, his excessive devotion to his plantation, Eva's lack of practical skills, and her separation from her mother, the story closes with the conventional nuptials, though details are conspicuously absent and the mood is somber: "The pink villa witnessed the wedding. Fanny never knew how she got through that day. She was calm; she did not once lose her self-control" (856). For Fanny, the wedding is an ordeal to be withstood, rather than an occasion to be celebrated. And her haunting question at the end of the story most emphatically undermines the narrative's romantic resolution. When Bartholomew observes, by way of consolation regarding Eva's future, that the two newlyweds have found "the sweetest thing life offers," Fanny asks plaintively, "And the mother?" (856). As her question suggests, Fanny's fate is left vague and dubious, despite the apparent closure offered by the marriage plot. In addition, those three final words may be read as a disputation of Bartholomew's pronouncement—perhaps the *mother* is really life's sweetest offering?—and leave the reader to wonder, along with Fanny. Now that Eva has traded her maternal past for a patriarchal future, what will become of her?

As in Woolson's other international fiction, the hostility of American culture toward women and other marginalized people is a pervasive and troubling theme in "A Pink Villa." Eva's future seems to be as bleak as those of the other women in Woolson's stories who end up silenced or creatively constrained, or worse. As I have argued, the ostensibly "modern" and "model" qualities of David Rod's pioneering spirit are ironized in the story, exposed as the dark underside of the American expansionist project and ideology. Read in light of Florida history and Woolson's woman-centered thematics, Eva's choice to leave the warmly constructed pink villa and her mother's care for a New World marriage with an aggressive profiteer seems destined to be a tragic mistake.

Notes

1. Constance Fenimore Woolson, "A Pink Villa," *Harper's Monthly* (November 1888): 843. Subsequent references to this story will be made parenthetically in the text.

2. Robert White, "Cultural Ambivalence in Constance Fenimore Woolson's Italian Tales," *Tennessee Studies in Literature* 12 (1967): 126.

3. Peter Caccavari, "Exile, Depatriation, and Constance Fenimore Woolson's Traveling Regionalism," *Women, America, and Movement*, ed. Susan L. Roberson (Columbia: University of Missouri Press, 1998), 33.

4. White, "Cultural Ambivalence in Constance Fenimore Woolson's Italian Tales," 122.

5. American Social History Productions, Inc., "Fair's Fair: McDonnell Argues for Acceptance of Aliens," *History Matters*, http://historymatters.gmu.edu/d/5044 (accessed May 29, 2002).

6. Patricia C. Griffin, "Blue Gold: Andrew Turnbull's New Smyrna Plantation," *Colonial Plantations and Economy in Florida*, ed. Jane G. Landers (Gainesville: University Press of Florida, 2000), 44.

7. Jane Quinn, *Minorcans in Florida: Their History and Heritage* (St. Augustine: Mission Press, 1975), 61.

8. Walt Whitman, *Leaves of Grass*, ed. Sculley Bradley and Harold Blodgett (New York: W. W. Norton, 1973), 229. Subsequent references will be made parenthetically in the text. "Pioneers! O Pioneers!" was first published in Whitman's 1865 *Drum-Taps*, then again in the 1867 "Drum Taps" sequel and in the 1871 and 1876 editions of *Leaves of Grass*.

9. Edward C. Williamson, *Florida Politics in the Gilded Age, 1877–1893* (Gainesville: University Press of Florida, 1976), 1.

Contributors

Anne E. Boyd is associate professor of English and Women's Studies at the University of New Orleans. She discusses Woolson at length in her book *Writing for Immortality: Women and the Emergence of High Literary Culture in America*. Her anthology, *Wielding the Pen: Writings on Authorship by American Women of the Nineteenth Century*, was published in 2009. Boyd is currently at work on a literary biography of Woolson.

Martin T. Buinicki is associate professor of English at Valparaiso University and author of *Negotiating Copyright: Authorship and the Discourse of Literary Property Rights in Nineteenth-Century America*. He has published essays in a number of books and journals, including Blackwell's *Companion to Mark Twain*, Scribner's *American History through Literature*, *American Literary History*, and *American Literary Realism*. Most recently, his article "'Average-Representing Grant': Whitman's General" was published in the *Walt Whitman Quarterly Review*. His book *Walt Whitman's Reconstruction* is forthcoming in the Iowa Whitman Series from the University of Iowa Press.

Kathleen Diffley is associate professor of English at the University of Iowa and past director of the Midwest Modern Language Association. The author of *Where My Heart Is Turning Ever: Civil War Stories and Constitution Reform, 1861–1876*, she has also edited *To Live and Die: Collected Stories of the Civil War*. Her essay on pictorial coverage of the Confederacy in the *Illustrated London News* appeared in a special issue of *Comparative American Studies* on "Writing the Civil War: Transnational Dimensions," which she coedited. She is completing a book about telling the war in a magazine culture shaped by market concerns.

Annamaria Formichella Elsden is professor of English at Buena Vista University in Storm Lake, Iowa. Her book on gender and travel, *Roman Fever: Domesticity and Nationalism in Nineteenth-Century American Women's Writing*, includes a chapter on Woolson's Roman stories. In addition, she has written on Harriet Beecher

Stowe in *Legacy*, on Margaret Fuller in *"The Only Efficient Instrument": Women and the Periodical 1830–1914*, and on Sophia Peabody Hawthorne in *Reinventing the Peabody Sisters*. She teaches a range of literature and writing courses and is currently at work on two novels.

Janet Gabler-Hover is professor of Nineteenth-Century American Literature and Feminist Theory in the Department of English at Georgia State University. She is the author of *Truth in American Fiction: The Legacy of Rhetorical Idealism* and *Dreaming Black / Writing White: The Hagar Myth in American Cultural History*, as well as the coeditor of *American History through Literature 1820–70 Volumes I–III*. She has also authored essays on many nineteenth-century American writers.

Caroline Gebhard is professor of English at Tuskegee University. Her research on nineteenth- and early twentieth-century femininity and masculinity includes essays on other American women writers such as Caroline Kirkland and Harriet Beecher Stowe. Her work on Woolson has appeared in *Constance Fenimore Woolson's 19th Century: Essays*, ed. Victoria Brehm, and *Haunted Bodies: Gender and Southern Texts*, ed. Anne Goodwyn Jones and Susan V. Donaldson. She has also coedited *Post-Bellum, Pre-Harlem: African American Literature and Culture, 1877–1919*. Currently she is at work on *Invisible Legacy: The Women of Tuskegee, 1881–1981*.

Michael Germana is assistant professor of English at West Virginia University and author of *Standards of Value: Money, Race, and Literature in America*. His essays on money in American literature have appeared in *American Literary History*, *American Periodicals*, and *Arizona Quarterly*.

Carolyn Hall is a doctoral candidate and Presidential Fellow at the University of Iowa, where she teaches nineteenth- and twentieth-century American and world literature in the General Education Literature Program. She has written in *Legacy* on Woolson's *For the Major* and anticipates completing a larger project on post–Civil War fiction dealing with the education of former slaves. She is specifically interested in the reflexive nature of postbellum definitions of American identity and the effort to delineate freedom for the newly free.

Sharon Kennedy-Nolle teaches in the Department of English at Iona College. A former president of the Constance Fenimore Woolson Society, she has published work in books and journals on Woolson and, more generally, on the literature and culture of the Civil War and Reconstruction. She has also introduced and edited a reissue of *Belle Boyd in Camp and Prison*. She is currently completing a book-length manuscript, *Owning Up to Citizenship: Freedpeople, Property Rights, and the Northern Literary Market, 1865–1890*.

John Lowe is Robert Penn Warren Professor of English and Comparative Literature at Louisiana State University, where he directs the Program in Louisiana and Caribbean Studies. His books include *Jump at the Sun: Zora Neale Hurston's Cosmic Comedy*, *The Future of Southern Letters*, *Bridging Southern Cultures*, and *Louisiana Culture from the Colonial Era to Katrina*. He has just completed two books, *Faulkner's Fraternal Fury: Sibling Rivalry, Racial Kinship, and Democracy* and *Calypso Magnolia: The Caribbean Side of the South*, which was supported by fellowships from the Virginia Foundation for the Humanities, the Louisiana Board of Regents, and the National Endowment for the Humanities.

Geraldine Murphy is professor of English and acting dean of the Humanities and the Arts at The City College of New York, CUNY. The recipient of an ACLS fellowship and a Fulbright Fellow in China, she has published numerous articles on Cold War culture, among other subjects. She discovered, edited, and recently published a previously unknown work by Lionel Trilling, *The Journey Abandoned: The Unfinished Novel*. Trilling sparked her interest in Woolson's *East Angels* by borrowing the name "Garda Thorne" for one of his characters.

Kevin E. O'Donnell is professor of Literature and Language and director of the Environmental Studies minor at East Tennessee State University. He edited a collection of historic travel writing, *Seekers of Scenery: Travel Writing from Southern Appalachia, 1840–1900*, and he has published articles on Environmental History, Appalachian Studies, and nineteenth-century American illustrated magazines.

John H. Pearson is professor of English and director of the General Studies Program at Stetson University in DeLand, Florida. His publications include *Frames of Reference: The Prefaces of Henry James* and articles on Emerson, Hawthorne, James, Woolson, nineteenth-century studies, and autobiography.

Timothy Sweet is professor of English at West Virginia University. His publications include *Traces of War: Poetry, Photography, and the Crisis of the Union*, *American Georgics: Economy and Environment in Early American Literature*, and articles on early, antebellum, and Native American literature.

Anthony Szczesiul is associate professor of English at the University of Massachusetts, Lowell, where he teaches courses in American literature, southern literature, and poetry. He has published articles in journals such as the *Walt Whitman Quarterly Review*, *American Transcendental Quarterly*, *Mississippi Quarterly*, *Style*, and the *European Journal of American Culture*. His first book, *Racial Politics and Robert Penn Warren's Poetry*, received a *Choice* "Outstanding Academic Title" award in 2003. His contribution for this volume is drawn from his current book project, titled *The Myth of Southern Hospitality: Discourse, Ethics, Politics*.

Cheryl B. Torsney, a past president of the Constance Fenimore Woolson Society, has been researching Woolson's work since 1983. She is the author of *Constance Fenimore Woolson: The Grief of Artistry*, editor of *Critical Essays on Constance Fenimore Woolson*, and author of a wide range of articles about all things Woolsonian. She is professor of English as well as vice president and dean of Hiram College in Ohio's Western Reserve—that is, Woolson country.

Index

Page numbers in **bold** indicate illustrations.

Abbott, John S. C., 113
Abolitionism, 59, 177, 196–97, 206
Academy, The, 261n6
Adams, Charles Francis, 24, 32n15
Advertising, 275–76
Africa, 39, 43, 45, 47, 51, 100, 108, 183, 185, 227, 252
African Americans, 8, 9, 10, 11, 12, 40, 45, 46, 48–49, 50, 51, 52, 60, 65, 66, 99, 100, 118, 148, 152, 153–54, 157–58, 161n21, 166–67, 169–70, 171, 174, 177–82, 184–89, 190n6, 191n11, 191n12, 206, 227, 233, 249–53, 255–58, 261n8, 262n12, 263n20, 263n23, 263–64n32, 264n33, 264n37
African Methodist Episcopal Church, 181
Agassiz, Louis, 145n28
Alabama, 143, 184
Alcott, Louisa May, 96
Alden, Henry Mills, 279
Aldrich, Thomas Bailey, 164, 175n9
Alexander, Adele, 257
Allen, James Lane, 39
Amazons, 198, 207
American Journal of Science and the Arts, 145n29
American Review, 73
American Revolution, 6, 130, 139–40, 160–61n16, 201
Anderson, Hendrik, 232
Andersonville, 8, 167, 168, 174
Andrews, Sidney, 59
Appalachia, 6, 45, 136–37, 145n28, 215, 220, 221, 224, 226, 271–72, 274, 278–79
Appletons' Journal, 4, 8, 9, 32–33n18, 90, 103n12, 104n26, 105n36, 105n39, 111, 131, 134, 135, 136, 139, 205, 215, 268–69, 270, 271

Arctic, the, 194, 205, 207
Ariosto, Ludovico, 52
Atlantic Monthly, 4, 8, 32–33n18, 90, 105n34, 163, 182, 187, 193n25, 196–97, 198, 208n1, 209n7, 251
Auerbach, Jeffrey A., 8, 210n20
Ayers, Edward L., 211n26, 255

Baer, John W., 106n46
Bankers' Magazine and Statistical Register, The, 33n19
Barbour, George M., 59
Beecher, Henry Ward, 270
Bellamy, Francis, 106n46
Benedict, Clare, 103n14, 105n43, 230n6
Benitez-Rojo, Antonio, 38, 39
Benson, C. D., 110
Bermingham, Ann, 201
Berry, Edward, 57
Berthold, Dennis, 144n3
Biblical reference, 18, 20–22, 23–25, 31–32n8, 32n9, 147, 161n23, 188
Bierce, Ambrose, 176n27
Black Atlantic, 39, 45
Black Bess, 111, 112
Blair, William A., 167, 175n19
Blight, David W., 4, 98, 152
Boime, Albert, 203
Boone, Daniel, 236, 277–79
Booth, Alison, 233
Boston Globe, 90
Boyd, Anne E., 146n40, 277
Boyesen, Hjalmar Hjorth, 35
Brathwaite, Edward Kamau, 37
Brazil, 38
Brehm, Victoria, 104n23, 122, 123n1, 195, 274–75
Breton, André, 43

297

Index

Brinton, Daniel, 135, 145n19
Brown, Joshua, 145
Brown v. Board of Education, 250
Bryant, William Cullen, 199, 210n14
Bunce, Oliver Bell, 131
Buonomo, Leonardo, 5, 72n20, 163, 174n6, 192n19
Buzard, James, 144n1

Cable, George Washington, 54n13, 69, 182
Caccavari, Peter, 207, 211n28, 285
California, 112, 115, 119, 121, 279
Campbell, Tunis, 255, 257, 264n35
Caribbean, the, 9, 37, 38, 39, 41, 44, 45, 46, 48, 49, 52, 54n15, 54n16, 99
Cary, Elizabeth, 100
Catholic World, 8
Catholicism, 37, 41, 42, 44, 63, 69, 197
Cemeteries, 11, 50, 59, 68, 162–76, 176n21
Century, 113, 244, 268, 279
Cesairé, Aimé, 40, 43
Cesairé, Suzanne, 43
Chameleons, 195, 198, **204**, 205–6, 208
Champney, J. Wells, 183
Chandler, David Leon, 271
Chegaray, Madame, 5, 219
Cheyfitz, Eric, 11, 180–81, 185, 188
Child, Lydia Maria, 96
Chopin, Kate, 69
Christian Advocate, 23–24, 32n14
Christian Recorder, 181–82, 191n11
Christian Union, 9, 109, 197, 270
Civil War, 3, 4, 11, 12, 74, 82, 90–102, 102n4, 105n45, 107, 108, 112, 113, 115, 118, 121, 122, 123n2, 148, 150, 158, 162, 164, 165, 166, 178, 179, 181, 182, 187, 189, 196, 235, 236, 249, 291
Cleopatra, 90–100, 103n21, 103–4n22, 104n26, 105n35
Cleveland Female Seminary, 20, 31n7, 247n18
Cleveland Herald, 92
Cleveland Leader, 117, 118
Cleveland Plain Dealer, 109
Clinton, Catherine, 103n19, 223
Cohn, Deborah, 178, 188, 189
Coinage Act: of 1834, 22; of 1873, 9, 22–24, 27, 28, 32n12, 32–33n18
Colonization, 40, 44, 45, 49, 59–60, 61, 63, 178, 179, 189, 192n20, 210n20, 286–91

Colorado, 132
Columbian Exposition, 122
Comment, Kristin M., 104n25
Condé, Maryse, 54n15
Confederacy, 46, 53–54n3, 60, 74, 76, 82, 91, 92, 93, 94, 99, 109, 111, 147, 162, 165–66, 167–69, 171, 172, 178, 191n7, 191n8, 191n9, 191n12, 219, 221, 222
Confederate Union, 224–25
Conjure, 49
Connecticut, 107, 163, 267
Conron, John, 201, 202
Consumption (tuberculosis), 54n13, 195, 196, 210n15
Cooke, Jay, 276
Cooper, James Fenimore, 3–4, 236, 277
Coulson, Victoria, 247n7
Craddock, Charles E. (Mary Noailles Murfree), 39
Creoles, 8, 37, 48, 69
Critic, The, 251
Crockett, Davy, 236
Cuba, 37, 41, 47, 48, 53, 132
Cushman, Charlotte, 90, 102n3
Cypresses, 42, 195, 198, 199, 203, **204**, 205, 206, 207, 208

Dante Alighieri, 52
Davis, Rebecca Harding, 136, 182
Davis, Theodore R., 131
Daws, Gavan, 114
De Fontaine, F. G., 271
De Soto, Hernando, 51
Dean, Sharon L., 6, 20, 45, 88n19, 104n23, 144n3, 185, 194, 195, 230n13, 274–75
DeBow's Review, 181–82, 191n9
Del Vitto, Carol, 87n6
Deleuze, Gilles, 48, 55n20
DeLoughrey, Elizabeth, 54n16
Derrida, Jacques, 149–50, 157
Dickinson, Emily, 104n25
Diffley, Kathleen, 91, 94, 102n6, 105n34, 145n18
Dixon, Thomas, 39
Doane, Mary Ann, 218, 228
Dodge, Mary Mapes, 125n22
Douglass, Frederick, 118, 197
Drago, Edmund L., 251

Duke, Basil W., 113
Duncan, Russell, 251

Early, Jubal A., 4
Economic concerns, 4, 9, 10–11, 12, 17–31, **27**, 31n6, 32n12, 32n14, 32n15, 32n17, 32–33n18, 33n19, 113–16, 118–19, 121, 136, 140–42, 153, 159n3, 178, 180, 182–84, 186, 187, 190n6, 191n7, 195, 196, 197, 202, 203, 223, 224, 250, 252–53, 257–58, 262n15, 263n19, 263–64n32, 264n33, 264n37, 267–80, 287–89
Edel, Leon, 217, 234
Eliot, George (Mary Ann Evans), 95
Emancipation Proclamation, 98
Emerson, Ralph Waldo, 48
England, 209n13, 266
Exile, 53n3, 179
Expatriates, 285–87

Faragher, John Mack, 277
Faust, Drew Gilpin, 223, 224, 253
Fenn, Harry, 131, 136, 139, **204**, 205–6, 207, 270, 271
Field Order #15, 180, 191n7, 257, 264n34
Flagler, Henry, 271
Fleissner, Jennifer, 226
Florida, 3, 4, 5, 6, 7, 9, 10, 11, 12, 37–53, 54n13, 54n16, 55n21, 57, 59, 62, 65, 68, 69, 73, 75, 76, 130, 131, 132, 134–36, 140, 194–208, 209n6, 210, 211, 232–46, 266, 270–71, 283, 285–92
Foner, Eric, 186
Foster, John T., 197
Foster, Sarah Whitmer, 197
Fox, James, Jr., 39
France, 116, 290
Franklin, Benjamin, 75
Frazier, Garrison, 180, 191n7
Free indirect discourse, 82
Free labor ideology, 186, 257, 259, 264n37
Free Soil Party, 107
Freedmen's Bureau, 8, 181, 186
Freedom school, 11, 177, 179–80, 189
Freemasonry, 75
Freud, Sigmund, 43, 217–18, 225
Fuller, Margaret, 233, 242–44, 248n20

Gabin, Jane S., 210n15

Galaxy, 4, 8, 32–33n18, 104n26, 268
Garvey, Ellen Gruber, 275, 281n21
Gebhard, Caroline, 89n22, 105n44, 249
Gendered tropes, 9, 10, 11–12, 62, 63, 74, 78, 81–82, 86, 92–93, 95–96, 97–98, 100–101, 103n14, 103n18, 158, 198, 215–29, 235, 238, 243–44, 246, 250, 252, 285–89, 290, 292
Genovese, Eugene D., 159n3
Geology, 10, 129–43, **140**, **142**, 144n13, 145n21, 145n28, 146n36, 146n37, 145n39
Georgia, 5, 8, 12, 61, 68, 147, 174, 191n7, 205, 250–60, 261n7, 261n8, 261n9, 261–62n10, 262n12, 262n15, 262n16, 262n17, 262n18, 263n20, 263n23, 264n33, 264n35, 264n37, 265n43, 279
Gilded Age, the, 12, 122, 235, 266, 267–68
Gilder, Richard Watson, 187, 191–92n13, 193n25
Glazener, Nancy, 187
Glissant, Édouard, 38, 40, 45, 53, 54n15
Goddard, Frederick B., 151–52
Gordon, Lyndall, 81, 232
Gosson, Renée K., 54n16
Gould, Stephen Jay, 143
Gouverneur, Marian, 219–20
Grand Army of the Republic, 169
Grant, Ulysses S., 90, 108, 125n23, 267–68
Grantham, Dewey W., 178
Gray, Francine du Plessix, 114
Gray, Richard, 59, 75, 77, 88n8
Great Lakes, 4, 9, 85, 91, 94, 125n25, 130, 132–34, **133**, 253, 272
Great South, The, 4, 131, 136, 141, 142, 146n39, 183–84, 192n16, 203, 205
Greenberg, Kenneth S., 155, 156, 159n3
Greenblatt, Stephen, 10, 75–76, 81
Greeson, Jennifer Rae, 4, 144n9, 183, 192n16
Gresham's Law, 22
Griffin, Patricia C., 288
Guattari, Félix, 48, 55n20
Guilford, Linda, 109, 247n18
Guyot, Arnold, 137, 139, 145n28

Haiti, 43, 45
Hall, Carolyn, 105n33
Halttunen, Karen, 217
Handley, George B., 54n16, 178, 189
Haralson, Eric L., 105n44
Harper's Bazar, 105n39

Harper's Monthly, 4, 6, 8, 32–33n18, 61, 73, 74, 90, 104n26, 105n39, 105n42, 113, 117, 129–30, 132, 134, 135, 136, 146n36, 146n38, 162, 163, 182, 201, 203, 210n20, 215, 217, 220, 233, 244, 249, 266, 267, 268–69, 274, 279, 292
Harper's Weekly, 92, 99, 102n11, 104n30, 113, 131, 197, 232
Harte, Bret, 182
Hawaii (Sandwich Islands), 10, 112–22, 124n9
Hawthorne, Nathaniel, 103n21, 248n20
Hayne, Paul Hamilton, 3, 15, 29, 90, 101, 102, 102n3, 103n14, 103n18, 109–10, 206
Hercules and Omphale, myth of, 98, 104n27
Heringman, Noah, 144n13
Hodgson, Telfair, 147–48, 159n2
Holland, Josiah Gilbert, 182–83, 191–92n13
Holmes, Francis Simmons, 141, 146n37, 146n43
Horne, Gerald, 118
Hospitality, 161n23; Southern, 11, 147–58, 159n3, 159–60n7
Howells, William Dean, 17, 31n1, 116, 127, 209n7, 251
Hoy, Lydia, 112
Hubbell, Jay B., 59, 72n14
Hunter-Gault, Charlayne, 103n21
Hybridity, 37, 57–58, 67–70, 195, 197, 257–58

Identity, 79–87
Imboden, J. D., 152
Immigration, 260, 264n37
Imperialism, 5, 9, 43, 56–60, 61, 62–70, 115, 117, 178–80, 183–85, 189, 190n2, 192n16, 196, 198, 203, 207, 209–10n13, 210n20, 227, 288–89, 295
Index, 191n9
India, 179
Indiana, 109
Ingalls, John J., 23
Inscoe, John C., 251
Irwin, William G., 116
Isaac, Rhys, 159n3
Italy, 9, 45, 85, 109, 122, 125n16, 232, 236–38, 242–43, 246, 266, 285, 287, 288, 289, 290, 291

Jackson, Andrew, 205
James, Henry, 10, 12, 40, 46, 52, 53, 61, 73–78, 81, 83, 87, 97, 103n21, 116, 217, 232–46, 247n4, 248n19, 248n20, 250; *The Ambassadors*, 97; *The American Scene*, 73–74, 76–78, 82, 238; *The Bostonians*, 217, 243, 244–46, 248n20; "A Chain of Cities," 237; *Daisy Miller*, 236, 238; *Hawthorne*, 236, 243; "The Madonna of the Future," 235; "Miss Woolson," 5, 88n13, 197, 229, 232, 234; *The Portrait of a Lady*, 53, 87, 234, 237, 238–40, 241, 242–43, 246, 248n20
Jameson, Anna, 97, 103–4n22
Jessamine, 47, 198
Jim Crow South, 250, 251, 255, 260
John, Arthur, 182
Johnson, Andrew, 251
Jones, Louise Coffin, 116
Jones, Suzanne W., 74

Kane, Elisha Kent, 205
Kant, Immanuel, 149
Kaplan, Amy, 60, 158, 182, 191n12
Kauai Historical Society, 112
Kemble, Frances, 55n23, 217
Kennedy, John Pendleton, 52, 55n23
Kennedy-Nolle, Sharon, 190n3
Kent, Charles William, 59
Kentucky, 10, 24, 91, 93, 99, 103n15, 108, 109, 277
Kern, John Dwight, 105n44, 220, 252, 261n6, 277
King, Clarence, 132
King, Edward, 4, 131, 136, 141, 142, 145n9, 145n21, 146n39, 183–84, 187, 192n16, 203, 205
Kipling, Rudyard, 179
Kreiger, Georgia, 239
Krén, Emil, 104n27
Kristeva, Julia, 81
Ku Klux Klan, 95, 141, 178, 187, 206, 208, 251

Labor, postwar, 114, 117–18, 223–24, 252, 253, 257, 259–60, 262n15, 264n37, 287–88, 289–90
Labor Standard, 287
Lacan, Jacques, 217
Ladd, Barbara, 67
Landscape, 62
Lanier, Sidney, 199, 201, 202, 210n15, 270
Larson, Jil, 76
Lawrence, D. H., 102
Lawrence, Kathleen, 248n20
Lawson, Benjamin S., 209–10n13
Lee, Robert E., 90, 99, 166
Levinas, Emmanuel, 149

Lewis, Edmonia, 103n21
Lewis, Nathaniel, 209n13
Lincoln, Abraham, 98, 107
Lippincott's, 8, 116, 160n8, 210n15
Literary World, 8, 17, 251
Littell's Living Age, 145n28
Little, Arthur, 99–100
Livingstone, David, 183
López, Alfred J., 187
Lost Cause, 4, 11, 40, 46, 92, 94, 149, 151, 152, 176n27
Louisiana, 54n13, 68, 183–84
L'Ouverture, Touissant, 45
Lowe, John, 53n3
Luraghi, Raimondo, 159n3

Mabie, Hamilton, 109, 213
MacLeod, Christine, 190n3
Maddex, Jack P., Jr., 160n13
Maine, 173
Makee, James, 115–16
Makee, Wilhelmina Harris, 116, **120**
Makee Sugar Company, 116
Maroons, 45, 54n15
Marra, Kim, 217
Martinique, 40, 43, 227
Maryland, 143
Marx, Dániel, 104n27
Marx, Leo, 144n6
Mason-Dixon Line, 163
Massachusetts, 91, 216, 236, 242, 244, 245
Mather, Samuel, 105n40, 109, 116, 119, 122, 125n25, 277
McDonnell, Joseph, 287–88
McKee, Kathryn, 5
Mediterranean, the, 288
Meindl, Christopher F., 203
Melville, Herman, 9, 43, 122
Memorial Day (Decoration Day), 157, 161n21, 163, 166–68, 169, 170–71, 174, 175n18, 175n19
Memory, sites of, 163–74, 175n9
Messiaen, Olivier, 54n13
Mexican-American War, 227
Mexico, 38, 53
Michaels, Walter Benn, 37
Michasiw, Kim Ian, 203
Michigan, 17–31, 78, 218

Miller, David C., 194
Miller, Joaquin, 198, 207, 209n12, 209–10n13
Minorcans, 41–42, 44, 56–57, 65, 66, 69, 195, 205, 206, 288
Mississippi, 108, 113
Mitchell, W. J. T., 210n20
Moers, Ellen, 247n18
Monroe Doctrine, 115
Monteith, Sharon, 74
Moonshiners, 45
Moore, Rayburn S., 55n23, 102n4, 105n44, 107, 108, 261n6
Morgan, John Hunt, 10, 91, 92, 93, 96, 98, 99, 101, 104n30, 105n41, 107–13, **110**, 119, 121–22
Morgan, John Pierpont, 122, 125n25
Morrison, Toni, 105n35, 191n8
Mott, Frank Luther, 144n4, 145n31, 183, 191–92n13
Muir, John, 132, 279
Murray, Lynn, 210n20

Nast, Thomas, 26, 27
Nation, 251
Native Americans, 6, 38, 40, 45, 46, 47, 49, 50, 51, 60, 134, 135, 136, 143, 180, 184, 195, 196, 198, 205, 206, 227, 259–60, 288–89, 291
New England, 8, 15, 40, 42, 46, 47, 48, 50, 165, 173, 187, 193n25, 220–21, 223, 225, 235, 236, 245
New Hampshire, 3, 8, 15, 66, 111, 136, 179, 188, 236, 241
New Jersey, 147–48, 264n35
New York, 3–4, 5, 63, 65, 123n2, 139, 182, 199, **200**, 201, 216, 218, 219, 236, 243, 268
New York Evening Post, 105n36, 105n39, 199, 260n6
New York Times, 92, 103n13, 125n25, 138–39, 145n29, 168, 175n18, 175n19, 181–82, 191n10, 260–61n6
Nietzsche, Friedrich, 88n21, 218–19, 228–29
Noll, Steven, 196
Nora, Pierre, 11, 163, 166, 169, 171, 174
North Carolina, 5, 6, **7**, 78–82, 121, 130, 131, 136–39, **138**, 175n19, 215–29, 266, 271–72, 273–75, 278–80
Norway, 114, 117
Novak, Barbara, 144n13
Nugent, Walter T. K., 20

O'Donnell, Kevin E., 215, 221
Ohio, 3, 10, 35, 91, 92, 104n30, 105n41, 107, 108, 109, 110, 111, 112–13, 115, 116, 123n2, 133, 236, 253–54, 256
Ohio Farmer, 113
Ohio Wesleyan College, 123n2
Olmstead, Frederick Law, 55n23
Outlook, The, 109
Overland Monthly, 132
Owen, David M., 176n27

Page, Thomas Nelson, 37, 38, 39, 40, 249
Pasadena Star-News, 119
Patriarchy, 233, 235, 238, 240–41, 243–44
Pattee, Fred Lewis, 194
Pennsylvania, 133, 194, 205, 207
Petit Trone, Esq., 119, **120**, 125n22
Picturesque, the, 4, 6–8, 131, 132–34, 139, 160–61n16, 196, 197–98, 199, 201–5, **204**, 207, 208, 209n13, 210n20, 236
Picturesque America, 131, 132, 136, 205, 270, 271
Plantation tradition, white, 12, 39, 45, 46, 52, 53–54n3, 64, 141–42, 143, 154–58, 184–89, 191n12, 192n19, 198, 215–29, 252–53, 255–56
Plessy v. Ferguson, 249, 251
Pollard, Edward A., 149, 150–54, 160n8, 160n13
Porte, Joel, 248n20
Powell, John Wesley, 132
Pratt, Mary Louise, 57, 62, 64
Presbrey, Frank, 275
Puerto Rico, 60

Quinn, Jane, 288

Rabinowitz, Howard N., 255
Race, issues of, 48, 49, 50, 51, 53, 55n21, 58, 60, 67–70, 99–101, 104n29, 105n33, 105n34, 118, 139, 148, 151–52, 154, 157–58, 161n21, 166–71, 177–89, 190n3, 195, 197–98, 249, 250, 251, 252, 255–60, 262n13, 263n20, 263n32
Railroads, 119, 121, 255, 267, 268, 269, 271–72, 274, 277, 278
Rainey, Sue, 145n15, 145n20
Rawlings, Marjorie Kinnan, 55n21
Raymond, Henry Jarvis, 191n10
Reciprocity Treaty, 113, 115, 117, 124n9
Reconstruction, 3–12, 17–31, 32n12, 32n15, 40, 59–60, 66, 74, 91, 95, 96, 103n19, 107, 131, 140–42, 148, 150, 154, 157–58, 160–61n16, 162, 163, 166–69, 173, 177–78, 183, 187–89, 196, 197, 199, 208, 211n28, 216, 222, 227, 233, 249, 250, 251–53, 255, 258, 260, 264n37
Redemption Era, 249, 251
Regionalism, 198, 207, 236, 245
Rehan, Ada, 217
Reid, Christian (Frances Fisher Tiernan), 271
Republican Party, 107, 191n10, 206
Reynolds, William, 115
Richmond Daily Examiner, 172
Richmond (Va.) State Journal, 168
Rinhart, Floyd, 209n6
Rinhart, Marion, 209n6
Romanticism, 41, 47, 209n13, 238, 242–45
Romine, Scott, 60
Rowe, Anne E., 177
Rowe, John Carlos, 103n21, 190n2
Royal Baking Powder, 275–76, **276**, 281n21
Royster, Francesca T., 99–100, 104n31, 105n32
Russia, 114

Safran, William, 53–54n3
Said, Edward, 53n3, 61
Saintsbury, George, 261n6
San Francisco Chronicle, 117–18
San Francisco Daily Morning Call, 115
Schmidt, Peter, 178, 189
Scholnick, Robert J., 183
Schurz, Carl, 117
Scott, Anne Firor, 219, 223, 225
Scribner's Monthly, 4, 8, 17, 32–33n18, 131, 132, 136, 146n39, 177, 182–83, 187, 191–92n13, 203, 268–69
Scudder, Horace, 251
Sedgwick, Ellery, 197, 209n7
Self-fashioning, 59, 74–87
Seward, William H., 113–15, 117
Seyd, Ernest, 23
Shakespeare, William, 10, 19, 25, 57, 90, 96–97, 99, 103–4n22, 104n23, 104n25, 104n26
Shapiro, Henry D., 144n2
Sherman, William Tecumseh, 12, 180, 191n7, 253, 262n18
Silber, Nina, 6, 12, 62, 73, 91, 92, 96, 102n5, 103n18, 103n19, 144n2, 146n34, 151, 153, 211n26, 254

Simmons, Lamaretta, 105n35
Simms, William Gilmore, 55n23
Slavery, 12, 44, 50, 98, 99, 117, 139, 143, 148, 151, 178–80, 181–82, 184–86, 189, 227, 252–53, 257, 262n12, 262n17, 263n23, 264n33
Smith, Andrew, 67, 70
Smith, James M., 251
Smith, Jon, 178, 188
Snakes, 43, 46, 51, 195, 198, **204**, 205, 206–7, 208, 209n12, 209–10n13
South Carolina, 3, 5, 6, **7**, 8, 59, 73, 76–78, 102, 121, 127, 130, 136, 139–43, 146n37, 160–61n16, 165, 191n7, **200**, 201, 216, 224, 252, 253, 266
Southern chivalry, myth of, 222–23
Southern Historical Society, 4
Spain, 53
Spalding, Rufus, 118
Spalding, Rufus P., 107, 109, 113, 115
Spalding, Thomas, 252–53, 262n16, 262n17
Spalding, Wilhelmina Makee, 119–20, **120**
Spalding, Zephaniah Swift, 10, 102n4, 107–23, **108**, **120**, 123n1, 123n2, 124n9, 124n12, 124–25n15, 125n16, 125n23
Spenser, Edmund, 52
Spreckels, Claus, 119
Sprengnether, Madelon, 218, 228
Staël, Madame de, 233, 242–43, 247–48n18, 248n19, 248n20
Stanford, Leland, 112
Stanley, Henry Morton, 183, 192n20
Stanton, Edwin, 191n7
Starke, Aubrey Harrison, 210n15
Stauffer, John, 96, 103n20
Stedman, Edmund Clarence, 139, 283
Stegner, Wallace, 274
Steinberg, Stephen, 186
Steinfeld, Robert J., 186
Stephan, Peter Morris, 20
Stephens, Lester D., 146n37
Sterne, Laurence, 131
Stoddard, Sandol, 123n2
Story, William Wetmore, 103n21
Stowe, Harriet Beecher, 55n23, 96, 197, 270; *Dred*, 43; *Palmetto Leaves*, 197, 199; *Uncle Tom's Cabin*, 43, 220–21
Sugar industry, 39, 47, 113–17, 119, 122, 124n11, 124n12, 289

Surrealism, 43
Swamp, the, 42–44, 46, 52–53, 54n13, 54n15, 55n23, 62, 135, 194–208, **204**, 209n6, 211n28, 240, 244
Swartz, Patti Capel, 111
Sweet, Timothy, 144n8
Swett, Katherine, 248n20
Swift, Zephaniah, 107

Tennessee, 41, 92, 104n30, 113, 170, 268, 272, 278
Thorpe, Thomas Bangs, 131, **204**, 205, 270, 271
Tocqueville, Alexis de, 180–81
Tod, David, 108
Tóibín, Colm, 232
Torsney, Cheryl B., 80, 88n13, 102n4, 103n18, 105n36, 218, 230n9
Tourism, 6, 11, 12, 57, 59, 62, 66, 73, 78, 81, 129–31, 150–54, 160–61n16, 195, 196, 197, 199, 201–6, **204**, 208, 209n6, 211n26, 221, 267, 271–72, 279
Trachtenberg, Alan, 269
Travel writing, 129–43, 144n3, 160–61n16, 178, 182–83, 201, 269–72, 275
Trefzer, Annette, 5
Tropiques, 43
Turnbull, Andrew, 288
Turner, Nat, 45
Turner, Thomas, 24
Twain, Mark (Samuel Clemens), 9, 115, 116, 118, 124n14, 153, 190n3, 267–68

United States Constitution, 197, 251
United States Postal Service, 51, 207, 257–58, 265n40, 269

VanBergen, Carolyn J., 19–20
Vermont, 65, 228
Virginia, 3, 5, 11, 63, 73, 76, 77–78, 82, 91, 150, 152–54
Voodoo/Vodun, 49, 52

Waldstreicher, David, 87n1
Walker, J. S., 116
Warner, Charles Dudley, 267–68
Washington, D.C., 91, 92, 93, 113, 115
Water lettuce, 207–8
Waud, Alfred, 131
Weaver, Elisha, 181, 191n11

Weekes, Karen, 33n20, 103n18, 167, 172, 195
Weir, Sybil B., 103n18
Wells, David A., 27
West Indies, 37, 41, 43, 53, 227
West Virginia, 112–13
Wharton, Edith, 217
White, Robert L., 285
Whitman, Walt, 289–90
Whitney, John P., 145n21
Wickham, Gertrude Van Rensselaer, 119–20, 125n22
Williamson, Edward C., 291
Wilson, Anthony, 55n23, 199
Winders, Jamie, 5, 60, 61, 65, 144n9, 178
Wolff, Cynthia Griffin, 230n6
Wood, Betty, 252
Wood engraving, 6, 145n31, 145n38, 182–83, 201, 202–3, 210n20, 268
Woodward, C. Vann, 255, 268
Woolson, Charles Jarvis, 4
Woolson, Charles Jarvis, Jr. (Charlie), 121, 125n24
Woolson, Constance Fenimore, 3, 6, 8, 12, 74–76, 90, 101, 105n37, 105n40, 105n44, 123n1, 149, 154–58, 233–34, 236, 241, 247n4, 249–51, 254, 255; "The Ancient City," 4, 6, 104n26, 134–36, 270–71; *Anne*, 103n18, 107–8, 113, 123n1, 216–17, 218, 219, 220, 228, 241–42, 272; "At Mentone," 104n26; "At the Château of Corrine," 101, 105n42, 238, 243–44; "Bro," 68, 118; "Cairo in 1890," 104n26; "Castle Nowhere," 9, 17–31, 105n43; *Castle Nowhere: Lake-Country Sketches*, 4, 17; critical response, 8–9, 17, 61, 90, 101, 105n36, 105n44, 163, 177, 229, 251–52, 260–61n6, 277–78, 286; "Crowder's Cove," 111; "Dolores," 69; "Duets," 104n26; *East Angels*, 12, 37, 39, 46–53, 103n18, 232–46, 248n20; "Felipa," 44, 56–59, 65, 70; "The Florida Beach," 104n26; "Flower in the Snow," 123n1; *For the Major*, 11–12, 75, 78–82, 86, 215–29; "The French Broad," 6, 7, 92, 102n9, 136–39, 271–72; "The Haunted Lake," 4, 199, **200**, 201; *Horace Chase*, 10, 12, 107, 118–22, 125n23, 266–80; "In Remembrance," 105n39; "In Search of the Picturesque," 201–3, **202**; "In the Cotton Country," 18, 29, 30, 62, 64, 70, 94, 118; "An Intercepted Letter," 101, 105n39; *Jupiter Lights*, 12, 74–75, 78, 82–86, 88n21, 89n22, 103n18, 249–60, 260n4; "King David," 8, 11, 18, 29, 30, 44–45, 66, 94–95, 103n16, 104n29, 118, 161n21, 177–89, 190n3; "Lake Superior," 132–34; "Matches Morganatic," 111–12; "Mentone," 105n39; "Miss Elisabetha," 65–66, 70; "Miss Grief," 101, 116; "The Oklawaha," 6, **7**, 203, 207–8, 211n29; "Old Gardiston," 8, 11, 18, 29–30, 64, 68, 94, 118, 149, 154–58; *Old Stone House, The*, 119, 123n1, 125n23; "A Pink Villa," 9, 122, 285–92; "Rodman the Keeper," 8, 11, 18, 29–30, 40–42, 53, 64, 68, 94, 118, 141–42, 154, 157–58, 161n21, 162–74; *Rodman the Keeper: Southern Sketches*, 10, 56–59, 62–70, 149, 163, 196, 198, 209n12; "Round by Propeller," 130, 134; "Sail-Rock, Lake Superior," 133, **134**; "Sister St. Luke," 39, 41–42, 62, 64, 69–70; "The South Devil," 11, 42–44, 46, 48, 62, 63, 69, 194–208; "St. Clair Flats," 97, 104n26; "To Certain Biographers," 101, 105n39; "Told in a Farm-House" ("Kentucky Belle"), 101, 102n3, 105n41, 105n44, 111; *Two Women, 1862*, 10, 90–102, 103n12, 105n42, 105n43, 111; "Up in the Blue Ridge," 45, 62, 68, 226; "Up the Ashley and Cooper," 6, **7**, 139–43, 160–61n16, **200**, 201; "A Voyage to the Unknown River," 69; "Wilhelmina," 100, 105n34, 108, 124n14
Woolson, Gary, 125n22
Woolson, Hannah Cooper Pomeroy, 3
Wright, Elizabethada A., 168, 172, 173, 174, 175n9
Wyatt-Brown, Bertram, 154–55, 156, 159n3
Wyman, Jeffries, 135

Young, Robert, 67

PS
3363
.W58
2021